# The Princeton Review

W0009373

# Cracking the ACT

## with Practice Tests on CD-ROM

GEOFF MARTZ, KIM MAGLOIRE, AND THEODORE SILVER

2003 EDITION

RANDOM HOUSE, INC.
NEW YORK

www.PrincetonReview.com

The Independent Education Consultants Association recognizes The Princeton Review as a valuable resource for high school and college students applying to college and graduate school.

Princeton Review Publishing, L.L.C.
2315 Broadway
New York, NY 10024
E-mail: booksupport@review.com

Library of Congress Cataloging-in-Publication Data

ISBN 0-375-76318-X

ACT is a registered trademark of ACT, Inc.

Editor: Jeff Soloway
Production Coordinator: Stephen White
Production Editor: Maria Dente

Manufactured in the United States of America.

9  8  7  6  5  4  3  2  1

2003 Edition

# ACKNOWLEDGMENTS

A test preparation course is much more than clever techniques and powerful computer score reports; the reason our results are so great is that our teachers care so much. Nine years ago a small group of Princeton Review instructors enthusiastically created a program to prepare students for the previous version of the ACT. We would like to thank John Cauman, Judy Moreland, Bill Lindsley, and Jim Reynolds for their commitment to the original ACT and PRA projects.

The completion of this book would not have been possible without the help and dedication of several individuals. We would like to thank Mike Freedman for his revision of the PRA, Linda Tarleton for her work on the reading chapter, Shawn Domzalski for his expert checking, Andrea Paykin, Jeff Soloway, Maria Dente, and Julian Ham for making our words look so good, and Rob Zopf for his patience. We would also like to thank David Owen for giving us a fine launch, and John Katzman for his unceasing faith in our work.

Special thanks to Adam Robinson, who conceived of and perfected the Joe Bloggs approach to standardized tests and many other successful techniques used by The Princeton Review.

# CONTENTS

# FOREWORD

If you were a college admissions officer, what would you look for in a potential student?

That's an easy question. We've asked hundreds of admissions folks, and their answers are always the same. They want students who can handle the workload, who have a curiosity and desire to learn, and who will add something to the campus—impressive math or science skills, athletic or artistic ability, or just great personalities. Because most good schools want a diverse student body, they will look for students with unusual backgrounds or skills.

Here's a tougher question. Let's say you already had records of the applicants' school performance over the past four years. *And* you had some essays they had written. *And* you had letters of recommendation from teachers and school counselors. *And* you had met with all the applicants for an hour to talk about their goals and their transcripts. What would you need, in addition to all of that, to see if the students were right for your college?

A. A measure of their raw intelligence

B. A measure of their reasoning ability

C. A national standard to check their grades in school

D. A rough prediction of their freshman year grades in college

E. Their parents' bank account balances

Most admissions officers answer (C). Every school has a different way of grading students and a different curriculum. Every school has teachers who are terrific but who are very tough graders. Colleges need some common measure against which they can judge students from hundreds of high schools. The important question, then, is whether a certain test can accurately measure what you've learned over your many years of study through high school.

How much does the ACT really measure? Only a small portion of what you have learned in school. The English test doesn't test anything you learned in English class; it only tests a very few rules of English grammar. The Mathematics test doesn't contain any geometric proofs, and you're never asked to show your work. In fact, the ACT measures many things that you didn't learn in school—or, at least, it measures those skills quite differently from the way you learned them in school. That's why it's important to prepare to take the test: You may know all the science in the world but still not understand how to tackle science problems in the way that they appear on the ACT.

All in all, we think that the ACT is a slightly better test than the SAT, if only for the fact that the ACT staff is open and helpful, and more student-friendly than the people at ETS. In fact, you should feel free to call them if you're confused about the testing process or about a specific question on the test.

And if they can't help you, feel free to call us.

—John Katzman
CEO
The Princeton Review

P.S. If you are paying attention to the problems colleges are having today, you might have answered (E) on that multiple-choice question. College has become very expensive. Don't let that discourage you, though. A college diploma will more than pay for itself in the job market, and with some good advice (speak to the financial aid people at the schools to which you're applying), grants, work, and some debt, almost everyone can still afford college.

# GET MORE FROM *CRACKING THE ACT* BY USING OUR FREE ONLINE TOOLS

Buyers of this book receive a free year-long subscription to *Cracking the ACT's* **online companion course**, which features the latest in interactive tools for test preparation. Go to www.PrincetonReview.com/cracking to register for all the free services we offer to help you improve your test score and find the right college. Once you've logged on, you'll be able to:

- **Learn Key Test-Taking Skills Through Our Distance Learning Tools**. Some of the key lessons of *Cracking the ACT* will be even clearer after you've spent some time seeing and hearing them presented online.

- **Practice New Techniques with Online Drills**. Once you've learned a new technique or concept, you can take online drills to practice and to gauge your mastery.

- **Research and Apply to the Best Colleges for You**. Through our award-winning college search site at www.PrincetonReview.com, you can access our complete library of information about US colleges, manage your application process, and even apply electronically to more than 800 colleges.

## YOU'RE IN COMPLETE CONTROL

Here's what you'll see once you've registered.

Practice will give you access to 4 full-length tests not available in your book, extra drills to help you sharpen your skills, and a score analysis of the two diagnostic tests that are in your book. Just click on a topic in the grey area, and then on the square or squares displayed in the white area to begin any Practice activity.

Your online tools are all brought together in one easy-to-use screen. Whether you're using the tests and drills located in the Practice area, the distance learning lessons in online lessons, or the college admissions tools in Your Colleges, you'll love every one of our well-organized online resources!

# PART I

# Orientation

# THE ACT

We at The Princeton Review have a reputation for test bashing that is pretty richly deserved. In general, we don't have many nice things to say about the tests we tackle or the organizations that write them. So it's a pleasure this time to take on what we feel is essentially a fair and good-hearted test, written by intelligent people who do not have a mean bone in their collective body.

The ACT measures what it says it does: academic achievement. It doesn't pretend to measure your analytic ability or your intelligence. The people at ACT admit that you can increase your score by preparing for the test. They even put out their own coaching book.

So if we ever seem to be poking fun at the test, or the people who write it, we want you to remember that it does not lessen our underlying affection and respect.

If there is any flaw in the ACT, it is that in its attempt to be fair, it has become a little, well, predictable. Of course, when we say that the ACT is a completely predictable test, we mean it in the nicest possible way. We *like* predictable tests.

## THE ACT IS A S~~TANDARD~~IZED TEST
### PREDICTABLE

From now on, whenever you see the word "standardized," think "predictable" instead. The ACT tests the same information the same way, year after year. For example, there are always 14 plane geometry questions on the ACT. Not 13, not 15. Exactly 14. There are exactly 10 questions on punctuation. You can count on it. Even the way they ask the questions is predictable, based on the need for a standardized product.

The review you will find in this book is based on the very specific knowledge you need to do well on this test. The test-taking strategies we have developed are designed to take advantage of the ACT's predictability.

## I HAVE GOOD GRADES IN SCHOOL.
## DO I NEED TO PREPARE?

Let's take the hypothetical case of Sid. Sid is valedictorian of his class, editor of the school paper, and the only teenager ever to win the Nobel Prize. To support his widowed mother, he sold more seeds from the back of comic books than any other person in recorded history. He speaks eight languages in addition to being able to communicate with dolphins and wolves. He has recommendations from Colin Powell *and* Bill Gates. So if Sid had a bad day when he took the ACT (the plane bringing him back from his Medal of Freedom award presentation was late), we are pretty sure that he is going to be just fine anyway. But Sid wants to make sure that when his colleges look at his ACT score, they see the same high-calibre student they see when they look at the rest of his application.

# I Have Lousy Grades in School. Is There Any Hope?

Let's take the case of Tom. Tom didn't do outstandingly well in high school. In fact, he has been on academic probation since kindergarten. He has caused four of his teachers to give up teaching as a profession, and he prides himself on his perfect homework record: He's never done any. Not ever. But if Tom aces his ACT, a college might decide that he is actually a misunderstood genius and give him a full scholarship.

Most of us, of course, fall between these two extremes. So is it important to prepare for the ACT?

If you were to look in the information bulletin of any of the colleges in which you are interested, we can pretty much guarantee that somewhere you would find the following paragraph:

> "Many factors go into the acceptance of a student by a college. Test scores are *only one* of these factors—grades in high school, extracurricular activities, essays, and recommendations are also important, and may in some cases outweigh test scores."
>
> (2002 University of Anywhere Bulletin)

Truer words were never spoken. In our opinion, just about *every* other element in your application "package" is more important than your test scores. The Princeton Review (among other organizations) has been telling colleges for years that scores on the ACT or the SAT are pretty incomplete measures of a student's overall academic abilities. Some colleges have stopped looking at test scores entirely, and others are downplaying their importance.

## So Why Should You Spend Any Time Preparing for the ACT?

Because, out of all the elements in your application "package," your ACT score is the easiest to *change*. The grades you've received up to now are written in stone. You aren't going to become captain of the football team or editor of the school paper overnight. Your essays will only be as good as you can write them, and recommendations are only as good as your teachers' memories of you.

On the other hand, in a few weeks you can radically change your score on the ACT (and the way colleges will look at your application). The test does not pretend to measure analytic ability or intelligence. It measures your knowledge of specific skills such as grammar, algebra, and reading comprehension.

## When It Comes to the ACT, *Nothing* Is Written in Stone

It doesn't matter how well you've done in school up to now. Good grades are not a guarantee that you will do well on the ACT. It doesn't matter if you've always been bad at taking standardized tests before. Colleges aren't going to see any of your scores from earlier standardized tests. It doesn't matter if you hate math in general or English in general or science in general. The ACT doesn't measure math in general. It measures the math that is on the ACT.

By reviewing the very specific knowledge that the people who write the ACT think is important, and by learning good test-taking strategies, it should be possible to increase your ACT score significantly. This is not just our opinion. Even the people who write the test agree.

## WHAT IS THE ACT?

The ACT is a multiple-choice standardized test that is supposed to measure your knowledge of some of the subjects taught in high school. With breaks, the test takes about three and a half hours. It is usually divided into four sections, which are always given in the same order.

### 1. English (45 minutes — 75 questions)

In this section you will see five essays on the left side of the page. Some words or phrases will be underlined. On the right side of the page, you will be asked whether the underlined portion is correct as written or whether one of the three alternatives listed would be better. This is a test of grammar, punctuation, sentence structure, and rhetorical skills. Throughout each passage there will also be questions about overall organization and style, or perhaps about how the writing could be revised or strengthened.

### 2. Math (60 minutes — 60 questions)

These are the regular multiple-choice math questions you've been doing all your life. The easier questions *tend* to come first—they test basic math proficiency. A good third of the test covers pre-algebra and elementary algebra. Slightly less than a third will cover intermediate algebra and coordinate geometry (graphing). Regular geometry accounts for less than a quarter of the questions, and there will be four questions (toward the end) about trigonometry.

### 3. Reading (35 minutes — 40 questions)

In this section there will be four reading passages of about 750 words each—the average length of a *People* magazine article, although maybe not as interesting. There is always one prose fiction passage, one social science passage, one humanities passage, and one natural science passage, and they are always in the same order from test to test. After each passage you will be asked ten questions.

### 4. Science Reasoning (35 minutes — 40 questions)

No specific scientific knowledge is necessary for the Science Reasoning Test. You won't need to know the chemical makeup of hydrochloric acid or any formulas. Instead, you will be asked to understand six sets of scientific information presented in graphs, charts, tables, and research summaries, and you will have to make sense of a disagreement between two scientists (sometimes three).

There may be one additional section on the ACT that you take. During this section, you will pay for the privilege of being a guinea pig while the test writers at ACT try out some experimental questions on you. This section typically comes at the end of the test and is usually very easy to recognize, as it is much shorter than a regular section—just 10 to 15 minutes long. In other words, it's not a big deal. This section usually shows up on the June test, and it won't count toward your score.

**Power Booking**

If you were getting ready to take a history test, you'd study history. If you were preparing for a basketball game, you'd practice basketball. So, if you're preparing for the ACT, study the ACT.

## Where Does the ACT Come From?

The ACT is written by a company that used to call itself American College Testing, but is now just called ACT. The company's main offices are in Iowa City, Iowa. The people at ACT have been writing a version of this test since 1959. Even if you aren't looking forward to taking the ACT this year, you would probably prefer it to the version they used to give. In the old days the test included detailed questions about topics like the Constitution of the United States, electrostatic forces, and planets in the solar system.

The people at ACT also write a number of other tests, including the medical school admission test (MCAT), a test for professional golfers, and a test for dieticians. Last year, about 1.1 million students took the ACT.

## How Is the ACT Scored?

Between two and seven weeks after you take the ACT, you and the colleges you have selected, if any, will receive your ACT scores in the mail. Unfortunately, ACT won't give anyone permission to reproduce its score report, but since its score report provides very limited information—basically, scores and percentile ranking—it is easy to describe.

Scores in each of the four sections of the test are reported on a scale of 1 to 36 (36 being the highest score possible). Next to each scaled score is a percentile ranking. Percentile ranking refers to the percentage of people who performed worse than you did on the test. For instance, a percentile ranking of 87 indicates that 86% of the people who took the test scored lower than you did, and 13% scored higher (86 + 13 + 1 (you) = 100%).

Some of the sections have subheadings as well. English is broken down into Usage/Mechanics and Rhetorical Skills. The subcategories may be of some marginal use to colleges; they are much more useful to you if you decide to take the test again, as a way to pinpoint your strengths and weaknesses. In these subheadings, scores are reported on a scale of 1 to 18 (18 being the highest score possible). They are also reported as percentiles. Finally, at the bottom of the page, you will find a composite score. This is an average of what you received on the four main sections.

> **Closed Loop**
>
> The ACT is a test of how well you take the ACT.

## Who Actually Receives the Scores?

You might think that your scores would be mailed directly to you at your home, but this is not always the case. If you take the June administration of the test, scores are mailed to colleges and to you. For all other administrations, scores are sent to colleges and to your high school counselor—not directly to you, unless your high school has given ACT permission to send them to you. You then get the scores from the counselor, unless you leave the High School Code field blank when signing up for the test. We've checked with ACT, and the people we talked to there said it does not matter if you choose not to provide a High School Code—your scores simply won't be sent to your high school. So, if you want your scores sent to your home (and not your high school), leave the High School Code blank. All colleges you list will get copies of your score whether you leave the High School Code blank or not.

There is one potential downside to not reporting your scores to your high school. If you're likely to receive a state-awarded scholarship on the basis of your ACT score, such a score is usually reported to the state's scholarship-awarding entity through—you guessed it—the high school. If you anticipate receiving such a score and are counting on such a scholarship (having taken at least one test as a reality check is a good idea), go ahead and provide your High School Code. As owners of your transcript, you and your parents can go to your high school and have a score removed from it later if you feel the score doesn't reflect your abilities. In any event, since ACT allows score choice (sending scores from just one testing date to colleges), the test scores on your high school transcript ultimately don't matter that much.

## WHEN SHOULD YOU TAKE THE ACT?

The test is given four or five times each year in most of the country, usually at 8:00 A.M. on a Saturday morning. In some states there are six administrations each year. Most students take the ACT in the spring of junior year or in the fall of senior year. A good case can be made for taking it at the earlier date. For one thing, you'll have a better idea of where you stand. If your score is about what you want, you can spend the summer visiting colleges, or getting started on your applications. If your score is lower than you want, you can use the summer to prepare to take the test again in the fall.

The main fall administration is in October. The following states, however, also offer an additional test date in September: Arizona, California, Florida, Georgia, Illinois, Indiana, Maryland, Nevada, North Carolina, Pennsylvania, South Carolina, Texas, and Washington. If you're a rising senior who lives in or near such a state, take advantage of the September administration! It's another shot at raising your scores, for admission or scholarship purposes. And if the commute creates a hardship, leave a day early and stay in a hotel or motel. No one should travel so far that stops at rest areas are required on the morning of the test.

You can obtain a registration packet at your high school guidance office, or by writing or calling ACT at:

> ACT Registration Department
> PO Box 414
> Iowa City, IA 52243
> (319) 337-1270

You can also register online via ACT's website at www.act.org
But before you decide on a test date, there is something you should know…

## Some ACT Test Dates Are Better than Others

On certain dates, the ACT offers what it calls "Test Information Release." If you take the ACT on one of these dates, you can, for a small fee, receive a copy of the test that you took, and for a small additional fee, a photocopy of your actual answer sheet. We strongly advise that you take the test on one of these dates. It is not unheard of for ACT to make a mistake in scoring. You certainly won't find out about this unless you can see the test you took and your own answers. For example, it is possible to fill in an oval on the answer sheet darkly enough for the human eye to see, but not darkly enough for the scantron machine that

### Flying Standby

You don't have to register in advance for the ACT. It is possible to register on the spot on the day of the test for an additional fee, but you *must* bring a completed registration booklet.

scores the test to read. In this case, if you point it out to them, for another small additional fee, ACT will hand-score your test, and change your grade if they made a mistake.

## What If I've Already Taken the ACT Once Before?

The nice folks at ACT allow you to decide which of your ACT scores they report to the colleges. If you want to have full control over this, it is a good idea *not* to take advantage of the four free score reports ACT will send to colleges directly after the test. Why send colleges scores you might not want them to see? While it costs a few extra dollars to get ACT to send scores to schools later, it is well worth being able to send the colleges your best results.

## How to Prepare for the ACT

The Princeton Review materials and test-taking techniques contained in this book should give you all the information you'll need to improve your score on the ACT. However, you will also need to practice our techniques and reinforce your review of math and verbal skills by taking some practice tests.

Other popular coaching books contain several complete practice ACTs. We would strongly advise you *not* to waste your time taking these tests. Unfortunately, the questions in these books are not real ACT questions. Some of them cover material that is not even on the real ACT. Others give the impression that the ACT is much easier or more difficult than it really is. In some cases, taking the practice tests offered in these books could actually hurt your score.

One reason these coaching books do not use real ACT questions is that the folks at ACT won't let them. They have refused to let anyone (including us) license actual questions from old tests. You may have chosen our book because it, too, contains a practice ACT. Rest assured that this test is *modeled very closely after actual ACTs*, with the proper balance of questions reflective of what the ACT actually tests.

Cynics might suggest that no one else can license ACTs because ACT has its own review book, which it sells for $17.00, called *Getting into the ACT: The Official Guide to the ACT Assessment*. Although *The Official Guide* doesn't contain a very full review section and its test-taking strategies are a little gentle (after all, it's hard to burgle your own house), we think their book is worth the price just for the two real tests it contains. We recommend that you either buy their book or ask your high school to send away to ACT for back copies of old tests. You should also get a copy of *Preparing for the ACT Assessment* from your counselor. It's free, and it contains a complete, real ACT.

## The ACT vs. the SAT

You may have to take the ACT anyway, but many of the schools you're interested in will also accept the SAT. We think the SAT is nowhere near as good a test as the ACT. Whereas the ACT says it measures "achievement" (which we believe *can* be measured), the SAT says it measures "ability" (which we don't think can be measured at all; and if it can, the SAT sure isn't doing it).

While we are obviously not tremendously fond of the SAT, you should know that some students end up scoring substantially higher on the SAT than they do on the ACT, and vice versa.

## What, Exactly, Are the Differences?

Currently, the Verbal sections of the SAT are designed primarily to test vocabulary. If you have a strong vocabulary but are weak on usage, it could be to your advantage to take the SAT. (The SAT will become more usage-oriented when the test changes in 2005.)

The Math sections on the SAT are trick oriented, with a heavier emphasis on arithmetic. However, there is currently no trigonometry and virtually no coordinate geometry. If your strengths lie in arithmetic, the SAT might get you a higher score.

To find out which test might be better for you, we have devised the PRA (Princeton Review Assessment), which appears at the back of this book.

## What Is the PRA?

The Princeton Review Assessment is a test that is used to predict your scores on both the ACT and the SAT. The test allows you to see whether it would be in your interest to take the SAT instead of (or as well as) the ACT. An answer key and score charts are provided on the pages right after the test. By following the step-by-step directions you can get approximate scores for both tests, and compare them using the conversion chart used by many colleges. In addition, the answer key tells you which types of question come from which test, so you can assess your performance on each directly.

Because it is brief, the PRA will only give you a possible range of scores. If there is only a slight discrepancy between your projected ACT and SAT scores, it certainly isn't worth taking both. However, if there's a big difference in favor of the SAT, you should consider taking the SAT as well.

## What Is The Princeton Review?

The Princeton Review is the world's leading test-preparation and education services company. We run courses at hundreds of locations worldwide, and offer web-based instruction at www.PrincetonReview.com. Our test-taking techniques and review strategies are unique and powerful. We developed them after studying all the real ACTs we could get our hands on and analyzing them with the most sophisticated software available. You can get in touch with us at 800-2Review.

## A Final Thought Before You Begin

The ACT does not measure intelligence, and it does not predict your ultimate success or failure as a human being. No matter how high or how low you score on this test initially—and no matter how much you may increase your score through preparation—you should *never* consider the score you receive on this or any other test a final judgment of your abilities.

# 1
# Triage

## WOULDN'T IT BE GREAT IF...

Wouldn't it be great if all the questions on the ACT were arranged in order of difficulty? Then you could do the easiest questions first and move on from there. That way you wouldn't waste a lot of time trying to answer difficult questions before you had answered all the easy questions, which count for the same number of points anyway.

Unfortunately, the ACT is not really organized that way.

According to the ACT writers we interviewed, the English section of the test is not in any order of difficulty. In the Math section, according to ACT literature, "most people find the first questions on the test easier . . . than the ones that come later" but these are only very rough guidelines. Many Princeton Review students find that some questions toward the end of the test are easier than most of the questions that preceded them.

**Equality**

Remember that easy questions are worth just as much as hard questions. So do the easy ones first!

## OH. BUT WHAT IF...

But what if, in the Science Reasoning and Reading sections, the *passages* were arranged in order of difficulty? Some of the test preparation books you can buy in bookstores maintain that they are. According to one ACT writer, this is true, ". . . only in an average sense. We believe in the *philosophy* that if students are running out of time, the questions they don't get to should be ones they would have difficulty with anyway. But students will find plenty of exceptions."

## OH. BUT...

It's no use. On the ACT, if you want to do the easy questions first, you're going to have to find them for yourself. We have a good way to think about this. We call it "Triage."

## TRIAGE

This is the medical term for the technique used by emergency room doctors when they have several emergencies at the same time. In order to save lives, the doctors treat the patients with the worst wounds or illnesses first, then progress downward in severity, until they finally get around to the patient with the scratch on his nose.

In ACT triage, we want you to learn to do exactly the same thing—*in reverse*. See that really tough algebra problem lying over there? Forget it, it's a goner. Send for the chaplain. Now this easy addition problem, on the other hand—this is one to do right now.

See that tough, horrible passage about European authoritarianism during the nineteenth century? Let's see if it's still breathing after we finish the one about Ronald Reagan's election in 1980.

## JUST ONE MORE MINUTE...

The temptation to get stubborn and stay with a particular problem can be very strong, especially when it is an early one. We've all had the experience of *thinking* we were on the verge of an answer. But if it takes you four minutes to solve question number five, that might mean you will never get a chance to look at several other questions later in the test that you would have found easy.

## "Oh, Yeah!"

We've also all had the experience of riding home in the car, and suddenly clapping our hand to our forehead as we finally realized exactly how to do question number five. By using triage, you can sometimes have this burst of revelation *before* the test is over, when you can still do something about it. So how does triage work exactly?

## Now, Later, Much Later

Do you want to do the problem NOW? That is the question you should constantly be asking yourself during the exam. If you finish reading a problem and immediately know how to solve it, then of course you should do it right away.

But what if you finish reading a problem and you aren't really certain how to begin? Put a circle around it and move on. This might seem hard to do at first, but it is one of the central tenets of good test taking, and it gets easier with practice. You aren't skipping the problem forever. You're just putting it at the back of the line.

## Two Passes

We want you to do each section in two passes. During the **first pass,** the object is to nail every single question that already has your name on it. By answering all the questions you're sure of, you will never have to hear the words, "O.K., pencils down," and know that there were several more questions you could have done if only there had been more time. You will already have done them.

## What Happens If I Think I Know How to Do It, But Then I Realize I Was Wrong?

Nobody's right all the time. As soon as you realize you're stuck, you should put a big circle around the question and move on. This is the time when people tend to get stubborn. They think, "But I've already spent so much time on this question. It would be a waste to skip it now."

## You Haven't Wasted the Time; You've Invested It

When you come back to this question on the second pass, you won't be starting from scratch. You'll already have read the question once. You might have made some notes in the margin. Perhaps reading it again will make you realize an important point you missed the first time. If not, throw it to the back of the line, and count your blessings: You could still be back there working on question number five!

## The Second Pass

Now, with about ten minutes left in the section, come back to the questions you circled for a **second pass.** Again, think ACT triage. Most of the "patients" in your emergency room have now been handled. Look over the remaining problems and ask yourself the same question: Which one do I want to do NOW? Obviously, none of them struck you as *easy* the first time or you would have done them on the first pass. On the other hand, among the remaining problems, some are probably more likely bets than others.

**First Pass, Second Pass**

On the first pass, do the questions you know how to do. On the second pass, do the questions you *think* you know how to do.

Sometimes when you read a question again, you suddenly realize what the point of the question really is. This will save you from having that "Oh, yeah!" revelation riding home in the car. But other times when you reread a question, you suddenly realize that you will hate this question for the rest of your life and you never, ever want to see it again. Fine. Throw it to the back of the list, and keep looking.

Sometimes you reject a question initially because you think it will take too much time. Well, now you have time. You've already locked in all the sure points, so maybe this is the question to do now.

## O.K., I'VE DONE ALL THE QUESTIONS I KNOW HOW TO DO AND ALL THE QUESTIONS I THINK I KNOW HOW TO DO. NOW WHAT?

You guess. Guessing on the ACT is so important that we've given it its own chapter.

# 2

# Guessing and POE

Imagine for a moment that you are a contestant on *Let's Make a Deal*. It's the final, big deal of the day. Monty Hall asks you, "Do you want curtain number one, curtain number two, or curtain number three?" As you carefully weigh your options, the members of the audience are screaming out their suggestions. But you can bet that there is one suggestion no one in the audience is going to shout to you:

"Skip the question!"

**Be Test Smart**

Many students with good grades get below-average scores because they refuse to guess.

It wouldn't make sense. You have a one in three shot of winning, and there is no penalty for guessing wrong. (Okay, you might have to cart home a lifetime supply of toilet paper.)

On the ACT, you don't even have to worry about the toilet paper, because there is no guessing penalty at all.

## YOU MUST ANSWER EVERY SINGLE QUESTION ON THE ACT

There are 215 questions on the ACT. If you went in to the test room, filled out your name, and then went to sleep for three and a half hours, your composite score would be just about what you might expect: 0.

However, if you went into the test room, filled out your name, went to sleep for three and a quarter hours, and then picked answer choice B 215 times, guess what your composite score would be? 12!

We would not recommend random guessing as an overall strategy (unless all you need is a 12—and that's only the first percentile), but you can see that it is in your interest to guess on every question.

Ah, but there's guessing and then there's guessing.

## HOW TO SCORE HIGHER ON THE ACT

Try the following question:

**1.** What is the French word for "eggplant"?

**Multiple Choice**

The ACT is a multiple-choice test. This means you don't have to come up with an answer; you just have to identify the correct answer from among the four or five choices provided.

What? You don't know? Well then, you'd better guess at random. (By the way, there are no questions about vegetables, French or otherwise, on the ACT. We're just using this question to make a point.)

If you really don't know the answer to a question, of course, you should always guess. But before you choose an answer at random, take a look at the problem the way you would see it on the ACT:

**1.** What is the French word for "eggplant"?
   A. のみもの
   B. すきやき
   C. Aubergine
   D. デザート

Suddenly the question looks a lot easier, doesn't it? You may not have known the correct answer to this question, but you certainly knew three answers that were incorrect.

# POE

The Process of Elimination (POE for short) will enable you to make your guesses really count. Incorrect answer choices are often easier to spot than correct ones. Sometimes they are logically absurd; sometimes they just sound wrong. While you will rarely be able to eliminate all the incorrect answer choices, it is often possible to eliminate one or two. And each time you can eliminate an answer choice, your odds of guessing correctly get better.

Try another question:

> 1. What is the Sioux word for "beautiful"?
>    A. Hopa
>    B. のみもの
>    C. Hunhe
>    D. デザート

This time you could probably only eliminate two of the answer choices. However, that meant you were down to a fifty-fifty guess—much better than random guessing.

The Process of Elimination is a tremendously powerful tool. We will refer to it in every single chapter of the rest of this book.

## A Moral Dilemma

What if someone approached you moments before the ACT began and offered to give you the answers to the test? You'd be shocked; SHOCKED! Right? But what if we told you that the person making the offer was the proctor running the test? The fact is that every student who takes the test gets to see virtually all the answers ahead of time; they're printed in the test booklet, right underneath each question.

# 3

# Taking the ACT

The best way to prepare for any test is to find out exactly what is going to be on it. This book will provide you with just that information. In the following chapters you will find a comprehensive review of all the question types on the ACT, complete information on all the subjects covered by the ACT, and some powerful test-taking strategies developed specifically for the ACT.

To take full advantage of the review and techniques, it's important that you practice on the test in this book, as well as on real ACT questions. We've already told you on page 8 how to obtain copies of real ACTs. Taking full practice tests will allow you to chart your progress (with accurate scores in each section), give you confidence in our techniques, and develop your stamina.

## THE NIGHT BEFORE THE TEST

Unless you are the kind of person who remains calm only by staying up all night to do last-minute studying, we recommend that you take the evening off. Go see a movie, or read a good book (besides this one), and make sure you get to bed at a normal hour. No final frantically memorized math formula or grammatical rule is going to make or break your score. A positive mental attitude comes from treating yourself decently. If you've prepared over the last several weeks or months, then you're ready.

If you haven't really prepared, there will be other opportunities to take the test, so get some rest and do the best you can. Remember, the colleges will only see the score you choose to let them see. No *one* ACT is going to be crucial. We don't think night-before-the-test cramming is very effective. For example, we would not recommend that you try going through this book in one night.

## ON THE DAY OF THE TEST

It's important that you eat a real breakfast, even if you normally don't. We find that about two-thirds of the way through the test, people who didn't eat something beforehand suddenly lose the will to live. Equally important, bring a snack to the test center. You will get a break, during which food is allowed. Some people spend the break out in the hallways comparing answers and getting upset when their answers don't match. Ignore the people around you, and eat your snack. Why assume they know any more than you do?

## WARMING UP

**Don't Leave Home Without 'Em**

- admissions ticket
- photo ID or letter of identification
- plenty of sharpened pencils
- a watch
- a calculator

While you're having breakfast, do a couple of questions from an ACT you've already seen to get your mind working. You don't want to use the first section of the real test to warm up.

At the test center, you'll be asked to show some form of picture ID or provide a note from your school, on school stationery, describing what you look like. The time is NOT announced during the test sections, so you should also bring a reliable watch—not the beeping kind—and, of course, several number two pencils, an eraser, and a calculator—the one you use every day. If you haven't changed the batteries recently (or ever!), you should do that before the test too.

When you get into the actual room in which you'll be taking the test, make sure you're comfortable. Is there enough light? Is your desk sturdy? Don't be afraid to speak up; you're going to be spending three and a half hours at that desk. And it's not a bad idea to go to the bathroom *before* you get to the room. It's a long haul to that first break.

## ZEN AND THE ART OF TEST TAKING

Once the test begins, tune out the rest of the world. That girl with the annoying cough in the next row? You don't hear her. The guy who is fidgeting in the seat ahead of you? You don't see him. It's just you and the test. Everything else should be a blur.

As soon as one section ends, erase it completely from your mind. It no longer exists. The only section that counts is the one you are taking right now. Even if you are upset about a particular section, erase it from your mind. Most people in the middle of taking the ACT are not great at assessing how a particular section went anyway. We once asked a group of students who were taking a practice test to write down at the end of each section how they thought they were doing compared to past tests. There was practically no correlation at all.

## KEEP YOUR ANSWERS TO YOURSELF

Please don't let anyone cheat off you. Test companies have developed sophisticated anti-cheating measures that go way beyond having a proctor walk around the room. We know of one test company that gets seating charts of each testing room. Their computers scan the score sheets of people sitting in the immediate vicinity for correlations of wrong answer choices. Innocent and guilty are invited to take the test over again, and their scores from the first test are invalidated.

## MISBUBBLING YOUR ANSWER SHEET

Probably the most painful kind of mistake you can make on the ACT is to bubble in A with your number two pencil when you really meant B. The proctor isn't allowed to let you change your answers after a section is over, so it is fairly important that you either catch yourself before the section ends, or—even better—that you don't make a mistake in the first place.

We suggest to our students that they write down their answers in their test booklet. This way, whenever you finish a page of questions in the test booklet, you can transfer all your answers from that page in a group. We find this cuts down the possibility of misbubbling, and it saves time as well. Of course, as you get near the end of a section, you should go back to bubbling question by question.

If you get back your scores from ACT and they seem completely out of line, you can ask the ACT examiners to look over your answer sheet for what are called "gridding errors." If you want to, you can even be there while they look. If it is clear that there has been an error, ACT will change your score. An example of a clear gridding error would be a section in which, if you moved all the responses over by one, they would suddenly all be correct.

**Write Now**

Feel free to write all over your test booklet. Don't do computations in your head—put them in the booklet. You paid for it; go nuts.

## How Much Time Do I Have to Cancel My Scores?

While ACT allows you to cancel your scores only at the test, you can stop scores from reaching colleges if you call ACT by 12 noon, Central Standard Time, on the *Thursday* following the test. The number to call is 319-337-1270. Also, if you've taken the ACT two or more times (something we heartily recommend), you can choose which score you want colleges to see when you request reports from ACT.

# PART II

# How to Beat
# the ACT English Test

## What's Good Writing?

Deciding what constitutes good writing is difficult. So much depends on the context, on what the writer is trying to accomplish—and on who is doing the deciding.

## Call Us Ignorant, but We Prefer "Four Score and Seven"

These days, there are even computer programs that are supposed to fix our writing. Mike Royko, the national columnist, once decided to try out one of these computer programs on Abraham Lincoln's Gettysburg Address, with predictably humorous results. "Four score and seven years ago" became "eighty-seven years ago" and it went downhill from there, turning a moving document of history into trite, conventional, standard written English.

## What the English Test Tests

The English Test measures how well you understand "the conventions of standard written English." There are five passages to read. Portions of the passages will be underlined, and you must decide whether these portions are correct as they stand, or whether one of the other answer choices is better.

On Your Mark...
75 questions; 45 minutes

These questions are designed to measure punctuation (10 questions), grammar (12 questions), and sentence structure (18 questions). Other questions are designed to see how you might revise and strengthen a passage (11 questions), whether you would change particular words for style or clarity (12 questions), or how you might "explain or support a point of view [more] clearly and effectively" (12 questions). There is a total of 75 questions to answer in 45 minutes.

## What Your Score Means

Good writing is, to some extent, a matter of opinion. No matter how well or how badly you do on the English Test, you should not feel that your ACT English score truly represents your ability to write. A good score does not make you the next Jane Austen; a bad score does not make you the next Bart Simpson.

We don't mean to imply that ACT is doing a bad job. It's tough to measure English skills, and we think the test writers have constructed a fine test. In the end, however, what the ACT English Test is measuring is how well you take the ACT English Test.

## Remember, This Is a Standardized Test

Every time the ACT is given, it tests the same things, in the same way. You don't need to be a strong writer to do well on this test. You *do* need to know what types of errors crop up again and again, and how to fix them.

We are going to review all punctuation, grammar, sentence structure, and rhetorical skills that are tested on this exam.

# What Do the Passages Look Like?

Here is part of a sample passage:

[1]

When studying a foreign language, <u>its</u>
    [1]

helpful to have a grasp <u>with</u> other foreign
    [2]

<u>languages, if only</u> because one has already
    [3]
learned what things are most important to
know how to say first.

[2]

I am proud to tell you that I can ask,
"Where is the bathroom?" in four different
languages. We both, however, admire the ac-
complishments of my clumsy friend, Al. He
can <u>says</u> he is sorry in fourteen different
    [4]

languages. [5]

1. **A.** NO CHANGE
   **B.** its'
   **C.** it's
   **D.** it, is

2. **F.** NO CHANGE
   **G.** of
   **H.** to
   **J.** OMIT the underlined portion

3. **A.** NO CHANGE
   **B.** languages. Only
   **C.** languages, only if
   **D.** language: only if

4. **F.** NO CHANGE
   **G.** say
   **H.** said
   **J.** says that

5. Suppose the author wants to add the
   following sentence to the essay:
   > My friend Alice can ask for directions in
   > five different languages.
   **A.** Before the first sentence of paragraph 2
   **B.** Before the second sentence of paragraph 2
   **C.** Before the third sentence of paragraph 2
   **D.** At the end of paragraph 2

---

Item 6 poses a question about the
preceding as a whole.

---

6. Considering the subject matter and tone of
   the passage, is the writer's use of the pronoun
   "I" appropriate?
   **F.** No, because the writer is speaking about
   the general experience of learning a language.
   **G.** No, because the writer is not just discussing her own experiences but also those
   of her friend.
   **H.** Yes, because this is an informal narrative,
   which needs a personal feel.
   **J.** Yes, because there is no way for the author
   to get across her thoughts without the
   personal pronoun.

Most of the questions refer to individual words or phrases in the passage; these words are underlined and numbered. A few of the questions (like question 5) ask you about the organization of a paragraph. You can tell what paragraph they ask about by looking for the question number in a box at the end of a paragraph. (See the number 5 in a box at the end of the passage?) You will also see a few questions (like question 6) that ask you about the passage as a whole. By the way, the answers are 1C, 2G, 3A, 4G, 5B, 6H.

## TRIAGE

In chapter 1, we introduced you to the concept of triage, and told you that it would be useful on every section of this test. In this section, the ACT writers have concocted their own brand of triage by organizing the questions so that the easier specific questions (on subjects like punctuation and grammar and sentence structure) tend to come first. At the end of each passage, there are a couple of tougher rhetoric questions based on the passage as a whole.

However, some rhetoric questions are sprinkled throughout the passages—and just because a question is at the beginning of a passage or because it only deals with a small mistake in grammar doesn't mean that you will necessarily spot the correct answer right away. If you are not sure what point of grammar, punctuation, or sentence structure is being tested, you might want to circle the question and move on.

In our students' experience, the format of this section—passages side by side with the questions—tends to make them want to guess too quickly. The impulse to pick the first answer that sounds good is sometimes very strong. After all, this *is* English, which for many of us is our first language.

The problem, of course, is that it is *not* English exactly—at least not the English we speak every day.

## ACT ISLAND

Imagine that a bunch of ACT writers were shipwrecked on a desert island about 20 years ago. Not having much to do, they go on writing tests, which they slip into empty bottles and cast into the sea. The tests regularly wash up on the coast of Iowa (yes, we know that Iowa is landlocked), where the national headquarters of ACT is located. The company is grateful and uses the tests regularly.

The only problem is that, after 20 years, the test writers' English is getting a little old-fashioned and stilted. Still, the company feels a lot of loyalty to these shipwrecked mariners and wouldn't dream of changing their tests.

If you make a lot of mistakes in this section, it is probably because you are relying on your ear—which is used to hearing a less formal English than is used on the ACT. A much better way to approach this section is to look for the specific errors that appear on the test all the time. By looking for these errors, you can take the guesswork out of your approach to the ACT English Test.

### LOOKING FOR CLUES

One of the best ways to look for errors is to search the answer choices for clues. The underlined portions are very short, usually only a few words, so it's easy to see how each choice is different from the others. These differences offer a strong indication of what is on the minds of the ACT writers.

**First Pass, Second Pass**

On your first pass, tackle all the errors you recognize. On your second pass, do the ones you don't.

**The Rules of ACT Island**

Don't just rely on your ears; look for specific errors.

Look at the following example:

27. **A.** NO CHANGE
    **B.** one goes
    **C.** you go
    **D.** he goes

Clearly, this question is about pronouns. Even if you had not spotted something wrong with the underlined portion of the passage as you read it, the answer choices are telling you to check to see which of these pronouns agrees with the noun referred to in the passage. (Don't worry if you are rusty on pronouns—we'll cover them in detail later in this section.)

In the sections that follow we will show you the key elements to look for in the passages and in the answer choices.

## What If There Is More than One Thing Wrong?

There is often more than one error in the underlined portion of a sentence. However, the best way to approach these questions is not to try to see everything at once. Find *one* error. Eliminate the answer choices that contain the same error. Then look among the remaining answer choices for the one you like best.

**What's Wrong?**
About 25% of the time
. . . absolutely *nothing*.

## No Change

Many of the questions in this section have NO CHANGE as the first of the answer choices. Just because this is a test is no reason to assume that there is always something wrong. NO CHANGE turns out to be the correct answer a bit less than a quarter of the time it is offered. So don't be afraid to select it.

## Omit the Underlined Portion

A few of the questions in this section will have "OMIT the underlined portion" as the last of the four answer choices. When this choice is offered it has a high probability of being correct—better than half the time on most of the tests we have looked at.

It is worth noting that when you do see OMIT, you should examine it very carefully.

## A Warning

To forestall the objections of the expert grammarians out there, let us say at the outset that this discussion is not designed to be an all-inclusive discussion of English grammar and usage. You are reading this chapter to do well on the English Test of the ACT. Thus, if we seem to oversimplify a point, or ignore an arcane exception to a rule, it's because we do not feel that any more detail is warranted.

## Before We Begin, Some Terminology

The ACT is not going to ask you to identify parts of speech or diagram a sentence, but it will be helpful for the discussion that follows if you know some basic definitions. Here's a simple sentence:

*Tom broke the vase.*

This sentence is made up of two nouns, a verb, and an article.

- A **noun** is a word used to name a person, place, thing, or idea.
- A **verb** is a word that expresses action.
- An **article** is a word that modifies or limits a noun.

In the sentence on the previous page, *Tom* and *vase* are both **nouns.** *The* is an **article.** *Broke* is a **verb.** *Tom* is the **subject** of the sentence because it is the person, place, or thing about which something is being said. *Vase* is the **object** of the sentence because it receives the action of the verb.

Here's a more complicated version of the same sentence:

> *Tom accidentally broke the big vase of flowers.*

We've added an adverb, an adjective, and a prepositional phrase to the original sentence.

- An **adverb** is a word that modifies a verb, an adjective, or another adverb.
- An **adjective** is a word that modifies a noun.
- A **preposition** is a word that notes the relation of a noun to an action or a thing.
- A **phrase** is a group of words that acts as a single part of speech. A phrase is missing either a subject or a verb or both.
- A **prepositional phrase** is a group of words beginning with a preposition.

In the sentence above, *accidentally* is an **adverb** modifying the verb *broke.* *Big* is an **adjective** modifying the noun *vase.* *Of* is a **preposition** because it shows a relationship between *vase* and *flowers.* *Of flowers* is a **prepositional phrase** that acts like an adjective by modifying *vase.*

Here's an even more complicated version of the same sentence:

> *As he ran across the room, Tom accidentally broke the big vase of flowers.*

Now, we've added a secondary clause containing a pronoun to the original sentence.

- A **pronoun** is a word that takes the place of a noun.
- A **clause** is a group of words containing a subject and a verb.

*Tom accidentally broke the big vase of flowers* is considered the **independent clause** in this sentence, because it contains the main idea of the sentence and could stand by itself. *As he ran across the room* is also a **clause** (it contains a subject and a verb), but because it is not a complete thought, it is called a **dependent clause.** This particular dependent clause is also known as an **adverbial clause** because it tells us something *about* the action that took place. *He* is a **pronoun** taking the place of *Tom.*

# 4

# Sentence Structure

Good sentence structure is about putting clauses and phrases—the essential building blocks of sentences—together in logical ways. Before we talk about the *errors* of sentence structure, let's spend a moment talking about correct structure. Here is that example again:

> *As he ran across the room, Tom broke the vase.*

This sentence consists of two clauses. Each clause has a subject and a verb. The second clause ("Tom broke the vase") is considered the main clause and is **independent,** because it can stand alone. The first clause ("As he ran across the room,") is called **dependent** because it can't.

You can easily change a dependent clause into an independent clause and vice versa. Often, all it takes is a single word.

> *He ran across the room.*

By removing "as" from the dependent clause, we suddenly have a sentence that can stand on its own. By adding an "as" to the second clause, we can instantly change it into a dependent clause.

> *As Tom broke the vase, . . .*

If we stuck these two new clauses together now, the meaning of the sentence would be very different. Could we have kept the meaning more or less the same and still made the first clause independent? Sure. Try this:

> *Tom ran across the room, breaking the vase.*

Now the first half of the sentence contains the main independent clause. We had to change "he" to "Tom" so the reader would know who the sentence was talking about. We also had to change the second half of the sentence from a clause into a modifying phrase. While a clause has a subject and a verb, a phrase generally has no subject.

## PUTTING THE PIECES TOGETHER

Proficient writers use a mixture of dependent clauses, independent clauses, and phrases to add variety to their writing and to create emphasis. By combining these building blocks in different ways, writers show the reader which thoughts are most important, and create a rhythm.

Here are the most often used structures:

- Independent clause (period) New independent clause (period)

  > *Jane lit the campfire. Frank set up the tent.*

- Independent clause (comma) AND independent clause (period)

  > *Jane lit the campfire, and Frank set up the tent.*

- Independent clause (semicolon) independent clause (period)

    *Jane lit the campfire; Frank set up the tent.*

- Independent clause (comma) dependent clause (period)

    *Jane lit the campfire, while Frank set up the tent.*

- Dependent clause (comma) independent clause (period)

    *As Jane lit the campfire, Frank set up the tent.*

All of these examples are correct. A writer might choose one over another to emphasize one thought over another. For example, in the last sentence, the writer is choosing to make "setting up the tent" the focus. Perhaps in the next sentence the tent is going to collapse with Frank inside it.

There are four main types of errors in sentence structure:

- sentence fragments
- run-ons and comma splices
- misplaced modifiers
- parallel construction

All of these errors are results of incorrect placement of the building blocks that make up sentences. Sentence structure on the ACT is closely tied to punctuation. The two are related because sentence structure errors can often be fixed through proper punctuation. In fact, you will find that by using punctuation clues from the answer choices, you will often be able to zero in on sentence structure errors in the passages.

## SENTENCE FRAGMENTS

A complete sentence must have a subject and a verb, and it must be able to stand alone. In other words it must be, or contain, an **independent clause**. Remember the very first example in this chapter?

    *Tom broke the vase.*

This is an independent clause. We can change it into a **dependent clause** by adding just one word.

    *When Tom broke the vase, ...*

Even though it still has a subject and a verb, this clause can no longer stand alone. It is now waiting for an independent clause to finish the sentence.

    *When Tom broke the vase, Sid ran to tell his Aunt Sally.*

**Fragments**

The ACT always contains. A few sentence fragments. Like these.

**Sentence Fragment Check**

Look out for...
- a dependent clause by itself
- punctuation changes in the answer choices

You can turn any independent clause into a dependent clause by *adding* one of these words to the beginning of it:

> when, where, why, how, if, as, because,
> although, while, despite, that, who, what

(You may see these words referred to in *The Official Guide to the ACT Assessment* or in grammar books as subordinating conjunctions, relative pronouns, or prepositions, but these terms are not important.)

By the same token, you can turn most dependent clauses into independent clauses by *taking away* these words.

## The First Sentence Fragment Type

There are two kinds of sentence fragments. The first is just a dependent clause waiting for a second half that isn't there. Here's an example:

The bride and groom drove away in their car. <u>As the</u> children ran behind, shouting and laughing.
1

1.  **A.** NO CHANGE
    **B.** While the
    **C.** During which the
    **D.** The

## Here's How to Crack It

The second "sentence" in the example isn't a sentence at all; it is a dependent clause, beginning with one of those words we told you to be on the lookout for—"as." Answer choices B and C repeat the error by using other words from the same list. The only answer that makes the clause independent is answer choice **D.**

Could we have combined the second "sentence" with the first to make a correct sentence? Yes, but in this case, ACT didn't give us that option: The period at the end of the *first* sentence wasn't underlined, so we couldn't change it.

## The Second Sentence Fragment Type

In the second type of sentence fragment question, the ACT writers ask you to *incorporate* the sentence fragment into the complete sentence that comes immediately before or after the fragment. In the example that follows, notice that the underlining extends from the end of one sentence through the beginning of the next sentence, and it includes the punctuation as well:

Although it will always be associated with Shakespeare's famous literary <u>character. The</u> castle at Elsinore was never home to Hamlet.
2

2.  **F.** NO CHANGE
    **G.** character, the
    **H.** character; the
    **J.** character. A

## Here's How to Crack It

The underlined portion of this passage includes pieces of two sentences and the punctuation in between. We have to check both "sentences" to make sure that they are complete. Let's check the first "sentence" first. Can it stand on its own?

No. It's a dependent clause. Aha! This is the error. Could we have removed the "Although" at the beginning to create an independent clause? Sure, but that isn't an option in this case because "Although" isn't underlined.

This time, the only way to fix the passage is to combine the dependent clause with the independent clause to form one big sentence. As we will discuss further in the punctuation review, you need a comma between a dependent and an independent clause. The only answer choice that contains a comma is choice **G**. This must be the correct answer.

## How Do You Spot a Sentence Fragment?

You will often be able to spot this type of error as you read the passage itself, now that you know to look for a dependent clause all by itself. However, if you don't see the error as you read the passage the first time, don't despair. There are three terrific clues waiting for you.

## The Answer Choices Contain Valuable Clues

If you're having trouble deciding whether a passage has a sentence construction error, it helps to look at the answer choices. They often contain great clues as to what is going on in the test writers' minds. For example, in the last question it might have helped to look at the differences in *punctuation* among the answer choices. Some of the choices break the two clauses into two sentences. Others combine them. This might make you ask, "Why would ACT be giving me this choice? Maybe this question is about sentence construction. Would it be better to combine the two clauses? Hmm. Let me check for sentence fragments."

Sometimes, of course, there will be no need to change the sentence at all. Remember, the answer NO CHANGE is right slightly less than a quarter of the time. However, the flip side of this is that NO CHANGE is wrong slightly more than three-quarters of the time.

## COMMA SPLICES AND RUN-ONS

In a **comma splice,** two independent clauses are jammed together into one sentence, usually with only a comma to try to hold them together.

> *Aunt Sally ran into the room, Tom was already gone.*

There are several ways to fix this sentence. The easiest way would be to break it up into two sentences.

> *Aunt Sally ran into the room. Tom was already gone.*

If there is a clear reason why one clause might be connected to the other (for example, if Tom has just broken Aunt Sally's vase), you can also fix it by putting a **conjunction** (such as "and" or "but") between the two thoughts.

> *Aunt Sally ran into the room, but Tom was already gone.*

If there is some connection between the two clauses, but it is not really a matter of cause and effect, you can break up the two thoughts with a semicolon instead of a period.

*Aunt Sally arrived home several hours later; Tom was already gone.*

A **run-on** sentence is pretty much the same thing as a comma splice, without the comma.

*Aunt Sally swept up the shards of glass she was furious.*

Again, the easiest way to solve the problem is to break up the sentence into two new sentences.

*Aunt Sally swept up the shards of glass. She was furious.*

A run-on sentence is often much longer than our example, running on and on, you might actually run out of breath if you read it out loud and then wonder whether perhaps it would have been better to split it up into more than one sentence. That last sentence, of course, was a run-on as well.

## Here's How They Look on the ACT

There is not much difference between the decision to enter politics and the decision to jump into a pit full of <u>rattlesnakes, in fact,</u> you might find a friendlier environment in the snake pit.

3. **A.** NO CHANGE
   **B.** rattlesnakes. In fact,
   **C.** rattlesnakes in fact
   **D.** rattlesnakes, in fact

## Here's How to Crack It

Check the punctuation. As soon as you see that one or more of the answer choices gives you the option of breaking the sentence up into two pieces, you should immediately consider whether there might be a comma-splice or run-on problem. Are the two clauses surrounding the punctuation both independent? Yes! This is probably a comma splice error. Now, the question is how to fix it. Only one of the answer choices breaks the long sentence into two little ones. Answer choice B is probably correct. Remember, however, that there are other ways to fix a comma splice; to be certain, try out the other answer choices in the sentence. Perhaps one of them will use a conjunction to bridge the two clauses. Is that the case here? No. Therefore, the correct answer is choice **B**.

The college's plans for expansion included a new science building and a new <u>dormitory if</u> the funding drive were successful there would be enough money for both.

4. **F.** NO CHANGE
   **G.** dormitory, if
   **H.** dormitory; if,
   **J.** dormitory. If

## Here's How to Crack It

If you could start from scratch, there would be lots of different ways to express the thoughts in this passage. However, as always, you must find the way that the ACT writers decided to use.

Again, the answer choices provide an immediate clue: In some, the sentence is broken up into two smaller sentences. Check to see if there are independent clauses on either side of the punctuation. Bingo: This is a run-on sentence. Which choices can we eliminate? F and G bite the dust. Both H and J successfully break up the two clauses. (Remember, a semicolon will often do the trick if the subjects of the two clauses are related.)

Is there anything else wrong with either of them? Come to think of it, the comma at the end of choice H is unnecessary. The correct answer is **J.**

## MISPLACED MODIFIERS

A modifying phrase needs to be near what it is modifying. If it gets too far away, it can get misplaced.

> *Sweeping up the shards of glass, the missing key to the jewelry box was found by Aunt Sally.*

As written, this sentence gives the impression that the *missing key* was sweeping up the shards of glass. When a sentence begins with a modifying phrase (a group of words without a subject), the noun being modified must follow the phrase. *Who* was sweeping up the shards of glass? Aunt Sally, of course. The correct version of this sentence would be:

> *Sweeping up the shards of glass, Aunt Sally found the missing key to her jewelry box.*

A more subtle version of the same type of error:

> *Ecstatic and happy, Aunt Sally's key opened the jewelry box for the first time in weeks.*

At first glance, it looks like the modifying phrase "ecstatic and happy" is modifying Aunt Sally. However, what is the real subject of this sentence, as written? The key. "Aunt Sally's" is actually modifying the key. A correct version of this sentence would be:

> *Ecstatic and happy, Aunt Sally was able to use her key to open the jewelry box for the first time in weeks*

Here's how a misplaced modifier might look on the ACT:

Walking to the pawnshop, <u>Bob's watch dropped into the sewer</u>.
5

**5. A.** NO CHANGE
   **B.** Bob's watch dropped in the sewer
   **C.** Bob dropped his watch into the sewer
   **D.** Bob's dropped his watch into the sewer

**Misplaced Modifier Check**

Look out for...

- modifying phrases followed by commas—is the noun being modified right after the comma?

### Here's How to Crack It

Bob's watch may have dropped into the sewer, but it certainly can't be walking to the pawnshop. So we've got to get Bob closer to the comma so it's clear that the first half of the sentence refers to him. Only **C** does that.

### How Do You Spot Misplaced Modifiers?

That's easy! If the underlined portion of the sentence is part of a modifying phrase, check to make sure it modifies the correct noun. If the underlined portion of the sentence includes the noun that is supposed to be modified, check to make sure it is the correct noun.

**Construction Shift Check**

Look out for...
• shifting phrases in the answerchoices

## CONSTRUCTION SHIFTS

A related type of error is what the ACT writers call construction shifts. These resemble misplaced modifiers in that the modifier is in the wrong place, but construction shifts require no words to be changed. Instead, the modifying word or phrase simply has to be moved over slightly:

Stepping to avoid the large puddle, I

<u>carefully</u> tripped and fell.
6

6. **F.** NO CHANGE
   **G.** (Place after *Stepping*)
   **H.** (Place after *and*)
   **J.** (Place after *fell*)

### Here's How to Crack It

These questions require just a little common sense. "Carefully" is an adverb. It must modify a verb. The only question for us is, which verb? Only a stunt man trips or falls "carefully." This effectively disposes of answer choices F, H, and J. If we put "carefully" after "stepping" does the sentence make sense? Yes, so the answer is **G**.

### How Do You Spot Construction Shifts?

That's easy. The answer choices in construction shifts are either presented as shown above, or like this:

<u>Stepping to avoid the large puddle, I carefully tripped and fell.</u>
7

7. **A.** NO CHANGE
   **B.** Stepping carefully over the puddle I tripped and fell.
   **C.** Stepping over the puddle I tripped and carefully fell.
   **D.** Stepping over the puddle I tripped and fell carefully.

In either case, it is easy to see that the only difference in each of the answer choices is the position of the word "carefully." This should alert you to consider the position of the modifier.

# PARALLEL CONSTRUCTION

There are two major types of parallel construction errors tested on the ACT. They both involve some kind of list. You might see a list of **verbs:**

> When Tom finally came home, Aunt Sally kissed him, hugged him, and gives him his favorite dessert after dinner.

The sentence above is wrong because all of the items on the list must be in the same tense. The first two verbs in the example above ("kissed" and "hugged") are in the past tense, but the third verb ("gives") is in the present tense. It is not "parallel" with the other two. The correct sentence should read:

> When Tom finally came home, Aunt Sally _kissed_ him, _hugged_ him, and _gave_ him his favorite dessert after dinner.

You also might see a list of **nouns:**

> Three explanations for Sid's locking himself in his room were _a desire_ to do his homework, _a sense_ that he needed to hone his college essays, and _hating_ his brother Tom, who always gets away with murder.

The sentence above is wrong because while "a desire" and "a sense" are both nouns, "hating" is a gerund, or a verb functioning as a noun. Is there a more noun-like way to say the same thing? If you said "a hatred," you were absolutely right. Now the sentence is parallel. Here's the corrected version:

> Three explanations for Sid's locking himself in his room were _a desire_ to do his homework, _a sense_ that he needed to hone his college essays, and _a hatred_ for his brother Tom, who always gets away with murder.

The lists do not have to have _three_ nouns or _three_ verbs. Sometimes there are only two:

> _To see_ the beauty of a sunset in Venice is _experiencing_ perfection.

This is wrong because if the first half of the sentence begins with the infinitive "to see," the second half of the sentence must do the same thing:

> _To see_ the beauty of a sunset in Venice is _to experience_ perfection.

## How Do I Spot Parallel Construction Problems?

That's easy. First, as you read the passage, be on the lookout for a series of actions or nouns. Now that you know what to look for, you may spot an error even without having to go to the answer choices. Second, look for changes in verb tense, or the way in which nouns are set up, among the answer choices.

**Parallel Construction Check**

Look out for...

- a series of nouns or actions

# SENTENCE CONSTRUCTION DRILL

In the drill below, you will find only questions that focus on sentence construction. Before you start, take a few moments to go back over the review material and techniques. If you don't spot an error as you read, remember that the answer choices may help to suggest the error you should look for.

When you see the gingerbread houses of Roskilde with their neatly thatched roofs, the gardens filled with <u>flowers, blooms,</u> and the
<sub>1</sub>
happy smiles on the fresh-faced inhabitants, it is difficult to believe that this town was once the home of a more warlike people— the Vikings.  Roskilde's main museum is devoted to those early <u>inhabitants, the Vikings</u>
<sub>2</sub>
once wandered throughout Europe, and by some reports, may have

<u>travel</u> all the way to North America as well.
<sub>3</sub>
The museum sits on a site at the edge of

Roskilde <u>fiord. Where</u> the Viking ships were
<sub>4</sub>
once launched on voyages of conquest and plunder. Until twenty years ago used only by the fishermen who still ply their trade in the fiord, <u>tourists now arrive in buses at the</u>
<u>craggy shoreline</u> to watch local artisans
<sub>5</sub>

build Viking ships <u>in the traditional manner.</u>
<sub>6</sub>
   High above the fiord is Roskilde Cathedral, built by the famous Viking King

Harold Blue-toothe <u>in the 1200s the king</u> is
<sub>7</sub>
said to have converted to Christianity when a visiting priest was able to cure his toothache.

1. **A.** NO CHANGE
   **B.** flowers and blooms,
   **C.** flowers; blooms
   **D.** flowers, blooms

2. **F.** NO CHANGE
   **G.** inhabitants the Vikings
   **H.** inhabitants. The Vikings
   **J.** inhabitants, the Vikings,

3. **A.** NO CHANGE
   **B.** travels
   **C.** traveled
   **D.** had traveled

4. **F.** NO CHANGE
   **G.** fiord. Where,
   **H.** fiord, where
   **J.** fiord; where

5. **A.** NO CHANGE
   **B.** the craggy shoreline must now be shared with tourists who arrive in buses
   **C.** tourists now arrive at the craggy shore line in buses
   **D.** the craggy shoreline must now share itself with tourists who arrive in buses

6. **F.** NO CHANGE
   **G.** (place after *artisans*)
   **H.** (place after *build*)
   **J.** (place after *watch*)

7. **A.** NO CHANGE
   **B.** in the 1200s. The king
   **C.** in the 1200s, the king
   **D.** in the 1200s, the king,

In one corner of the cathedral is a column on which the heights of some other famous historical figures who visited the cathedral are recorded. The tallest (over seven feet tall, if the markings are to be believed) was Peter the Great; the shortest was a King of <u>Siam; who</u>[8] one hopes was only a boy at the time.

8. **F.** NO CHANGE
   **G.** Siam. Who
   **H.** Siam, whom
   **J.** Siam, who

## Here's How to Crack It

**Question 1:** Did you notice as you were reading that the passage begins with a *list* of nice things about the town of Roskilde? Lists often mean **parallel construction**. Because this is a list of *things,* or nouns, we need to check if everything on the list is presented in the same way. The list is composed of

- the gingerbread houses of Roskilde with their neatly thatched roofs

- the gardens filled with flowers

- blooms

- the happy smiles on the fresh-faced inhabitants

Which one of these seems a little out of place? Each of them begins with "the" except for the third item on the list. And come to think of it, the third item is a lot shorter. Is "blooms" by itself a nice thing about Roskilde or does it really belong with the gardens back in the previous item on the list?

Let's look at the answer choices. We see several ways to connect the two nouns. Different constructions of the nouns in the answer choices indicates that this could be a parallel construction problem (or possibly a misplaced modifier). Answer choice A implies that there are four items on the list, but these items are not set up the same way. Let's get rid of it. Choice D is essentially just the same, but even worse, there is no comma after "blooms." Choice C splits the sentence in two. Can the second half of the sentence stand on its own? No way. Answer choice B puts the blooms back in the garden, and it clears up all problems of parallel construction. The correct answer is **B.**

**Question 2:** The answer choices here provide an immediate clue: One of the choices breaks the sentence up into two pieces, while the others leave it intact. Changes in punctuation may mean a **comma splice.** They don't always, of course, but we should always check. Can the clauses on both sides of the punctuation stand alone? Yes, they can. Aha! This is definitely a comma splice. We are now probably giving serious thought to answer choice H, which splits the sentence in two.

However, since there is more than one way to fix a comma splice, we should check the other answer choices just to see if any of them are better than H. Choice G takes the comma splice and removes the comma, turning it into a run-on sentence. This is no better. Choice J merely inserts another pause after "the Vikings," which does not help matters. The correct answer is **H.**

**Question 3:** Here the sentence, which is partially underlined, contains a *list* of actions:

> The Vikings a) once wandered and b) may have travel

Are the two verbs in the same tense? No. What did we really need here? If you said "traveled" you are absolutely correct.

If you missed this as you were reading it the first time, the answer choices provided great clues. Each was just another form of a verb. Any time you see verb changes in the answer choices, you should immediately think of **parallel construction**. Each choice is in a different tense. Just read through them until you get a match with "wandered." The correct answer is **C.**

**Question 4:** Punctuation again! Three of the choices break up the sentence, one doesn't. Let's see which is better this time. Again, we ask ourselves, can the clauses on both sides of the punctuation stand by themselves? This time, the answer is no. The clause that begins "Where the Viking ships..." is dependent. This is a **sentence fragment.** We need to combine the two thoughts. Our only option is answer choice **H.**

**Question 5:** The answer choices here give us a choice of nouns. This could be a parallel construction problem or it could be a misplaced modifier. Since there is no list in this case, let's check for a misplaced modifier. How does the sentence begin?

> *"Until twenty years ago used only by the fishermen who still ply their trade in the fiord,..."*

This is a long modifying phrase. The noun that comes next in the sentence must be what is being modified. Are "tourists" what the fishermen used until twenty years ago? No! This is a **misplaced modifier.** We can eliminate answer choices A and C. In choice D, the shore must share itself. Can a shore do something like that? In choice B, the construction indicates that the fishermen and the tourists must do the sharing. The correct answer is **B.**

**Question 6:** We can spot the *type* of error ACT is looking for this time by going straight to the answer choices. This is one of those **construction shift** questions. Let's move "in the traditional manner" around in the sentence and find the best fit. You say it was just fine where it was? You're right. The answer is **F.** NO CHANGE.

**Question 7:** More punctuation! Again, our choices either put the sentence together or break it apart. Can the two phrases on either side of the punctuation stand on their own? The answer this time is "yes." We have another run-on sentence. There is only one choice that breaks the two clauses up: The correct answer is **B.**

**Question 8:** More of the same. Can "who one hopes was only a boy at the time," stand on its own? No. We are down to choices H and J. The correct answer is **J.** How do you decide between "who" and "whom"?

To find out, let's review the elements of basic grammar.

# 5

# Grammar and Usage

The grammar questions on the ACT test your ability to recognize the proper (or improper) uses of the different parts of speech. We will not review *all* the rules of grammar (several books exist on the subject if you're really interested, one of which is our *Grammar Smart*). Instead, we will go over the grammatical rules that are tested most frequently on the ACT: noun-pronoun agreement, pronoun case agreement, subject-verb agreement, verb tense, proper placement of adjectives and adverbs, and correct use of idioms.

## PRONOUNS

Pronouns—words such as *he*, *she*, *it*, and *they*—are used to replace nouns. The ACT writers like to see if you understand the rules of pronouns—there will probably be two or three pronoun questions on the test you take.

### The First Pronoun Rule: Agreement

A pronoun must always agree with the noun it refers to. Sound straightforward? Try to spot the error in the sentence below.

> *Any young boy who watched the first moon landing probably spent the next few years wishing that they could become an astronaut.*

In spoken English, people make pronoun agreement errors all the time. In written English, you have to be more precise. As you look at the sentence above, try to decide which noun is being referred to by the word "they." If you decided that "they" was referring to "boy," you were absolutely correct. However, since "boy" is singular, the pronoun referring to "boy" has to be singular as well. "He" would more correctly refer back to "boy."

> *Any young boy who watched the first moon landing probably spent the next few years wishing that he could become an astronaut.*

The charts below contain some commonly used singular and plural pronouns.

| Singular Pronouns | | |
|---|---|---|
| **Subject** | **Object** | **Possessive** |
| I | me | mine |
| you | you | yours |
| he | him | his |
| she | her | hers |
| it | it | its |

| Plural Pronouns | | |
|---|---|---|
| **Subject** | **Object** | **Possessive** |
| we | us | ours |
| you | you | yours |
| they | them | theirs |
| | | |
| | | |

Here's another example:

> *Neither of the two young girls with whom I watched the first*
> *moon landing expressed their feelings out loud, but I knew*
> *that all three of us wanted to be astronauts.*

Neither and either are considered singular. Therefore, in this sentence, it is incorrect to use the possessive pronoun "their." We should use "her" instead.

> *Neither of the two young girls with whom I watched the first*
> *moon landing expressed her feelings out loud, but I knew that*
> *all three of us wanted to be astronauts.*

The following indefinite pronouns are all singular:

| | | |
|---|---|---|
| anybody | each | somebody |
| anyone | everybody | someone |
| | everyone | |

Let's look at an example in ACT format:

Although the American bald eagle has

been on the endangered species list for years,

they have been sighted in wildlife preserves
<sub>1</sub>

much more frequently during the past two

years.

1. **A.** NO CHANGE
   **B.** they are
   **C.** it can be
   **D.** it has been

## Here's How to Crack It

As you read the sentence, look to see if there is a pronoun in the underlined portion. If you find one, check to make sure the pronoun agrees with the noun to which it refers. What does the "they" refer to here? Obviously, it must refer to "the American bald eagle." Although the sentence is clearly talking about the American bald eagle in its *general* sense, we need to use a singular pronoun to agree with the singular noun. Thus, we can eliminate choices A and B. Choices C and D both contain the correct pronoun, "it." How do we decide which one to pick? Note the difference between C and D. Choice C uses the present tense, while choice D uses a type of past tense. According to the sentence, when were these birds sighted? "In the past two years." Which answer do you want to pick? If you said choice **D,** you were absolutely correct.

Even if you missed the pronoun as you read the sentence, you almost certainly would have noticed that the *answer choices* offered you two different pronouns. The answer choices are always great clues to what might be going on in the ACT writers' minds.

## The Second Pronoun Rule: Case

If a pronoun is the subject of a sentence, it must be expressed as a subject. Subject pronouns include *I, we, you, he, she, it, they*, and *who*. If a pronoun is the object of a sentence, or the object of a preposition, it must be expressed as an object. Object pronouns include *me, us, you, him, her, it, them*, and *whom*.

Which choice best fits the sentence below?

*(She/her) bought a souvenir NASA sweatshirt.*

Since the person who buys the shirt is the subject of the sentence, the correct pronoun is "she."

*Jane bought a souvenir NASA sweatshirt for (he/him).*

Since the person who receives the shirt is the object of the preposition "for," the correct pronoun is "him."

ACT's favorite pronoun case errors involve the use of *who* and *whom*, both of which are called relative pronouns. Let's look at a correct example first:

*The TV announcer, who was quite an expert, told us many interesting facts about the lunar mission.*

The group of words "who was quite an expert" is functioning here as an adjective describing the TV announcer. Is this group of words a phrase or a clause? You may remember that a phrase cannot contain a subject but a clause must contain both a subject and a verb. In this group of words, the relative pronoun "who" functions as a subject, which means that this group of words is a clause. You should always use "who" when the relative pronoun is functioning as the subject of a clause, or as the subject of the entire sentence. " . . . whom was quite an expert" would be completely wrong here.

Now try an incorrect example:

*Before the moon landing, the TV announcer gave some additional background on the astronauts, about who we were all quite interested.*

If you spot *who* following a preposition (in this case, "who" follows the word "about") on the ACT, it will almost certainly turn out to be incorrect. In most cases, a pronoun following a preposition is supposed to be the object of that preposition. The sentence should read:

*Before the moon landing, the TV announcer gave some additional background on the astronauts, about whom we were all quite interested.*

### Pronoun Check

Look out for...
- pronouns in the answer choices — should the pronoun be singular or plural? Is the pronoun being used as a subject or an object?

Let's try an example in ACT format:

The students, <u>who had been studying the space program</u>, were thrilled to witness the lunar landing.

2. **A.** NO CHANGE
   **B.** about whom had been studying the space program,
   **C.** whom had been studying the space program,
   **D.** who had been studying the space program

## Here's How to Crack It

The group of words "who had been studying the space program" is functioning as an adjective clause describing the students. Is "who" the subject of this adjective clause? Yes, it is, so we are down to answer choices A (NO CHANGE) and D, both of which contain the correct form of the pronoun—"who." How do the two remaining choices differ? Answer choice A contains a comma after "program" while choice D does not. Is the comma necessary? We look back at the passage and see that a comma precedes the clause, which is a nonrestrictive clause. (You'll learn in the punctuation section that a nonrestrictive clause is not necessary in order for the sentence to make sense.) Here, "The students were thrilled to witness the lunar landing" would be perfectly acceptable. Nonrestrictive clauses require commas on either side of them, so answer choice **A**, NO CHANGE, is correct.

## How Do You Spot Pronoun Errors?

Look for pronouns! Whenever you see a pronoun in the underlined portion of the sentence—or in the *answer choices*—you must first determine which noun the pronoun is replacing. If the pronoun is replacing a singular noun, it must be singular; if it is replacing a plural noun, it must be plural.

If the pronoun is being used as a subject, it must be in its subject form. If the pronoun is being used as an object, it must be in its object form.

If *who* or *whom* appears in the underlined portion of the passage—or in the answer choices—you must determine whether the pronoun is the subject or the object of the clause in which it appears. If it is the subject, *who* is correct. If it is the object, *whom* is correct. Generally, if the relative pronoun follows a preposition, the correct form will be "whom."

## SUBJECT-VERB AGREEMENT

The verb of a sentence must always agree with its subject. If a sentence contains a singular subject, the verb that goes with it must also be singular. If a sentence contains a plural subject, then the verb that goes with it must also be plural. Let's look at an example:

> *The best moment during a broadcast filled with many great moments were when the astronaut stepped out of the lunar lander and bounced on the moon.*

> **Reminder**
>
> Don't forget that many indefinite pronouns are singular. These are words such as *each, either, somebody, anyone, everyone,* and *neither.*

The subject of this sentence is "moment," which is singular. See if you can find the main verb of the sentence. If you said "were" you were absolutely correct. Since the subject is singular, the verb should also be singular. The correct form of the verb is "was."

> *The best moment during a broadcast filled with many great moments was when the astronaut stepped out of the lunar lander and bounced on the moon.*

Now if the original sentence had been written like this...

> *The best moment were when the astronaut stepped out of the lunar lander and bounced on the moon.*

...the error would have been a *lot* easier to spot.

ACT writers like to stick lots of modifying phrases and clauses between the subject and the verb, in the hope that you will forget what the subject was by the time you get to the verb. The best way to check subject-verb agreement is to put mental parentheses around all the words between the subject and the verb so you can see if they really agree.

## PRONOUN-VERB AGREEMENT

Sometimes, the subject of a sentence turns out to be a pronoun; don't let that throw you. The verb must still agree with the subject, even if it is just a pronoun. Let's look at an example:

SIDEBAR

**Subject/Verb Agreement Check**

Look out for...

• a verb in the underlined portion of the sentence—do the answer choices contain different forms of the verb?

> *Each of these moments have played in my mind again and again as I try to recapture the excitement of that momentous day in June.*

The subject of this sentence is "each," which you'll recall is singular (along with *either, neither, anyone,* and *everybody, everyone*). The verb is "have played," which is plural. The subject (in this case a pronoun) and the verb don't agree. How do you fix the sentence?

> *Each of these moments has played in my mind again and again as I try to recapture the excitement of that momentous day in June.*

## How Do You Spot Subject-Verb Agreement Errors?

That's easy. Isolate the subject and the verb of the sentence. To see the relationship between the subject and the verb, try putting parentheses around any words, phrases, or clauses in between. As always, remember that the answer choices themselves can provide valuable clues. If the underlined portion of a sentence contains a verb, you should check to see whether the answer choices contain different forms of that verb. If they do, you have a potential subject-verb error.

# VERB TENSE

Verb tense tells us when the action of the sentence is taking place—in the past, in the present, or in the future. Let's review the different verb tenses.

The **present tense** indicates an action that is happening right now:

> *He runs the 440 in 50 seconds.*

The simple **past tense** indicates an action that took place entirely in the past:

> *He ran the 440 in 50 seconds last week.*

The **present perfect tense** indicates an action that started in the past, but that may continue into the present:

> *He has run the 440 in under 50 seconds in the last four races.*

The **past perfect tense** indicates an action that happened in the past and that preceded another action also in the past:

> *He had run 100 yards of the race when he twisted his ankle.*

The **future tense** indicates an action that will take place at some point down the road:

> *He will run the race next Saturday.*

The **future perfect tense** indicates that an action will be completed by a definite time in the future:

> *He will have finished the race by next Sunday.*

## How Does the ACT Test Verb Tense?

The ACT writers don't care whether you know the names of the verb tenses, or even, sometimes, whether you know in which tense a particular passage should be written.

What the ACT writers want to see is whether you can spot *inconsistencies* in verb tense (they are testing a form of agreement here). If a verb in a non-underlined portion of the sentence is in one tense, the verb in the underlined portion will tend to be in the same tense. What's wrong with the following sentence?

> *Sam is walking down the street when he found a large suitcase.*

The verbs "is walking" and "found" are in two different tenses. "Is walking" is in the present tense, and "found" is in the past tense. One or the other has to change.

**Verb Agreement Check**

Look out for...
- a verb in the underlined portion of the sentence—does it agree with the subject? Is the verb's tense consistent with the other verbs in the sentence?

The new sentence can either read:

> *Sam is walking down the street when he finds a large suitcase.*

> or

> *Sam was walking down the street when he found a large suitcase.*

On the ACT, you generally will not be asked to make a decision as to which tense (in this case, past or present) would be most appropriate for the sentence. Only one of the verbs will be underlined, and it will be up to you to look at the other verb in the sentence, or the verbs in surrounding sentences, to decide how to change the underlined verb.

## How Do You Spot Verb Agreement Errors?

That's easy. If you see a verb in the underlined portion of the sentence—or in any of the answer choices—you should immediately anticipate that the error could be one of two types: subject-verb agreement (which we've already spoken about) or tense.

You should begin by asking yourself whether the verb agrees with its subject.

If that is not the problem, then ask yourself whether the verb's tense is consistent with the tense of other verbs in the sentence or in surrounding sentences. If there is an inconsistency, then you've probably spotted the error.

## ADJECTIVES AND ADVERBS

Adjectives modify nouns. Adverbs modify everything else—verbs, adjectives, and other adverbs. The ACT sometimes tests to see whether you know the difference between adjectives and adverbs. You may remember from grade school a method that often helps to decide if a word is an adjective—simply put the word you aren't sure about into the following sentence: "He (or she or it) is very." If the word fits the blank, then the word is an adjective. Let's try it out.

> *He is very <u>intelligent</u>.*

> *He is very <u>intelligently</u>.*

**Adjectives and Adverbs**

Adjectives and adverbs can usually be distinguished from each other by the "He is very —" test (if the word fits, it's an adjective) or by their form (most adverbs end in -ly).

*Intelligent* fits the blank in the first sentence, so *intelligent* must be an adjective. *Intelligently* does not fit the blank in the second sentence. In fact, *intelligently* is an adverb. You can often recognize an adverb by the "-ly" at the end of the word.

> *She thinks intelligently.*

A comparative adjective is often used when a sentence is comparing two things.

> *Juanita is taller than Jane.*

> *("Taller" is a comparative adjective.)*

In general, if an adjective has only one syllable, you can make it comparative by adding an "-er" to the end of the word. If an adjective has more than one syllable, you can usually make it comparative by adding a "more" or a "less" in front of the adjective.

> *Sid is more careful than Tom.*

> *Tom is less careful than Sid.*

A comparative adverb is often used when a sentence is comparing two actions.

> *Juanita dances more gracefully than Jane.*

> *("More gracefully" is a comparative adverb.)*

To make most adverbs comparative, you also need to add a "more" or "less" in front of the adverb.

> *Sid behaves more correctly than Tom does.*

> *Tom behaves less correctly than Sid does.*

When more than two things are being compared, a sentence often needs a superlative adjective.

> *Of the many men in the room, John is the strongest.*

> *("Strongest" is a superlative adjective.)*

To make a comparison among three or more people or things, add "-est" to the adjective. When more than two actions are being compared, a sentence often needs a superlative adverb.

> *Compared to the other boys in the school, Sid behaves the most correctly.*

> *("Most correctly" is a superlative adverb.)*

## IDIOMATIC EXPRESSIONS

Why do we say, "I am in love *with* you," instead of, "I am in love *for* you?" The answer is

> *"Well, just because!"*

Each idiomatic expression is a law unto itself. There are no general rules to go by. Of course, it would be difficult to memorize every single idiom in the English language, at least on short notice. Fortunately, it turns out that you already know most of the idioms that come up on the ACT.
Here's an example:

> *My sculpture is based after Rodin's* Thinker.

Do you base something "after?" No, the correct expression is

> *My sculpture is based on Rodin's* Thinker.

**Idioms**

Idioms are expressions that require the use of a specific preposition. Fortunately, you'll be familiar with most of the idioms on the test. The best way to spot them is to look for prepositions in the answer choices.

## How Do You Spot Idiomatic Errors?

You already know most of the idiomatic expressions likely to appear on the ACT. The only problem will be spotting the error in the first place. As always, the answer choices provide excellent clues. Let's see how that last example would have looked like on the ACT.

My sculpture <u>is based after</u> Rodin's  
<sub>3</sub>  
*Thinker.*

3. **A.** NO CHANGE  
   **B.** is based over  
   **C.** is based on  
   **D.** based on

## Here's How to Crack It

Even if you didn't spot the error as you read the sentence, when you went to the answer choices you would have noticed that the question seemed to be mostly concerned with the preposition that followed the word "based."

The best way to check out a potential idiom error is to try making up your own sentence using the idiomatic expression.

*My term paper is based after the discoveries of Edison.*

Does that sound correct? No! We need to say "is based on . . . " Answer choice D, while it uses the correct idiomatic expression, is a sentence fragment. Thus the best answer is choice **C**.

# GRAMMAR DRILL

In the drill below, you will find questions focusing only on grammar. Before you start, take a few moments to go back over the review material and techniques. If you don't see an error as you read, examine the answer choices for clues to which error you should look for.

Have you ever had a day when you realized in retrospect that it would have been better <u>if one had</u> stayed in bed? Yesterday
<sub>1</sub>
was one of those days. I

1. **A.** NO CHANGE  
   **B.** if you had  
   **C.** if one has  
   **D.** had one

woke up at 10:30 to find that my alarm clock <u>has failed</u> to go off. I was already an hour
<sub>2</sub>
and a half late for work. I jumped into my clothes and ran to my car, only to discover that I had left the lights <u>on the previously</u>
<sub>3</sub>
<u>evening</u> and the car wouldn't start. Each of the first three taxis I saw <u>were</u> too far away
<sub>4</sub>
to hail. The taxi driver

2. **F.** NO CHANGE  
   **G.** have failed  
   **H.** had failed  
   **J.** having failed

3. **A.** NO CHANGE  
   **B.** on the evening previously  
   **C.** on the evening previous  
   **D.** on the previous evening

4. **F.** NO CHANGE  
   **G.** was  
   **H.** are  
   **J.** is

who finally picked me up didn't have change
 ‾‾‾‾‾‾‾‾‾‾‾‾‾
      5
for a ten dollar bill. When I finally arrived at
the office, my boss was not only furious that
I was late, and she was also mad that I had
           ‾‾‾‾‾‾‾
              6
forgotten to bring the report I had been preparing at home. Of all the bad days I have
experienced in my life, this was the worse.
                         ‾‾‾‾‾‾‾‾‾‾‾‾‾
                              7

5. **A.** NO CHANGE
   **B.** whom finally picked me up
   **C.** whom picked me up finally
   **D.** who finally picks me up

6. **F.** NO CHANGE
   **G.** and her
   **H.** but her
   **J.** but she

7. **A.** NO CHANGE
   **B.** was the more worse
   **C.** was the worst
   **D.** was the worser

## Here's How to Crack It

**Question 1:** Looking at the answer choices, you might notice that there are two potential errors to check: pronoun agreement and tense. Why? Because the answers contained two different pronouns and two different verb tenses. Let's check pronouns first. In the original underlined portion of the sentence, "one" is a pronoun. Does it agree with the other pronouns in the same sentence? Not really. The author begins the passage by addressing "you." It is confusing and incorrect to change to "one" in the same sentence. Which answer choice avoids the use of "one"? The correct answer is **B**.

**Question 2:** Checking the answer choices, we see that the question seems to revolve around verb tense. The sentence is describing something that happened yesterday, so we can expect that the sentence should be in some form of the past tense. Two events take place in this sentence. The author woke up, and the alarm clock failed to go off. Which of these two events happened first, thus causing the other? If you said that the failure of the alarm clock took place before the author woke up, you were absolutely correct. When two events occur in the past, but one occurs before the other, the sentence requires the past perfect. The correct answer is choice **H**.

**Question 3:** The answer choices here offer us the choice of the adverb "previously" or the adjective "previous." To decide which is correct, we need to know what "previously" (or "previous") is referring to. The word being modified here is "evening," which we all know is a noun. The correct modifier of a noun is an adjective. This eliminates choices A and B. Now, does an adjective normally precede or follow the noun it modifies? The correct answer is **D**.

**Question 4:** The answer choices here indicate that we have to consider either of two errors: tense or subject-verb agreement. Let's check subject-verb agreement first. Find the subject of the sentence. If you said the subject was "each" you were absolutely correct. "Of the first three taxis I saw" is modifying "each." Now, check the verb. "Each . . . were." In our review, we said that the word "each" is always singular—but the verb in this case is plainly plural. Aha! we have found the error. Check the answer choices to see which ones are singular.

Our only remaining choices are G, *was*, and J, *is*. In what general tense is this passage written? Check the tense of the verbs in surrounding sentences. The correct answer is choice **G.**

**Question 5:** Clearly this question is testing our understanding of the "who/whom" issue. Remember that the difference between the pronouns "who" and "whom" lies in whether they are being used as subjects or objects in the clause or phrase that contains them. "Who finally picked me up" is a clause modifying the taxi driver. What is the subject of the clause? If you said "who" you are absolutely correct. Thus, "who" is fine just the way it is. We can eliminate choices B and C, both of which contain "whom." Now let's see what the difference is between choices A and D. Again, it comes down to tense. Is this passage being told in the present tense? No. The correct answer is **A.** NO CHANGE.

**Question 6:** The answer choices are offering you a variety of options having to do with "and" or "but." This is an idiom question. Try making up your own sentence using the idiomatic expression in question.

*My sister Jane is not only stupid...*

How would you finish this sentence? Or put it this way: What would be *the next word* in the sentence after "stupid?"

*My sister Jane is not only stupid*, but *she is also a pain.*

Choices F and G bite the dust. The answer is either H or J. In the sentence you just made up, did you use "she" or "her" after the "but?" Chances are you used "she." "She is also a pain" is a clause. Since "she" is the subject of the clause, we have to use the subject form, "she," instead of the object form, "her." The same is true for the sentence in the passage. The correct answer is choice **J.**

**Question 7:** This question is about the proper use of the superlative. The answer choices (including "worser" and "worst") give you a pretty good indication that this is the case. If you are discussing two bad options, you would have to decide which of them was *worse*. If you are discussing three or more bad options, you would have to decide which of them was *the worst*. The correct answer is choice **C.**

# 6
# Punctuation

Punctuation marks generally signal pauses and transitions. While you've probably learned dozens of punctuation rules over the last eight years or so, you'll only need to know a select few for the ACT. In this chapter we'll show you only the rules you'll need to know.

## COMMAS

More than half of the punctuation questions on the ACT concern the proper use of commas (,). Too few commas in a sentence can create confusion as to where one thought ends and another begins. Too many commas break up the flow of a sentence.

### THE FIRST COMMA RULE: THE SERIAL COMMA

Commas are used to separate items in a series. Let's look at an example:

> *When Mary walked into the classroom she saw a school teacher, a doctor, a woman eating a bagel and a bird.*

**Reminder**

Don't forget that some of the punctuation questions will be correct *as is*. Many punctuation questions on the ACT concern commas.

A comma should be placed after each item in a series. Thus, we need a comma after the phrase "a woman eating a bagel." As this sentence stands, you might get the impression that the woman was eating the bird as well!

In some writing, it is acceptable to omit the comma before the "and" in a series of three or more items. However, the ACT test writers prefer a more formal version of English (no surprise there), so use a comma to separate every item in a series, including the last one.

> *When Mary walked into the classroom she saw a school teacher, a doctor, a woman eating a bagel, and a bird.*

### How Do You Spot Serial Comma Errors?

To spot serial comma errors, look at the entire sentence, not just the portion that is underlined. What you are searching for is a series or list of three or more items or actions. If you spot one of these series, make sure there is a comma after each item in the series except the last.

### THE SECOND COMMA RULE: SEPARATING CLAUSES AND PHRASES

The ACT also tests your ability to use commas correctly when two clauses, or a clause and a phrase, appear in the same sentence.

### Two Independent Clauses

As you'll recall from the sentence structure chapter, independent clauses are those that could form a complete sentence on their own. Identify the two independent clauses in the sentence below:

> *Mary wondered why there was a bird in the classroom and she decided to ask the teacher what the bird was doing indoors.*

When two independent clauses appear in the same sentence, they are usually joined by a conjunction (a word like *and, or, but, for, nor,* or *yet*). Thus, the two independent clauses above are, "Mary wondered why there was a bird in the classroom," and "She decided to ask the teacher what the bird was doing indoors." A comma belongs before the conjunction that joins the two independent clauses.

> *Mary wondered why there was a bird in the classroom, and she decided to ask the teacher what the bird was doing indoors.*

## An Independent Clause and a Dependent Clause

Commas are also used to separate independent clauses from dependent clauses. You'll remember that a dependent clause is one that cannot stand on its own as a sentence. Identify the dependent clause in the sentence below:

> *Before Mary could reach the teacher she saw the woman offer the bird part of the bagel.*

The first clause, "Before Mary could reach the teacher," cannot stand by itself, and therefore is a dependent clause. "She saw the woman offer the bird part of the bagel" can stand by itself, so it is an independent clause. The two must be separated by a comma.

> *Before Mary could reach the teacher, she saw the woman offer the bird part of the bagel.*

## An Independent Clause and a Modifying Phrase

Commas are also used to separate independent clauses from modifying phrases of more than just a couple of words. A modifying phrase modifies, or describes, something else, usually a noun. Identify the modifying phrase in the sentence below:

> *Hungry and excited the bird snapped up the bagel.*

"Hungry and excited" is a modifying phrase (it modifies the noun "bird"). "The bird snapped up the bagel" is an independent clause. The two must be separated by a comma.

> *Hungry and excited, the bird snapped up the bagel.*

## How to Spot Comma Errors in Clause/Phrase Separation

As you saw in the last example, sometimes the error can be the *lack* of a comma, which you might think would be very difficult to spot. Fortunately, as always, the answer choices provide you with excellent clues. If some of the answer choices insert a comma into the sentence while others don't, that is reason enough to check to see whether we need to separate two clauses or a clause and a phrase.

### Comma Check

Look out for...
- words and phrases in a series
- introductory phrases and words
- mid-sentence phrases that are not essential to the sentence

## The Third Comma Rule: Separating "Restrictive" and "Nonrestrictive" Elements

A "restrictive" clause or phrase is essential to the meaning of a sentence, and it should not be separated from the rest of the sentence by commas.

> *People who snore are advised to sleep on their side.*

"Who snore" is essential to the meaning of this sentence. The sentence is not saying that *all* people should sleep on their side, just the ones who snore.

A "nonrestrictive" clause or phrase is not essential to the meaning of a sentence. It merely adds a parenthetical thought, and thus needs to be separated from the rest of the sentence by commas.

> *My father, who snores loudly, always sleeps in his longjohns.*

Identify the nonrestrictive clause in the sentence below:

> *Mary who by now was very confused stopped in front of the woman.*

The nonrestrictive clause is "who by now was very confused." This clause modifies the noun that precedes it—in this case, "Mary"—but is not essential to the meaning of the sentence. "Mary stopped in front of the woman" can stand on its own. To set off the clause from the rest of the sentence, you need to surround it with a *pair* of commas.

> *Mary, who by now was very confused, stopped in front of the woman.*

Identify the restrictive clause in the sentence below:

> *"Only a person who is a little peculiar would feed a bagel to a bird!" thought Mary.*

"Who is a little peculiar" is a restrictive clause, because it adds essential information to the sentence. Thus, it does *not* require separation by commas.

### How Do You Spot a Restrictive/Nonrestrictive Comma Error?

As always, the answer choices provide you with a very small "menu" of options to choose from. If you see differences in punctuation among the choices, check to see whether the underlined portion of the sentence is part of a restrictive or nonrestrictive phrase or clause.

# SEMICOLONS

Semicolons (;) are punctuation marks used to put two or more clauses together to form one big sentence. A semicolon falls somewhere between a heavy comma and a light period.

## When Do You Use a Semicolon?

Use a semicolon instead of a period to connect two related independent clauses. Identify the two independent clauses in the sentence below:

> *Just then, the woman screamed the bird jumped up and perched on her head.*

The first independent clause is "Just then the woman screamed." The second independent clause is "The bird jumped up and perched on her head." In the absence of a conjunction (these two could be connected by a comma and the word *and*), a semicolon is used to join the two independent clauses. Of course, it would have been equally correct to put a period after the first independent clause; however, the use of a semicolon suggests to the reader that the two clauses are closely related.

> *Just then, the woman screamed; the bird jumped up and perched on her head.*

## How Do You Spot a Semicolon Error?

If the underlined portion *or any of the answer choices* contains a semicolon, you should ask yourself whether the sentence contains two related independent clauses not joined by a conjunction. If it does, the semicolon is probably correct. You might be wondering how you would decide if the ACT gave you a choice between a semicolon and a period. Don't worry. The test writers know that semicolons and periods are often interchangeable, and we've never seen them offer that choice.

### Semicolon Check

Look out for...
- answer choices that contain two related independent clauses

# COLONS

Colons (:) are usually used after a complete statement to introduce a list of related details. The list can have many items or just one. In the following sentence, try to decide where the statement ends and the details begin:

> *Maria just purchased all the camping supplies for our trip, a backpack, a sleeping bag, and a pair of hiking boots.*

"Maria just purchased all the camping supplies for our trip" is the complete statement in the sentence above. (It is also an independent clause.) "A backpack, a sleeping bag, and a pair of hiking boots" are the related details. A colon belongs between the two:

> *Maria just purchased all the camping supplies for our trip: a backpack, a sleeping bag, and a pair of hiking boots.*

### Colon Check

Look out for...
- an underlined phrase that contains a list

## How Do You Spot a Colon Error?

If the underlined phrase *or the answer choices* contain a colon, you should ask yourself the question on the following page.

Is a list of some kind introduced by an independent clause?

If so, a colon preceding the list or statement is correct. If not, a colon is probably incorrect.

## DASHES

Dashes (—) separate a word or group of words from the rest of the sentence. Dashes are used either to indicate an abrupt break in thought, or to introduce an explanation or afterthought.

In the example below, which group of words should be separated from the rest of the sentence?

> *I tried to express my gratitude not that any words could be adequate but she just nodded and walked away.*

The clause "not that any words could be adequate" must be isolated from the rest of the sentence.

> *I tried to express my gratitude—not that any words could be adequate—but she just nodded and walked away.*

When the group of words that needs isolating is in the middle of a sentence, dashes function like a pair of less formal parentheses. However, when the phrase that needs isolating is at the end of the sentence instead, only one dash is required.

> *Just outside the door to the cabin we heard the howling of wolves— a sound that made our hair stand on end.*

**Dashes Often Travel in Pairs**

Dashes (like parentheses) are used to set off a phrase that is not essential to the meaning of the sentence.

## HOW DO YOU SPOT DASH ERRORS?

If the underlined portion *or any of the answer choices* contains a dash, compare the dash to the punctuation marks available in the other answer choices. Also check the non-underlined portion of the passage for dashes that might be linking up with this one to isolate a clause or phrase. Ask yourself whether the sentence contains a sudden break in thought, an explanation, or an afterthought. Remember that if the group of words that need isolating is in the middle of the sentence, there should be a *pair* of dashes. If the group of words is at the end of the sentence, there should be only one.

## APOSTROPHES

An apostrophe (') is used either to indicate possession or to mark missing letters in a word.

When it is used to indicate possession, it appears either right before or right after the "s" at the end of the possessive noun.

> *Peter's new car is extremely expensive.*
> *Women's issues will be important in the next election.*
> *The girls' room will be renovated this summer.*

The apostrophe tells us that the car belongs to Peter. If the noun in possession is singular—as in the case of Peter—the apostrophe falls before the "s." If it is plural and it doesn't end in "s"—as in the case of women—the apostrophe falls before the "s." If it is plural and it ends in "s"—as in the case of "girls"—the apostrophe falls after the "s." Note: Don't worry too much about the plural nouns—ACT seems more interested in your ability to form singular possessives correctly.

The ACT folks also seem very interested in whether you know when an apostrophe is *unnecessary*—some apostrophe questions require you to *drop* an apostrophe. Remember, in order for the apostrophe to be correct when forming a possessive, the noun containing it must be followed by another noun, or an adjective and a noun.

> *Peter's new car*
> *Women's issues*
> *Girls' room*

If the noun containing the apostrophe is followed by a verb, no apostrophe is needed.

> *Students must have identification cards.*

The apostrophe is also used to indicate missing letters in a word.

> *I'm sorry. I couldn't make it to your party.*

In the sentences above, the apostrophe takes the place of "a" (*I'm* instead of *I am*) and the place of "o" (*couldn't* instead of *could not*). Words that use apostrophes in this way are called contractions. Common contractions include: *don't, isn't, won't,* and *can't.*

## Its/It's/Its'

The most common apostrophe error you'll see tested on the ACT is misuse of *it's* and *its*, which have their own special rules.

The word *it's*—with an apostrophe—is only used when you want to say "it is" or "it has."

> *It's important.* (It is important.)
> *It's been nice talking to you.* (It has been nice talking to you.)

The word *its*—without an apostrophe—is (in this case only) the possessive form of the word "it."

> *The baby bear could not find its mother.*

We realize this is a little confusing, because you usually use an apostrophe to form the possessive. The ACT writers realize this is confusing too—that's why this error is on the test! Possessive pronouns (such as his, her, your, our) never take apostrophes.

The word *its'* isn't a word at all. That doesn't stop ACT from throwing it in once in a while to try to trip you up. Most ACT English Tests have at least one made-up word on them somewhere.

## How Do You Spot Apostrophe Errors?

If a word in the underlined portion *or any of the answer choices* contains an apostrophe, you should ask yourself whether the apostrophe is being used to form a contraction, or to make a noun *followed by another noun* possessive. In either case, the apostrophe is probably correct. Any other use of an apostrophe is probably wrong.

Unless . . .

You see the words *it's* or *its* in the underlined portion *or any of the answer choices*. In this case, remember the special rules we've just discussed.

## WHAT ABOUT !(")*?

It seems that the ACT test writers just aren't that interested in whether you know how to use exclamation points, parentheses, asterisks, and question marks correctly. They mention in their guide that the ACT tests some of these points, but not one of the real ACTs in *The Official Guide* contains any such questions.

Quotation marks sometimes surround words in the underlined portion and the answer choices, but when they do appear they show up in every answer choice (you aren't given the option of removing them), and seem intended to distract you from some other error.

As a result, we think you're safe spending your time worrying about other kinds of punctuation. The most common punctuation errors on the ACT deal with commas, semicolons, colons, dashes, and apostrophes: Learn how to use *these* correctly, and you should be covered punctuation-wise.

**Pronouns Most Frequently Misused**

The ACT writers will sometimes try to confuse you by presenting both a possessive pronoun and the same pronoun in a contraction as answer choices. Do you know the difference between these words?

*whose, who's, its, it's*

## PUTTING IT ALL TOGETHER

### How Do You Spot Punctuation Errors?

That's easy. Look for changes in punctuation among the answer choices. These changes tell you what the ACT writers are up to.

Look at the following example:

> **A.** NO CHANGE
> **B.** cities environmental problems
> **C.** city's environmental problems
> **D.** citys' environmental problems

Clearly, this question is about proper use of the apostrophe. Read the entire sentence and use the rules you've learned in this chapter to pick the best answer.

### One Last Note

There are some forms of punctuation that can be used interchangeably. As we stated above, a semicolon can sometimes take the place of a period. Dashes can sometimes be used instead of parentheses. Sometimes a colon could be replaced by a dash. We haven't discussed these possibilities at length because on the ACT you will never be asked to make a decision between two correct alternatives.

If two kinds of punctuation could both be considered correct, only one will appear among the answer choices. After all, questions can't have two right answers, can they?

# PUNCTUATION DRILL

In the drill below, you will find questions that focus only on punctuation. Before you start, take a few moments to go back over the review material and techniques. If you don't spot an error as you read, remember to use the answer choices to help you determine what the problem might be.

## Passage I

My most memorable vacation as a child was a trip I took to the Grand Canyon with my grandfather. I was only eleven at <u>the time; and</u> I'd never been outside the city of
<sub>1</sub>

1. **A.** NO CHANGE
   **B.** at the time and
   **C.** at the time, and
   **D.** at the time. And

Boston. My <u>grandfather, a true adventurer,</u> decided that it was time for me to discover
<sub>2</sub>
the great West. My romantic picture of the

2. **F.** NO CHANGE
   **G.** grandfather, a true, adventurer,
   **H.** grandfather: a true adventurer
   **J.** grandfather, a true adventurer

<u>West complete with cowboys and Indians</u>
<sub>3</sub>
was a little out of date, but the incredible

3. **A.** NO CHANGE
   **B.** West—complete with cowboys and Indians—
   **C.** West—complete with cowboys and Indians
   **D.** West; complete with cowboys and Indians,

scenery took my breath away. <u>On our first day we</u> decided that the best way to explore
<sub>4</sub>
the vast beauty of the canyon would be to take a mule-packed trip down one of the

4. **F.** NO CHANGE
   **G.** On our first day we,
   **H.** On our first day, we
   **J.** On, our first day, we

trails. As I rode along <u>on my mules back,</u> I
<sub>5</sub>
noticed that each rock stratum displayed a

5. **A.** NO CHANGE
   **B.** on my mules' back
   **C.** on our mules' back
   **D.** on my mule's back

distinctive <u>hue; gray</u> and violet in some
<sub>6</sub>
places, dark brown and green in others. The rock layers of the Grand Canyon are mostly

6. **F.** NO CHANGE
   **G.** hue. Gray
   **H.** hue, gray
   **J.** hue: gray

made of <u>limestone, freshwater shale and</u>

<u>sandstone</u>. The Grand Canyon was truly

magnificent.

7. **A.** NO CHANGE
   **B.** limestone, freshwater, shale, and sandstone.
   **C.** limestone, freshwater shale, and sandstone.
   **D.** limestone freshwater shale and sandstone.

As I looked up from the floor of the canyon,

<u>it's imposing</u> peaks made me realize how
small I really was.

8. **F.** NO CHANGE
   **G.** its imposing
   **H.** its' imposing
   **J.** its, imposing

## Here's How to Crack It

**Question 1:** In the underlined portion, the semicolon breaks up two independent clauses. Of course, that is acceptable behavior for a semicolon, but only if there is no conjunction between them. Thus, we can get rid of answer choice A. Looking at the answer choices, none of the alternatives gets rid of the conjunction. Therefore, we cannot break the two clauses into two separate sentences. This allows us to eliminate choice D. When you have two independent clauses linked by a conjunction, what kind of punctuation is required? If you said a comma, you were absolutely right. The correct answer is **C**.

**Question 2:** Notice that the underlined portion contains two commas. When do we need two commas in a sentence? When we want to set off a clause or phrase that describes a noun in more detail, but that is not vital to the meaning of the sentence (a nonrestrictive element). Let's remove the phrase "a true adventurer" from the sentence. Do we lose any vital information? No. Therefore, the correct answer choice is **F**. If you weren't sure how to correct the underlined portion, you could have looked at your answer choices. Answer choice G has three commas. Do they make the sentence any clearer? No. The comma after the word "true" is unnecessary. Answer choice H is incorrect because a colon should come after a complete thought and precede a list of related details. Answer choice J supplies only *one* comma. Remember, nonrestrictive elements need a *pair* of commas.

**Question 3:** Since the wording is exactly the same in each of the answer choices, it is easy to see that this question can only concern punctuation. Choice D creates an incomplete sentence: "My romantic picture of the West;" Since this cannot stand alone, we can forget choice D. The phrase "complete with cowboys and Indians" is supposed to be a parenthetical description of the author's vision of what the West would be like. As the underlined sentence stands, it is unclear where the main clause ends and the parenthetical thought begins, so cross off choice A. If there had been a pair of parentheses in one of the answer choices, that could well have been the correct answer, but there were no parentheses in any of the choices. What is another way to surround a parenthetical thought? If you suggested dashes, you were absolutely correct. Now, look at the difference between choices B and C. In B, there are *two* dashes surrounding the parenthetical thought. In choice C, there is only one at the beginning of the phrase. The correct answer is choice **B**.

**Question 4:** Again, we can be pretty sure that this is a question about punctuation. Let's look at the entire sentence. It begins with a long introductory phrase, followed by an independent clause. Do we need any punctuation between a long phrase and a clause? Sure. We need a comma. The only answer choice that correctly positions the comma between the phrase and the clause is choice **H.**

**Question 5:** If you look at the answer choices, you'll realize that this question is concerned with proper use of the apostrophe. Whose back is it? It is the mule's back. We need the possessive form here. Thus, choice A is immediately gone. Choice C uses the pronoun "our." Does this agree with the first part of the sentence? It could, but look at "back." Do "mules" have only one "back?" Nope. So **C** is out. In choice B, "mules'" gives the impression that she is riding more than one mule at the same time. The correct answer is choice **D.**

**Question 6:** This sentence contains an independent clause followed by a list of related details, so the best punctuation mark to connect the two is the colon. A period or semicolon would be inappropriate since the sentence does not contain two independent clauses. So, answer choices F and G are eliminated. A comma would not be sufficient: The related details should be set off in order to separate the hue from its description. So, answer choice H is eliminated. The best answer to this question is choice **J.**

**Question 7:** Here we have a series of items that need commas. Eliminate answer choice D, because it doesn't have any commas. The original sentence, answer choice A, is missing a comma after the word "shale." In answer choice B, the adjective "freshwater" is split from the noun "shale." Commas should be placed after the words "limestone" and "shale." Therefore, the correct answer choice is **C.**

**Question 8:** Does the sentence require the word "its" or "it's?" If you use the word "it's," the sentence would be the same as: *It is* imposing peaks. This is clearly wrong. The word "its" refers to the Grand Canyon. Thus, answer choice F is wrong. A comma is unnecessary after the word "its" in J because it would break up the thought of the sentence. Two down and two to go. Is an apostrophe needed after the word "its?" Definitely not! There is no such word as "its'." Therefore, the correct answer choice is **G.**

# 7

# Rhetorical Skills

Thirty-five of the 75 ACT English questions test rhetorical skills. These questions are not necessarily harder than the types we've been discussing up to now; they're just different. Rather than ask you about specific points of grammar, rhetoric questions get into the realm of style and editing. A few will concern the passage as a whole—save these for last. For the most part, the test writers have placed those at the end of the passage anyway.

*The Official Guide to the ACT* suggests two strategies for rhetoric questions with which, frankly, we disagree.

First, *The Official Guide* suggests that you read or skim the entire passage quickly for content, and then start answering the questions. We think this is a waste of time. You don't get any points for *reading* these passages. The proctor is not going to walk around the room saying, "Ah, excellent reading form there. Five points." You get points for *answering questions* correctly. Since most of the questions (including many of the rhetoric questions) can be answered just by looking at the particular sentence that contains the underlined portion related to that question, you might as well wade in there and start racking up points.

Second, *The Official Guide* suggests that it might be a good idea to answer the general rhetoric questions first. The *Guide* points out that if a general question asks you to rearrange the order of paragraphs, your new order will make it easier for you to answer other questions. Unfortunately, we think it's equally distracting to try to read a passage for content when every other sentence has something grammatically wrong with it.

The ACT writers break rhetorical skills down into three subcategories: strategy, organization, and style.

## STRATEGY

There are 12 strategy questions on the ACT; many of these concern **transitions.** Transition questions pop up throughout the passage, not just at the end. They are probably the easiest of the rhetorical skills questions.

A transition is sometimes needed at the *beginning* of a clause, sentence, or paragraph, as the writer attempts to move smoothly from one thought to another. Writers use what are called sentence connectors to get from one thought to the next. There are only three main kinds of sentence connectors in the world: **but, also,** and **thus.** Try filling in each of the blanks below with one of these three words.

Fred and Sue were looking forward to going to dinner at a Chinese restaurant with their friends, _____ their friends wanted to go to an Italian restaurant.

When European children hear the word "Chicago," the first thing they think of is gangsters; _____ it must be a disappointment to them when they get off the plane and see that no one is wearing spats or carrying a tommy gun.

The campers were very tired. _____ they were very hungry.

### Here's How to Crack It

There's a food fight brewing in the first sentence. To indicate that the friends are in disagreement with Fred and Sue, we need a word implying *contradiction.* That word is "but."

In the second sentence, we want to imply a *cause and effect* relationship. The first part of the sentence is meant to cause the second half. The word that suggests this is "thus."

The third example connects two sentences. Surely the two are related, but much less directly than in either of the first two examples. Our transition word needs to stress that the second idea is an addition to the first. The word is "also."

Of course there are lots of different ways of saying *but*, *thus*, and *also*. Here's a partial list:

> **but (contradiction)**—however, quite the contrary, despite, rather, notwithstanding, contrarily, on the other hand, on the contrary, although, yet, nevertheless
>
> **thus (cause and effect)**—hence, and so, therefore, consequently, for example, because of, finally, in conclusion
>
> **also (in addition)**—in addition, for example, furthermore, another, and, first, second, moreover, by the same token, besides, so too, similarly

**The Big Three Transitions:**
but, also, thus

Each of these words has a slightly different shade of meaning—we don't mean to imply that all the "but" words, for example, are interchangeable. On the other hand, the answer choices in a transition question generally won't give you a choice between four different kinds of *buts*. Your choice will be between a *but* and three *also*s, or a *thus* and three *buts*.

## How Do You Spot Transition Questions?

The underlined portion in a transition question is almost always at the *beginning* of a new clause, sentence, or paragraph.

The answer choices themselves will help you to spot transition questions. They are, invariably, made up of different sentence connectors from the list we just gave you. You have to decide which sentence connector is appropriate.

Now go back to the passage. Think **but, thus,** or **also.** Which type of sentence connector would be most appropriate to express the transition from one thought to the other? Look at the answer choices again to see which version of the sentence connector you want is available to you this time. Here's an example:

Funds provided by the Stafford program are not considered scholarships; <u>so too,</u> they are part of the extended student loan system.
   1

1. **A.** NO CHANGE
   **B.** in addition,
   **C.** rather,
   **D.** moreover

## Here's How to Crack It

There are two clues that might immediately point you in the right direction on this question: The underlined portion is at the *beginning* of a new clause; it also contains one of the sentence connectors we just listed. If you still aren't sure what type of question this is, look at the other answer choices. What do we see? More sentence connectors. This is a transition question.

As the passage stands, what type of transition is being used? "So too" is an **also.** Is this what we need? No. The next clause is not an *additional* thought, but rather a contrary thought. If we eliminate any answer choices that contain **also**s, A, B, and D all bite the dust. The answer must be **C**.

Note that in this case it might have been harder to decide among the answer choices if one of them had been a **thus.** Fortunately, that was not an option.

**Transition Check**

Look out for...
• underlining at the *beginning* of sentences.

## THE OTHER STRATEGY QUESTIONS

Other strategy questions read as if they were lifted from the Reading Test section of the ACT.

• Which of the following answers best summarizes the main point of the passage?

• Is the use of formal English appropriate in the context of this passage?

• If the passage were revised to present conflicting viewpoints, which of the following changes would best represent the other side of the author's argument?

## ORGANIZATION

There are three kinds of organization questions. The first asks you to check the placement of an underlined word or phrase in a sentence and possibly relocate it according to what the underlined word or phrase should logically modify. The second asks you to reorder sentences within a paragraph. The third asks you to reorder paragraphs within the passage as a whole. Let's talk about sentences within a paragraph first. Here's an example:

[1] Van Gogh, particularly in his later paintings, creates thick swirls of paint that perhaps mirror the emotional storm raging within. [2] DuFevre piles the paint onto the canvas in thick swatches that rise off the canvas by a good half inch at times. [3] Perhaps the most telling similarity between Van Gogh and DuFevre, the little-known modern surrealist, lies in their use of brushstrokes. [4] It is almost as if he is challenging Van Gogh to a contest to determine who was more emotionally disturbed.

2. Which of the following ordering of sentences will make the paragraph most logical?
   F. NO CHANGE
   G. 1, 3, 2, 4
   H. 1, 4, 3, 2
   J. 3, 1, 2, 4

## Here's How to Crack It

Although you might not think so at first, these questions are actually easier when they ask you to reorder *all* of the sentences in the paragraph as they do here. Rather than trying to figure out the order of all four sentences, why not figure out which of the sentences ought to come *first*. This should eliminate several of the answer choices and make your job much easier. Read through the sentences again looking for the thought that is capable of launching the entire paragraph. We need the topic sentence—the main idea that the other sentences support.

If you think the main idea is in Sentence [3], you are absolutely correct. The third sentence suggests a similarity between two painters that is explained and amplified in the other sentences. Which of the answer choices has Sentence [3] in the lead-off position? Only one. The answer must be choice **J**.

If you can't decide which of the choices comes first, another trick is to pair sentences that you can connect in some way. For example, in the paragraph on the previous page, you might have looked at Sentence [4] and noticed that the pronoun "he" could only refer to DuFevre. This implies that Sentence [4] comes right after Sentence [2]. This would eliminate answer choices F and H.

## ORDERING WHOLE PARAGRAPHS

When the ACT writers ask you to reorganize the paragraphs in a passage, they always position the question at the end of the passage after all the other specific questions. That's exactly where this question belongs. Don't spend large amounts of time rereading the entire passage. If you were struck by something strange in the ordering of paragraphs during the first read, go back and look at that place; otherwise, do some quick elimination and guess.

Again, you don't need to be sure of the position of *all* the paragraphs in order to do some quick elimination. Look for either the first paragraph or a pair of paragraphs that you are pretty sure go together, and use POE.

Here's a small-scale example. Let's assume that you've worked a passage and summarized each of the paragraphs in your head. Here are the summaries:

### Summary of Paragraph 1:

Most people believe eating healthy,

nutritious food is good for you.

### Summary of Paragraph 2:

Carrying the heavy boxes home, I pulled

a muscle.

### Summary of Paragraph 3:

I recently went to the health food store and

bought big boxes of wheat germ, carrot juice,

and tofu.

**Organization Check**

Look out for...

• words like "ordering," "organize," and "summary"

**Summary of Paragraph 4:**

But you can take this health kick too far, as I discovered.

3. Which of the following ordering of paragraphs best organizes this passage?
   A. NO CHANGE
   B. 1, 4, 3, 2
   C. 4, 2, 1, 3
   D. 2, 3, 4, 1

## Here's How to Crack It

There are several ways to approach this question. You could look for the first paragraph of the passage. You could try to establish some relationship between any two of the paragraphs. You could try to spot the last paragraph of the passage. Let's begin by trying to establish some relationship between any two paragraphs. In this passage, is there any observable cause and effect going on? Yes. Lifting the boxes caused a pulled muscle in the narrator. He couldn't pull the muscle until after he bought the boxes, which means Paragraph 2 must come after Paragraph 3. This option exists in only one of the answer choices. It begins to look as if answer choice B must be correct. To check, we can look to see what answer B offers us as the beginning and end paragraphs. However, bear in mind that you don't want to spend too much time on any one question. Reading an entire passage again with a new beginning is a laborious task. Bubble in **B** on your answer sheet and move on.

## STYLE

The largest number of style errors stems from **redundancy.** Put simply, redundancy means saying the same thing twice.

## HOW TO SPOT REDUNDANCY

Some redundancy errors are easier to see than others. Here are a couple of easy examples:

> *Cheap and inexpensive gifts can be found in the shopping district.*

> *Weak and without strength, the old car could not make it up the hill.*

In both of the examples above, two adjectives are saying exactly the same thing. Since there is really no need for both, the best way to correct the sentences would be to remove one of the superfluous adjectives.

> *Inexpensive gifts can be found in the shopping district.*
> *The weak, old car could not make it up the hill.*

Slightly more difficult:

> *After birth, the newborn babies are weighed by a nurse.*
> *In the year 1992…*

These examples would be perfectly acceptable in normal speech. However, newborn babies have obviously just been born, and 1992 is already a year. To fix these sentences, simply remove one of the superfluous items.

> *After birth, the babies are weighed by a nurse.*
> *In 1992…*

A comprehensive list of all the possible redundancies would be too long to do you any good. All you have to do in questions like these is spot the redundancy, and that's easy enough. Look for repetition in the underlined portion of the sentence or among the answer choices. When you see it, expunge it ruthlessly.

The Vietnam veterans were recently

<u>memorialized by a memorial</u> sculpture in
 4

Washington.

4.  **F.**  NO CHANGE
    **G.**  memorialized by a
    **H.**  memorialized with a new memoria
    **J.**  memorialized in a recent

## Here's How to Crack It

This is an obvious case of redundancy. We need to find an answer choice that does not repeat itself. Choice J seems possible until we realize that "recently memorialized in a recent sculpture" merely makes the same error with another word (recently). The only possible answer is choice **G**.

## THE OTHER STYLE QUESTIONS

A small number of style questions relate to the tone of the passage overall, and to the suitability of individual words. Some deal with issues of irrelevancy, wordiness, or slang. There are relatively few of these questions, and again, we counsel that unless you have a strong feeling that you have a handle on these questions, you circle them and come back to them later.

**Redundancy Check**

Look out for...

- redundancy—Oh, and check for sentences that say the same thing twice, too.

# SUMMARY

1.  Do the questions in order, leaving only tougher rhetoric questions for the end. If you're having trouble with a particular question, leave it and come back. Often a later question will help you with an earlier one.

2.  Search the answer choices for clues. Note how the choices differ from each other, and use that information to determine the error(s) being tested.

3.  Look for one error at a time. It is a good idea to first narrow the choices down on the basis of errors in sentence structure and grammar, then use punctuation to make your selection between the remaining choices. For instance, if the choices offer you a list of items or actions, first check for parallel construction, then look for correct use of serial commas.

4.  Don't forget that NO CHANGE is correct a little less than a quarter of the time—if you can't find anything wrong with the underlined portion, it may be correct as written.

5. If "OMIT the underlined portion" is offered as an answer choice, examine it very closely. It has a high probability of being correct.

6. Read carefully—it is easy to overlook a comma or apostrophe when you're working quickly.

7. Leave nothing blank. There's no wrong answer penalty.

## RHETORIC DRILL

[1]

The golden age of television means many things to many people, and to the small band of actors, writers, and directors who
1

would rise to prominence in the late 50s and early 60s, without a doubt it meant the "live" television shows such as *Playhouse 90*
2

where many of them initially worked for the first time.
3

[2]

[1] Each week, a new "teleplay" was created from scratch—written, cast, rehearsed, and performed. [2] *Playhouse 90* was truly a remarkable training ground for the young talents. [3] Such future luminaries as Paddy Chayefsky, Marlon Brando, and Patricia Neal worked long hours honing to a knife edge their craft. [4] In some cases, when there were problems with the censors,
4
it would have to be created twice.

1. **A.** NO CHANGE
   **B.** thus to
   **C.** but to
   **D.** In addition to

2. **F.** NO CHANGE
   **G.** prominent famousness
   **H.** famous prominence
   **J.** famousness

3. **A.** NO CHANGE
   **B.** initially for the first time worked
   **C.** for the first time worked initially
   **D.** worked for the first time.

4. **F.** NO CHANGE
   **G.** to an edge
   **H.** edges
   **J.** OMIT the underlined portion

5. Which of the following sequences would best organize the sentences in Paragraph 2?
   **A.** NO CHANGE
   **B.** 1, 2, 4, 3
   **C.** 2, 1, 4, 3
   **D.** 3, 4, 1, 2

[3]

Despite the frantic pace, accidents hap-
6
pened frequently. David Niven once revealed
that, during an early show, he inadvertently
locked his costume in his dressing room two
minutes before air time. As the announcer
announced the opening credits, the sound of
axes splintering the door to Niven's dressing
room could be heard in the background.

6. **F.** NO CHANGE
   **G.** Due to
   **H.** In spite of
   **J.** Thus

Items 7, 8, and 9 ask questions about
the passage as a whole.

7. If the writer wished to make the tone
   of Paragraph 3 more lighthearted, she
   could change the word "accidents" to
   **A.** NO CHANGE
   **B.** casualties
   **C.** mishaps
   **D.** grave errors

8. Which of the following would best
   summarize the passage as a whole?
   **F.** The golden age of television meant
   many things to many different
   people.
   **G.** Early television shows such as
   *Playhouse 90* provided the training
   ground where talented new enter-
   tainers could learn their craft.
   **H.** The golden age of television had
   many amusing moments.
   **J.** The rise of Paddy Chayefsky, Marlon Brando, and Patricia Neal helped
   to make *Playhouse 90* a success.

9. Which of the following sequences of
   paragraphs would make the structure of
   the passage as a whole the most logical?
   **A.** NO CHANGE
   **B.** 3, 2, 1
   **C.** 3, 1, 2
   **D.** 2, 3, 1

## Here's How to Crack It

**Question 1:** The underlined portion and the answer choices all contain sentence
connectors. This is a **transition** question. Do we need an *also*, a *but*, or a *thus*? It
seems pretty clear we need a *but*. The answer is **C**.

**Question 2:** Several of the answer choices here seem to use similar words. We should consider **redundancy** immediately. G and H are clearly redundant. Answer choice J ("famousness") is incorrect. Thus, the best answer is **F,** NO CHANGE.

**Question 3:** The underlined portion and the answer choices all seem to contain similar words, so again we should consider **redundancy.** There is no need to say both "initially" and "for the first time" in the same sentence. Answer choice **D** is the only choice that does not do this.

**Question 4:** At first this might strike you as an idiom question. In fact, **style** questions often resemble idiom questions. The metaphor of an actor sharpening his or her skills is effective, but how far do we want to take it? Is it necessary to say "to a knife edge" to get the point across? The answer is **J.** OMIT the underlined portion.

**Question 5:** As with all **organization** questions, we should try to spot either the beginning sentence, or any pair of sentences we can link together. There is a certain cause and effect visible between Sentence [1] and Sentence [4]. Which of the answer choices puts them next to each other in that order? Only one. The answer would seem to have to be C. Does that make sense? Let's read the paragraph in the new order just to be sure. It begins by saying *Playhouse 90* was a training ground. Each week a new teleplay was created from scratch. Sometimes, it was created twice. Future stars worked there in order to get experience. The paragraph seems to hold together. The answer is **C.**

**Question 6:** We see more sentence connectors, so we are again prepared for **transition.** "(Blank) the frantic pace, accidents happened frequently." Let's try out the words in the answer choices. Could "despite" fill in the blank? No. We want more of a causal word. Answer choice **G,** "Due to," is the correct answer.

**Question 7:** How do we change the **tone** of Paragraph [3] with one word? Well, "accidents" sounds a little drastic. Which choice minimizes the sound of that word? If you said **C,** "mishaps," you were absolutely correct.

**Question 8:** This is one to leave for last. **Summary** questions always take a while. Answer choice F merely repeats the first half of the first sentence of the passage, entirely missing *Playhouse 90*. Answer choice G seems really good. Answer choice H concentrates on the third paragraph only. Answer J concentrates solely on the three actors and writers mentioned. Are they the primary focus of the passage? Not really. The answer is **G.**

**Question 9:** Another question to leave until the end. **Organization of paragraphs** requires an overview of the entire passage. As always, try to find one paragraph you feel you can label as first or last, and proceed from there. The correct answer is **A,** NO CHANGE.

# PART III

# How to Beat the ACT Mathematics Test

## What to Expect in the Math Section

You will have 60 minutes to answer 60 multiple-choice questions based on "...
topics covered in typical high school classes." For those of you who aren't sure if
you went to a typical high school, these questions break down into rather precise
areas of knowledge.

There are always exactly:

- 24 problems from pre-algebra and elementary algebra
  *Questions based on definitions of terms (integers, prime numbers,
  etc.), fractions, decimals, ratios, percents, averages, word problems,
  quadratic equations.*

- 18 problems from intermediate algebra and coordinate
  geometry
  *Questions based on exponents, square roots, factoring, writing equa-
  tions, inequalities, simultaneous equations, and graphing.*

- 14 problems from geometry
  *Questions based on angles, lengths, triangles, parallel lines, area,
  perimeter, circles, and volume.*

- 4 problems from basic trigonometry
  *Questions based on SOHCAHTOA, and some other relatively easy
  trigonometry formulas.*

## What Not to Expect in the Math Section

You won't find calculus of any kind. For those of you who may have taken the
SAT, you also won't find any of the devious tricks that plague that test. The ACT,
by contrast, is pretty straightforward.

## The Princeton Review Approach

Because the test is so predictable, the best way to prepare for ACT Math is with

1. a thorough review of the very specific information and question
   types that come up again and again

2. an understanding of The Princeton Review test-taking
   strategies and techniques

In each chapter of the Math Test you'll find a mixture of review and technique,
with a sprinkling of ACT-like problems. At the end of each chapter will be a
summary of the chapter and a drill designed to pinpoint your math test-taking
strengths and weaknesses. In addition to working through the problems you'll
find in this book, we strongly suggest you practice our techniques on some real
ACT practice tests. We'll begin with some general strategy.

## EASY, MEDIUM, DIFFICULT

Sixty minutes for 60 questions. This seems fairly straightforward, but don't let the symmetry of these two numbers fool you; some problems will take much less than a minute—and others could take forever if you let them.

The first few questions are designed to be easier than the rest of the test, then the questions get a bit tougher for the remainder of the section. At least, this is ACT's intention. However, what the people at ACT think is easy may not strike you the same way. Similarly, you might find some of the problems in the middle or end of the test to be a piece of cake.

So you are going to have to figure out for yourself which are the easy, medium, and difficult questions in this section.

## MATH TRIAGE

In chapter 1 we introduced the concept of triage. Let's apply this concept to ACT Math. Here's a problem:

1. Cynthia, Peter, Nancy, and Kevin are all carpenters. Last week, each built the following number of chairs:

   Cynthia–36   Peter–45   Nancy–74   Kevin–13

   What was the average number of chairs each carpenter built last week?
   A. 39
   B. 42
   C. 55
   D. 59
   E. 63

## NOW, LATER, MUCH LATER, NEVER

**First Pass**

Do the problems you're sure you know how to do.

**Second Pass**

Do the problems you *think* you know how to do.

**Third Pass**

If there's time, take a crack at the ones you have no idea how to do. Be sure you don't leave any blanks on your answer sheet.

Do you want to do this problem *now*? That is the question you should constantly be asking yourself during the exam. If you finish reading a problem and immediately know how to solve it, then of course you should do it right away.

If you finish reading a problem and immediately know that you will never, ever understand that question, then write R.I.P. next to it, pick an answer at random, and never look at it again (remember: Never leave a question blank).

If you aren't sure, you *might* want to *start* doing the problem to see if something will jog your memory. However, if you look at your watch and see that 30 seconds have gone by and you still don't have a handle on the problem, it's time to throw it to the back of the line. Put a big circle around it and move on. You haven't wasted the 30 seconds, you've invested them. When you come back to the question later, after you've done all the problems that you found easy, you will already have read it once, thought about it, and perhaps made some beginning calculations. You won't be starting from scratch at all.

## I'm Almost Done...

The temptation to get stubborn and stay with a particular problem can be very strong. But if it takes you four minutes to solve question 5, then it might mean that you don't have the time to do several problems later on that you might have found easier. As we mentioned in chapter 1, you might have the "oh, yeah!" revelation on this problem before you finish the section!

**An Easy Problem**

has one or two steps.

## That Was an Easy One

Of course, to solve the problem about the four carpenters, you were probably not going to have to depend on a revelation. Did you want to do it right away? Sure. It's a moderately easy average problem.

### Here's How to Crack It

To find the average of a group of numbers, add the numbers together and divide by the number of terms.

$$\frac{\text{sum of everything}}{\text{number of things}} = \text{average}$$

In this case, the thing we don't know is the average, but we do know everything else, so let's put the numbers into our formula:

$$\frac{36 + 45 + 74 + 13}{4} = \text{average}$$

(By the way, we will cover average problems more fully in chapter 9. The answer to this question is **B**.)

How do you distinguish an easy problem from a tough one? In part by deciding whether it can be done in one or two steps, or whether it will require three or more steps.

## Here's a Medium ACT Problem

22. Four carpenters built an average of 42 chairs each last week. If Cynthia built 36 chairs, Nancy built 74 chairs, and Kevin built 13 chairs, how many chairs did Peter build?
    F. 24
    G. 37
    H. 45
    J. 53
    K. 67

**A Medium Problem**

has two or three steps.

This is still an average problem, but it is less straightforward now and will require an extra step to get the final answer.

### Here's How to Crack It

Let's put the information we have into the same formula we used before:

$$\frac{36 + 74 + 13 + \text{Peter}}{4} = 42$$

You might want to substitute the variable x for Peter. Note that medium and difficult average problems often give you the number of terms and the average. What they don't give you—and the important thing to figure out—is the **sum** of the numbers to be averaged.

If we multiply both sides by 4, we get the sum of all four numbers.

$$36 + 74 + 13 + \text{Peter} = 168$$

To find out Peter's number of chairs, we just have to add the other numbers and subtract from 168. $168 - 123 = 45$. The answer is **H**.

## HERE'S A HARD ACT PROBLEM

**A Difficult Problem**

has three or four steps.

41. Four carpenters each built an average of 42 chairs last week. If no chairs were left uncompleted and if Peter, who built 50 chairs, built the greatest number of chairs, what is the **least** number of chairs one of the carpenters could have built, if no carpenter built a fractional number of chairs?

   A. 18
   B. 19
   C. 20
   D. 39.33
   E. 51

The concept *behind* this question is really no more difficult than either of the first two problems. It is still about averages. But now there are several more steps involved, including a small leap of faith. You can tell it's more difficult than the first two questions partly because of the language it uses: "If no chairs were left uncompleted" is closing a potential loophole. Easy problems are usually too simple to have loopholes. "What is the *least*" implies the need for reflection.

### Here's How to Crack It

Let's put what we know into the same formula we have used twice already:

$$\frac{50 + x + y + z}{4} = 42$$

The only individual we know something specific about is Peter. We've represented the other three carpenters as $x$, $y$, and $z$. Since the sum of all four carpenters' adds up to 168, we now have:

$$50 + x + y + z = 168$$

By itself, an equation with three variables can't be solved, so unless we can glean a bit more information from the problem, we're stuck, and it's time to put a circle around the problem and move on.

Let's assume you skipped the problem temporarily, and you have now come back to it after completing all the problems you thought were easy.

The problem asks for the *least* number of chairs one carpenter could build. To figure this out, let's have the other two carpenters build the *most* number of chairs they could build. According to the problem, Peter constructed 50, and no one else built as many as he did. So let's say two of the other carpenters constructed 49 each—the largest possible amount they could build and still have built fewer than Peter. By making carpenters $x$ and $y$ construct as many chairs as possible, we can find out the *minimum* number of chairs carpenter $z$ would have to make.

Now the problem looks like this:

$$50 + 49 + 49 + z = 168$$

If we add $50 + 49 + 49$ and subtract it from 168, then $z = 20$, and the correct answer choice is **C**.

## PROCESS OF ELIMINATION

Even if you weren't sure how to do that last problem, you might have been able to eliminate two answer choices right away using the major technique we introduced in chapter 2: POE. Remember, ACT doesn't take away any points for wrong answers, so it is in your interest to guess on every question you can't solve using other methods. But your guesses will be a lot more valuable if you can eliminate some of the answer choices first. The problem said Peter built the greatest number of chairs—50 of them. Therefore, could any of the other carpenters have built *more* than that? No, so answer choice E didn't make sense. And because no carpenter built a fractional number of chairs, D didn't make sense either.

## COMMON SENSE

You can frequently get rid of several answer choices in an ACT Math problem without doing any complicated math. Let's look at an example:

3. There are 600 school children in the Lakeville district. If 54 of them are high school seniors, what is the percentage of high school seniors in the Lakeville district?

   A. .9%
   B. 2.32%
   C. 9%
   D. 11%
   E. 90%

### Here's How to Crack It

This is not an advanced problem. ACT wants us to write a simple equation, and we will review just how to do that in the arithmetic chapter. But before we do any heavy math, let's see if we can get rid of some answer choices using common sense.

**Cross Off the Crazy Answers**

What's the average of 100 and 200?

A. ~~500~~
B. 150
C. ~~a billion~~

The question asks us to find a percentage of 600. Just to get a rough fix on where we are, what is 10% of 600? If you said 60, you were right. To find 10% of anything, you simply move the decimal point over one place to the left. If 60 is 10%, then 54 must be slightly less than 10%. Which answer choices don't make sense? D and E don't work because we need something less than 10%. On the other hand, we need something only *slightly* less than 10%. Could the answer be A or B? No. On this problem, it was just as easy to eliminate wrong answers as it was to solve for the right answer. The answer is **C**.

On most ACT problems, you will be able to eliminate only one or two answer choices by using common sense, but it's still vital that you always think about what a reasonable answer might be for a particular problem—*before* you solve it mathematically. This is because the ACT has some trap answers waiting for you.

## PARTIAL ANSWERS

**Pop Quiz**

Q: What percent of the math ACT tests trigonometry?

Sometimes students think they have completed a problem before the problem is actually done. The test writers at ACT like to include trap answer choices for these students. Here's an example:

4. A bus line charges $5 each way to ferry a passenger between the hotel and an archeological dig. On a given day, the bus line has a capacity to carry 255 passengers from the hotel to the dig and back. If the bus line runs at 90% of capacity, how much money did the bus line take in that day?
   F. $1147.50
   G. $1275
   H. $2295
   J. $2550
   K. $2625

## Here's How to Crack It

The first step in this problem is to determine how much money the line would make if it ran at total capacity. If there were 255 passengers, each of whom paid $10 (remember, the bus company charges $5 each way), that would be $2550.

If you were in a hurry, you might decide at this point that you were already done and go straight to the answer choices. And there is answer choice J, beckoning seductively. Unfortunately, of course, J is not the right answer. The bus line is only running at 90% of capacity. To get the real answer, we have to find 90% of $2550.

You also might have missed, or put aside temporarily, the information that each passenger has to pay coming *and* going, in which case you might have multiplied 255 by 5 to get $1275, and then found 90% of that, $1147.50—which just happens to be answer choice **F**.

Both answer choices F and J were partial answers. Students who picked one of these answers did not make a mistake in their math, nor did they misunderstand the overall concept of the problem; they simply stopped before they were completely finished. All you had to do to $1147.50 to get the right answer was double it, so that you included both trips. All you had to do to $2550 to get the right answer was to take 90% of it. The answer is **H**.

## How to Avoid Partial Answers

You can prevent yourself from picking partial answers by doing two things.

1. Slow down. It isn't going to help to do a problem so quickly that you miss important information.

2. When you finish a problem, always reread the last line to make sure you've answered the question the ACT writer asked.

## Are Partial Answers Fair?

You might decide that it is not very sporting of ACT to try to trip up students with partial answer choices. On the other hand, if this had been a short-answer test, students might well have made exactly the same mistake on their own. Besides, if partial answers represent the downside of multiple choice testing, there is a tremendous upside as well: Let's see how POE could have helped us on this last problem.

## You Bet!

POE allows us to eliminate crazy answer choices. Remember, we said the first step in the problem was to find out how much total money was taken in on that day. If you read carefully, you realized that each of the 255 passengers had to pay $10. This is a total of $2550. To get the final answer, of course, we had to get 90% of $2550. Was it necessary to work the problem out exactly? Let's look at the answer choices.

J, $2550, represents the total capacity. It is a trap, so eliminate it. The correct answer must be a bit less than $2550. Could the answer be **K**, $2625? Impossible.

We know the answer should be a bit less than $2550. Could it be as small as F, $1147.50, or G, $1275? No way. It has to be **H**.

**Pop Quiz**

A: 4 questions out of 60 is equal to roughly 6.67%.

## Can I Use My Calculator?

You sure can, and you should. Though the folks who write the ACT state that none of the math questions *require* a calculator, the fact is the math on the test has become steadily more complex since calculators were first allowed. The test writers clearly expect you to have a calculator.

Furthermore, there are plenty of questions on the test that will go much more quickly and smoothly *if* you know how to use your calculator properly. As we go through the math in this book, we'll be pointing out which questions are particularly calculator friendly and telling you just what you need to be able to do with your calculator in order to succeed. The key, of course, is that you need to know how to use your calculator before the test begins. So when we tell you to make sure that you can do a certain type of operation on your calculator, be sure to check right away.

We thought about including little tutorials on how to use your calculator to do different things, such as factor quadratics, but because there are so many different types of calculators out there, that wasn't practical. So, if you need help learning how to use your calculator, ask a friend, ask your math teacher, check out the manufacturer's website, or read the instruction book that came with the calculator.

Whatever calculator you decide to get, be sure it can do the following: handle positive, negative, and fractional exponents; use parentheses; graph simple functions; convert fractions to decimals and vice versa; and change a linear equation into $y = mx + b$ form. One model we've found to be pretty easy to understand and effective on the ACT is the TI-83.

## RED HERRINGS

Of the 60 problems in this section, perhaps as many as two will contain extra information that is not, strictly speaking, necessary to solve the problems. The test writers want to see if you can distinguish important information from filler. Since there are so few of these questions, it isn't necessary to examine each new piece of information with a magnifying glass to see if it might be a red herring. In almost every problem on the ACT, you will need *all* the information given in order to solve it. However, if you're staring at a particular number that doesn't seem to have anything to do with the solution of the question you're doing—well, every once in a while it might not. Here's an example:

5. Susan's take-home pay is $300 per week, of which she spends $80 on food and $150 on rent. What fraction of her take-home pay does she spend on food?

   A. $\frac{2}{75}$

   B. $\frac{4}{15}$

   C. $\frac{1}{2}$

   D. $\frac{23}{30}$

   E. $\frac{29}{30}$

## Here's How to Crack It

The last line tells us what we need to do. A fraction is a part over a whole. In this case, the whole is $300. The part is the amount of money spent on food:

**Pop Quiz**

Q: Is 0 positive or negative?

$$\frac{\$80}{\$300} \text{ which reduces to } \frac{4}{15}$$

Where does the $150 fit in? It doesn't. The question isn't asking about rent. The test writers just threw that in to confuse you. Note that if you got confused and found the fraction of the take-home salary that was paid in rent, $150/$300, you would pick answer choice C. The correct answer is **B.**

# SUMMARY

1. The Math Test of the ACT contains 60 questions to do in 60 minutes. It breaks down into

   - pre-algebra and elementary algebra—24 questions

   - intermediate algebra and coordinate geometry—18 questions

   - geometry—14 questions

   - trigonometry—4 questions

2. To answer the greatest number of questions correctly, use triage to decide whether to do a problem now, or whether to wait until later. Triage enables you to decide if a problem is easy, medium, or hard. Easy problems generally have only one or two steps. Medium problems generally have two or three steps. Difficult problems have more steps and may call for further analysis.

3. You can use the Process of Elimination, or POE, to cancel out wrong answer choices. Sometimes it is easier to get rid of wrong answers than to find the correct answer.

   - Incorrect answers are sometimes partial answers—answers you arrive at on the way to the final solution if you quit before you are really done.

   - Incorrect answers sometimes don't really make sense if you look at them in the cold light of day. Frequently, you can eliminate answer choices because they are nowhere near what common sense says the answer would have to be.

   - Incorrect answers are sometimes based on red herrings—pieces of information that are not really necessary to solve the problem.

4. Be sure you put an answer down for every question—even the ones you don't have time to do. There's no penalty for wrong answers.

**Pop Quiz**
A: 0 is neither positive nor negative.

# 8

# Basics

Look at the following problem:

1. How many even prime numbers are there between 0 and 100?
   A. 0
   B. 1
   C. 2
   D. 3
   E. 4

This is a very easy problem—provided you know what the terms "even" and "prime" mean. Without a knowledge of these terms, the problem is impossible. Let's begin our math review by going over all the basic math terms and operations covered on the ACT. By the way, the answer to the question is **B**.

# BASIC TERMS

**Pop Quiz**

Q: Is 0 even or odd?

Q: Is 0 a prime number?

## REAL NUMBERS

Real numbers are all the numbers you think of when you think of numbers: 5, $\frac{1}{4}$, 7.9, 100, –43, $\sqrt{2}$, etc. They include everything *except* imaginary numbers, which only appear occasionally on the ACT. An example of an imaginary number is $i$, which is the square root of –1.

## RATIONAL NUMBERS

Any number that can be written as a whole number, a fraction (an integer over another integer), or as a repeating decimal is a rational number. This means that 5, $\frac{1}{5}$, and $.33\overline{3}$ are rational numbers. In fact, most of the numbers you'll see on the ACT are rational numbers.

## IRRATIONAL NUMBERS

An irrational number cannot be written as an integer over another integer. $\pi$ is irrational. Like other irrational numbers, it goes on forever. While you may think of $\pi$ as 3.14, it can be written out to as many decimal places as you feel like writing down: 3.141592 etc.—and as many places as you take it, you will never find a repeating pattern.

Other irrational numbers? Any square root of a number that does not have a perfect square root. For example, $\sqrt{3}$ or $\sqrt{2}$. By contrast, $\sqrt{4}$, which simplifies to 2, is a rational number.

## INTEGERS

Integers include everything *except* what we normally think of as fractions or decimals: 2, 134, –56, 0, and 7 are all integers. $\frac{1}{2}$, 6.7, and $\frac{-31}{2}$ are not.

## POSITIVE AND NEGATIVE

Positive numbers are to the right of the 0 on the number line above. Negative numbers are to the left of zero on the number line above. Zero itself is neither negative nor positive.

Note that positive numbers get bigger as they move away from 0. Negative numbers get smaller. For example, –3 is smaller than –1.

There are three rules regarding the multiplication of positive and negative numbers. They are:

positive × positive = positive
positive × negative = negative
negative × negative = positive

When you add a positive number and a negative number, you're subtracting the number with the negative sign in front of it from the positive number.

$$5 + (–3) = 2$$

When you add two negative numbers, you're adding the two numbers as if they were positive and then putting a negative sign in front of the sum.

$$–3 + –4 = –7$$

## EVEN AND ODD NUMBERS

Even numbers are integers that can be divided evenly by 2:

–4, –2, 0, 2, 4, 6, etc.

Odd numbers are integers that cannot be divided evenly by 2:

–5, –3, –1, 1, 3, 5, etc.

Note that 0 is even. There are several rules regarding multiplication and addition of even and odd numbers. They are:

$$\text{even} \times \text{even} = \text{even}$$
$$\text{odd} \times \text{odd} = \text{odd}$$
$$\text{even} \times \text{odd} = \text{even}$$
$$\text{even} + \text{even} = \text{even}$$
$$\text{odd} + \text{odd} = \text{even}$$
$$\text{even} + \text{odd} = \text{odd}$$

## DIGITS

**Pop Quiz**

Q: What's the only even prime?

There are ten digits: 0, 1, 2, 3, 4, 5, 6, 7, 8, 9.

The number 364 has three digits—3, 6, and 4. In this number, the 4 is called the **ones** digit, or **units** digit. The 6 is called the **tens** digit. The 3 is called the **hundreds** digit.

The number 4.56 has three digits—4, 5, and 6. The 4 is called the ones digit or **units** digit. The 5 is called the **tenths** digit, and the 6 is called the **hundredths** digit.

## PRIME NUMBERS

A prime number can be divided evenly by two, and only two, distinct factors—1 and itself. Thus 2, 3, 5, 7, 11, and 13 are all prime numbers. The number 2 is the only even prime number. Neither 0 nor 1 is a prime number. There are no negative prime numbers.

## ABSOLUTE VALUE

The absolute value of a number is the distance between that number and 0 on the number line. The absolute value of 6 is expressed as $|6|$.

$$|6| = 6$$
$$|-6| = 6$$

## VARIABLES AND COEFFICIENTS

In the expression $3x + 4y$, $x$ and $y$ are called **variables** because we don't know what they are. 3 and 4 are called **coefficients.**

# BASIC OPERATIONS

## DIVISIBILITY RULES

If a number can be divided evenly by another number, it is said to be divisible by that number. A good way to save time actually dividing is to know the rules of divisibility for some common numbers. The rules are on the following page.

1. A number is divisible by 2 if its units digit can be divided evenly by 2 (in other words, if it is even). 46 is divisible by 2. So is 3,574.

2. A number is divisible by 3 if the sum of its digits can be divided evenly by 3. We can quickly determine that 216 is divisible by 3 because the sum of the digits (2 + 1 + 6) is divisible by 3.

3. A number is divisible by 4 if the number formed by its last two digits (tens digit and units digit) is also divisible by 4. Thus, 316 is divisible by 4 because 16 is divisible by 4. 728 is also divisible by 4 because 28 is divisible by 4.

4. A number is divisible by 5 if its last digit (units place) is either 0 or 5. For example, 60, 85, and 15 are all divisible by 5.

5. A number is divisible by 6 if it is also divisible by the factors of 6: 2 and 3. For example, 228 is divisible by 6 because it is even (divisible by 2) and the sum of its digits is divisible by 3.

6. A number is divisible by 9 if the sum of its digits can be divided evenly by 9. For example, 873 is divisible by 9 because the sum of the digits (8 + 7 + 3) is divisible by 9.

## OPERATIONS

- **Sum** is the result of addition.

  *The sum of 3 and 4 is 7.*

- **Product** is the result of multiplication.

  *The product of 5 and 2 is 10.*

- **Difference** is the result of subtraction.

  *The difference between 7 and 3 is 4.*

- **Quotient** is the result of division.

  *If you divide 14 by 7, the quotient is 2.*

## FACTORS AND MULTIPLES

A number is a **factor** of another number if it can be divided evenly *into* that number. Is 3 a factor of 15? Yes, because 3 can be divided evenly into 15. The complete list of factors of 15 is 1, 3, 5, and 15.

A number is a **multiple** of another number if it can be divided evenly *by* that number. For example, multiples of 15 include 15, 30, 45, and 60.

All integers have a limited number of factors and an infinite number of multiples. You can remember this with the following mnemonic: Factors, Few; Multiples, Many.

What is the only factor of 15 that is also a multiple of 15? 15.

# STANDARD SYMBOLS

| Symbol | Meaning |
|:---:|:---|
| = | is equal to |
| ≠ | is not equal to |
| < | is less than |
| > | is greater than |
| ≤ | is less than or equal to |
| ≥ | is greater than or equal to |

# EXPONENTS

An exponent is a short way of writing the value of a number multiplied several times by itself. $4 \times 4 \times 4 \times 4 \times 4$ can also be written as $4^5$. This is expressed aloud as "4 to the fifth power." The lower and larger number (4) is called the **base,** and the upper number (5) is called the **exponent**. There are several rules to remember about exponents.

## MULTIPLYING NUMBERS WITH THE SAME BASE

When you multiply numbers that have the same base, you simply add the exponents.

**Pop Quiz**

Q: If a number is divisible by 2 and by 3, it's also divisible by...

$$6^2 \times 6^3 = 6^{(2+3)} = 6^5 \qquad \left(y^2\right)\left(y^3\right) = y^{(2+3)} = y^5$$

## DIVIDING NUMBERS WITH THE SAME BASE

When you divide numbers that have the same base, you simply subtract the bottom exponent from the top exponent.

**The Strange Powers of Powers**

Parentheses can have very important consequences on exponents: Remember to distribute powers to everything within parentheses. For example: $(3x)^2 = 9x^2$, not $3x^2$. Many students carelessly forget that they must also square the 3. If the parentheses surround a fraction, the exponent applies to both the numerator and the denominator.

$$\frac{4^7}{4^2} = 4^5 \qquad \frac{x^7}{x^2} = x^5 \qquad \frac{y^3}{y^5} = \frac{1}{y^2} = y^{-2}$$

## NEGATIVE POWERS

In that last example, we also wrote the result as $y^2$. A negative power is simply the reciprocal of a positive power. (The reciprocal of 3 is $\frac{1}{3}$.)

$$3^{-1} = \frac{1}{3} \qquad 3^{-2} = \frac{1}{9} \qquad 3^{-3} = \frac{1}{27}$$

## FRACTIONAL POWERS

When a number is raised to a fractional power, the numerator (the number above the line in a fraction) functions like a real exponent, while the denominator (the number below the line in a fraction) tells you what power radical to make the number. (Radicals will be defined on page 98.)

$$9^{\frac{1}{2}} = \sqrt{9} = 3 \qquad 8^{\frac{2}{3}} = \sqrt[3]{8^2}$$

## RAISING A POWER TO A POWER

When you raise a power to a power, you simply multiply the exponents.

$$(4^2)^6 = 4^{(2 \cdot 6)} = 4^{12} \qquad (y^3)^2 = y^{(3 \cdot 2)} = y^6$$

## THE ZERO POWER

Anything to the zero power is 1.

$$4^0 = 1 \qquad x^0 = 1$$

## THE FIRST POWER

Anything to the power of 1 is itself.

$$5^1 = 5 \qquad y^1 = y$$

## DISTRIBUTING EXPONENTS

When several numbers are inside parentheses, the exponent outside the parentheses must be distributed to all of the numbers within.

$$(4y)^2 = 4^2 y^2 = 16y^2$$

## BUT WATCH OUT FOR...

There are several operations that *seem* like they ought to work with exponents but don't.

Does $x^2 + x^3 = x^5$? NO!

Does $x^4 - x^2 = x^2$? NO!

Does $\dfrac{x^2 + y^3 + z^4}{x^2 + y^3} = z^4$? NO!

You would expect that raising a number to a power would increase that number, and usually it does, but there are exceptions.

- If you raise a positive fraction of less than 1 to a power, it gets smaller.

$$\left(\frac{1}{2}\right)^2 = \frac{1^2}{2^2} = \frac{1}{4}$$

- If you raise a negative number to an odd power, the number gets smaller (unless it is between 0 and –1).

$$(-3)^3 = (-3)(-3)(-3) = -27$$

(remember, –27 is smaller than –3)

- If you raise a negative number to an even power, the number becomes positive.

$$(-3)^2 = (-3)(-3) = 9$$

# RADICALS

**Roots Are Positive on the ACT**

When you're asked for the square root of any number, supply the positive root only. Although $5^2$ and $(-5)^2$ both equal 25, 5 is the only square root of 25.

The **square root** of a positive number $x$ is the number that, when squared, equals $x$. For example, the square root of 16 equals 4 because $4 \times 4 = 16$. On the ACT, you will not have to worry about negative square roots—for our purposes, the square root of 16 is just 4.

The symbol for a positive square root is $\sqrt{\phantom{x}}$. A number inside the $\sqrt{\phantom{x}}$ is also called a radical.

$$\sqrt{16} = 4$$
$$\sqrt{9} = 3$$

The **cube root** of a positive number $x$ is the number that, when cubed, equals $x$. For example, the cube root of 8 equals 2 because $2 \times 2 \times 2$ equals 8.

$$\sqrt[3]{8} = 2$$
$$\sqrt[3]{27} = 3$$

**Pop Quiz**

Q: What number is both a factor and a multiple of 21?

Be sure that you know how to use your calculator to find more than just square roots and simple exponents like $4^2$. The ACT is going to have fractional exponents, negative exponents, and all sorts of weird roots, and you'll need to be able to solve them quickly and accurately. Can you do the two examples above on your calculator? What about questions 4 and 5 in the drill at the end of this chapter? If you can't, be sure to learn how.

There are several rules to remember about radicals:

- $\sqrt{x} + \sqrt{x} = 2\sqrt{x}$

  For example, $2\sqrt{5} + 20\sqrt{5} = 22\sqrt{5}$
- $\sqrt{x} \cdot \sqrt{y} = \sqrt{xy}$

For example, $\left(\sqrt{12}\right)\left(\sqrt{3}\right) = \sqrt{36}$ or 6.

$$3\sqrt{5} \cdot 6\sqrt{2} = 18\sqrt{10}$$

- $\sqrt{\dfrac{x}{y}} = \dfrac{\sqrt{x}}{\sqrt{y}}$

For example, $\sqrt{\dfrac{3}{16}} = \dfrac{\sqrt{3}}{\sqrt{16}} = \dfrac{\sqrt{3}}{4}$

- To simplify a radical, try factoring.

$$\sqrt{32} = \sqrt{16}\sqrt{2} = 4\sqrt{2}$$

$$2\sqrt{5} + 4\sqrt{125} = 2\sqrt{5} + 4\left(\sqrt{25}\right)\left(\sqrt{5}\right) =$$

$$2\sqrt{5} + (4)(5)\left(\sqrt{5}\right) = 22\sqrt{5}$$

- The square root of a positive fraction less than 1 is actually larger than the original fraction.

For example, $\sqrt{\dfrac{1}{4}} = \dfrac{1}{2}$

- Always try to have a ballpark idea of how big the number you are dealing with actually is. $\sqrt{63}$ is a bit less than $\sqrt{64}$ or 8.

$\sqrt[3]{9}$ is a bit more than $\sqrt[3]{8}$ or 2.

Some good approximations to remember:

$\sqrt{2} \approx 1.4$

$\sqrt{3} \approx 1.7$

# BASICS DRILL

Pop Quiz
A: 21

1. Which of the following expresses the prime factorization of 54?

   A. $9 \times 6$
   B. $3 \times 3 \times 6$
   C. $3 \times 3 \times 2$
   D. $3 \times 3 \times 3 \times 2$
   E. $5.4 \times 10$

2. $\dfrac{(-5)(4)|-6|}{-3} =$

   F. $-120$
   G. $-40$
   H. $40$
   J. $60$
   K. $120$

3. The number 1134 is divisible by all of the following except

   A. 3
   B. 6
   C. 9
   D. 12
   E. 14

4. $(-2)^3 + (3)^{-2} + \dfrac{8}{9} =$

   F. $-7$

   G. $-1\dfrac{7}{9}$

   H. $\dfrac{8}{9}$

   J. $1\dfrac{7}{9}$

   K. $12$

5. $27^{\frac{2}{3}}$

   A. $-9$
   B. $-4$
   C. $9$
   D. $18$
   E. $81^3$

6. For all $x \neq 0$, $y \neq 0$, $\dfrac{(xy)^3 z^0}{x^3 y^4} =$

   F. $\dfrac{1}{y}$

   G. $\dfrac{z}{y}$

   H. $z$

   J. $xy$

   K. $xyz$

7. When is $\dfrac{11-a}{2}$ an integer?

   A. Only when $a$ is negative
   B. Only when $a$ is positive
   C. Only when $a$ is odd
   D. Only when $a$ equals 0
   E. Only when $a$ is even

8. How many even integers are there between $-4$ and 4?

   F. 1
   G. 3
   H. 4
   J. 5
   K. 7

**9.** If the four-digit number 47*w*6 is divisible by 6
(*w* represents the tens digit), which of the following
could be the value of *w*?

   A.  2
   B.  3
   C.  4
   D.  6
   E.  8

**10.** If $9^x = \dfrac{1}{3}$ , then $x =$

   F.  $-3$

   G.  $-2$

   H.  $-1$

   J.  $-\dfrac{1}{2}$

   K.  $-\dfrac{1}{3}$

## Here's How to Crack It

**Question 1:** Answer choice C does not equal 54, so we can eliminate it right away. Answers A, B, and E all equal 54, but each of these choices includes a factor that is not prime. The correct answer is **D**.

**Question 2:** The absolute value of –6 is 6, so after we multiply, the numerator equals –120. If you picked answer choice F, it was because you thought you were already done, but we haven't finished the problem yet. We still have to divide by the denominator, –3. A negative number divided by a negative number must be positive, so we can cancel out choices F and G. The correct answer is **H**.

**Question 3:** We could just divide each of these numbers into 1134, but there's a shortcut: Think rules of divisibility. Is 1134 divisible by 3? Yes. By 6? Yes. By 9? Yes. 12 breaks down in two factors: 3 and 4. We already know the number is divisible by 3. Is it divisible by 4? NO! If you don't remember these rules, go back and review divisibility. The correct answer is **D**.

**Question 4:** $(-2)^3$ equals –8. $(3)^{-2}$ equals $\dfrac{1}{9}$ . $\dfrac{1}{9} + \dfrac{8}{9}$ equals 1. –8 + 1 = –7. The correct answer is **F**.

**Question 5:** The cube root of 27 equals 3. 3 squared equals 9. The correct answer is **C**.

**Question 6:** $(xy)^3$ equals $x^3y^3$. Anything to the zero power equals 1, so *z* disappears from the numerator. The correct answer is **F**.

**Question 7:** To make this expression an integer, we need an even numerator. Why? Because it is going to be divided by 2. How can we ensure that the numerator of this fraction is even? The value $a$ must be odd. The correct answer is **C.** Another, perhaps simpler, way to approach this question is to plug in numbers and see what happens. Use the answer choices to help you decide what numbers to try. First, let's try 2, which is positive and even. If we put 2 in for $a$, we get $\frac{9}{2}$, which isn't an integer, so we can cross out E and B. Try 0 next, since that's an easy number to work with. $\frac{11}{2}$ isn't an integer, so 0 doesn't work, so D is out, too. We're down to A, negative and C, odd. Let's try 3 for $a$. That gives $\frac{8}{2}$, which is 4, which is an integer. So $a$ doesn't have to be negative, but does have to be odd, so C is the answer.

**Question 8:** Just count on your fingers. Is 0 even? Yes. The correct answer is **G.**

Note: If you chose J, it's because you read "between –4 and 4" as "between –4 and 4, inclusive" i.e., including –4 and 4 themselves. Sometimes a math test is actually a vocabulary test...

**Question 9:** For the four-digit number to be divisible by 6, it must also be divisible by the prime factors of 6: 2 and 3. We already know it is divisible by 2, because the last digit is even. If the sum of the four digits is divisible by 3, so is the entire number. Which of the answer choices makes the four-digit number divisible by 3? The correct answer is **C.**

**Question 10:** If you get confused by the fractional roots or negative roots, you might start by trying the simpler answer choices first. A negative power is just the reciprocal of a positive power. Putting answer choice F into the equation gives us $\left(\frac{1}{9}\right)^3$. Does that equal $\frac{1}{3}$? No way. We can use the same method to eliminate answers G and H. If you aren't sure how to put answer choices J and K into the equation, just guess. At this point, the odds are fifty-fifty. Then go back and review fractional powers. The correct answer is **J.** You could also have tried the answers in the question. Only one of them will work.

# 9
# Arithmetic

Did you know that the ACT tests ancient history? You don't believe us? O.K., when was the last time you took a test in school that asked you to add fractions or subtract decimals? We're talking fourth grade here. Because it's been so long, we think it's a good idea for you to read through this chapter carefully (even the part about adding fractions). Sometimes specific rules from a subject you learned a long time ago can vanish from your mind when you need them most. Also, the test writers at ACT sometimes like to take simple concepts and construct hard problems around them.

Here are the specific arithmetic (and related) topics tested on the ACT:

1. Order of operations

2. Fractions

3. Decimals

4. Ratios

5. Percentages

6. Averages

7. Charts and Graphs

8. Combination

In this chapter, we will first discuss the fundamentals of each topic and then show you how ACT constructs questions based on those fundamentals.

## CALCULATORS

Students are permitted (but not required) to use calculators on the ACT. You should definitely bring a calculator to the test. Remember—we'll be pointing out the calculator-friendly questions and telling you what you need to be able to do with your calculator on the ACT. Be sure to confirm that you can do each of the operations we mention. If it's been a while since you used your calculator in that way, put it through its paces again.

## ORDER OF OPERATIONS

In a problem that involves several different operations, the operations must be performed in a particular order. Here's an easy way to remember the order of operations:

Please Excuse My Dear Aunt Sally

First, you do operations enclosed in Parentheses; then you take care of Exponents; then you Multiply, Divide, Add, and Subtract. Most calculators follow the correct order of operations, but you have to be sure to enter the equations into your calculator correctly. Now's the time to test your calculator's ability to handle order of operations (and your ability to push tiny buttons properly).

Try this one:

$$((-5)+4)^2\left(\frac{8}{2}\right)+4-8=$$

How about this one?

$$(-8)+\left(\frac{8}{2}\right)(4-5)^2+4 =$$

If your calculator follows order of operations, then you should have gotten the same answer both times: 0.

**The Associative Law:** In adding a string of numbers, you can add them in any order you like. The same thing is true when you are multiplying a string of numbers.

> $5 + 6 + 7$ is the same as $7 + 6 + 5$
>
> $2 \times 3 \times 4$ is the same as $3 \times 4 \times 2$

**The Distributive Law:** Some combinations of addition and multiplication can be written in two different formats—which often proves extremely useful in finding ACT answers. The distributive law states that:

> $a(b + c) = ab + ac$
>
> and that
>
> $a(b - c) = ab - ac$

**What Comes First?**

Perform all operations within parentheses first. The distributive law is something of an exception; it gives you two ways to get the same result.

If a problem gives you information in "factored" format, which is $a(b + c)$, you should distribute it immediately. If the information is given in distributed form, which is $ab + ac$, you should factor it. An ACT problem might look like this:

**1.** For all $x \neq -2$, $\dfrac{2x+4}{x+2} = ?$

    **A.** $x + 2$
    **B.** $x$
    **C.** $2$
    **D.** $x + 4$
    **E.** $4$

## Here's How to Crack It

Let's use the distributive property on the numerator of this fraction, and rewrite it in factored form:

$$\frac{2(x+2)}{(x+2)}$$

$\dfrac{(x+2)}{(x+2)}$ equals just one. Therefore, we can cancel out both terms and the answer must be choice **C**.

# FRACTIONS

Fractions can be thought of in two ways. A fraction is just another way of expressing division. The expression $\frac{1}{2}$ means 1 divided by 2. $\frac{x}{y}$ is nothing more than $x$ divided by $y$. A fraction is made up of a numerator and a denominator. The numerator is on top, the denominator is on the bottom. Just think, the denominator starts with "$d$," just like *downstairs*.

$$\frac{1}{2} \quad \frac{\text{numerator}}{\text{denominator}}$$

The other way to think of a fraction is as a part over a whole.

$$\frac{1}{2} \quad \frac{\text{part}}{\text{whole}}$$

In the fraction $\frac{1}{2}$ we have one part out of a total of two parts.

In the fraction $\frac{3}{7}$ we have three parts out of a total of seven parts.

**Fraction Reduction**

In any fraction involving large numbers, try to reduce the fractions before you do anything else.

## REDUCING FRACTIONS

To reduce a fraction, see if the numerator and the denominator have a common factor. It may save time to find the largest factor they share, but this isn't crucial. Whatever factor they share can now be canceled. Let's take the fraction $\frac{6}{8}$. Is there a common factor? Yes, 2.

$$\frac{6}{8} = \frac{\cancel{2} \times 3}{\cancel{2} \times 4} = \frac{3}{4}$$

Get used to reducing all fractions (if they can be reduced) before you do any work with them. It saves a lot of time and prevents errors that crop up when you try to work with big numbers. If your calculator can reduce fractions (and many of them can), review (or learn) how to use that function now.

## COMPARING FRACTIONS

Sometimes a problem will involve deciding which of two fractions is bigger. If your calculator can convert fractions to decimals at the touch of a button, that's the way to compare them. If not, keep reading, and we'll explain how to do it by hand.

Which is bigger, $\frac{2}{5}$ or $\frac{4}{5}$? Think of these as parts of a whole. Which is bigger, two parts out of five, or four parts out of five? $\frac{4}{5}$ is clearly bigger. In this case it was easy to tell because they both had the same whole, or the same denominator.

What about this one? Which is bigger, $\frac{2}{3}$ or $\frac{3}{7}$? To decide, we need to find a common whole, or denominator. You change the denominator of a fraction by multiplying it by another number. In order to keep the entire fraction the same, however, you must multiply the numerator by the same number.

Let's change the denominator of $\frac{2}{3}$ into 21.

$$\frac{2 \times 7}{3 \times 7} = \frac{14}{21}$$

$\frac{14}{21}$ still has the same value as $\frac{2}{3}$ (it would reduce to $\frac{2}{3}$), because we multiplied the fraction by $\frac{7}{7}$, or one.

Let's change the denominator of $\frac{3}{7}$ into 21 as well.

$$\frac{3 \times 3}{7 \times 3} = \frac{9}{21}$$

$\frac{9}{21}$ still has the same value as $\frac{3}{7}$ (it would reduce to $\frac{3}{7}$), because we multiplied the fraction by $\frac{3}{3}$, or one.

Now we can compare the two fractions. Which is bigger, $\frac{14}{21}$ or $\frac{9}{21}$? Clearly $\frac{14}{21}$ (or $\frac{2}{3}$) is bigger than $\frac{9}{21}$ (or $\frac{3}{7}$). Why did we decide on 21 as our common denominator? The easiest way to get a common denominator is to multiply the denominators of the two fractions you wish to compare: $7 \times 3 = 21$.

Let's do it again. Which is biggest?

$$\frac{2}{3} \text{ or } \frac{4}{7} \text{ or } \frac{3}{5}$$

To compare these fractions directly you need a common denominator, but finding a common denominator that works for all three fractions would be complicated and time consuming. It makes more sense to compare these fractions two at a time. Let's start with $\frac{2}{3}$ and $\frac{4}{7}$. An easy common denominator is 21.

$$\frac{2}{3} \qquad\qquad\qquad \frac{4}{7}$$

$$\frac{2 \times 7}{3 \times 7} = \frac{14}{21} \qquad\qquad \frac{4}{7} \times \frac{3}{3} = \frac{12}{21}$$

Since $\dfrac{2}{3}$ is bigger, let's compare it with $\dfrac{3}{5}$. This time, the easiest common denominator is 15.

$$\dfrac{2}{3} \qquad\qquad \dfrac{3}{5}$$

$$\dfrac{2}{3} \times \dfrac{5}{5} = \dfrac{10}{15} \qquad\qquad \dfrac{3}{5} \times \dfrac{3}{3} = \dfrac{9}{15}$$

So $\dfrac{2}{3}$ is bigger than $\dfrac{3}{5}$, which means it's also the biggest of the three.

## THE BOWTIE

A more streamlined way to do this is to use the **Bowtie.** Let's compare the last two fractions again. We get the common denominator by multiplying the two denominators together:

$$\dfrac{2}{3} \to \dfrac{3}{5} = \dfrac{}{15}$$

We get the new numerators by multiplying as shown below:

$$\overset{\textcircled{10}}{\phantom{x}}\quad\overset{\textcircled{9}}{\phantom{x}}$$
$$\dfrac{2}{3} \bowtie \dfrac{3}{5} = \dfrac{}{15}$$

So $\dfrac{2}{3}$ is bigger.

**ECD**

Your teachers wanted you to calculate the Least Common Denominator (LCD) of a fraction. They even made you "show your work." The ACT doesn't care. This gives you the luxury of finding the Easiest Common Denominator by using the Bowtie.

## ADDING AND SUBTRACTING FRACTIONS

Now that we've reviewed finding a common denominator, adding and subtracting fractions is simple. Let's use the Bowtie to add $\dfrac{2}{5}$ and $\dfrac{1}{4}$.

$$\overset{\textcircled{8}}{\phantom{x}}\quad\overset{\textcircled{5}}{\phantom{x}}$$
$$\dfrac{2}{5} \bowtie \dfrac{1}{4} \to \dfrac{8+5}{20} = \dfrac{13}{20}$$

Let's use the Bowtie to subtract $\dfrac{2}{3}$ from $\dfrac{5}{6}$.

$$\overset{\textcircled{15}}{\phantom{x}}\quad\overset{\textcircled{12}}{\phantom{x}}$$
$$\dfrac{5}{6} \bowtie \dfrac{2}{3} \to \dfrac{15-12}{18} = \dfrac{3}{18} \text{ or } \dfrac{1}{6}$$

## MULTIPLYING FRACTIONS

**Half Empty or Half Full?**

On the ACT, always think about what's left over. If a pizza is three-quarters eaten, there's still one quarter left.

To multiply fractions, line them up and multiply straight across.

$$\dfrac{5}{6} \times \dfrac{4}{5} = \dfrac{20}{30} = \dfrac{2}{3}$$

Was there anything we could have canceled or reduced *before* we multiplied?

Yes. We could cancel the 5 on top and the 5 on the bottom. What's left is $\dfrac{4}{6}$, which reduces to $\dfrac{2}{3}$.

Sometimes rusty students think they can cancel or reduce in the same fashion *across an equal sign*. For example:

$$\frac{\cancel{5}x}{6} = \frac{4}{\cancel{5}} \quad \text{No!}$$

You *cannot* cancel the 5s in this case, or reduce the $\frac{4}{6}$. When there is an equal sign, you have to cross multiply, which yields $25x = 24$, so $x$ in this case would equal $\frac{24}{25}$.

## DIVIDING FRACTIONS

To divide one fraction by another, just invert the second fraction and multiply:

$$\frac{2}{3} \div \frac{3}{4} \text{ is the same thing as } \frac{2}{3} \times \frac{4}{3} = \frac{8}{9}$$

You may see this same operation written like this:

$$\frac{\frac{2}{3}}{\frac{3}{4}}$$

Again, just invert and multiply. Try the next example:

$$\frac{6}{\frac{2}{3}}$$

Think of 6 as $\frac{6}{1}$, so we do the same thing:

$$\frac{6}{1} \times \frac{3}{2} = \frac{18}{2} = 9$$

### Fractional Calculators

Many calculators can add, subtract, multiply, and divide fractions and return the answer as a fraction. If yours can, it will save you lots of time on the ACT.

## CONVERTING TO FRACTIONS

An integer can always be expressed as a fraction by making the integer the numerator and 1 the denominator. $8 = \frac{8}{1}$.

Sometimes the ACT gives you numbers that are mixtures of integers and fractions, for example $3\frac{1}{2}$. It is often easier to work with these numbers by converting them completely into fractions. Here's how you do it: Since the fraction is being expressed in halves, let's convert the integer into halves as well. $3 = \frac{6}{2}$. Now just add the $\frac{1}{2}$ to the $\frac{6}{2}$. $3\frac{1}{2} = \frac{7}{2}$.

## Now, How Does the ACT Test Fractions?

An ACT fraction problem combines several of the elements we've just discussed. Here's a typical problem:

1. After $\dfrac{4\frac{1}{3}}{2\frac{3}{5}}$ has been simplified to a single fraction in lowest terms, what is the denominator?

    A. 2
    B. 3
    C. 5
    D. 9
    E. 13

## Here's How to Crack It

First, let's convert the mixture of integers and fractions into fractions. $4\frac{1}{3} = \frac{13}{3}$, $2\frac{3}{5} = \frac{13}{5}$. Remember, to divide fractions, simply flip and multiply $\frac{13}{3} \times \frac{5}{13}$. The 13s cancel, leaving $\frac{5}{3}$. The answer is choice **B**.

More complicated fraction problems might test your ability to recognize that every fraction implies another fraction—what's left over. If a glass is $\frac{3}{5}$ full, what part of the glass is empty? $\frac{2}{5}$.

2. On Friday, Jane does one-third of her homework. On Saturday, she does one-sixth of the remainder. What fraction of her homework is still left to be done?

    F. $\dfrac{4}{9}$

    G. $\dfrac{1}{2}$

    H. $\dfrac{5}{9}$

    J. $\dfrac{5}{6}$

    K. $\dfrac{7}{12}$

## Here's How to Crack It

Jane did $\frac{1}{3}$ on Friday. How much is still left to be done? That's right: $\frac{2}{3}$. On Saturday she did $\frac{1}{6}$ *of the remainder*. In math, the word "of" always means multiply, so let's set it up on the next page.

| Friday | Saturday |
|---|---|
| $\dfrac{1}{3} \times 1$ | $\dfrac{1}{6} \times \dfrac{2}{3} = \dfrac{2}{18}$ |
| $\dfrac{1}{3}$ done | $\dfrac{2}{18}$ or $\dfrac{1}{9}$ done (on Saturday). |

If we find a common denominator so we can add up what she's done, we get

$$\frac{3}{9} + \frac{1}{9} = \frac{4}{9}$$

So altogether, she has done $\dfrac{4}{9}$ of the assignment. If you thought you were done at this point, you might have picked answer choice F, but the question doesn't ask how much was done, but rather how much remained *undone*. How much is left? $\dfrac{5}{9}$. The answer is choice **H**.

## POE Notes

In that last problem, answer choice F was a *partial* answer designed to catch people who thought they were done before they really were. Choice G, on the other hand, was designed to catch people who slightly misunderstood the question. If you missed the words "of the remainder" as you read the question, you probably added $\dfrac{1}{6}$ to $\dfrac{1}{3}$, and you got $\dfrac{1}{2}$.

# DECIMALS

Most simple decimal problems are easier to figure out on a calculator than on paper. However, unless you understand the theory behind them, it is easy to make a mistake.

A fraction can be written as a decimal and vice versa. Take the fraction $\dfrac{3}{5}$. Remember what we said before: A fraction is just another form of division.

$$\frac{3}{5} = 3 \div 5 = .6 \qquad\qquad 5\overline{)3.0}^{\,.6}$$

You can also express any decimal as a fraction.

$$.4 = \frac{4}{10} = \frac{2}{5} \qquad\qquad .03 = \frac{3}{100}$$

The test writers frequently ask questions using decimals but want answers as a fraction, or vice versa, so the ability to go back and forth between the two is essential to succeeding on the test. If your calculator can do this for you, be *sure* you know how to use that function.

## ADDING AND SUBTRACTING DECIMALS

To add or subtract decimals, just line up the decimal points, and proceed as if it were regular addition or subtraction. To add 9.25, 3.2, and 8.567:

```
   9.250
   3.200
 + 8.567
 ───────
  21.017
```

**Stay in Line**

When adding or subtracting decimals, keep all decimal points lined up.

It helped to add zeros to fill out the decimal places of the numbers with fewer digits. 3.2 is the same as 3.200.

## MULTIPLYING DECIMALS

To multiply decimals, simply ignore the decimal points, and multiply your numbers. When you've finished, count all the digits to the right of the decimal points in the original numbers you multiplied. Now place the decimal point in your answer so that there are the same number of digits to the right of it.

Here's an example:

$$
\begin{array}{r}
2.32 \\
\times\ .03 \\
\hline
.0696
\end{array}
$$

$3 \times 232 = 696$. There were a total of four digits to the right of the decimal point in the original numbers, so now we place the decimal so that there are four digits to the right in the answer.

## DIVIDING DECIMALS

**Place Value**

Compare decimals place-by-place, going from left to right.

The best way to divide one decimal by another is to convert the number you are dividing *by* (in mathematical terminology, the divisor) into a whole number. You do this simply by moving the decimal point as many places as necessary.

This works as long as you also remember to move the decimal point in the number that you are *dividing* (in mathematical terminology, the dividend) the same number of spaces.

Here's an example: To divide 12 by .6, set it up the way you would an ordinary division problem:

$$.6\overline{)12}$$

To convert .6 into a whole number, move the decimal point over one place to the right. Now, you must move the decimal place in 12 one place as well. Now the operation looks like this:

$$6\overline{)120} \quad 6\overline{)120}^{\,20}$$

# SCIENTIFIC NOTATION

The purpose of scientific notation is to express very large numbers or very small numbers without endless strings of zeroes.

$$3.24 \times 10^2$$

All you have to do to simplify this expression is move the decimal point over to the right by the same number as the power of ten. In this case, two places. If the power of ten is negative, you move the decimal point to the left instead.

$$
\begin{array}{l}
3.24 \times 10^3 = 3240 \\
3.24 \times 10^2 = 324 \\
3.24 \times 10^{-1} = .324 \\
3.24 \times 10^{-2} = .0324
\end{array}
$$

An ACT scientific notation problem might look like this:

1. $\left(9\times10^{-3}\right)-\left(2\times10^{-2}\right)=?$
   A. −0.007
   B. −0.07
   C. −0.011
   D. −0.11
   E.   0.11

## Here's How to Crack It

$$9\times10^{-3}=.009$$
$$2\times10^{-2}=.02$$

$$\begin{array}{r} .009 \\ -\ .02 \\ \hline -.011 \end{array}$$

The answer is **C**.

# RATIOS

There are relatively few ratio problems on the ACT. The important thing to remember is the difference between a ratio and a fraction. While a fraction is a $\dfrac{\text{part}}{\text{whole}}$, a ratio is a $\dfrac{\text{part}}{\text{part}}$.

Take the ratio of $\dfrac{4\text{ cats}}{3\text{ dogs}}$. What is the whole of this ratio? If you said the total number of animals, or 7, you were absolutely correct. So what fractional part of the animals is dogs? Let's change the ratio $\left(\dfrac{\text{part}}{\text{part}}\right)$ into a fraction $\left(\dfrac{\text{part}}{\text{whole}}\right)$. The part made up of dogs is 3. The whole is 7. Thus the fractional part of the animals that are dogs is $\dfrac{3}{7}$.

Other ratio problems don't need to be converted to fractions:

1. If the ratio of $2x$ to $5y$ is $\dfrac{1}{20}$, what is the ratio of $x$ to $y$?

   A. $\dfrac{1}{40}$

   B. $\dfrac{1}{20}$

   C. $\dfrac{1}{10}$

   D. $\dfrac{1}{8}$

   E. $\dfrac{1}{4}$

### Ratio vs. Fractions

Keep in mind that a ratio compares part of something to another *part*. A fraction compares part of something to the whole thing.

## Here's How to Crack It

$$\frac{2x}{5y} = \frac{1}{20}$$

To isolate $\frac{x}{y}$ on the left side of this equation, what do we have to do to it?

Let's multiply both sides by $\frac{5}{2}$.

$$\frac{5}{2} \times \frac{2x}{5y} = \frac{1}{20} \times \frac{5}{2}$$

$$\frac{x}{y} = \frac{5}{40}$$

$\frac{5}{40}$ reduces to $\frac{1}{8}$. The answer is choice **D.**

# PERCENTAGES

A percentage is just a fraction in which the denominator equals 100. Fifty percent means $\frac{50}{100}$ or $\frac{1}{2}$. Since fractions can be expressed in different ways, $\left( \frac{1}{2} = \frac{2}{4} = \frac{25}{50} = \frac{50}{100} \right)$, any fraction can be turned into a percentage. To do this, you set the fraction equal to $\frac{x}{100}$ and solve for $x$. If four out of five dentists recommend a particular brand of toothpaste, what percentage of the dentists recommend the toothpaste?

$$\frac{\text{part}}{\text{whole}} = \frac{4}{5} = \frac{x}{100}$$

We cross multiply, and find that $x = 80$.

## PERCENTAGE SHORTCUTS

In the last problem, we could have saved a little time if we had realized that $\frac{1}{5} = 20\%$. Therefore, $\frac{4}{5}$ would be $4 \times 20\%$ or 80%. Below are some fractions and decimals whose percent equivalents you should know.

$$\frac{1}{5} = .2 = 20\%$$

$$\frac{1}{4} = .25 = 25\%$$

$$\frac{1}{3} = .\overline{33} = 33\frac{1}{3}\%$$

$$\frac{1}{2} = .5 = 50\%$$

Another fast way to do percents is to move the decimal place. To find 10% of any number, move the decimal point of that number over one place to the left.

$$10\% \text{ of } 500 = 50$$

$$10\% \text{ of } 50 = 5$$

$$10\% \text{ of } 5 = .5$$

To find 1% of a number, move the decimal point of that number over two places to the left.

$$1\% \text{ of } 500 = 5$$

$$1\% \text{ of } 50 = .5$$

$$1\% \text{ of } 5 = .05$$

You can use a combination of these last two techniques to find even very complicated percentages, by breaking them down into easy-to-find chunks.

- 20% of 500: 10% of 500 = 50, so 20% is twice 50, or 100

- 30% of 70: 10% of 70 = 7, so 30% is three times 7, or 21

- 32% of 400: 10% of 400 = 40, so 30% is three times 40, or 120

  1% of 400 = 4, so 2% is two times 4, or 8

  Therefore 32% of 400 = 128

Here's what an ACT percentage problem might look like:

1. At a restaurant, diners enjoy an "early bird" discount of 10% off their bill. If a diner orders a meal regularly priced at $18, and leaves a tip of 15% of the discounted meal, how much does he pay in total?
   A. $13.50
   B. $16.20
   C. $18.63
   D. $18.90
   E. $20.70

## Here's How to Crack It

10% of 18 = $1.80. If we subtract this from the cost of the meal, we have the discounted price of $16.20. This is answer choice B, but we aren't done yet. The diner leaves a tip of 15% of the $16.20.

| | |
|---|---|
| 10% of 16.20 is | $1.62 |
| 5% is half again of that, or | 0.81 |
| | $2.43 |

The diner's total cost is $16.20 plus $2.43, which equals $18.63, or answer choice **C**.

## POE Notes

Even before you began this problem you could have eliminated one answer choice through POE. Did you spot it? Answer choice A was way too small. The diner is getting a discount of only 10% off the $18.00 and he must still pay the tip, which will add a bit more money. Could the answer be as low as $13.50? Nope. Cross off answer choice A.

Even if you didn't notice that answer choice A was too small, once you figured out that 10% of $18.00 was $16.20, you could have eliminated answer choices A and B, because there was still the tip to pay, so the total had to be bigger than $16.20.

# AVERAGES

To find the average of a set of $n$ numbers you simply add the numbers and divide by $n$. For example, the average of 9, 12, and 6 is

$$\frac{9+12+6}{3} = \frac{27}{3} \quad \text{or} \quad 9$$

Whenever you see the word average, you should think:

$$\frac{\text{sum of everything}}{\text{number of things}} = \text{average}$$

An ACT average problem might look like this:

3. Over 9 games, a baseball team had an average of 8 runs per game. If their average number of runs for the first 7 games was 6 runs per game, and the same number of runs was scored in each of the last 2 games, how many runs did they score during the last game?

A. 5
B. 15
C. 26
D. 30
E. 46

## Here's How to Crack It

Let's put the information from the first line of this problem into our trusty average equation:

$$\frac{\text{sum of everything}}{9} = 8$$

What is the sum of everything for these 9 games? $9 \times 8$, or 72.

Now let's put the information from the second line into the average equation:

$$\frac{\text{sum of everything}}{7} = 6$$

What is the sum of everything for these 7 games? $7 \times 6$, or 42.

If all 9 games added up to 72, and 7 of these games added up to 42, then the remaining 2 games added up to 72 minus 42, or 30. In case you are feeling smug about having gotten this far, the ACT writers made 30 answer choice D.

But of course, if you read the last line, you know that they only want the runs they scored in the last game. Since the same number of runs was scored in each of the last two games, the answer is $\frac{30}{2}$ or 15, answer choice **B**.

# THE WEIGHTED AVERAGE

ACT writers have a particular fondness for "weighted average" problems. First, let's look at a regular unweighted average question:

> If Sally received a grade of 90 on a test last week and a grade of 100 on a test this week, what is her average for the two tests?

Piece of cake, right? The answer is 95. You added the scores and divided by 2. Now, let's turn the same question into a weighted average question:

> If Sally's average for the entire year last year was 90, and her average for the entire year this year was 100, is her average for the two years combined equal to 95?

The answer is, "not necessarily." If Sally took the same number of courses in both years then yes, her average is 95. But what if last year she took 6 courses while this year she took only 2 courses? Can you compare the two years equally? ACT likes to test your answer to this question. Here's an example:

> **1.** The starting team of a baseball club has 9 members who have an average of 12 home runs apiece for the season. The second-string team for the baseball club has 7 members who have an average of 8 home runs apiece for the season. What is the average number of home runs for the starting team and the second-string team combined?
> 
> **A.** 7.5
> **B.** 8
> **C.** 10
> **D.** 10.25
> **E.** 14.2

## Here's How to Crack It

The ACT test writers want to see whether you spot that this is a weighted average problem. If you thought the first string team was exactly equivalent to the second string, then you merely had to take the average of the two averages, 12 and 8, to get 10. In weighted average problems, the ACT test writers always include the average of the two averages among the answer choices—and it is always wrong. 10 is answer choice C. Cross off C.

The two teams are not equivalent because there are different numbers of players on each team. To get the true average, we'll have to find the total number of

**Playing the Averages**

**Arithmetic mean:** the only average that requires arithmetic.
**Median:** the one in the middle—like the median strip on the highway.
**Mode:** you're looking for the element that appears most. Get it? MOde, MOst.

home runs and divide by the total number of players. How do we do this? By going to the trusty average formula as usual. The first line of the problem says that the 9 members on the first team have an average of 12 runs apiece.

$$\frac{\text{sum of everything}}{9} = 12$$

### The Missing Number

The ACT loves to leave out "the sum of everything" on average problems. You aren't done until you've found it.

So the sum of everything is $9 \times 12$, or 108.

The second sentence says that the 7 members of the second team have an average of 8 runs each.

$$\frac{\text{sum of everything}}{7} = 8$$

So the sum of everything is $7 \times 8$, or 56.

Now, we can find the true average. Add all the runs scored by the first team to all the runs scored by the second team: $108 + 56 = 164$. This is the true sum of everything. We divide it by the total number of players ($9 + 7 = 16$).

The answer is 10.25, or answer choice **D.**

## POE Notes

While we could eliminate answer choice C in that last problem because it represented the "unweighted" average, there were several other answers we might have eliminated through POE. If the average of the first team was 12 and the average of the second team was 8, it stood to reason that the correct answer would be somewhere between those two numbers. Could the answer really have been higher than 12? Answer choice E bites the dust. Could the answer really have been equal to or lower than 8? Answer choices A and B also fall by the wayside.

## CHARTS AND GRAPHS

Since calculators were added to the arsenal you're allowed to bring with you when you take the ACT, more and more of the test has been composed of questions on which calculators are of little or no use. Questions based on charts and graphs are great examples of this. On this type of question, your math skills aren't really being tested at all; what ACT is interested in is your ability to read a simple graph (not unlike on the Science Reasoning Test, which we'll get to later). All of the questions we have seen in this format have been very direct. If you can read a simple graph, you can always get them right. What's most important on questions like these is paying attention to the labels on the information. Let's take a look at a graph on the next page.

Average monthly rainfall for Belleville, IL.

3. Between which two months was the change in total rainfall the greatest?

   A. May and June
   B. June and July
   C. July and August
   D. August and September
   E. September and October

## Here's How to Crack It

The ACT test writers want to see if you can decipher the information presented in the graph. Before you read the question, then, you need to take a look at the graph. What is measured here? It says on the bottom: the monthly rainfall in Belleville, IL. You should look at the values along the left side and bottom of the graph, too. When you do, you'll see that the rain is measured in inches (left hand side), and the measurements were made each month (bottom).

Now for the question. In order to determine which two months had the greatest change, we need to compare the change between each pair of months, discarding the smaller ones until we only have one left. The difference from May to June is about 3, and that's bigger than June to July and September to October, so B and E are out. July to August is bigger still, though, so A is out, leaving only C and D. It should be pretty apparent that the August to September change is bigger than the July to August change, though, so the right answer must be **D**.

Though most questions involving graphs on the Math Test are this simple, you may see slightly more complicated variations. Here's another question based on the same bar graph:

Average monthly rainfall for Belleville, IL.

24. Based on the information presented in the graph above, what is the approximate average monthly rainfall in Belleville, IL for the period given?

    **F.**  2
    **G.**  3
    **H.**  4
    **J.**  5
    **K.**  8

## Here's How to Crack It

As with the last question, the first thing you want to do is examine the graph and figure out what information is being given to you and how it is being presented. Since you already did that for this graph, we'll skip that step on this one.

This question combines graph reading with average calculation, so the next thing you'll have to do is estimate the rainfall for each month. Since the question uses the word "approximate," you don't have to worry too much about making super-exact measurements of the heights of the bar graphs—eyeballing it and rounding to the closest value given on the left hand side will be good enough to get you the right answer. Do that now before you read the next sentence . . . To us, it looks like about 2 inches fell in May and September, and around 3 fell in October. July saw about 4, June roughly 5, and August about 8. Your estimates should be the same as ours. If they're not, go back now and figure out why not.

You probably need to be a little more careful in your estimating—use another piece of paper as a guide if necessary (you can use your answer sheet in this manner when taking the real ACT).

Now it's just a matter of calculating the average. Find the total first:

$$2 + 2 + 3 + 4 + 5 + 8 = 24$$

There are 6 months, so divide the total by 6 to find the average:

$$\frac{24}{6} = 4$$

So, the answer is 4, or, answer choice **H**.

# COMBINATIONS

Combination problems ask you how many different ways a number of things could be chosen or combined. The rule for combination problems on the ACT is:

The number of combinations is the **product** of the number of things you have to choose from.

Here's an example:

4.  At the school cafeteria, students can choose from 3 different salads, 5 different main dishes, and 2 different deserts. If Isabel chooses one salad, one main dish, and one desert for lunch, how many different lunches could she choose?

    **F.**  10
    **G.**  15
    **H.**  25
    **J.**  30
    **K.**  50

## Here's How to Crack It

Isabel is going to choose her lunch by choosing one of each of the items. The numbers of items she has to choose from are 3, 5, and 2. The number of possible combinations she could choose from is always the product of the number of things she can choose from, so there are $3 \times 5 \times 2 = 30$ possible lunch combinations. Therefore, the answer is **J**.

# SUMMARY

1. The six main topics of arithmetic are

   - order of operations

   - fractions

   - decimals

   - percentages

   - ratios

   - averages

2. Your calculator can be an extremely powerful tool on the ACT. Having a command of 9 or 10 simple operations on the calculator will raise your score and lower your blood pressure significantly.

3. Arithmetic operations must be performed in a particular order. Here's an easy way to remember the order of operations: **P**lease **E**xcuse **M**y **D**ear **A**unt **S**ally. First, you do operations enclosed in **p**arentheses; then you take care of **e**xponents; then you **m**ultiply, **d**ivide, **a**dd, and **s**ubtract.

4. When you add or multiply a group of numbers, you can put them in any order that suits you. This is called the associative law.

5. The distributive law states that $a(b + c) = ab + ac$ and that $a(b - c) = ab - ac$. On the ACT, if you see a problem in one form, you will make the problem much easier by immediately putting it in the other form.

6. A fraction can be thought of as a $\dfrac{\text{part}}{\text{whole}}$.

7. You must know how to reduce, multiply, divide, compare, add, and subtract fractions. The Bowtie is a great method for doing all of the last three items mentioned, but your calculator is even better—if you know how to use it.

8. Every fraction implies another fraction—what is left over. If a glass is $\dfrac{3}{5}$ empty, it is $\dfrac{2}{5}$ full.

9. A decimal is just another way to express a fraction.

10. You must know how to add, subtract, multiply, and divide decimals, as well as be familiar with scientific notation.

11. A ratio is different in one respect from a fraction: A ratio is a $\dfrac{\text{part}}{\text{part}}$. If the ratio of cats to dogs is $\dfrac{3}{4}$, the whole is 7.

12. A percentage is just a fraction in which the denominator is equal to 100. Most percentage problems can be set up to look like this: $\dfrac{\text{part}}{\text{whole}} = \dfrac{x}{100}$

13. In average questions, you should immediately think:

$$\frac{\text{sum of everything}}{\text{number of things}} = \text{average}$$

14. The ACT has a particular fondness for weighted averages. Be on the lookout for them.

15. The number of possible combinations is the product of the number of things you have to chose from.

# ARITHMETIC DRILL

**1.** The ratio of boys to girls at the Milwood school is 4 to 5. If there are a total of 27 children at the school, how many boys attend the Milwood school?

A. 4
B. 9
C. 12
D. 14
E. 17

**2.** Linda computed the average of her biology test scores by adding the totals of the 5 scores together and dividing by the number of tests. She discovered her average score was an 88. Unfortunately, she completely forgot one entire test on which she scored an 82. What is the true average of Linda's biology tests?

F. 82
G. 85
H. 86
J. 87
K. 88

**3.** In the process of milling grain, 3% of the original is lost due to spillage, and another 5% of the original is lost because of mildew. If the mill starts out with 490 tons of grain, how much (in tons) remains to be sold after milling?

A. 425
B. 426
C. 420.5
D. 440
E. 450.8

4. $5\frac{1}{3} - 6\frac{1}{4} = ?$

F. $\dfrac{-11}{12}$

G. $\dfrac{-1}{2}$

H. $\dfrac{-2}{7}$

J. $\dfrac{1}{2}$

K. $\dfrac{9}{12}$

**5.** $1,245 \div .05 = ?$

    **A.**    200
    **B.**  2,490
    **C.**  2,500
    **D.** 24,900
    **E.** 25,000

## Here's How to Crack It

**Question 1:** A ratio is a $\dfrac{\text{part}}{\text{part}}$. Since the only actual number of students that we have is a whole, we will need to convert the ratio into a fraction. If the ratio is $\dfrac{4}{5}$, then the whole is 9. The equation we need is $\dfrac{4}{9} = \dfrac{x}{27}$. $x = 12$ and the answer is **C**.

**Question 2:** First, let's do some quick elimination. The average of the first 5 tests is 88. Since the sixth test is less than 88, the final average must also be less than 88. Scratch answer choice K. Now, let's get to work. As expected, the key number in this average question is the sum of all the tests. If on the first 5 tests she had an average of 88, the sum of all five tests is $5 \times 88$, or 440. She scored 82 on the sixth test. To get the true average, we add 82 to 440, which equals 522. Dividing 522 by 6—the total number of tests—we get 87. The correct answer is **J**.

**Question 3:** The mill lost a total of 8%. To find the correct answer, we just have to take away 8% of 490. That isn't much. In fact, it's just a bit less than 10%. Can we eliminate any answer choices? 10% of 490 is 49. 490 minus 49 is 441. The correct answer must be a little more than 441. There is only one answer greater than 441. The correct answer is **E**.

**Question 4:** First, let's convert these numbers into improper fractions. $5\dfrac{1}{3}$ equals $\dfrac{16}{3}$. $6\dfrac{1}{4}$ equals $\dfrac{25}{4}$. Clearly, when we subtract the second number from the first, the result will be negative. Cross off answer choices J and K since they are both positive. To find the exact answer, we need a common denominator. How about 12? The first number becomes $\dfrac{64}{12}$. The second number becomes $\dfrac{75}{12}$. The correct answer is **F**. You could have used the Bowtie to get this answer.

**Question 5:** If you picked answer choice B, you forgot to take away two decimals from *both* numbers before you divided. The correct answer is **D**.

# 10
## Algebra

Algebra is all about solving for an unknown quantity. The unknown is usually represented by a variable such as $x$ or $y$. There are two general kinds of algebra questions on the ACT. The first kind asks you to solve for a particular $x$. The second kind asks you to solve for a more cosmic $x$ (don't worry, we'll explain). Let's begin with the particular.

## WHEN $x$ HAS A PARTICULAR VALUE: THE BASIC EQUATION

Here is a simple example of a basic equation:

$$3x + 7 = 28$$

There is only one number in the world that will satisfy this equation. To find it, we need to isolate $x$ on one side of the equation and get all of the numbers on the other side. To get rid of the 7 that is being added on the left side, we must do the opposite of addition and **subtract** 7 from the left side. However, in order to avoid changing the entire equation, we also have to subtract 7 from the right side. Whatever is done to one side must also be done to the other.

$$\begin{array}{r} 3x + 7 = 28 \\ -7 \quad -7 \\ \hline 3x = 21 \end{array}$$

In order to get rid of the 3 that is being multiplied on the left side, we must do the opposite of multiplication and **divide** the left side by 3. If we are dividing the left side by 3, we must also divide the right side by 3.

$$\frac{3x}{3} = \frac{21}{3} = 7$$

$$x = 7$$

But in this last problem, we left out one very important thing: ACT questions always have multiple–choice answers. Let's look at this question the way it would have appeared on the actual test:

1. If $3x + 7 = 28$, what is $x$?
   A. 4
   B. 5
   C. 6
   D. 7
   E. 8

You might say, "Well, what's the difference? It's the same problem." But in fact, it's not the same problem at all.

## Most Particular *x* Problems Can Also Be Solved
## *Backward*

Algebra is a wonderful discipline, and we *do* want you to be able to solve problems like the one above algebraically, particularly when they are easy. However, there is another way to do most particular *x* problems, a way that can, in some cases, save you huge amounts of time and trouble. It's called "Working Backward."

If we asked you to *guess* the value of *x* in this question, it might take you a long, long time. After all, there's only going to be one number in the whole world that satisfies this equation, and there is a limitless supply of numbers to choose from. Or is there?

In fact, on the ACT, there are always just five: the five possible answer choices—and one of them has to be the correct answer. Let's try doing the problem backward. To do this, you take the answer choices one at a time, and put them into the equation to see which one makes the equation work. Which choice should we begin with?

The one in the middle. Numeric answers are always presented in order on this test, from least to greatest. There are three steps to **Working Backward**:

1. Start with the middle answer—choice C or H.

2. If it's too big, go to the next smallest choice.

3. If it's too small, go to the next larger choice.

Here's the problem again:

1. If $3x + 7 = 28$, what is *x*?
   A. 4
   B. 5
   C. 6
   D. 7
   E. 8

## Here's How to Crack It

Let's start with answer choice C: $3(6) + 7$ equals only 25. Could this be the right answer? No, it's *supposed* to equal 28. Do we need a smaller or a larger *x*? Since we need a larger number, we can immediately knock out answer choices A and B. Let's try answer choice **D**. 3 times $(7) + 7 = 28$. Bingo! We have our answer.

Note that if answer choice D had still been too small, the only possible answer would have been choice E, and you would not have had to check it. Remember, if you've eliminated 4 wrong answers, what's left *must* be right. One of the great things about Working Backward is that you will usually have to do only two actual calculations. You start with C. If C is correct, you're done. If C is too big, then you're down to A and B. Now you try B. If B is correct, you're done. If it isn't, you're still done. The answer must be the only remaining choice: A.

Now, we know that many of you are thinking, "This technique is a waste of time. It would have been way easier to just solve for *x*." You know what? You're right. On this example, solving for *x* would have been easier, but if you don't learn how to do the Working Backward technique on easy questions, you won't be able to do it effectively on more complex questions (and, believe us, the questions get *much* more complex). So do yourself a favor and use Working Backward on these easy questions so that you have a good feel for it when it's time to do the tough ones.

## LET'S DO IT AGAIN

Here's another problem:

> **2.** If $600 was deposited in a bank account for one year and earned interest of $42, what was the interest rate?
>
> **F.** 6.26%
> **G.** 7.00%
> **H.** 8.00%
> **J.** 9.00%
> **K.** 9.50%

### Here's How to Crack It

Of course, we *could* write an equation. On the other hand, one of these answer choices is correct, and all we have to do is find out which one it is. Why not work backward?

We'll start, as always, in the middle, this time with H. If the interest rate is 8%, then 8% of $600 should equal $42. Remember the quick way to do percents we taught you in arithmetic? What's *one* percent of 600? That's right, 6. So what is eight percent? 8 times 6, which equals $48. Is this the correct answer? It's a little too big. We wanted $42. Great, we can cross out H, and while we're at it, we might as well cross off answers J and K—they're even bigger. Let's try G. What is 7% of 600? One percent is 6, so seven percent would be 7 times 6, or $42. Yes! We're done. The answer is **G.**

## HOW DO YOU KNOW WHEN TO WORK BACKWARD?

You can *always* work backward when you see numbers in the answer choices, and when the question asked in the last line of the problem is relatively straightforward. For example, if there are numbers in the answer choices, and the question asks, "What is $x$?" you can work backward.

However, if the question asks instead, "What is the difference between $x$ and $y$?" then you probably don't want to work backward. In this case, the answers won't give us a value to try for either $x$ or $y$.

## THE REVERSE QUESTION

Sometimes, the ACT test writers will make your job even easier by giving you the value for the variable within the question itself:

> **1.** What is the value of $3x^2 + 5x - 7$ when $x = -1$?
>
> **A.** −15
> **B.** −9
> **C.** −1
> **D.** 5
> **E.** 15

**Which Way?**

Sometimes, it's hard to tell which way to work backward after eliminating C. Should you go higher or lower? Don't fret, just pick a direction and try. Find a choice with an easy-to-manipulate number. It may turn out to be wrong, but it won't take long to find out. It may also tell whether to go higher or lower.

## Here's How to Crack It

There is still only one number in the world that will satisfy this question, and—in this case—you know what $x$ is supposed to be. This time the ACT writer is asking you to find the value of the entire polynomial. (A polynomial is a type of equation.) These problems are about as easy as this test gets.

Note that it would be pointless to work backward on this problem, since the answer choices don't give you possible values for $x$, but rather for the entire polynomial. Simply plug –1 into the polynomial and solve:

$$3(-1)^2 + 5(-1) - 7 =$$
$$3 \quad -5 \quad -7 = -9$$

## NOW THERE'S A CHOICE

When you are asked to find a particular value for $x$, you have a choice: You can solve for $x$ or you can work backward. There are times when one technique is more suitable than the other, but as we cover different algebra topics in this chapter—factoring, quadratics, inequalities—we will keep returning to the concept of Working Backward. You will find it extremely useful, particularly on the more difficult questions that you might not want to take the time to solve the old-fashioned way. That's why we now want you to practice Working Backward on the easier questions.

## WHEN x HAS NO PARTICULAR VALUE: THE COSMIC EQUATION

Now let's look at the following problem:

1. What is 5 more than the product of 4 and a certain number $x$?
   A. $4x - 5$
   B. $4x$
   C. $-x$
   D. $5x - 4$
   E. $4x + 5$

In this problem, there is *no* one value for $x$. $x$ could be 5 or 105 or –317. In fact, the ACT writers are asking you to create an expression that will answer this question no matter what the "certain number" is.

In other words, this is kind of a cosmic problem. The correct answer choice will be correct *for any value of $x$*. There are two methods for approaching cosmic problems.

## ONE METHOD IS TRANSLATION

The people at ACT would like you to write a mathematical translation of the words they've written in English. This is not that hard, as it turns out. Unlike an English-French Dictionary or a Chinese-English Dictionary, the ACT English-Math dictionary is very short. In fact, here it is, in its entirety:

| ACT English ⟶ | ACT Math |
|---|---|
| is<br>(any form of the verb to be)<br>is the same as | = |
| of<br>product<br>times | × (multiplication) |
| what<br>a certain number | $x, y, z$ (your favorite variable)<br>$x, y, z$ |
| percent | over 100 |
| 30 percent | $\dfrac{30}{100}$ |
| more than | + (addition) |
| less than | − (subtraction) |

Let's translate the problem word for word:

Does this look like any of the answer choices? Yes, answer choice **E**.

While translation is a fine way to solve this problem, we want you to try thinking about cosmic problems in a slightly different way. If this problem is truly cosmic—if the correct answer is correct for *every* value of "a certain number"—then it should be correct for *any* value you can think of, right?

## THE OTHER METHOD IS PLUGGING IN

Why don't we pick our own value? Let's make $x = 7$. (Why? Why not? We could have just as easily chosen 5 or 12 or whatever you like. Try it and see.) The advantage of using a specific number is that our minds do not think naturally in terms of variables. We don't go into a store and ask for an $x$-pack of soda. We have a specific number in mind. There are three steps involved in **Plugging In:**

1. Pick numbers for the variables in the problem (and write them down).

2. Using your numbers, find an answer to the problem.

3. Plug your numbers into the answer choices to see which choice equals the answer you found in step 2.

Here's the problem again:

1. What is 5 more than the product of 4 and a certain number $x$?
   A. $4x - 5$
   B. $4x$
   C. $-x$
   D. $5x - 4$
   E. $4x + 5$

## A Few More English/Math Terms

| Words | Math |
| --- | --- |
| more than | + (addition) |
| the sum of | + (addition) |
| increased by | + (addition) |
| is added to | + (addition) |

## Here's How to Crack It

Let's make $x = 7$. In the space over the $x$ in the problem above, write down "7." Now, let's figure it out. Reread the question with "7" for the $x$. The product of 4 and 7 is 28. 5 more than 28 is 33. So, if $x = 7$, then the answer to the question is 33. We're done. All we have to do now is check to see which of the answer choices equals 33.

- Let's start with A. Since $x = 7$, $4(7) - 5 = 23$. Not the answer.
- Let's look at E. Since $x = 7$, $4(7) + 5 = 33$. The answer is **E.**

You might be thinking, "Wait a minute. It was easier to solve this problem algebraically. Why should I plug in?" There are a couple of reasons:

1. This was an easy problem. Plugging In makes even difficult problems easy, so you should learn how to do it by practicing on the easy ones, just as we advised with the Working Backward technique for particular $x$ problems.

2. The test writers at ACT try to anticipate how you might mess up this problem using algebra. If you make one of these common mistakes, your answer will be among the answer choices, and you will pick it and get it wrong.

## How Do You Spot a Cosmic Problem?

Any problem with variables in the answer choices is a cosmic problem. You may not choose to plug in on every one of these, but you *could* plug in on *all* of them. However, there are also some cosmic problems that do *not* have variables in the answer choices. For example:

1. At a baseball game, *h* hot dogs are divided equally among 9 people, but there are 2 hot dogs left over. If there were (*h* + 5) hot dogs for the 9 people, how many hot dogs would be left over?

   A. 3
   B. 4
   C. 5
   D. 7
   E. 9

### Here's How to Crack It

At first glance, you might think this was a "Working Backward" question. However, the question is not asking how many hot dogs there were, but how many were *left over*. This would be difficult to solve by Working Backward.

The real clue to solving this problem is that it never tells you how many hot dogs there were in the first place. The number is represented by a variable. In other words, this is a cosmic problem too. Let's plug in. Why don't we make *h* = 12?

You say we can't? Oh, good point. The problem tells us that after we share the number *h* among 9 people there are 2 hot dogs left over. 12 would give us a remainder of 3, one too many. What would be a good number for *h*? 11 would be fine. What other number could we use? 20 would work, because 20 divided by 9 also leaves a remainder of 2.

Let's stick with 11. Write the 11 in near the *h* in the problem above, so you don't forget which number you chose. Now, the problem wants to know how many hot dogs would have been left over if the original number had been (*h* + 5). If *h* = 11, then (*h* + 5) equals 16. If there are 9 people who share these 16 hot dogs, how many are left over? 7. The answer is choice **D**.

Would the problem have worked if we had chosen another number? Sure, as long as we chose a number that when divided by 9 gives a remainder of 2. Let's try it with *h* = 20. They want to know how many hot dogs would be left over if there had been (*h* + 5) hot dogs or 25. 9 goes evenly into 25 twice, with a remainder of…you guessed it—7.

## Some Numbers Are Better Than Others

In that last problem, only certain numbers could be plugged in for *h*—numbers that agreed with the conditions set forth in the problem.

In most cosmic problems, you can pick any number you like. However, there are some numbers that work better than others. In general, you might want to stick to small numbers just because they're easier to work with. If a problem is about days and weeks, 7 might be a particularly good number. If the problem is about percents, 100 is probably a good number.

Some numbers to avoid are 0, 1, and numbers that are already being used in the problem. Why? If you plug in one of these numbers, you may find that more than one answer choice appears to be correct.

## So Now There's Another Choice

When $x$ has *no* particular value, you also have a choice: You can translate or you can plug in. There are times when one technique is more suitable than the other, but as we cover the different algebra topics in this chapter we will keep returning to the concept of Plugging In.

## Factoring

Many ACT problems involve factoring of one kind or another. Here is the most basic kind of factoring problem:

$$x^2 + 7x + 12 = ?$$

If your calculator can solve quadratics, now's the time to make sure you know how to put it through its paces.

To factor this expression by hand, put it into the following format, and start by looking for the factors of the first and last terms.

$$x^2 + 7x + 12 =$$
$$(\quad)(\quad) =$$
$$(x\quad)(x\quad) =$$
$$(x\ 3)(x\ 4) =$$
$$(x+3)(x+4) =$$

The ACT test writers might use that last expression to make a problem like this:

1. If $\dfrac{x^2 + 7x + 12}{(x + 4)} = 5$, then = ?

    A. 1
    B. 2
    C. 3
    D. 5
    E. 6

This is a specific $x$ question. If we factor the top expression as we did a moment ago, we get:

$$\frac{(x+3)(x+4)}{(x+4)} = 5$$

Now we can cancel the $(x + 4)$s, with the result that $x + 3 = 5$. To get rid of the 3, we subtract it from both sides. Now $x = 2$, and the answer is **B**.

### The ACT's Favorite Factors

Train yourself to recognize these quadratic expressions instantly in both factored and unfactored form. Here they are:

$x^2 - y^2 = (x + y)(x - y)$
$x^2 + 2xy + y^2 = (x + y)^2$
$x^2 - 2xy + y^2 = (x - y)^2$

Learn them, love them. Better yet, if your calculator can factor quadratics, use these to make sure that you know how to use that function.

## POE Notes

1. If you were having trouble factoring $x^2 + 7x + 12$, it might have helped to wonder why—of all the numbers in the world—ACT picked $(x + 4)$ as the denominator of its problem. It was almost bound to be one of the factors of the polynomial in the numerator.

2. Note that like all specific $x$ problems, this could also have been solved by Working Backward.

   1. If $\dfrac{x^2 + 7x + 12}{(x + 4)} = 5$, then $x = ?$

      A. 1
      B. 2
      C. 3
      D. 5
      E. 6

The question asks, "what is $x$?" Let's start with answer choice C—3.

$$\frac{(3)^2 + 7(3) + 12}{(3 + 4)}$$
$$= \frac{9 + 21 + 12}{7}$$
$$= \frac{42}{7}$$
$$= 6$$

Since the answer was supposed to be 5, we know that we need a smaller $x$. Eliminate answer choices C, D, and E. Let's try 2:

$$\frac{(2)^2 + 7(2) + 12}{(2 + 4)}$$
$$= \frac{4 + 14 + 12}{6}$$
$$= 5$$

Again, the answer is choice **B**.

The same kind of equation could have been used in a **cosmic problem**:

1. For all $x \neq -3$, which of the following is equivalent to the expression $\dfrac{x^2 - x - 12}{x + 3}$?

   F. $x - 4$
   G. $x - 2$
   H. $x + 2$
   J. $x + 4$
   K. $x + 6$

Again, we could solve this by factoring:

$$x^2 - x - 12 =$$

$$(\quad)(\quad)$$
$$(x\quad)(x\quad)$$
$$(x\quad4)(x\quad3)$$
$$(x-4)(x+3)$$

Therefore we can write the problem as $\dfrac{(x-4)(x+3)}{x+3}$.

The $(x+3)$s cancel and we get $(x-4)$, or answer choice **F.**

## POE Notes

1. As in the preceding problem, if you were having trouble factoring $x^2 - x - 12$, it might have helped to wonder why—of all the numbers in the world—ACT picked $(x+3)$ as the denominator of its problem. It was almost bound to be one of the factors of the polynomial in the numerator.

2. Because this was a cosmic problem (variables in the answer choices), we also could have done this problem by Plugging In.

Here's how. Let's choose a value for $x$. How about 3?

$$\frac{(3)^2 - (3) - 12}{(3+3)}$$
$$= \frac{9 - 3 - 12}{6}$$
$$= \frac{-6}{6}$$
$$= -1$$

Now all we had to do was plug 3 (our value for $x$) into the answer choices to see which one gets us the answer –1. Let's try choice **F,** $x - 4$. Bingo!

$$3 - 4 = -1$$

## FACTORING: ADVANCED PRINCIPLES

More advanced factoring problems set a factorable expression equal to zero. This is called a **quadratic equation.**

$$x^2 + 7x + 6 = 0$$
$$(\quad)(\quad) = 0$$
$$(x\quad)(x\quad) = 0$$
$$(x\quad6)(x\quad1) = 0$$
$$(x+6)(x+1) = 0$$

Quadratic equations often have *two* values that solve the equation. In this example, $x$ could be either –6 or –1. These two solutions are sometimes called the **roots** or zeroes of the equation. Let's try an ACT-type quadratic equation:

**1.** What is the positive value of $x$ in the equation
$2x^2 - 4x - 6 = 0$?

A. –1
B. 2
C. 3
D. 4
E. 6

## Here's How to Crack It

Before we can factor the expression the way we did in the previous problems, we need to reduce it. Look to see if all of the terms have any factor in common. Yes, each of the terms can be divided by 2.

$$\frac{2x^2}{2} - \frac{4x}{2} - \frac{6}{2} = \frac{0}{2}$$

Let's rewrite the equation:

$$2\left(x^2 - 2x - 3\right) = 0$$

Now we can factor. The expression becomes:

$$2(x + 1)(x - 3) = 0$$

$x$ could equal –1, or 3. Unfortunately, both our values are among the answer choices. Which one is correct? If we reread the question, we realize that we were asked to find the *positive* value of $x$. Therefore, the answer is 3, answer choice **C**.

## POE Notes

1. Because the problem asked us for a *positive* value, we should have crossed out answer choice A even before we factored the expression. If we had done this, we would not have been tempted by it when we finished factoring and discovered it was one of the solutions to the problem.

2. This was a particular $x$ problem. That's right, you could have worked backward. Start with answer choice C, and put it back into the equation. Does $2(3)^2 - 4(3) - 6 = 0$ ? It sure does. The answer must be **C**.

**A note of warning:** When you work backward with a quadratic problem, remember that there may be two solutions. The problem will usually find a way to ask you for only one of them, but sometimes the test writers will ask you for the *sum* or the *product* of the two solutions. Remember what we said before: If a question asks, "what is $x$?" you can work backward; if a question asks, "what is $x + y$?" then you probably can't.

## The ACT's Three Favorite Quadratics

The test writers are really fond of three quadratic equations in particular. The first is called the difference of perfect squares (although the name isn't important):

$$x^2 - y^2 = (x + y)(x - y)$$

For some reason, they use this one all the time, and you should just memorize it. The idea is that whenever you see this expression in the form on the left, you should immediately put it into the form on the right. If you see it in the form on the right, you should immediately put it into the form on the left. That's all there is to it. Here's an example:

1. If for all $x \neq -3, \dfrac{x^2 - 9}{x + 3} = 12,$ then $x = ?$

    A. 10
    B. 15
    C. 17
    D. 19
    E. 20

### Here's How to Crack It

Do you recognize the form of the numerator? Great, so let's factor it:

$$\frac{(x + 3)(x - 3)}{(x + 3)} = 12$$

Now we can cancel the $(x + 3)$ terms and are left with $(x - 3)$. The answer is 15, or answer choice **B**.

### POE Notes

Could you have worked backward to solve this problem? Yes, although it wouldn't have been much fun squaring those large numbers. In this case it was definitely faster to solve by factoring—if you recognized the difference of perfect squares.

The two other quadratic equations ACT test writers are fond of are these:

$$x^2 + 2xy + y^2 = (x + y)^2$$
$$x^2 - 2xy + y^2 = (x - y)^2$$

As with the difference of perfect squares, the important thing is to recognize the two forms that each of these equations takes. Whichever form is used in the problem, the solution lies in immediately putting it into its *other* form. Memorize both forms and look for them on the test.

## SIMULTANEOUS EQUATIONS

If you see one equation with two variables, can you solve for either variable? For example, if $x + y = 4$, do we know exactly what $x$ and $y$ equal? No. If $x$ is 2 then $y$ is 2, but if $x$ is 3 then $y$ is 1. You can *never* solve one equation with two variables. However, if there are *two* equations, each of which contains the same two variables, then you can solve using a process known as **simultaneous equations**. An easy problem might look like this:

If $4x + 2y = 5$ and $6x - 2y = 15$, then what is $x$?

To solve, set one equation above the other and add or subtract one equation to or from the other so that one of the variables disappears.

$$4x + 2y = 5$$
$$\underline{+6x - 2y = 15}$$
$$10x \quad\quad = 20$$
$$\text{so, } x = 2.$$

In more difficult simultaneous equations, you'll find that neither of the variables will disappear when you try to add or subtract the two equations. In such cases, you must multiply both sides of one of the equations by some number in order to get the coefficient in front of the variable you want to disappear to be the same in both equations.

This sounds more complicated than it really is. A difficult problem might look like this:

**2 Variables —
2 Equations**

You can't solve one equation with two variables. But if you have two different equations with the same two variables, you're in business.

1. What is the value of $y$ in the system of equations below?
   $$3x + 4y = 5 \quad\quad 6x + 2y = 2$$

   A. $\dfrac{4}{3}$

   B. $\dfrac{8}{3}$

   C. 6

   D. 7

   E. 9

## Here's How to Crack It

Line up the two equations:
$$3x + 4y = 5$$
$$6x + 2y = 2$$

Since we want to end up with a value for $y$, we need to make $x$ disappear. To do this, let's multiply the entire top equation by 2. Now we have:
$$6x + 8y = 10$$
$$6x + 2y = 2$$

When we subtract one equation from the other, all the $x$s will disappear.
$$6x + 8y = 10$$
$$\underline{-6x + 2y = 2}$$
$$6y = 8$$

$y = \dfrac{8}{6}$ *or* $\dfrac{4}{3}$, and the answer is choice **A**.

## INEQUALITIES

There is one difference between an inequality and an equality. You solve both in exactly the same way, except that when you multiply or divide both sides of an inequality by a *negative* number, the direction of the inequality sign flips. Here's an example:

$$3x + 7 > 28 \qquad\qquad -3x + 7 > 28$$
$$\underline{-7 \quad -7} \qquad\qquad \underline{-7 \quad -7}$$
$$3x > 21 \qquad\qquad -3x > 21$$
$$\frac{3x}{3} > \frac{21}{3} \qquad\qquad \frac{-3x}{-3} < \frac{21}{-3}$$
$$x > 7 \qquad\qquad x < -7$$

Because most inequalities on the ACT involve graphing, we will be discussing them in more detail in the Graphing and Coordinate Geometry chapter.

## SUMMARY

1. There are two main types of algebra questions on the ACT: particular value questions, which ask you to solve for a particular $x$, and no particular value questions, otherwise known as cosmic problems.

2. On particular value questions you can use algebra OR you can work backward from the answer choices. Working Backward is frequently easier. When you work backward, begin with the middle answer choice to see whether you need a larger number or a smaller number. You can always work backward if you see specific numbers in the answer choices and the question in the last line is relatively straightforward.

3. On cosmic problems, you can use algebra OR you can plug in. Plugging In is frequently easier. You can always plug in if you see variables in the answer choices, or if the problem itself does not depend on specific numbers.

4. You must know how to factor quadratic equations. ACT's favorites are $x^2 + 2xy + y^2 = (x + y)^2$, $x^2 - 2xy + y^2 = (x - y)^2$, and $x^2 - y^2 = (x + y)(x - y)$. Remember that many quadratic problems can be solved by Working Backward or Plugging In. The best approach, of course, may be to let your calculator do the work for you. However, this can be a more complicated calculator function, so be sure you know how to use it now, before it's too late.

5. In solving simultaneous equation problems, add or subtract one equation to or from another so that one of the two variables disappears.

6. When you solve for an inequality, remember that if you multiply or divide by a negative number, the sign flips.

# ALGEBRA DRILL

1. If $x = -3$, then $\dfrac{(x + 3)(x - 3)}{9} = ?$

   A.  0
   B.  1
   C.  3
   D.  5
   E.  6

2. What is the largest value of $x$ that solves the
   equation $x^2 - 4x + 3 = 0$ ?

   F.  1
   G.  2
   H.  3
   J.  4
   K.  5

3. If $x + 2y = 8$ and $\dfrac{x}{2} - y = 10$, then $x = ?$

   A.  –7
   B.   0
   C.  10
   D.  14
   E.  28

4. For all $x \neq -9$, $\dfrac{x^2 + 6x - 27}{(x + 9)}$

   F.  $x + 9$
   G.  $x - 3$
   H.  $x + 3$
   J.  $2x - 4$
   K.  $2x + 3$

5. If 2 less than 3 times a certain number is the same as 4
   more than the product of 5 and 3, what is the number?

   A.   7
   B.  10
   C.  11
   D.  14
   E.  15

**6.** A certain number of books are to be given away at a promotion. If $\frac{2}{5}$ of the books are distributed in the morning, and $\frac{1}{3}$ of the remaining books are distributed in the afternoon, what fraction of the books remain to be distributed the next day?

F. $\frac{1}{5}$

G. $\frac{2}{5}$

H. $\frac{1}{3}$

J. $\frac{5}{7}$

K. $\frac{8}{9}$

## Here's How to Crack It

**Question 1:** If $x = -3$, then the first term of the denominator $(x + 3)$ equals 0. 0 times any number equals 0, so the correct answer is **A**.

**Question 2:** If we factor the equation we get $(x - 3)(x - 1) = 0$. $x$ could be either 3 or 1. Since we are being asked for the larger value, the correct answer is **H**. Note that you could have worked backward on this question, starting with K, because the question wants you to find the "largest value."

**Question 3:** Since this question contains two equations with two different variables, this is a simultaneous equations question. Let's get rid of the fraction in the second equation. Multiply the entire equation by 2. We get:

$$x + 2y = 8$$
$$x - 2y = 20$$

If we add the two equations together, we get $2x = 28$, or $x = 14$. The correct answer is **D**.

**Question 4:** If we factor, we get:

$$\frac{(x + 9)(x - 3)}{(x + 9)}$$

The $(x + 9)$s cancel out, so the correct answer is **G**. Note that you could have plugged in on this question. Also, you could have used the denominator to help you factor the numerator.

**Question 5:** The correct translation of the equation is $3x - 2 = 5(3) + 4$. Thus, the correct answer is **A.**

**Question 6:** "A certain number" sounds pretty cosmic to us. This is a Plugging In question. Let's pick a number of books. Since we will be dividing by 5 and by 3, a good number might be 15. $\frac{2}{5}$ of 15 = 6. If 6 are gone, then 9 remain to be given out. In the afternoon, $\frac{1}{3}$ of 9 are given out: This equals 3. If 3 are given out in the afternoon, that leaves 6. The question asks for the **fraction** of books that remain. Every fraction is a part over a whole. The part is 6; the whole is 15. $\frac{6}{15}$ reduces to $\frac{2}{5}$. The correct answer is **G.**

# 11

# Geometry

Geometry questions account for a greater percentage of the ACT Math Test than do any other type of question. However, the amount of actual information being tested is extremely small. You can forget most of the geometry you learned in high school: There will be no proofs, no theorems, and virtually no problems in three dimensions. Instead, you will find a few concepts being tested over and over again. All of these concepts will be covered in this chapter, along with illustrations of how the ACT writers use the concepts to construct their questions.

Even if geometry was your least favorite subject in school, you should count on getting most of the ACT geometry questions correct after you've finished reading this chapter. They just aren't that tough.

Before we begin our review, however, ask yourself the following important questions:

## TO SCALE OR NOT TO SCALE?

That is the question. In the instructions to the math portion of the ACT, the test writers say that the diagrams are "NOT necessarily drawn to scale." On the other hand, in the ACT's own *Official Guide*, one of the suggested strategies is to use the diagrams to estimate the correct answer. The book says that "some of the figures are reasonably accurate."

We didn't think measuring the diagrams would be a very successful strategy if some of them were accurate and some of them weren't. So, we carefully measured the diagrams on every geometry problem of every ACT test we could get our hands on. The results? EVERY diagram was drawn EXACTLY to scale. When we asked an ACT spokesperson about this, he said that ACT diagrams were never intended to be misleading, but that there might be rare instances in which it was impossible to draw a problem to scale. Since we couldn't find a single one of these problems, you should consider it a very rare possibility, indeed.

### POE and Crazy Answers

In the previous chapters you've seen how POE can be used to prevent picking careless or partial answers when you know how to do a problem. You've also seen how POE can narrow down the range of reasonable answers when you *don't* know how to do a problem and just need to guess.

In geometry, because the problems are *always* drawn to scale, it will be possible to get very close approximations of the correct answers *before you even do the problems*.

## HOW BIG IS ANGLE *NLM*?

### All a Matter of Degree

| | |
|---|---|
| Degrees in a circle: | 360 |
| Degrees in a line: | 180 |
| Degrees in a perpendicular angle: | 90 |
| Degrees in a triangle: | 180 |
| Degrees in a quadrilateral: | 360 |

Obviously, you don't know exactly how big this angle is, but it would be easy to compare it to an angle whose measure you *did* know exactly. Let's compare it to a 90 degree angle:

Angle *NLM* is clearly a bit less than 90°. Now look at the following problem, which asks about the same angle *NLM*:

1.  In the figure above, *O*, *N*, and *M* are collinear. If the lengths of $\overline{ON}$ and $\overline{NL}$ are the same, and the measure of angle *LON* is 30° and angle *LMN* is 40°, what is the measure of angle *NLM*?

    A.  40
    B.  80
    C.  90
    D.  120
    E.  150

## Here's How to Crack It

This is a relatively easy problem, and we will be showing you its geometric solution later in the chapter (as well as explaining terms like "collinear," and which angle is meant by angle *LON)*.

For now, however, let's focus on eliminating answer choices that don't make sense. We've already decided that ∠*NLM* is a bit less than 90°, which means we can eliminate answer choices C, D, and E. How much less than 90°? 40° is less than half of 90°. Could angle *NLM* be that small? Of course not. The answer to this question must be **B.**

In this case, it wasn't necessary to do any real geometry at all in order to get the question right. Why did the ACT writers make the other answers so crazy? They wanted to include some partial answers for people who tried to do the problem geometrically, but who stopped before they were really done.

For example, a student who used the information that segments $\overline{ON}$ and $\overline{NL}$ were the same might have realized that triangle *ONL* is isosceles (has two equal sides), and that ∠*ONL* is equal to 120°. This was a possible first step to getting the correct answer geometrically. However, if the student felt carried away with his or her own brilliance at getting this far and looked straight to the answers, the folks at ACT wanted 120° to be one of the possible answer choices.

## LET'S DO IT AGAIN

2. In the figure above, if $\overline{AB}$ = 27, $\overline{CD}$ = 20, and the area of triangle *ADC* = 240, what is the area of polygon *ABCD*?
   F.   420
   G.   480
   H.   540
   J.   564
   K.   1128

## Here's How to Crack It

Again, we will be solving this problem using geometry a little later in the chapter. For now, let's concentrate on eliminating crazy answers. This polygon is not a conventional figure, but if we had to choose one figure that the polygon resembled, we might pick a rectangle. Try drawing a line at a right angle from the line segment $\overline{AB}$ so that it touches point *C*, thus creating a rectangle. It should look like this:

The area of polygon *ABCD* is equal to the area of the rectangle you've just formed, plus a little bit at the top. The problem tells you that the area of triangle *ADC* is 240. What is the area of the rectangle you just created? If you said 480, you are exactly right, whether you knew the geometric rules that applied or whether you just measured it with your eyes.

So the area of the rectangle is 480. Roughly speaking then, what should the area of the polygon be? A bit more. Let's look at the answer choices. F and G are either less than or equal to 480. Get rid of them. H and J both seem possible. They are both a bit more than 480. Let's hold on to them. Answer choice K seems pretty crazy. We want more than 480, but 1128 is ridiculous.

Thus, on this problem, which was of medium difficulty, we were able to eliminate three of the five answer choices without doing any real geometry. Now what should you do? If you know how to do the problem, you do it. If you don't or if you are running out of time, you guess and move on.

## IMPORTANT APPROXIMATIONS

In some cases, you may want to estimate problems that contain answer choices with radicals or $\pi$. Here are some useful approximations:

$$\sqrt{2} \approx 1.4$$
$$\sqrt{3} \approx 1.7$$
$$\pi \approx 3$$

## WHAT SHOULD I DO IF THERE IS NO DIAGRAM?

Draw one! It's always easier to understand a problem when you can see it in front of you. If possible, draw your figure to scale so that you can estimate the answer as well.

# GEOMETRY REVIEW

By using the diagrams ACT has so thoughtfully provided, and by making your own diagrams when they are not provided, you can often eliminate several of the answer choices. In some cases you'll be able to eliminate every choice but one. Of course, you will also need to know the actual geometry concepts that ACT is testing. We've divided our review into four topics.

1. Angles and lines

2. Triangles

3. Four-sided figures

4. Circles

# ANGLES AND LINES

Here is a line:

A line extends forever in either direction. This line, called $l_1$, has three points on it: *A*, *B*, and *C*. These three points are said to be **collinear** because they are all on the same line. The piece of the line in between points *A* and *B* is called a line **segment**. ACT will refer to it as segment *AB* or simply $\overline{AB}$. *A* and *B* are the **endpoints** of segment *AB*.

A line forms an angle of 180°. If that line is cut by another line, it divides that 180° into two pieces that together add up to 180°:

In the previous diagram, what is the value of *x*? If you said 60°, you were correct. To find ∠*x*, just subtract 120° from 180°.

An angle can also be described by points on the lines that intersect to form the angle, and the point of intersection itself, with the middle letter corresponding to the point of intersection. For example, in the previous diagram, ∠*x* could also be described as ∠*LNP*. On the ACT, instead of writing out "angle *LNP*," they'll use math shorthand and put ∠*LNP* instead. So, "angle *x*" becomes ∠*x*.

If there are 180° above a line, there are also 180° below the line, for a total of 360°.

When two lines intersect, they form four angles, represented below by letters *A*, *B*, *C*, and *D*. ∠*A* and ∠*B* together form a straight line, so they add up to 180°.

Angles like these are called **supplementary**. ∠*A* and ∠*C* are opposite from each other, and always equal each other, as do ∠*B* and ∠*D*. Angles like these are called **vertical** angles.

In the figure above, what is the value of ∠x? If you said 80°, you're right. Together with the 100° angle, x formed a straight line. What is the value of ∠y? If you said 80°, you're right again. These two angles are vertical and must equal each other. The four angles together add up to 360°.

When two lines meet in such a way that 90° angles are formed, the lines are called **perpendicular.** The little box at the point of the intersection of the two lines below indicates that they are perpendicular. It stands to reason that all four of these angles have a value of 90°.

When two lines in the same plane are drawn so that they could extend into infinity without ever meeting, they are called **parallel.** In the figure below, $l_1$ is parallel to $l_2$. The symbol for parallel is ||.

When two parallel lines are cut by a third line, eight angles are formed, but in fact, there are really only two—a big one and a little one. Look at the diagram below:

If ∠A = 110°, then ∠B must equal 70° (together they form a straight line). ∠D is vertical to ∠B, which means that it must also equal 70°. ∠C is vertical to ∠A, so it must equal 110°.

The four angles ∠E, ∠F, ∠G, and ∠H are in exactly the same proportion as the angles above. The little angles are both 70°. The big angles are both 110°.

Try the following problem:

1. In the figure above, line *L* is parallel to line *M*. Line *N* intersects both *L* and *M*, with angles *a*, *b*, *c*, *d*, *e*, *f*, *g*, and *h* as shown. Which of the following lists includes all the angles that are supplementary to ∠*a*?

   A. Angles *b*, *d*, *f*, and *h*
   B. Angles *c*, *e*, and *g*
   C. Angles *b*, *d*, and *c*
   D. Angles *e*, *f*, *g*, and *h*
   E. Angles *d*, *c*, *h*, and *g*

## Here's How to Crack It

An angle is supplementary to another angle if the two angles together add up to 180°. Since ∠*a* is one of the eight angles formed by the intersection of a line with two parallel lines, we know that there are really only two angles: a big one and a little one. ∠*a* is a big one. Thus only the small angles would be supplementary to it. Which angles are those? The correct answer choice is **A**.

# TRIANGLES

A triangle is a three-sided figure whose inside angles always add up to 180°. The largest angle of a triangle is always opposite to its largest side. Thus, in triangle *xyz* below, *xy* would be the largest side, followed by *yz*, followed by *xz*. On the ACT, "triangle *xyz*" will be written Δ*xyz*.

The ACT likes to ask about certain kinds of triangles in particular:

An **isosceles** triangle has two equal sides. The angles opposite those sides are also equal. In the isosceles triangle above, if $\angle A = 50°$, then so does $\angle C$. If $\overline{AB} = 6$, then so does $\overline{BC}$.

An **equilateral** triangle has three equal sides and three equal angles. Since the three equal angles must add up to 180°, all three angles of an equilateral triangle are always equal to 60°.

A **right triangle** has one inside angle that is equal to 90°. The longest side of a right triangle (the one opposite the 90° angle) is called the **hypotenuse.**

Pythagoras, the Greek mathematician, discovered that the sides of a right triangle are always in a particular proportion, which can be expressed by the formula $a^2 + b^2 = c^2$, where $a$ and $b$ are the shorter sides of the triangle, and $c$ is the hypotenuse. This formula is called the **Pythagorean Theorem.**

There are certain right triangles that the test writers at ACT find endlessly fascinating. Let's test out the Pythagorean Theorem on the first of these:

$$3^2 + 4^2 = c^2$$
$$9 + 16 = 25$$
$$c^2 = 25 \;\; so \;\; c = 5$$

The ACT writers adore the 3-4-5 triangle, and use it frequently, along with its multiples, such as the 6-8-10 triangle and the 9-12-15 triangle. Of course, you can always use the Pythagorean Theorem to figure out the third side of a right triangle—as long as you have the other two sides—but since ACT problems almost invariably use "triples" like the ones we've just mentioned, it makes sense just to memorize them.

The ACT's most commonly used right-triangle triples:

| |
|---|
| 3-4-5 (and its multiples) |
| 5-12-13 |
| 7-24-25 |

## TWO SMALL NOTES OF CAUTION

1.  Is this a 3-4-5 triangle?

No, because the hypotenuse of a right triangle must be its *biggest* side—the one opposite the 90 degree angle. In this case, we must use the Pythagorean Theorem to discover side $c$: $3^2 + c^2 = 16$. $c = \sqrt{7}$.

2.  Is this a 5-12-13 triangle?

No, because the Pythagorean Theorem—and triples—apply only to *right* triangles. We don't know anything about the third side of this triangle.

**Pythagoras' *Other* Theorem**

Pythagoras also developed a theory about the transmigration of souls. So far, this has not been proven.

# THE ISOSCELES RIGHT TRIANGLE

As fond as the test writers are of triples, they are even fonder of two other right triangles. The first is called the **isosceles right triangle.** The sides and angles of the isosceles right triangle are always in a particular proportion:

You could use the Pythagorean Theorem to prove this (or you could just take our word for it). Whatever the value of the two equal sides of the isosceles right triangle, the hypotenuse is always equal to one of those sides times $\sqrt{2}$. Here are two examples:

# THE 30-60-90 TRIANGLE

The other right triangle tested frequently on the ACT is the **30-60-90** triangle, which also always has the same proportions:

**Be on the Lookout...**

for problems in which the application of the Pythagorean Theorem is not obvious. For example, every rectangle contains two right triangles. That means that if you know the length and width of the rectangle, you also know the length of the diagonal, which is the hypotenuse of both triangles created by the diagonal.

You can use the Pythagorean Theorem to prove this (or you can just take our word for it). Whatever the value of the short side of the 30-60-90 triangle, the hypotenuse is always twice as big. The medium side is always equal to the short side times $\sqrt{3}$. Here are two examples:

Because these triangles are tested so frequently, it makes sense to memorize the proportions, rather than waste time deriving them each time they appear.

## TWO MORE NOTES OF CAUTION

1.  In the isosceles right triangle below, are the sides equal to $3\sqrt{2}$?

No. Remember, in an isosceles right triangle, hypotenuse = the side $\times \sqrt{2}$. In this case, 3 = the side $\times \sqrt{2}$. If we solve for the side, we get $\frac{3}{\sqrt{2}}$ = the side.

For arcane mathematical reasons, we are not supposed to leave a radical in the denominator, but we can multiply top and bottom by $\sqrt{2}$ to get $\frac{3\sqrt{2}}{2}$.

**2.** In the right triangle below, is $x$ equal to $4\sqrt{3}$?

No. Even though it is one of ACT's favorites, you have to be careful not to see a 30-60-90 where none exists. In the triangle above, the short side is half of the *medium* side, not half of the hypotenuse. This is some sort of right triangle all right, but it is not a 30-60-90. The hypotenuse, in case you're curious, is really $4\sqrt{5}$.

## AREA

The **area** of a triangle can be found using the following formula:

$$\text{area} = \frac{\text{base} \times \text{height}}{2}$$

with height being the perpendicular line from the base of the triangle to its highest point.

In all three of the above triangles, the area is:

$$\frac{8 \times 4}{2} = 16$$

## TWO FURTHER NOTES OF CAUTION

1. Sometimes the height of a triangle can be *outside* the triangle itself, as we just saw in the second example.

2. In a right triangle, the height of the triangle can also be one of the sides of the triangle, as we just saw in the third example. However, be careful when finding the area of a *non-right* triangle. Simply because you know two sides of the triangle does not mean that you have the height of the triangle.

## SIMILAR TRIANGLES

Two triangles are called similar if their angles have the same degree measures. This means their sides will be in proportion. For example, the two triangles below are similar.

Because the sides of the two triangles are in the same proportion, you can find the missing side, $x$, by setting up a proportion equation.

$$\begin{array}{ccc} & \text{small triangle} & \text{big triangle} \\ \dfrac{\text{short leg}}{\text{hypotenuse}} & \dfrac{2}{4} = & \dfrac{4}{x} \\ & x = 8 & \end{array}$$

## ACT TRIANGLE PROBLEMS

Most of the triangle problems on the ACT combine *several* of the triangle concepts we've just gone over. Be flexible, and look for clues as to which concepts are being tested. Here are some triangle problems as they might appear on the ACT:

1. In the figure above, $O$, $N$, and $M$ are collinear. If the length of $\overline{ON}$ and $\overline{NL}$ are the same, and the measure of $\angle LON$ is 30° and $\angle LMN$ is 40°, what is the measure of $\angle NLM$?

   A. 40°
   B. 80°
   C. 90°
   D. 120°
   E. 150°

## Here's How to Crack It

We saw this problem at the beginning of the chapter, and managed to solve it without using any geometry. Now let's solve it geometrically. Since $\overline{ON}$ is equal to $\overline{NL}$, we know that $ONL$ is isosceles. If $\angle O = 30°$ then so does $\angle OLN$, and therefore $\angle ONL$ is equal to 120°. Because this angle and $\angle LNM$ add up to a straight line, $\angle LNM$ must be equal to 60°. $\angle LNM$ plus $\angle LMN$ add up to 100°, meaning that the angle we are looking for ($NLM$) is equal to 80° and the answer is **B.** Alternatively, in $\triangle OLM$, $\angle OLM$ must equal 110°, and $\angle OLN$ makes up 30°, leaving 80° for $\angle NLM$.

**2.** In the figure above, if $\overline{AB} = 27$, $\overline{CD} = 20$, and the area of $\triangle ADC = 240$, what is the area of polygon $ABCD$?

   **F.**    420
   **G.**   480
   **H.**   540
   **J.**    564
   **K.**  1128

## Here's How to Crack It

Again, we saw this problem at the beginning of the chapter, and managed to eliminate three of the five answer choices through POE. Now let's solve it geometrically. The polygon in question is made up of two triangles. We are told that the area of $\triangle ADC$ is 240.

The formula for the area of a triangle $= \dfrac{\text{base} \times \text{height}}{2}$

We don't know the base of this triangle, but we do know the height and the total area. Can we figure out the base? Of course.

$$\frac{(b)(20)}{2} = 240$$

$$b = 24$$

Now let's look at the other triangle. We need to find its area, because the sum of the areas of the two triangles equals the area of the polygon we are looking for. If we turn the polygon on its side so that $\overline{BA}$ is on the bottom, we have the base of the $\triangle ABC$. Do we know the height? Yes! The base of $\triangle ADC$ also happens to be equal to the height of $\triangle ABC$: 24.

All that's left is to plug the base and height into the area formula to get the area of $\triangle ABC$.

$$\frac{(27)(24)}{2} = 324$$

The area of the polygon is $324 + 240 = 564$, or answer choice **J.**

3.  In the figure above, square *ABCD* is attached to △*ADE* as shown. If ∠*EAD* is equal to 30°, and $\overline{AE}$ is equal to $4\sqrt{3}$, then what is the area of square *ABCD*?

A.  $8\sqrt{3}$

B.  16

C.  64

D.  72

E.  $64\sqrt{2}$

## Here's How to Crack It

The triangle in this diagram is a 30-60-90. Since angle *A* is the short angle, the side opposite that angle is equal to 4 and the hypotenuse is equal to 8. Because that hypotenuse is also the side of the square, the area of the square must be 8 times 8, or 64. This is answer choice **C.** If you forgot the ratio of the sides of a 30-60-90 triangle, go back and review it—you'll need it.

## POE Notes

If you didn't remember the ratio of the sides of a 30-60-90 triangle, could you have eliminated some answers using POE? Of course. Let's see if we can use the diagram to eliminate some answer choices.

The diagram tells us that $\overline{AE}$ has length $4\sqrt{3}$. Remember the important approximations we gave you earlier in the chapter? A good approximation for $\sqrt{3}$ is 1.7. So $4\sqrt{3}$ = approximately 6.8. We can now use this to estimate the sides of square *ABCD*. Just using your eyes, would you say that $\overline{AD}$ is longer or shorter than $\overline{AE}$? It's a bit longer. You decide and write down what you think it might be. To find the area of the square, simply square whatever value you decided the side equaled. This is your answer.

Now, all you have to do is see which of the answer choices still make sense. Could the answer be A? $8\sqrt{3}$ equals roughly 13.6. Is this close to your answer? No way. Could the answer be answer choice B, which is 16? Still much too small. Could the answer be answer choice C, which is 64? Quite possibly. Could the answer be 72? It might be. Could the correct answer be $64\sqrt{2}$? An approximation of radical 2 = 1.4, so $64\sqrt{2}$ equals 89.6. This seems rather large. Thus, on this problem, by using POE we could eliminate answer choices A, B, and E.

## FOUR-SIDED FIGURES

The interior angles of any four-sided figure (also known as a quadrilateral) add up to 360°. The most common four-sided figures on the ACT are the rectangle and the square, with the parallelogram and the trapezoid coming in a far distant third and fourth.

**Your Friend the Triangle**

Since a quadrilateral is really just two triangles, its interior angles must measure twice those of a triangle: 2(180) = 360.

A **rectangle** is a four-sided figure whose four interior angles are each equal to 90°. The area of a rectangle is base times height. Therefore, the area of the rectangle above is 8 (*base*) × 5 (*height*) = 40. The perimeter of a rectangle is the sum of all four of its sides. The perimeter of the rectangle above is 8 + 8 + 5 + 5 = 26.

A **square** is a rectangle whose four sides are all equal in length. You can think of the area of a square therefore as **side squared**. The area of the above square is 6 (*base*) × 6 (*height*) = 36. The perimeter is 24.

A **parallelogram** is a four-sided figure made up of two sets of parallel lines. We said earlier that when parallel lines are crossed by a third line, eight angles are formed, but that in reality there are only two—the big one and the little one. In a parallelogram, 16 angles are formed, but there are still, in reality, only two.

The area of a parallelogram is also *base × height,* but because of the shape of the figure, the height of a parallelogram is not necessarily equal to one of its sides. Height is measured by a perpendicular line drawn from the base to the top of the figure. The area of the parallelogram above is 9 × 5 = 45.

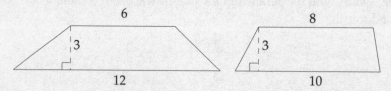

A **trapezoid** is a four-sided figure of which two sides are parallel. Both of the figures above are trapezoids. The area of a trapezoid is the *average of the two parallel sides × the height,* or $\frac{1}{2}$ *(Base 1 + Base 2)(Height),* but on ACT problems involving trapezoids there is almost always some easy way to find the area without knowing the formula (for example, by dividing the trapezoid into two triangles and a rectangle). In both trapezoids above, the area is 27.

# CIRCLES

The distance from the center of a circle to any point on the circle is called the **radius.** The distance from one point on a circle, through the center of the circle, to another point on the circle is called the **diameter.** The diameter is always equal to twice the radius. In the circle on the left below, *AB* is called a **chord.** *CD* is called a **tangent** to the circle.

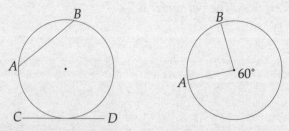

The curved portion of the right-hand circle between points *A* and *B* is called an **arc.** The angle formed by drawing lines from the center of the circle to points

$A$ and $B$ is said to be **subtended** by the arc. There are 360° in a circle, so that if the angle we just mentioned equaled 60°, it would take up $\frac{60}{360}$ or $\frac{1}{6}$ of the degrees in the entire circle. It would also take up $\frac{1}{6}$ of the area of the circle and $\frac{1}{6}$ of the outer perimeter of the circle, called the circumference.

The formula for the **area** of a circle is $\pi r^2$.

The formula for the **circumference** is $2\pi r$.

In the circle below, if the radius is 4, then the area is $16\pi$, and the circumference is $8\pi$.

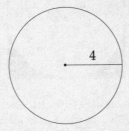

The key to circle problems on the ACT is to look for the word or phrase that tells you what to do. If you see the word circumference, immediately write down the formula for circumference, and plug in any numbers the problem has given you. By solving for whatever quantity is still unknown, you have probably already answered the problem.

1. If the area of a circle is 16 meters, what is its radius in meters?

   A. $\frac{8}{\pi}$

   B. $12\pi$

   C. $\frac{4\sqrt{\pi}}{\pi}$

   D. $\frac{16}{\pi}$

   E. $144\pi^2$

## Here's How to Crack It

As soon as you see the word "area," start thinking $\pi r^2 = 16$. The problem is asking for the radius, so you have to solve for $r$. If you divide both sides by $\pi$ you get:

$$r^2 = \frac{16}{\pi}$$

$$r = \sqrt{\frac{16}{\pi}}$$

$$= \frac{4}{\sqrt{\pi}}$$

$$= \frac{4\sqrt{\pi}}{\pi}$$

The correct answer choice is **C**.

**Geometry Hint**

If there isn't a diagram, draw
one yourself.

2.  In the figure above, the circle with center $O$ is inscribed
    inside square *ABCD* as shown. If a side of the square
    measures 8 units, what is the area of the shaded region?
    **F.**  $8 - 16\pi$
    **G.**  $8\pi$
    **H.**  $16\pi$
    **J.**  $64 - 16\pi$
    **K.**  $64\pi$

## Here's How to Crack It

Since the side of the square measures 8 units, what is the area of the square? 64
square units. Okay, hold that thought.

## POE Notes

Before we do any more real math, let's take a moment to look at the diagram.

What portion of the entire square would you say is shaded? Could it be as much

as $\frac{1}{2}$? No, so we're looking for an answer that is less than half of 64—in other

words, less than 32. Most of the answer choices are in terms of $\pi$, but a rough

approximation of $\pi$ is 3. Let's go through the choices and see if there are any we

can eliminate.

**F.**  $8 - 16(3) = -40$. This is clearly crazy. You can't have a negative area.

**G.**  $8(3) = 24$. Let's hold on to this one.

**H.**  $16(3) = 48$. No. We need an answer less than 32.

**J.**  $64 - 16(3) = 16$. Let's hold on to this one too.

**K.**  $64(3) = 192$. This is larger than the entire square. No way.

You can use POE to eliminate three of the choices. If you're running out of time, or don't remember how to do the problem geometrically, guess and move on.

To solve the problem the way ACT expects you to, you must find the area of the circle and subtract it from the square. What is left over is the shaded region. The formula for the area of a circle is $\pi r^2$. Do we know the radius of this circle? Sure. Because the circle is inscribed in the square, the side of the square has the same measure as the diameter of the circle. In other words, the radius of the circle is 4, and the area of the circle is $16\pi$. Subtracting the area of the circle from the area of the square, we get $64 - 16\pi$, which is answer choice **J**.

# SUMMARY

1. If there is no diagram included in a problem, you should draw your own.

2. There are several things to know about angles and lines.

   A. A line is a 180-degree angle.

   B. When two lines intersect, four angles are formed, but in reality there are only two.

   C. When two parallel lines are cut by a third line, eight angles are formed, but in reality there are still only two (big ones and small ones).

3. There are several things to know about triangles.

   A. A triangle has three sides and three angles, the sum of which equals 180°.

   B. An isosceles triangle has two equal sides, and two equal angles opposite those sides.

   C. An equilateral triangle has three equal sides, and three equal angles, all of which equal 60°.

   D. A right triangle has one 90-degree angle. In a right triangle problem you can use the Pythagorean Theorem to find the lengths of sides.

   E. Some common right triangles are 3-4-5, 6-8-10, 5-12-13, 7-24-25.

   F. ACT writers also like the isosceles right triangle, whose sides are always in the ratio $s:s:s\sqrt{2}$, and the 30-60-90 triangle, whose sides are always in the ratio $s:s\sqrt{3}:2s$.

   G. Similar triangles have the same angle measurements, and sides that are in the same proportion.

   H. The area of a triangle is equal to $\dfrac{\text{base} \times \text{height}}{2}$.

4. Four-sided objects are called quadrilaterals and have four angles, which add up to 360 degrees. There are several important things to remember.

   A. The area of a rectangle, a square, or a parallelogram can be found using the formula: $base \times height = area$.

   B. The perimeter of any object is the sum of the lengths of its sides.

   C. The area of a trapezoid is equal to the average of the two bases times the height.

5. In a circle problem, the two important things to remember are:

   A. Area = $\pi r^2$

   B. Circumference = $2\pi r$

# GEOMETRY DRILL

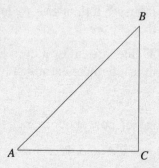

1. In *ABC* above, $\angle A = \angle B$, and angle *C* is twice the measure of $\angle B$. What is the measure, in degrees, of $\angle A$?
   A. 30
   B. 45
   C. 50
   D. 75
   E. 90

**2.** In the figure above, $l_1 \parallel l_2$. Which of the labeled angles must be equal to each other?

   **F.** $A$ and $C$

   **G.** $D$ and $E$

   **H.** $A$ and $B$

   **J.** $D$ and $B$

   **K.** $C$ and $B$

**3.** In the figure above, right triangles $ABC$ and $ACD$ are drawn as shown. If $\overline{AB} = 20$, $\overline{BC} = 15$, and $\overline{AD} = 7$ then $\overline{CD} = ?$

   **A.** 21

   **B.** 22

   **C.** 23

   **D.** 24

   **E.** 25

**4.** If the area of circle $A$ is $16\pi$, then what is the circumference of circle $B$ if its radius is $\dfrac{1}{2}$ that of circle A?

   **F.** $2\pi$

   **G.** $4\pi$

   **H.** $6\pi$

   **J.** $8\pi$

   **K.** $16\pi$

5. In the figure above, $\overline{MO}$ is perpendicular to $\overline{LN}$, $\overline{LO}$ is equal to 4, $\overline{MO}$ is equal to $\overline{ON}$, and $\overline{LM}$ is equal to 6. What is $\overline{MN}$?

A. $2\sqrt{10}$

B. $3\sqrt{5}$

C. $4\sqrt{5}$

D. $3\sqrt{10}$

E. $6\sqrt{4}$

## Here's How to Crack It

**Question 1:** Let's say $\angle A$ equals $x°$. $\angle B$ also equals $x°$. $\angle C$ is therefore $2x°$. We have a total of $4x°$. Since there are $180°$ in a triangle, $4x = 180$. $x$ equals 45, and therefore the correct answer is **B**. Note that you could have worked backward on this problem.

**Question 2:** When two parallel lines are cut by a third line, there are really only two angles formed—a big one and a little one. We need to find an answer choice with two big angles or two little angles. Remember, any answer choice with $\angle D$ in it must be wrong because this angle is not formed by two parallel lines being cut by a third. The correct answer is **F**.

**Question 3:** You could use the Pythagorean Theorem to solve this question, but you will be done much faster if you know the triples ACT likes to use. The triangle on the left is a multiple of 3-4-5 triangle: 15-20-25. The triangle on the right is a 7-24-25 triangle. The correct answer is **D**.

**Question 4:** The radius of circle $A$ is 4. If circle $B$ has a radius that is half of circle A, its radius is 2. Therefore the circumference is $4\pi$. The correct answer is **G**.

**Question 5:** This time we have to use the Pythagorean Theorem, because all we know about $\triangle LMO$ is that it is a right triangle. Using the Pythagorean Theorem, we find that MO is equal to $\sqrt{20}$ or $2\sqrt{5}$. $\triangle MON$ is an isosceles right triangle, so the hypotenuse is equal to the side times $\sqrt{2}$. The correct answer is **A**.

# 12

# Graphing and Coordinate Geometry

Coordinate geometry, the fancy name for graphing, is a way of thinking about an equation, or the solutions to an equation, as a kind of picture. The simplest equations involve only one variable and can be represented on a number line. These equations often involve inequalities.

## GRAPHING INEQUALITIES

Here's a simple inequality:

$$3x + 5 > 11$$

As you know from reading the algebra chapter of this book, you solve an inequality in the same way that you solve an equality. By subtracting 5 from both sides and then dividing both sides by 3, you get the expression:

$$x > 2$$

This can be represented on a number line as shown below:

**An Open Circle**

On the number line, a hollow circle means that point is *not* included in the graph.

The open circle at 2 indicates that $x$ can include every number greater than 2, but not 2 itself, or anything less than 2.

If we had wanted to graph $x \geq 2$, the circle would have to be filled in, indicating that our graph includes 2 as well:

**A Solid Dot**

On the number line, a solid dot means that point *is* included in the graph.

Many calculators can solve and graph inequalities just as easily as they solve equations with one variable. If yours can, you might want to make sure you know how to use that function. Because there aren't many inequalities on the ACT, you'll probably be okay if you decide to do them all by hand.

An ACT graphing problem might look like this:

1. Which of the following represents the range of solutions for inequality $-5x - 7 < x + 5$ ?

## Here's How to Crack It

The test writers want you first to simplify the inequality, and then figure out which of the answer choices represents a graph of the solution set of the inequality. To simplify, isolate $x$ on one side of the inequality.

$$
\begin{array}{r}
-5x-7 < x+5 \\
\underline{-x \qquad -x} \\
-6x-7 < \quad 5 \\
\underline{+7 \qquad +7} \\
-6x \quad < \quad 12
\end{array}
$$

Now, divide both sides by –6. Remember that when you multiply or divide an inequality by a negative, the sign flips over.

$$
\frac{-6x}{-6} < \frac{12}{-6}
$$
$$
x > -2
$$

Which of the choices answers the question? If you chose answer choice **B**, you're right!

## POE Notes

You could have done this (and most other inequality graphing problems) just as easily by Working Backward. Look at the possible answer choices. The test writers at ACT tend to surround the correct answer with at least one *almost* correct answer. Why don't we begin by checking to see if any numbers appear more than once as origin points in the answer choice graphs? The only number that repeats here is –2, which appears in answer choices B and C. Let's plug –2 into our inequality and pretend for a moment that it is an equality.

$$
\text{Does } -5(-2)-7 = (-2)+5 ?
$$
$$
10-7 = 3 ?
$$

Yes! Now, to decide whether the answer is B or C, just pick a number that is in one answer but not the other. For example, in answer choice C, –4 is part of the solution set but it is not included in B. By plugging –4 into the inequality, we will see if answer choice C is correct. If it isn't, then the answer is B.

$$
-5(-4)-7 < (-4)+5
$$
$$
20-7 < 1
$$
$$
13 < 1
$$

Is this true? No, so the answer must be **B**.

> **Flip Flop**
>
> Remember that when you multiply or divide an inequality by a negative, the sign flips.

## GRAPHING IN TWO DIMENSIONS

More complicated graphing questions concern equations with two variables, usually designated $x$ and $y$. These equations can be graphed on a Cartesian grid, which looks like this:

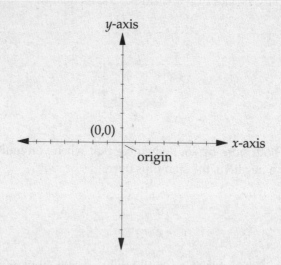

Every point $(x,y)$ has a place on this grid. For example, the point $A$ (3,4) can be found by counting over on the $x$–axis 3 places to the right of (0,0)—known as the origin—and then counting on the $y$-axis 4 places up from the origin, as shown below. Point $B$ (5,–2) can be found by counting 5 places to the right on the $x$–axis and then down 2 places on the $y$-axis. Point $C$ (–4,–1) can be found by counting 4 places to the left of the origin on the $x$-axis and then 1 place down on the $y$–axis.

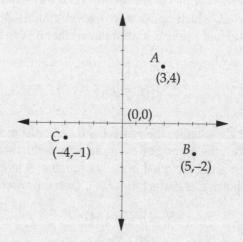

The grid is divided into four quadrants, which go counterclockwise for no good reason.

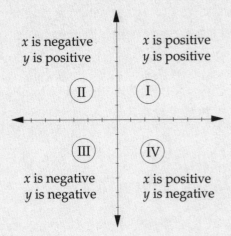

- In the first quadrant, $x$ and $y$ are both positive.
- In the second quadrant, $x$ is negative, but $y$ is positive.
- In the third quadrant, $x$ and $y$ are both negative.
- In the fourth quadrant, $x$ is positive, but $y$ is negative.

**Note:** This is when your graphing calculator (if you have one) will really get a chance to shine. Practice doing all the ACT coordinate geometry questions on your calculator now and you'll blow them away when you actually take the test.

## GRAPHIC GUESSTIMATION

A few questions on the ACT might involve actual graphing, but it is more likely that you will be able to make use of graphing to *estimate* the answer to a question that ACT test writers think is more complicated.

1. Point $B$ (4,3) is the midpoint of line segment $\overline{AC}$. If point $A$ has coordinates (0,1), then what are the coordinates of point $C$?
   A. (–4,–1)
   B. (4,1)
   C. (4,4)
   D. (8,5)
   E. (8,9)

## Here's How to Crack It

You may or may not remember the midpoint formula: The ACT writers are expecting you to use it to solve this problem. We'll go over it in a moment, along with the other formulas you'll need to solve coordinate geometry questions. However, it is worth noting that by drawing a rough graph of this problem, you can get the correct answer without the formula.

Plot the two points from the problem on your calculator. If you don't have a graphing calculator, use the grid we've provided below.

$B$ is supposed to be the midpoint of a line segment $AC$. Draw a line through the two points you've just plotted and extend it upward until $B$ is the midpoint of the line segment. It should look like this:

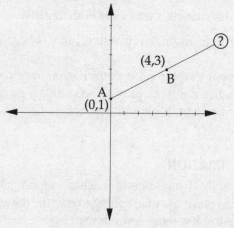

The place where you stopped drawing is the approximate location of point $C$. Now let's look at the answer choices to see if any of them are in the ballpark.

   **A.**  $(-4,-1)$: These coordinates are in the wrong quadrant!

   **B.**  $(4,1)$: This point is way below where it should be.

   **C.**  $(4,4)$: This point does not extend enough to the right.

   **D.**  $(8,5)$: Definitely in the ballpark. Hold on to this answer choice.

   **E.**  $(8,9)$: Possible, though the $y$-coordinate seems a bit high.

Which answer choice do you want to pick? If you said answer choice **D**, you were right.

By the way, the folks giving the exam will not allow you to bring graphing paper (or any other kind of scrap paper) with you to the real test, so get used to making your graphs and other calculations in the test booklet. A full column, labeled "DO YOUR FIGURING HERE." is provided on every page of the Mathematics Test.

# THE IMPORTANT COORDINATE GEOMETRY FORMULAS

By memorizing a few formulas, you will be able to answer virtually all of the coordinate geometry questions on this test. Remember, too, that in coordinate geometry you almost *always* have a fallback—just graph it out.

The following formulas are listed in order of importance:

## THE *Y*-INTERCEPT FORMULA

$$y = mx + b$$

By putting $(x,y)$ equations into the formula above, you can find two pieces of information that ACT likes to test: the **slope** and the **y-intercept.** Most graphing calculators will put an equation into y-intercept form at the touch of a button.

The **slope** is a number that tells you how sharply a line is inclining, and it is equivalent to the letter **m** in the equation above. For example, in the equation $y = 3x + 4$, the number 3 (think of it as $\frac{3}{1}$) tells us that from any point on the line, we can find another point on the line by going up 3 and over to the right 1.

In the equation $y = -\frac{4}{5}x - 7$, the slope of $-\frac{4}{5}$ tells us that from any point on the line, we can find another point on the line by going up 4 and over 5 to the left.

The **y-intercept,** equivalent to the letter **b** in the equation above, is the point at which the line intercepts the y-axis. For example, in the equation $y = 3x + 4$, the line will strike the y-axis at a point 4 above the origin. In the equation $y = 2x - 7$, the line will strike the y-axis at a point 7 below the origin. A typical ACT $y = mx + b$ question might give you an equation in another form and ask you to find either the slope or the y-intercept. Simply put the equation into the form we've just shown.

> **To Find the x-intercept**
>
> Set y equal to zero and solve for x.

1. What is the slope of the line based on the equation
   $5x - y = 7x + 6$?
   A. –2
   B. 0
   C. 2
   D. 6
   E. –6

## Here's How to Crack It

Isolate $y$ on the left side of the equation. You can have your graphing calculator do this for you, or you can do it by hand by subtracting $5x$ from both sides.

$$
\begin{array}{r}
5x - y = 7x + 6 \\
\underline{-5x \quad\quad -5x} \\
-y = 2x + 6
\end{array}
$$

We aren't quite done. The format we want is $y = mx + b$, *not* $-y = mx + b$. Let's multiply both sides by $-1$.

$$(-1)(-y) = (2x + 6)(-1)$$
$$y = -2x - 6$$

The slope of this line is $-2$, so the answer is **A**.

## THE SLOPE FORMULA

You can find the slope of a line, even if all you have are two points on that line, by using the slope formula:

$$\text{slope} = \frac{\text{change in } y}{\text{change in } x}$$

**The Slippery Slope**

A line going from bottom left to upper right has a positive slope. A line going from top left to bottom right has a negative slope.

1. What is the slope of the straight line passing through the points $(-2,5)$ and $(6,4)$ ?

A. $-\dfrac{1}{16}$

B. $-\dfrac{1}{8}$

C. $\dfrac{1}{5}$

D. $\dfrac{2}{9}$

E. $\dfrac{4}{9}$

## Here's How to Crack It

Find the change in $y$ and put it over the change in $x$. The change in $y$ is the first $y$-coordinate minus the second $y$-coordinate. (It doesn't matter which point is first and which is second.) The change in $x$ is the first $x$ minus the second $x$:

$$\frac{y[1] - y[2]}{x[1] - x[2]} \qquad \frac{5 - 4 = 1}{-2 - 6 = -8}$$

The correct answer choice is **B**.

## MIDPOINT FORMULA

If you have the two endpoints of a line segment, you can find the midpoint of the segment by using the midpoint formula.

$$\left(x[m], y[m]\right) = \frac{x_1 + x_2}{2}, \frac{y_1 + y_2}{2}$$

It looks a lot more intimidating than it really is.

To find the midpoint of a line, just take the *average* of the two $x$ coordinates, and the *average* of the two $y$ coordinates. For example, the midpoint of the line segment formed by the coordinates (3,4) and (9,2) is just:

$$\frac{(3+9)}{2} = 6 \ and \ \frac{(4+2)}{2} = 3$$

$$or \ (6,3)$$

Remember the first midpoint problem we did? Here it is again:

1. Point $B$ (4,3) is the midpoint of line segment $\overline{AC}$. If point $A$ has coordinates (0,1) then what are the coordinates of point $C$?
   A. (–4,–1)
   B. (4,1)
   C. (4,4)
   D. (8,5)
   E. (8,9)

## Here's How to Crack It

You'll remember that it was perfectly possible to solve this problem just by drawing a quick graph of what it ought to look like. However, to find the correct answer using the midpoint formula, we first have to realize that, in this case, we already *have* the midpoint. We are being asked to find one of the endpoints.

The midpoint is (4,3). This represents the average of the two endpoints. The endpoint we know about is (0,1). Let's do the $x$-coordinate first. The average of the $x$-coordinates of the two endpoints equals the $x$-coordinate of the midpoint. So $\frac{(0+?)}{2} = 4$. What is the missing $x$-coordinate? 8. Now, let's do the $y$-coordinate. $\frac{(1+?)}{2} = 3$. What is the missing $y$-coordinate? 5. The answer is **D**

If you had trouble following that last explanation, just remember that you already understood this problem (and got the answer) using graphing. Never be intimidated by formulas on the ACT. There is usually another way to do the problem.

## THE DISTANCE FORMULA

We hate the distance formula. We keep forgetting it, and even when we remember it, we feel like fools for using it because there are much easier ways to find the distance between two points. We aren't even going to tell you what the distance formula is. If you need to know the distance between two points, you can always think of that distance as being the hypotenuse of a right triangle. Here's an example:

1. What is the distance between the points $A$ (2,2) and $B$ (5,6) ?
   A. 3
   B. 4
   C. 5
   D. 6
   E. 7

### Here's How to Crack It

Let's make a quick graph of what this ought to look like.

If we extend lines from the two points to form a right triangle under the line segment *AB*, we can use the Pythagorean Theorem to get the distance between the two points. What is the length of the base of the triangle? 3. What is the length of the height of the triangle? 4. So what is the length of the hypotenuse? 5. Of course, as usual, it was one of the triples of which ACT is so fond. The answer is **C.** You could also have popped the points into your calculator and had it calculate the distance for you.

## CIRCLES, ELLIPSES, AND PARABOLAS, OH MY!

You should probably have a *vague* idea of what the equations for these figures look like; just remember that there are very few questions concerning these figures, and when they do come up you can almost always figure them out by graphing.

The standard equation for a circle looks like this:

$$(x - h)^2 + (y - k)^2 = r^2$$
$(h,k)$ = center of the circle
$r$ = radius

The standard equation for an ellipse (just a squat-looking circle) looks like this:

$$\frac{(x - h)^2}{a^2} + \frac{(y - k)^2}{b^2} = 1$$
$(h,k)$ = center of the elipse
$2a$ = horizontal axis
$2b$ = vertical axis

The equation for a parabola (just a U-shaped line) looks like this:

$$y = x^2$$

1. If the equation $x^2 = 1 - y^2$ were graphed in the standard $(x,y)$ coordinate plane, the graph would represent which of the following geometric figures?
   A. square
   B. straight line
   C. circle
   D. triangle
   E. parabola

## Here's How to Crack It

If you're familiar with what the equations of the various elements in the answer choices are supposed to look like, you may be able to figure out the problem without graphing at all. (On the other hand, that's why you bought a graphing calculator in the first place...) Let's consider what we know about the equations of geometric figures. If an equation has only $x$ and $y$, we know that the graph of the equation is a straight line. (Think back to the $y = mx + b$ problems we did earlier.) However, in this equation, both $x$ and $y$ are squared, so we can rule out answer choice B. There is no equation for a square, so we can rule out answer choice A. Similarly, there's no equation for a triangle, so D is out. If only one of the variables were squared, this might be a parabola, but in this problem both are squared, which means we can eliminate answer choice E. We are left with answer choice **C**.

## Estimating Note

Of course, we could also just plug some numbers into the equation and plot them out on a homemade $(x,y)$ axis in the scratchwork column of the test booklet. Let's try this on the grid below.

The easiest way to start is to let one of the variables equal 0. If $x = 0$, then $y$ must equal 1. So one point of this equation is $(0,1)$. If we let $y = 0$, then $x$ must equal 1. So another point of this equation is $(1,0)$. Plot out some other points of the equation. How about $(-1,0)$ and $(0, -1)$? What kind of geometric figure does it appear that we have? If you said a circle, you were absolutely correct.

## SUMMARY

1.  In graphing an inequality, solve for the variable, and look for the number-line graph that expresses the equation. Remember, you can often work backward on inequality graphing questions. Remember to flip the inequality when you divide or multiply by a negative.

2.  Graphing on an $(x,y)$ axis is most useful as a way to estimate the correct answers to coordinate geometry questions.

3.  Some coordinate geometry questions can be solved by putting them into the format $y = mx + b$, where m is the slope of the line and b is the $y$ intercept. Your calculator should be able to do this for you.

4.  Some coordinate geometry questions can be solved by using the slope formula.

$$\text{slope} = \frac{\text{change in } y}{\text{change in } x}$$

5.  Other coordinate geometry questions can be solved using the midpoint formula.

$$(x[m], y[m]) = \frac{x_1 + x_2}{2}, \frac{y_1 + y_2}{2}$$

6.  If you don't have a graphing calculator, you can always find the distance between two points by drawing a line between them and making it the hypotenuse of a right triangle.

7.  Every once in a while, ACT asks a question based on the equations of circles, ellipses, and parabolas. If you need a very high score, it might help to memorize these equations, but remember, these questions can frequently be done by using graphing to estimate the correct answer.

## GRAPHING AND COORDINATE GEOMETRY DRILL

1. Which of the following represents the solution of the inequality $-3x - 6 > 9$?

2. What is the midpoint of the line segment whose endpoints are represented on the coordinate axis by the points (3,5) and (−4,3)?

    F.   (−2,−5)

    G.  $(-\frac{1}{2}, 4)$

    H.  (1,8)

    J.  $(4, -\frac{1}{2})$

    K.  (3,3)

3. What is the slope of the line represented by the equation $10x + 2x = y + 6$?

    A.  10
    B.  12
    C.  14
    D.  15
    E.  16

4. What is the length of the line segment whose endpoints are represented on the coordinate axis by the points (−2,−1) and (1,3) ?

    F.  3
    G.  4
    H.  5
    J.  6
    K.  7

5. What is the slope of the line that contains the points (6,4) and (13,5) ?

    A.  $-\frac{1}{8}$

    B.  $-\frac{1}{9}$

    C.  $\frac{1}{7}$

    D.  1

    E.  7

## Here's How to Crack It

Question 1: We can immediately cancel choices B and D because the equation does not contain a greater-than-or-equal-to sign. If you chose answer choice C, you forgot that the sign flips when you multiply or divide an inequality by a negative number. The correct answer is E.

**Question 2:** If you don't remember the formula for finding a midpoint, just make a rough graph. Which quadrant should the answer be in? If you said the second, you were absolutely correct. The $x$-coordinate should be negative, the $y$-coordinate should be positive. Which answer choices are possible? There's only one. The correct answer is **G**.

**Question 3:** We need to put this into the standard $y = mx + b$ form. In this case, the equation becomes $y = 12x - 6$. The slope is 12, and the answer is **B**.

**Question 4:** Forget the distance formula. Instead, try sketching out a graph. Make the line between the two points the hypotenuse of a right triangle. It turns out to be a 3-4-5 triangle. The correct answer is **H**.

**Question 5:** Just use the slope formula—the difference in $y$ over the difference in $x$. The correct answer is **C**.

# 13

# Trigonometry

There are only four trigonometry questions on the ACT. Two of these questions are among the easiest on the test, and you should plan to do them even if you never took trigonometry. The other two might be easy and might not. If all four trig questions are based on right triangle relationships (SOHCAHTOA), you'll be able to do all four pretty quickly. But sometimes two of the four questions test your ability to graph trig functions. These might be trickier.

The easier trigonometry questions on this test involve the relationships between the sides of a right triangle. In the right triangle below, the angle $x$ can be expressed in terms of the ratios of different sides of the triangle.

The **sine** of angle $x = \dfrac{\text{length of side opposite angle } x}{\text{length of hypotenuse}}$

The **cosine** of angle $x = \dfrac{\text{length of side adjacent angle } x}{\text{length of hypotenuse}}$

The **tangent** of angle $x = \dfrac{\text{length of side opposite } x}{\text{length of side adjacent } x}$

There is a very handy acronym to remember all this:

## SOHCAHTOA

**S**ine is **o**pposite over **h**ypotenuse. **C**osine is **a**djacent over **h**ypotenuse. **T**angent is **o**pposite over **a**djacent. So in the triangle below, the sine of angle θ [*theta*, a Greek letter] would be $\dfrac{4}{5}$. The cosine of angle θ would be $\dfrac{3}{5}$. The tangent of angle θ would be $\dfrac{4}{3}$.

Sine, cosine, and tangent are often abbreviated as sin, cos, and tan, respectively.

# YOU'RE ALMOST DONE

There are three more relationships to memorize. They involve the reciprocals of the previous three.

$$\text{The } \textbf{cosecant} = \frac{1}{\text{sine}}$$

$$\text{The } \textbf{secant} = \frac{1}{\text{cosine}}$$

$$\text{The } \textbf{cotangent} = \frac{1}{\text{tangent}}$$

And two more little things, while we're at it:

$$\sin^2\theta + \cos^2\theta = 1$$

$$\frac{\sin\theta}{\cos\theta} = \tan\theta$$

To make matters even better, a good calculator has buttons for all of these functions (sometimes cosecant, secant, and cotangent are represented by $\sin^{-1}$, $\cos^{-1}$, and $\tan^{-1}$, respectively). Let's try a couple of problems:

1. What is $\sin\theta$, if $\tan\theta = \frac{4}{3}$?

 A. $\frac{3}{4}$

 B. $\frac{4}{5}$

 C. $\frac{5}{4}$

 D. $\frac{5}{3}$

 E. $\frac{7}{3}$

## Here's How to Crack It

It helps to sketch out the right triangle and fill in the information we know.

What kind of right triangle is this? That's right—a 3-4-5. Now, we need to know the sine of angle θ: opposite over hypotenuse, or $\frac{4}{5}$, which is answer choice **B**.

1. For all θ, $\dfrac{\cos\theta}{\sin^2\theta + \cos^2\theta} = ?$

    **A.** sin θ
    **B.** csc θ
    **C.** cot θ
    **D.** cos θ
    **E.** tan θ

## Here's How to Crack It

Sin $^2$θ + cos $^2$θ always equals 1. $\frac{\cos}{1} = \cos$. The answer is **D**.

2. In a right triangle shown above, sec θ is $\frac{25}{7}$. What is sin θ?

    **F.** $\dfrac{3}{25}$

    **G.** $\dfrac{5}{25}$

    **H.** $\dfrac{7}{25}$

    **J.** $\dfrac{24}{25}$

    **K.** $\dfrac{25}{7}$

## Here's How to Crack It

The secant of any angle is the reciprocal of the cosine, which is just another way to say that the cosine of angle θ is $\frac{7}{25}$.

Secant $= \dfrac{1}{\cos}$ so $\dfrac{1}{\cos} = \dfrac{25}{7}$, which means that cos $= \dfrac{7}{25}$.

Cosine means adjacent over hypotenuse. Let's sketch this out:

As you can see, we now have two sides of a right triangle. Can we find the third side? If you said this was one of the triples we told you about before, you were absolutely correct, although you also could have derived this by using the Pythagorean Theorem. The third side must be 24. The question asks for sin θ. Sine = opposite over hypotenuse, or $\frac{24}{25}$, which is answer choice **J**.

# HARDER TRIGONOMETRY

When graphing a trig function, such as sine, there are two important coefficients, A and B, as shown here: A{sin (B)}.

The two coefficients A and B govern the amplitude of the graph (how tall it is) and the period of the graph (how long it takes to get through a complete cycle), respectively. If there are no coefficients, then that means A = 1 and B = 1 and the graph is the same as what you'd get when you graph it on your calculator.

- Increases in A increase the amplitude of the graph. It's a direct relationship.

That means if A = 2, then the amplitude is doubled. If A = $\frac{1}{2}$, then the amplitude is cut in half.

- Increases in B decrease the period of the graph. It's an inverse relationship.

That means if B = 2, then the period is cut in half, which is to say the graph completes a full cycle faster than usual. If B = $\frac{1}{2}$, then the period is do ubled.

You can add to or subtract from the function as a whole, and also to the variable, but neither of those actions changes the shape of the graph, only its position and starting place.

Here's the graph of sin $x$—what are the amplitude and period?

The simple function sin $\theta$ has an amplitude that goes from –1 to 1, for a total of 2, while its period is $2\pi$, which means that every $2\pi$ on the graph (as you go from side to side) it completes a full cycle. That's what you see in the previous graph.

This graph is also a sine function, but it's been changed. What is the function graphed here?

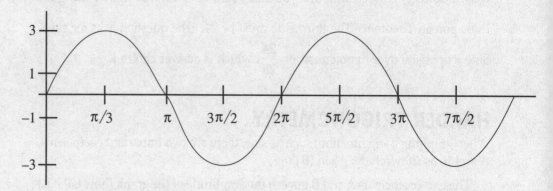

You have three things to check when looking at this graph: Is it sin or cos, is the period changed, and is the amplitude changed?

- This is a sin graph, since it has a value of 0 at 0. Cos has a value of 1 at 0.

- It makes a complete cycle in $2\pi$, so the period isn't changed. B = 1, in other words.

- The amplitude is triple what it normally is, so A = 3. The function graphed, therefore, is 3 sin $\theta$.

How about here?

Once again, there are three things to check.

- This is a sin graph, since it has a value of 0 at 0. Cos has a value of 1 at 0.

- It makes a complete cycle in π, so the period has changed—it's half of what it usually is. Since B has an inverse effect, that means B = 2.

- The amplitude is triple what it normally is, so A = 3. The function graphed, therefore, is 3 sin2 θ.

Let's try some practice questions.

**49.** As compared to the graph of $y = \cos x$, which of the following has the same period and three times the amplitude?

A. $y = \cos 3x$
B. $y = \cos \dfrac{1}{2}(x + 3)$
C. $y = 3 \cos x$
D. $y = 1 + 3 \cos x$
E. $y = 3 + \cos x$

## Here's How to Crack It

Recall that the coefficient on the outside of the function changes the amplitude and the one on the inside changes the period. Since the question states that the period isn't changed, you can eliminate A and C. The amplitude is three times greater, you're told, so since there's a direct relationship between A and amplitude you want to have a 3 on the outside of the function. That leaves only **D** as a possibility.

**52.** Which of the following equations describes the equation graphed above?

F.  2 cos *x*
G.  1 + 2 cos *x*
H.  cos 2*x*
J.  1 + cos 2*x*
K.  1 + 2 cos 2*x*

## Here's How to Crack It

At first it looks like this graph has an amplitude of 3, but if you look closer you'll see that though the top value is 3, the bottom value is –1, which means that the whole graph has been shifted up. Since F and H don't add anything to the function (which is how you move a graph up and down), they're out. The period of this graph is half what it usually is, so B = 2, which eliminates G. Since the amplitude is changed also, you can eliminate J. The answer is **K**.

## SUMMARY

1. There are only four trigonometry questions on the ACT. At least two will deal with right triangles, and they are relatively easy if you know a few formulas.

2. SOHCAHTOA will help you remember most of the formulas:

$$\text{Sine} = \frac{\text{opposite}}{\text{hypotenuse}}; \text{cosine} = \frac{\text{adjacent}}{\text{hypotenuse}}; \text{tangent} = \frac{\text{opposite}}{\text{adjacent}}.$$

3. The cosecant $= \frac{1}{\text{sine}}$, the secant $= \frac{1}{\text{cosine}}$, and the cotangent $= \frac{1}{\text{tangent}}$.

4. $\sin^2\theta + \cos^2\theta = 1$.

5. $\frac{\sin\theta}{\cos\theta} = \tan\theta$.

# TRIGONOMETRY DRILL

**1.** In $\triangle ABC$ below, the tan θ equals

A. $\dfrac{5}{12}$

B. $\dfrac{12}{13}$

C. $\dfrac{17}{12}$

D. $\dfrac{12}{5}$

E. 3

**2.** If the cotangent of an angle θ is 1, then the tangent of angle θ is

F. −1

G. 0

H. 1

J. 2

K. 3

**3.** If $x + \sin^2 \theta + \cos^2 \theta = 4$, then $x = ?$

A. 1

B. 2

C. 3

D. 4

E. 5

## Here's How to Crack It

**Question 1:** This is a 5-12-13 triangle. The tangent of an angle is opposite over adjacent. The correct answer is **D**.

**Question 2:** The cotangent of an angle is the reciprocal of the tangent. If the tangent is 1, then so is the cotangent. The correct answer is **H**.

**Question 3:** $\sin^2 \theta + \cos^2 \theta$ always equals 1. Therefore, $x$ must equal 3. The correct answer is **C**.

# PART ◆ IV

# How to Beat the ACT Reading Test

The ACT Reading Test presents four passages and 40 questions. That's ten questions per passage. You get 35 minutes for the whole section, which means you have about nine minutes to cover each passage and the questions that follow it.

The passages are edited bits of books and magazines, and according to ACT, they're "typical of what a college freshman might be required to read . . ." And the questions? ACT says they test your ability to "understand" the passages.

## BUT THAT'S NOT REALLY TRUE

No one ever achieved a great insight by spending eight or nine pressured minutes reading an isolated fragment of a book or article. Serious writers don't intend their work to be read in fragments, or in so hurried a fashion as Reading Tests require. (Imagine that you were asked to read a *fragment* of the history of the relations between the United States, Germany, and Japan during the twentieth century. Suppose, in particular, that you're only asked to read about their cooperative relations in the years 1985–1990. You'd be missing the history of their relationship during the years 1940–1945—World War II—which means you'd be missing a rather important piece of the story.)

Furthermore, serious readers take time to think about the things they read. How far would Albert Einstein have gotten if someone had interrupted his reading every eight or nine minutes to announce that he should "close his book because time is up"? As a college student, you'll be asked not only to read, but also to think about what you read—and then to reread—and then to think some more. Any professor will tell you that understanding takes thought, and thought usually takes time.

When you take the ACT Reading Test you're not asked to understand. You're not asked to do anything you'll ever do in college. You're just asked to take a "reading test."

## THE ACT READING TEST: CRACKING THE SYSTEM

You'll raise your reading score if you're "wise" to the test and if you think strategically. We're first going to show you how ACT Reading questions are built. Then we'll show you how to use that knowledge to select correct answers. You'll learn to:

1. Attack the passages in the order that best suits you.

2. See through the camouflage that hides correct answer choices.

3. Identify incorrect answer choices and eliminate them quickly.

4. Answer questions without really reading passages.

5. Put all of these techniques together in order to approach every passage and question with a step-by-step strategy that leads systematically to the correct answer.

**The ACT Reading Test Format**

4 Passages; 40 questions: 35 minutes

## Reading Test Triage: Ordering the Passages

The Reading Test has four passages, one each from the fields of:

1. prose fiction
2. social science
3. the humanities
4. natural science

**The Reading Test Covers the Following Topics:**

- Prose Fiction (excerpts from short stories and novels)
- Social Sciences (history, economics, psychology, political sciences, and anthropology)
- Humanities (art, music, architecture, and dance)
- Natural Sciences (biology, chemistry, physics, and physical sciences)

Students differ in their abilities to tackle these different passage types and it's important that you decide which passages are easiest and hardest for you. That way you can decide which passages to do first (the easier ones) and which to do last (the harder ones).

**Natural science passages** are filled with lots of details and dry technical descriptions.

> It is further noteworthy that the terrestrial vertebrate's most significant muscles of movement are no longer located lateral to the vertebral column as they are in the fish, but rather in ventral and dorsal relation to it. This trend in terrestrial evolution is highly significant and means that the terrestrial vertebrate's principle movements are fore and back, not side to side. The trend is well documented in the whale, an aquatic animal whose ancestors are terrestrial quadrupeds. The whale, in other words, has "returned" to the sea secondarily, after an ancestral stage on the land. Unlike the fish, and in accordance with its ancestry, it propels itself by moving the tail up and down, not side to side. In a sense, the whale moves itself by bending up and down at the waist. Indeed, that very analogy is recalled by the mythical mermaid figure who seems to represent a humanlike line returned to the water secondarily like the whale.

The questions usually track the text pretty closely and don't require you to make inferences.

**Reading Test Triage**

If you have a knack for particular passage types, great! Do them first. If not, look at the topics, as well as the questions and answer choices. Some will be straightforward, while others will look like true pains.

1. Which of the following best represents a general trend associated with mammalian evolution?
   A. Enhancement of bodily movement from right to left and left to right
   B. Minimization of muscle groups oriented lateral to the vertebral column
   C. The development of propulsive fins from paired limbs
   D. Secondary return to the sea

Some people have a flair for the ACT's natural science passages, and some people find them extremely tedious and difficult. (And by the way, it isn't necessarily good science students who do well with these passages nor poor science students who have trouble with them.) If among all of the passage types you find natural science the easiest, you should make it a rule to address the natural science passage first. If, on the other hand, you find natural science passages the most difficult, save them for last.

The **prose fiction passage** is kind of opposite to the natural science passage. It tells a fictitious story and it's supposed to be packed with hints and suggestions about characters and their motivations.

Allen's grandmother was readying herself to leave. She was, in fact, putting the final touches on her makeup which, as always, looked to Allen as though someone had thrown it on her face with a shovel. Mrs. Mandale then placed her newly purchased bracelet over her wrist when a look of troubled ambivalence came over her. "Perhaps this bracelet isn't right for me," she said. "I won't wear it."

Waiting, now, for thirty minutes, Allen tried to be tolerant. "It is right for you," he said. "It matches your personality. Wear it." The bracelet was a remarkable illustration of poor taste. Its colors were vulgar and the conformation lacked any sign of thoughtful design. The truth is it did match his grandmother's personality. All that she did and enjoyed was tasteless, and induced in Allen a quiet hopelessness.

Prose fiction questions often require that you "read between the lines" and draw inferences about the way characters feel or behave.

1. Allen most likely encouraged his grandmother to wear her bracelet because he:
   A. found it colorful and approved of its appearance.
   B. found its appearance pathetic and wished his grandmother to look pretty.
   C. was impatient with his grandmother for spending time worrying about the bracelet.
   D. felt the bracelet matched his grandmother's personality.

Some people have a flair for these kinds of passages and questions. Others find them unclear and confusing. If you find literature passages easiest, do them first. If you find them most difficult, do them last.

**Social science and humanities passages** are sort of a cross between natural science and prose fiction. Often, the author has views about the subject he or she is discussing, and you might be asked to draw inferences about them. You might also be asked questions about details.

Religion is so fundamental a part of human existence that one might easily forget to ask how it started. Yet it had to start somewhere and there had to be a time when human beings or their apelike ancestors did not entertain notions of the supernatural. Hence the historian should want to probe the origins of religious belief.

It is doubtful that morality played a part in the beginnings of religious belief. Rather, religion is traceable to a far more fundamental human and animal characteristic. Storms, floods, famine, and other adversities inspired *fear* in the hearts of primitive peoples as well they should have. Curiously, humankind early took the position that they might somehow subject such catastrophes to their control. Specifically, they believed they might control it by obedience and submission

**Fiction Passages**

Most prose fiction passages are primarily concerned with five things:
- Who
- What
- When
- Where
- Why

and by conforming their behavior to its mandates. Worship, ritual, sacrifice of life, and property became means through which early peoples sought to cajole the powers and avoid the blights and miseries they dreaded. As Petronius, in Lucretius's tradition remarked, "it was fear that first made the gods."

1. According to the passage, natural disasters contributed to the development of religion by:
   A. motivating human beings to acquire some command over their environment.
   B. making human beings distinguish themselves from animals.
   C. causing human beings to sacrifice their lives and goods.
   D. providing a need for ritual and tradition.

2. The author believes that the origins of religion:
   F. are extremely easy to ascertain and understand.
   G. should not be questioned by historians because religion is fundamental to civilized life.
   H. are directly tied to apelike subhuman species.
   J. should be the subject of serious historical inquiry.

Mark Twain had magnificent style, and with *The Adventures of Huckleberry Finn* he built the gateway to American fiction. *Huckleberry Finn* treats extraordinarily serious themes and it reflects the author's coming of age. Although they don't represent truly mature works, other Twain Mississippi River stories, published before Huck Finn, afford Americans a clear, collective picture of pre-Civil War life in the Mississippi Valley.

With the coming and going of the Civil War, however, Twain adopted a revised agenda and this was reflected in the style and subject matter of his writing. The postwar era demanded that he address himself to the nation's social squalor. His work was more intellectualized, artificial, and at times angry. The author himself had faced several personal tragedies in series and these too might have contributed to the metamorphosis.

1. According to the passage, which of the following statements is true of *The Adventures of Huckleberry Finn*?
   A. It appeared after the publication of other Mark Twain stories describing life on the Mississippi River.
   B. It was the first full-length book that Mark Twain published.
   C. It would have been quite different if Mark Twain had not suffered personal tragedy.
   D. It had no serious themes and addressed no serious issues.

**2.** In the author's opinion, *The Adventures of Huckleberry Finn*:

    **F.** should not be read by children.

    **G.** contributed less to American literature than did Twain's postwar writings.

    **H.** is less adult in its subject matter than were Twain's postwar writings.

    **J.** reveals that Mark Twain had grown since writing his early Mississippi River stories.

You should order your work according to its degree of difficulty for you.

If you find literature passages especially easy and science passages especially tough, you should probably address the passages in this order:

| | |
|---|---|
| 1 | Prose Fiction |
| 2/3 | Social Science / Humanities (either order) |
| 4 | Natural Science |

If you find *both* literature and natural science particularly difficult, do the social studies and humanities passages first (in either order) and then do the literature and science passages in this order:

| | |
|---|---|
| 1/2 | Social Sciences / Humanities (either order) |
| 3/4 | Prose Fiction / Natural Science (either order) |

If you find both prose fiction and natural science passages especially easy, order your work like this:

| | |
|---|---|
| 1/2 | Prose Fiction/ Natural Science (either order) |
| 3/4 | Social Science / Humanities (either order) |

## How to Tell Which Passages You Find Easy and Hard

What do you do if you dislike all of the passages equally, or show no particular —or, for that matter, consistent—knack for particular passage types? The subject matter of the passages may be dull, but in the end, you should base your ordering of the passages on

- **the user-friendliness of the topics themselves**

"Wait a minute!" you say. "I thought you said that if I show no particular knack for particular passage types...." True, but...

Let's say you notice that a social science or humanities passage is historical in nature. Chances are that events will be presented in chronological order, making the passage easy to navigate. Or let's say you've recently learned about lasers in physics class and, lo and behold, the natural sciences passage is about lasers. Chances are that you'll be able to eliminate answers or even answer some of the questions based on what you've learned. You don't have to love a topic to take advantage of familiarity with it. In fact, being too enamored of a topic can work against you. Remember, you get points for answering questions correctly, not for understanding the passages, and certainly not for reading over them with great interest.

- **the user-friendliness of the questions and answer choices**

Many students who dislike all the passages pretty much equally find this an especially helpful guideline. Look at the questions. Do many of them direct you to particular lines in the passage, refer to dates, refer to proper nouns, or refer to italicized words? If so, a passage with several such questions will usually be much easier to manage. Look at the answer choices. Are they relatively straightforward, or do they resemble miniature novels? A passage with several longwinded questions and/or answer choices will always take more time to complete.

Now that we've talked about the ordering of the passages and questions, let's talk about the whole point of taking the ACT—finding right answers.

## THE RIGHT ANSWER MIGHT BE CAMOUFLAGED

Look at these two phrases:

> "rationally conceived idea"
> "concept born of reason"

The two phrases don't have a single word in common, but if you think about it you'll probably agree that they mean the same thing. Lots of ACT Reading questions test your ability to see that one sentence or phrase means more or less the same as another even though the wording is quite different. They test whether you can see that a sentence has been *paraphrased*, which means—reworded.

## READ THIS PASSAGE; IT'S VERY SHORT

**Correct Answer Choices May Be Disguised**

Look for answer choices that re-word parts of the passage.

> Regardless of personal religious belief, no true student of history can emerge from study without a scholarly appreciation for the significant role of religion in the development of human civilization.

Now that you've read the passage, answer this question:

1. Which of the following represents the author's belief regarding religion and the study of history?
   A. Many historians develop a deep suspicion of totalitarian societies and the way in which they abuse human rights.
   B. Most historians have a profound distaste for ancient documents and torn papers.
   C. True historians develop an appreciation for the role of religion in the course of human development.
   D. Few historians develop insight into the manner in which political leaders gain power.

It's pretty easy to see that **C** is right, and that A, B, and D are wrong. Choice C features the author's words and accurately reflects his meaning. Options A, B, and D are extreme and have nothing whatsoever to do with anything in the passage. This question is pretty straightforward. The wrong answers are clearly wrong and the right answer is clearly right.

## MANY ACT QUESTIONS AREN'T LIKE THAT

ACT questions won't always provide you with a correct answer that reprints the author's own words. Instead, the author's statements will be camouflaged by *rewording*. That means you must be on the lookout for answer options that don't seem right because the author's sentences have been reworded. Let's take the question we just answered and turn it into an ACT question by rewriting the answer choices.

1. Which of the following represents the author's belief regarding the role of religion in the study of history?
   A. Few historians have gained a complete appreciation for the development of religion.
   B. Historians should not allow their personal religious beliefs to affect the historical conclusions with which they emerge.
   C. Serious historians regard religious belief as an important force in man's social evolution.
   D. A true student of religious history should not ignore a general study of human development.

Answer choice C is still the correct answer, but that's not so easy to figure out anymore. Unless you're on the lookout for camouflage, you might not appreciate the similarity between these two statements:

1. ...no true student of history can emerge from study without a scholarly appreciation for the significant role of religion in the development of human civilization. 

   *and*

2. Serious historians regard religious belief as an important force in man's social evolution.

These two statements don't have a single word in common. Yet, when you think about it:

| "serious historians" | *is camouflage for* | "true student of history" |
| "important force" | *is camouflage for* | "significant role" |
| "man's social evolution" | *is camouflage for* | "development of human civilization" |

Answer choice C presented the author's statements—camouflaged.

## SEE THROUGH THE CAMOUFLAGE

You'll raise your ACT score if you learn first to recognize camouflage, and then to see through it. So, let's practice. Each of the very short readings below comes from an ACT-type passage. We want you to

- read each one

- think carefully about what it means

- *with that meaning in mind* consider the meaning of each answer choice

- determine which one constitutes the author's statements—camouflaged

> The human condition is unequal, distributing its gifts and penalties according to a wildly haphazard scheme. A person is not what he deserves to be but, simply—what he is.

1. According to the passage, it is true that the human condition:
   A. is a precious gift and should not be treated haphazardly.
   B. does not allocate its burdens and benefits according to merit.
   C. will become more predictable as human beings learn to appreciate it.
   D. is sometimes unjust, due to fundamental aspects of human nature.

## Here's How to Crack It

### What does the author say?

The author says that life's pleasures and hardships are not given out fairly—according to what people deserve. Instead, they're given out randomly. The author is saying that you don't get what you deserve. You just get what you get.

With that in mind, let's look at the answer options and see which one makes the same statement in a different way.

### What do the choices mean?

Answer choice A means that life is a very valuable thing and that people should not be careless with it.

### That's not what we're looking for.

Answer choice B says just what the author has said—in different words. Think about it:

| | | |
|---|---|---|
| "allocate" | *is camouflage for* | "distributing" |
| "burdens and benefits" | *is camouflage for* | "gifts and penalties" |
| "merit" | *is camouflage for* | "deserves" |

Answer choice C means that people who appreciate life will find that it offers fewer surprises.

**The author did not say that.**
Answer choice D means that human nature is the cause of life's unfairness.

**Interesting, but that's not what the author wrote.**
Only answer choice **B** comes close to expressing the author's meaning.

**That's why it's right.**

> Poverty, deformity, illness, loss, weakness, and mistreatment impose themselves relentlessly on individual lives. That circumstance begs the historian to ask why humans have for the most part accepted the situation so peaceably.

1. The passage indicates that persistent poverty and illness:
   A. are caused partially by humanity's overriding concern with acceptance and peace.
   B. are due in some part to faulty understanding of history.
   C. should make historians question the role of the individual in human affairs.
   D. should provoke historical inquiry into humanity's willingness to tolerate adversity.

## Here's How to Crack It

**What does the author say?**
The author says, first of all, that people have always had a lot of trouble in their lives. He then says that historians should try to figure out why they're so willing to put up with it.

**What do the choices mean?**
Answer choice A means that people have trouble because they're too concerned with peace.

**Ridiculous, but more important, it's not what the author wrote.**
Answer choice B means that people have trouble because they don't understand history.

**Not so ridiculous, but the author made no such statement.**
Answer choice C means that all of this trouble should make historians try to figure out the place of individuals in society.

**Whatever that means, it's not what we're looking for.**
Now look at answer choice D. It's just what the doctor ordered. It's the author's statement—camouflaged. Think about it:

| | | |
|---|---|---|
| "should provoke historical inquiry" | *is camouflage for* | "begs the historian to ask" |
| "willingness to tolerate adversity" | *is camouflage for* | "why humans…accepted the situation so peaceably" |

So answer choice **D** is right.

> Religious belief allows the unlucky on some very important level to treat their misery as insignificant in the grand scheme of things, for they look to something higher: the approval of their God and the faith that they will not in the end be forsaken.

1. The passage states that religious belief helps people by:
   A. allowing them to accept the idea that they have been forsaken.
   B. providing them with faith that they will overcome their difficulties.
   C. diminishing the importance they might place on their day–to–day pain.
   D. emphasizing that spiritual strength is more significant than luck.

## Here's How to Crack It

### What does the author say?
The author says that religious belief helps people whose lives are difficult. It causes them to focus on the wish to please their God, which means that they place relatively little importance on the troubles they face in their lives.

### What do the choices mean?
Answer choice A means that religious believers don't mind being forsaken.

### Sorry, not what we're looking for.
Answer choice B means that religion helps people believe they'll get over their problems.

### Sounds good, but it's not the meaning we're after.
Answer choice C means that religious believers don't think their troubles are so important.

### That's what the author said!
Choice C represents the author's statements camouflaged. Think about it:

| "diminishing the importance" | is camouflage for | "treat…as insignificant" |
|---|---|---|
| "pain" | is camouflage for | "misery" |

Answer choice D means that religious believers think spiritual strength is more important than luck.

### The author doesn't say anything like that.
Only answer choice **C** reflects the author's meaning.
### That's why it's right.

# 14

# Distracters

# GETTING WISE TO DISTRACTERS

## PROCESS OF ELIMINATION

You'll raise your ACT Reading score if you're good at spotting not only right answers but wrong answers too. In the standardized test business, wrong answers are called "distracters," and that's a perfect name for them. Distracters are designed to misdirect your thinking—to break your concentration and throw you off course. Even if you have a pretty good grasp of the passage and the question you're trying to answer, distracters can make you lose sight of both. But if you're wise to distracters, you can quickly eliminate them and make your way rapidly to the right answer.

## FOUR KINDS OF DISTRACTERS

You should know about the four kinds of distracters that show up on the ACT Reading Test. We're going to show you how each one operates so you'll know how to use them to your advantage.

## DISTRACTER TYPE 1: DISTORTIONS

Many distracters steal words directly from the passage and use them to create a statement that does *not* reflect the content of the passage. These distracters use the author's words but *distort* his meaning, so we call them distortions.

Read this statement:

> *"Tom loves going to the movies with Mary."*

It's easy to write a bunch of sentences that do not reflect the statement's meaning, even though they use the words "Tom," "love," "movies," and "Mary." For example, consider this:

> *"Tom fell in love with Mary at the movies."*

or this:

> *"Tom and Mary love movies."*

or this:

> *"Tom and Mary generally enjoy seeing movies about love."*

If you think about *meaning*, not one of these statements resembles the one with which we started. Each *distorts* the original by taking its words and rearranging them. Yet they all sort of "sound like" the original because they use the same words.

Each one of the distortions we just read would make a good ACT distracter. Suppose you've just read an ACT passage that contains the statement we just worked with: "Tom loves going to the movies with Mary." Now imagine that you get a question like this:

> 1. According to the passage, which of the following statements is true regarding Tom and Mary?
>    A. Tom fell in love with Mary at the movies.
>    B. Tom enjoys viewing motion pictures with Mary as his companion.
>    C. Tom and Mary generally enjoy seeing movies about love.
>    D. Both Tom and Mary love going to the movies.

Notice that answer choices A, C, and D use words that come straight from the passage. *They're all wrong*. Which one is right? Answer choice **B**: It presents the author's meaning—in camouflage.

## Don't Let Distortions Trap You

Don't be fooled by answer choices that take words and phrases directly from the passage. Be suspicious of them: They're often distortions.

Look at these four excerpts from ACT-like passages. Each one is followed by five statements. Three of the five are distortion distracters. The other two accurately reflect the author's meaning; they *don't* distort. For each passage, decide which three statements distort and which two do not.

Read this natural science excerpt:

> As an explanation for the age and origin of the solar system, the nebular hypothesis lost ground at the turn of the twentieth century over questions about the distribution of angular momentum.

What does the author say?

- The nebular hypothesis was intended to explain the age and origin of the solar system.

- It lost influence at the beginning of the twentieth century.

- That happened because people raised questions about the distribution of angular momentum, and the nebular hypothesis did not provide adequate answers.

**Use Process of Elimination (POE)**

Look for 4 types of distracters on the ACT Reading Test:
- Distortions
- The Switch
- Extremes
- Answer choices that sound too nice

| Now evaluate these statements: | Distorts | Does Not Distort |
|---|---|---|
| 1. According to the nebular hypothesis, the solar system was created by distributions of angular momentum. | ☐ | ☐ |
| 2. The nebular hypothesis came under question at the beginning of the twentieth century. | ☐ | ☐ |
| 3. The nebular hypothesis was challenged because of issues related to angular momentum. | ☐ | ☐ |
| 4. Knowledge about the solar system's angular momentum was first distributed in the twentieth century. | ☐ | ☐ |
| 5. The nebular hypothesis was poorly understood until the twentieth century, when theories of angular momentum gained ground. | ☐ | ☐ |

**Important**

Distortions are often words in the passage that are used out of context. Eliminate them.

**Statements 1, 4, and 5 distort** the author's meaning. The words come straight from the passage, but the meanings definitely do not. The author does *not* say that

- the distribution of angular momentum created the solar system

- someone first distributed knowledge about angular momentum in the twentieth century

- people didn't understand the nebular hypothesis until the twentieth century

**Statements 2 and 3 do not distort.** The author *does* say that

- the nebular hypothesis was questioned (lost ground) at the beginning of the twentieth century

- the nebular hypothesis was questioned because of concerns relating to angular momentum

Read this social science excerpt:

> With revolutionary improvements in health care technologies, modern medicine's expansive arsenal has undoubtedly created an improved state of national health. Although the incidence of degenerative disease is on the rise, that is primarily because degenerative diseases are characteristic of old age and the population is living, on average, longer than did its parents and grandparents.

**What does the author say?**

- There has been great progress in medicine.

- It's true that there's more degenerative disease around than there used to be.

- That's because degenerative diseases usually affect the elderly, and people are living long enough to *get* these diseases.

| Now evaluate these statements: | Distorts | Does Not Distort |
|---|---|---|
| 1. Modern medicine has increased the individual's average life span. | ☐ | ☐ |
| 2. Revolutionary health care techniques have produced degeneration in the state of national health. | ☐ | ☐ |
| 3. Few people doubt that degenerative disease tends to increase longevity. | ☐ | ☐ |
| 4. Today's health care technologies have bettered the national health. | ☐ | ☐ |
| 5. With today's tools and techniques the physician can cure degenerative diseases that once caused early death. | ☐ | ☐ |

**The Switch**

Look out for...
- changes in the wording in the answer choices
- a "flip" in the meaning of the sentence

**Statements 2, 3, and 5 distort** the author's meaning. The words are familiar, but they've been rearranged to say something that has nothing to do with the passage. The author does *not* say

- modern medicine has had a negative effect on health care

- most people think degenerative disease makes for longer life

- modern medicine allows physicians to cure degenerative diseases

**Statements 1 and 4 do not distort.** The author *does* say

- modern medicine has increased the average life span

- modern medicine has improved the national health

Read this prose fiction excerpt:

> Mrs. Mandale's physician repeatedly reminded his patient of her diabetes and had ordered her on several occasions to lose weight. Hence, Allen found himself escorting her once each week to her weight-watching group.

Mrs. Mandale was not among the heavier women in her group. She never announced her weight, however, because, "a true lady did not discuss such personal matters." The group was one of Mrs. Mandale's few pleasures, but she feared walking unaccompanied in the city at night and asked that Allen take her each week to "group." She pointed out that she had done much for him, that her very health was involved, and that he should be willing to extend himself for her.

## What does the author say?

- Allen's grandmother has diabetes.

- For that reason her doctor ordered her to lose weight.

- To lose the weight she participates in a weight-watching group.

- She's not one of the heavier women in the group.

- Even so, she won't reveal her weight, because she thinks true ladies shouldn't discuss such personal issues.

- The weight-watching group is one of Mrs. Mandale's few pleasures.

- The weight-watching group is conducted at night and Mrs. Mandale does not like to walk in the city by herself at night.

- Mrs. Mandale thinks she's done a lot for Allen so she asks him to take her to her weight-watching group each week.

**Half-and-Half**

Beware of answer choices that are half good, half bad. They're also traps.

| Now evaluate these statements: | Distorts | Does Not Distort |
|---|---|---|
| 1. Mrs. Mandale is willing to reveal her weight only because she weighs less than others in her weight-watching group. | ☐ | ☐ |
| 2. The doctor recommends that Allen's grandmother not walk alone at night. | ☐ | ☐ |
| 3. Mrs. Mandale finds her weight reduction group more enjoyable than most of her other activities. | ☐ | ☐ |
| 4. Mrs. Mandale thinks that other women in her weight-watching group are not as ladylike as she is. | ☐ | ☐ |
| 5. Mrs. Mandale believes she has been a positive force in her grandson's life. | ☐ | ☐ |

**Statements 1, 2, and 4 distort** the author's meaning. The key words come straight from the passage, but the statements are distortions. The author does *not* say that

- Mrs. Mandale is willing to reveal her weight (He says just the opposite.)

- the doctor advised Mrs. Mandale against walking alone at night

- Mrs. Mandale believes herself to be more of a lady than the other women in the group

**Statements 3 and 5 do not distort.** The author *does* say that

- the weight-watching group is one of the few pleasures Mrs. Mandale has

- Mrs. Mandale thinks she has done a lot for her grandson

Read this humanities excerpt:

> Before the Civil War, Frances Ellen Watkins Harper was the best known of black abolitionist writers. Her greatest true novel, *Iola Leroy,* or *Shadows Uplifted,* appeared in 1892. The work was transitional: It treats both the pre-Civil War and post-Civil War periods. Although it describes the evils of slavery, its principle purpose was considerably different from some of the earlier novels for which Mrs. Harper became famous. In *Iola Leroy,* Mrs. Harper wished to promote justice and interracial tolerance. For that reason, the novel treats some issues with more idealism than realism.
>
> Referring to her own novel, Mrs. Harper wrote: "I have woven a story whose mission will not be in vain if it awakens in the hearts of our countrymen a stronger sense of justice and a more Christlike humanity."

## What does the author say?

- Mrs. Harper was a black abolitionist writer—the most famous of her time.

- Her earlier novels dealt primarily with the evils of slavery.

- Her best novel was *Iola Leroy,* which was also called *Shadows Uplifted.*

- That novel dealt with the periods before and after the Civil War—*Iola Leroy* dealt with the evils of slavery, but Mrs. Harper primarily intended the novel to promote justice and tolerance among races.

- Because that was her purpose, she sometimes treated issues not in a realistic manner, but in an idealistic manner.

| Now evaluate these statements: | Distorts | Does Not Distort |
|---|---|---|
| 1. *Iola Leroy* depicts situations occurring before and after the Civil War. | ☐ | ☐ |
| 2. Frances Ellen Watkins Harper was not well known as an abolitionist until the appearance of her first true novel, *Iola Leroy*. | ☐ | ☐ |
| 3. Although best known as abolitionist literature, Mrs. Harper's prewar novels usually concerned justice, not slavery. | ☐ | ☐ |
| 4. Mrs. Harper was well-known before the Civil War but in the postwar period her fame diminished considerably. | ☐ | ☐ |
| 5. Frances Ellen Watkins Harper opposed slavery before the war and attempted to improve relations among blacks and whites after the war. | ☐ | ☐ |

**Statements 2, 3, and 4 distort** the author's meaning. The words come right out of the passage, but the meanings have nothing to do with it. The author definitely does *not* say that

- *Iola Leroy* was Mrs. Harper's *first* true novel, or that Mrs. Harper was not well-known until that novel appeared

- Mrs. Harper's prewar novels concerned justice and not slavery

- Mrs. Harper lost fame after the Civil War

**Statements 1 and 5 do not distort.** The author *does* indicate that:

- *Iola Leroy* concerned both the pre-Civil War and post-Civil War periods

- Mrs. Harper was an abolitionist before the war and that her postwar novel *Iola Leroy* was intended to improve relations among the races

## DISTRACTER TYPE 2: THE SWITCH

Some ACT distracters take the truth and switch it around. We call this "the switch." Don't let it fool you. For instance, read this:

> 1. Professor Thorne generally explains a technological discovery first in terms of its history and then in terms of the science on which it was founded.

We've learned that Professor Thorne discusses history *first*, and science *second*.

Now, look at this statement:

> 2. Professor Thorne generally explains a technological discovery first in terms of the science on which it was founded, and then in terms of its history.

Statement 2 looks like Statement 1, but it's backward. Professor Thorne is doing things in the wrong order: science first and history second. Statement 2 takes the truth and turns it around. That's the essence of "the switch."

## But the ACT Writers Get Sneaky

When the ACT writers throw a switch into the answer choices, they don't always write something like Statement 2, which takes the author's statement and literally reverses the order of its words. Sometimes they *change* the wording and at the same time, turn the meaning upside down. Read Statement 1 again, and then look below at Statement 3.

> 3. After Professor Thorne describes the scientific aspects of a technological breakthrough he explains the historical context in which the breakthrough was made.

It's not so easy to see at first, but Statement 3 is a switch. It doesn't use the words "first," or "then," and it begins with the word "after." But think about what it says. Professor Thorne discusses history *after* discussing science. That would mean that he discusses science first and history second. That's opposite to what you're told in the passage.

Now read this:

> 4. Irrespective of population, every state elects two members to the United States Senate. The most populous state and the least populous state thus have equal representation in that important legislative body. In contradistinction, the House of Representatives is population based and the number of representatives elected by any state depends on the number of citizens residing in it.

Here's a switch:

> 5. Representation in the United States Senate is dependent on state population.

From Statement 4 we learned that

- representation in the Senate is *not* based on population.
- representation in the House *is* based on population. Statement 5 is exactly opposite to the original. It's a switch.

### Use Process of Elimination (POE)

Sometimes it's easier to find the correct answer by eliminating the wrong answer choices. If you can eliminate answer choices with the following distracters: distortions, the switch, extreme wording, and answer choices that are too nice, you'll increase your chance of getting the right answer!

## Eliminate the Switch

You're looking at a question. You spot two distortions and you eliminate them. That leaves you with two choices and you aren't sure which is right. One thing you should do is determine whether one of them is a switch. If it is, then the *other* one is right. Here are two passage excerpts, each one followed by two to three questions. For each question, determine which answer choice is the switch.

Read this social sciences excerpt:

> Twenty or thirty thousand years ago *Homo Sapiens* was an uncommon animal, wandering alone or in small groups in a constant search for food. Primitive humans lived by the hunt, and modern nutritionists like to
> 5 observe that with meat as dietary staple, they were seldom iron-deficient as are many farm-based populations today. But the absence of iron deficiency was perhaps the only advantage to the hunting lifestyle of the time. The hunter, it should be remembered, may find himself
> 10 the hunted, and by anything approaching our own standards today, primitive human life was unstable and incessantly hazardous.
>
> In this regard, however, the advent of agriculture improved the human condition. Between ten and twenty
> 15 thousand years ago human beings discovered the use of herding and of growing, which apparently served as inspiration to man's mechanical facilities. Relatively crude weapons of hunt were replaced by more refined farming implements. To be sure, farming is subject to
> 20 the uncertainties of weather and climate but it ultimately allows humans a greater degree of control over their food supply and relieves them from the dangers of the hunt.

1. In terms of the tools and implements made by primitive man, the passage suggests that:
   A. farming tools were less sophisticated than hunting weapons.
   B. [Already eliminated]
   C. agriculture is associated with more advanced tool-making skills.
   D. [Already eliminated]

Look at answer choice A. It says farming tools are less sophisticated than hunting weapons. Now look at the passage, lines 18–19. It says that hunting implements were crude and that farming implements were more refined. Choice A has it backward—it's a switch. Eliminate it!

2. According to the passage, a life based on agriculture:
   A. [Already eliminated]
   B. provides humans with more iron than is provided by hunting.
   C. [Already eliminated]
   D. offers a greater degree of certainty than does a hunting lifestyle.

Look at answer choice B. It says that agriculture provides more iron than does hunting. The author does discuss iron deficiency, but she says that hunters were *not* iron deficient, and that farmers *are*. Choice B is a switch. Eliminate it!

Read this natural science excerpt:

In certain critical respects the magnificence of science lies not in its discovery of what is true but in its identification of that which is not. Pivotal points in scientific learning are those at which some long-held assumption is openly examined and exposed as a
5  falsehood. Copernicus, Kepler, Galileo, and ultimately Newton established that the sun, not the earth, is the fixed center of the solar system and that the earth orbited the sun, thus invalidating the views of Aristotle and Ptolemy, which were largely unquestioned before
10  that time.

Toward the turn of the last century, Michelson, Morley, Lorentz, and Einstein successfully challenged a host of assumptions about the absolute quality of space and time. Then, in the nineteen twenties, theories
15  put forward by Heisenberg, Schrodinger, and Dirac together created the science of quantum mechanics and thus destroyed time-honored views about position and velocity. Even Einstein had difficulty accepting Heisenberg's theory, which dealt a lethal blow to the cherished
20  notion, advocated especially by LaPlace, that science could aspire to complete knowledge of the state of the universe and thus predict its future.

In 1929 Hubble, versed in the writings of Olbers a hundred years before him, showed that the universe
25  was finite but expanding and more or less did away with the prevailing belief that the universe had either to be finite and static or infinite.

1. According to the passage, Ptolemy differed from Copernicus in that:
   A. Ptolemy envisioned a stationary earth and Copernicus did not.
   B. [Already eliminated]
   C. [Already eliminated]
   D. Ptolemy postulated that the earth followed an orbit about the sun and Copernicus did not.

Look at answer choice D. It says that Ptolemy imagined the earth orbiting the sun, and that Copernicus did not imagine the earth orbiting the sun. Now look at lines 6–10 of the passage. They tell us that Copernicus (and others) did *not* believe in a fixed earth. They thought the earth orbited the sun. That view invalidated Ptolemy's view. In other words, Ptolemy thought otherwise. He thought the earth was fixed and that the sun orbited the earth. Choice D is a switch. Eliminate it!

2. According to the passage, Heisenberg's theory:
   A. [Already eliminated]
   B. challenged traditional beliefs about position and velocity.
   C. described a universe that could be understood and predicted.
   D. [Already eliminated]

Look at answer choice C. It says that Heisenberg's principle makes the universe seem predictable. Now read the passage, lines 20–23. They say that Heisenberg's theory *dealt a blow* to the idea that science could attain complete knowledge of the universe and predict its future. Heisenberg's principle *destroyed* the belief that science might completely understand the state of the universe. That means choice C is a switch. Eliminate it!

## Sometimes the Switch Involves a Sneaky Word Substitution

Sometimes the switch involves the substitution of a wrong word (or name) for a right one. The answer choice looks correct, but isn't because one word doesn't belong. Recall the natural science passage and look at this question:

3. The Aristotelian conception of the solar system was:
   A. inconsistent with Newtonian and Galilean insights.
   B. at odds with Copernican and Ptolemic views.
   C. [Already eliminated]
   D. [Already eliminated]

Look at answer choice B. It indicates that Aristotle's views were different from those of Ptolemy and Copernicus. Now look at lines 6–11 of the passage. They tell us that Copernicus, Kepler, Galileo, and Newton challenged the views of Aristotle and Ptolemy. In other words, Aristotle and Ptolemy believed one thing and the other four, including Copernicus, believed another. "Copernican" belongs in the answer choice, but "Ptolemic" does not. Answer choice B is a switch. Eliminate it!

## Sometimes the Switch Gives You a Simple Shortcut to the Right Answer

If the answer choices happen to feature two statements that are basically opposites, then one of them is usually right (and the other, of course, is the switch). That means you can eliminate the remaining two answer options automatically.

For instance, consider the natural science excerpt we just read, and look at these answer choices:

4. Blah, blah, blah…
   A. important in that it shows certain propositions to be true.
   B. important in that it shows certain propositions to be false.
   C. less precise than most scientists believe.
   D. extremely misleading to those who fail to question its premises.

Notice that answer choices A and B are opposites. Without even looking at the question you can conclude that one of them is the right answer. Why? Because the ACT writers are predictable that way. They tend not to present opposing statements unless one of them is right. Answer choices C and D are wrong, and you can eliminate them.

Now, let's look at the question:

4. In the first paragraph the author makes the point
   that natural science can be:
   A. important in that it shows certain propositions to be true.
   B. important in that it shows certain propositions to be false.
   C. less precise than most scientists believe.
   D. extremely misleading to those who fail to question its premises.

## Here's How to Crack It

You know that either answer choice A or B is right. Eliminate C and D. At this point, even if you guessed wildly between A and B you'd stand a fifty-fifty chance of being right. But you don't have to guess wildly. In the first sentence of the paragraph the author states that "In certain critical respects the magnificence of science lies not in its discovery of what is true but in its identification of that which is not." Answer choice B makes the same statement—in camouflage. Answer choice A is the switch. Answer choice **B** is right.

## DISTRACTER TYPE 3: EXTREMES

If an answer choice indicates that something is *always* so, *invariably* so, or *never* so—it's usually wrong. We call such choices *extremes* and you should be very suspicious of them.

Words like "completely," "perfectly," and "absolutely" also signal an extreme.

Extremes tend to be wrong because they're usually *debatable*, and the ACT writers know that. Think about these statements:

> *Patients who are chronically depressed never enjoy their lives.*

Never? *Ever?* It's pretty hard to prove the truth of such a statement.

It's one thing to say that depressed patients *have difficulty* enjoying their lives or that they *tend not* to enjoy their lives. But to say they *never* enjoy their lives just can't be correct.

> *A political leader should seek to make peace at all costs.*

*All* costs? No matter what? That's pretty tough to defend. Such a statement is too debatable to constitute a right answer on the ACT.

> *In order to lead a productive life a citizen must devote all of his energy to his work.*

### Extreme Answer Choices

Look out for answer choices that are too extreme to be the correct answer. These are the best answer choices to eliminate. These answer choices include words such as *always*, *completely*, and *absolutely*.

*All* of his energy? Come on. That statement is too easy to dispute and the ACT writers know it. They can't call it correct.

Extreme statements are easy to write and they're very useful to standardized test writers. When a standardized test writer has trouble thinking of a wrong answer choice for one of her questions, she constructs an extreme.

Without reading any passage, consider this question and determine which answer choice is an extreme.

1. The author's claim that "cause is relative only to perspective" introduces his argument that:
   A. mental well-being depends on physical strength.
   B. how something is perceived depends on its nature.
   C. psychological health requires a perfect upbringing.
   D. psychiatric condition depends on numerous factors, environmental and internal.

## Here's How to Crack It

Answer choice C is extreme. The idea that anything has to be "ideal" or "perfect" or "absolutely precise" or "completely objective" or "totally honest" is usually contrary to ACT philosophy. Eliminate it!

Look at this question and determine which answer choice or choices are extremes.

2. The author believes that practicing psychiatrists:
   F. cannot possibly help patients unless they are completely objective.
   G. are hopelessly confused over the genesis of mental illness.
   H. are scientists notwithstanding the uncertainties that surround psychiatry.
   J. should for the time being treat mental disease in terms of environment.

Answer choices F and G are extremes. The phrases "cannot possibly," "completely objective," and "hopelessly confused" should tip you off.

Read this next question and determine which answer choice or choices are extremes.

3. According to information presented in the third paragraph, an individual organism will not survive to reproductive age unless:
   A. all of its compensatory mechanisms are in ideal balance.
   B. it has adequate homeostatic and feedback responses.
   C. it is capable of complete adaptation to every form of stress.
   D. other individuals of the same species fail to reproduce.

Answer choices A and C are extremes. "Ideal balance," "complete adaptation," "every...stress" are the tip-offs.

# Distracter Type 4: Choices That Sound Too "Nice"

Some distracters will appeal to you simply because they sound "nice," even though they have little to do with the question or the passage. Such distracters might draw on something you already know, or on the surface they might just seem reasonable and correct. Think for instance, about statements like these:

> *Ultimately, the voting public knows its own best interest.*

> *Structure is important, but it should not be imposed in such a way as to stifle creativity.*

> *The ideal society is one that allows for individual difference, but at the same time creates a people united in interest.*

> *All people have a right to live and die with dignity.*

These thoughts are so "nice" and "sensible" as to seem practically beyond challenge. Some students read them and think, "this must be right." Sometimes these kinds of statements do represent the correct answer. But at other times they don't. When you find yourself drawn to such an answer choice, you should check back with the question and ask yourself whether the answer choice is just a sweet and easy sentiment or whether it really *answers* the question you are asked.

For example, look at this prose fiction excerpt and consider the question that follows.

> "And then the men!" said Jonathan, "the men coming aboard drunk, and having to be pounded sober!..." "Well, what can you do?" he went on. "If you don't strike, the men think you're afraid of them...." Jonathan Tinker was plainly part of the horrible tyranny which we all know exists on shipboard; and his listener respected him the more that, though he had heart enough to be ashamed of it, he was too honest not to own it.

1. Jonathan's listener respected him because he believed:
   A. [Already eliminated]
   B. Jonathan did not attempt to conceal his participation in maritime abuse.
   C. Jonathan had a good heart and basically cared for his men.
   D. [Already eliminated]

Look at answer choice C. What could be more correct than a good heart and an honest concern for other people? Answer choice C is tempting, but it isn't right. Nice or not, the author does not state that the listener's respect for Jonathan had anything to do with a good heart or a concern for his men. Read the last two lines of the passage. The listener respected Jonathan because he had the honesty to "own" his acts. He acknowledged his participation in the tyranny.

## Too Nice

Don't automatically fall for answer choices that sound "too nice." Check to see if the statement was actually made in the passage. If not, eliminate this answer choice.

Read this social studies excerpt:

The thought that older citizens might be denied health care on the basis of cost effectiveness is very troublesome and probably not acceptable to modern American society. Yet there is precedent for such policies in other westernized

5 nations. In Sweden, for example, where the overwhelming majority of health care is funded by the government, patients over the age of 55 are not eligible for long-term life-saving renal dialysis. The nation has made a decision to invest a certain amount of its resources in renal dialysis and it does

10 not consider it sensible to provide the service to kidney patients over a certain age. Because Sweden is founded largely on egalitarian principles, a citizen over 55 is not permitted access to renal dialysis even if he is willing to pay for it on his own. The society does not believe that wealth should

15 play a role in longevity. Recently, the United States has inaugurated a number of systems aimed at controlling health care costs and avoiding waste. These include requirements that patients obtain a second opinion before undergoing surgery and utilize review systems aimed at shortening hospital

20 stays. To date, however, no agency or insurer in the United States premises its willingness to pay for health care on the age or the youth of the patient.

1. In Sweden, which of the following measures is designed to promote egalitarianism?
   A. [Already eliminated]
   B. The Swedish government denies certain life-saving medical resources to older citizens.
   C. [Already eliminated]
   D. The Swedish government attempts to provide the same health care to all citizens regardless of wealth or age.

## Here's How to Crack It

Look at answer choice D. Very, very attractive. What could be nicer than equal health care for all? But look at lines 5–15. In Sweden, we are told, citizens over 55 are denied access to renal dialysis. D is wrong, and **B** is right.

# 15

# The Four–Step System

Now that you've learned how to recognize right and wrong answer choices, we're going to teach you a four-step process that leads you systematically to correct answers. We take time to explain each step slowly, so we can be sure you learn it. Because of that you might at first think our system lengthy or cumbersome. It isn't. It's streamlined and efficient. When we're all through, you'll see how speedily it works. (Think about how long it takes to tie a shoe. Now think about how long it would take to tell—not show—someone how to tie a shoe.)

We'll begin by answering the following simple question:

## Why Are ACT Passages Hard to Follow?

You know how to read. So why is it so tough to read an ACT passage? It's tough, first of all, because the passage is pulled out of the middle of some larger work: You're reading it out of context. It's also tough to read an ACT passage because you don't know why you're reading it. You don't know what you're looking for or what you're supposed to "understand."

Stop thinking about the ACT for a second and suppose someone offers you a $20/hour job. She points from her office window to a building sitting on a nearby lot. Then she hands you a key and says, "Check the place out and come back with a report."

That sounds easy enough, except for one thing.

## You Don't Know What You're Looking For

What are you supposed to "check out?" The landscaping? The driveway? Are you looking for chipped paint? Leaky pipes? Broken windows?

You have no idea. So you roam around the place. An hour goes by and you roam back to your boss's office. She asks:

"Are there any mice in the basement?"

You tell her you don't know.

"In a whole hour you couldn't look in the basement and see if there were any mice?"

Of course you could have, but you didn't know she wanted you to. You had a simple job, and you blew it. Why? Because you never really knew what the job was. You didn't know what you were supposed to do.

The same sort of thing holds true for ACT Reading passages. The passages are usually tough to read because you don't know what you're supposed to look for. They become much easier if you solve that problem. Having said that, we're ready to tell you about the first two steps of our system.

**Step #1:**
**Identify the**
**Critical Words**

As you read each question, underline the key words or phrases that tell you the focus of the question.

# STEP 1: FIND THE CRITICAL WORDS AND PHRASES

Step 1 should take you about 30 seconds and here's what it's all about. Before you read the passage, look at the questions (but not the answer choices) and underline their critical words or phrases. Look, for instance, at the question on the following page. (We'll help you ignore the answer choices by turning them all into "blah, blah, blah.")

1. Jeremy Bentham probably would have said that lawyers:
      A. blah, blah, blah...
      B. blah, blah, blah...
      C. blah, blah, blah...
      D. blah, blah, blah...

The question has some pretty ordinary words like "probably," "would," "have," and "that." We might find those words in a lot of different questions. The critical words special to this question are: "Jeremy Bentham" and "lawyers." So, when we say "critical words," we mean the words, phrases, or names that kind of stand out and tell you what the question's about. Look at this question and underline the critical words or phrases:

   2. The author states that the common law differs from the civil law in that:
      F. blah, blah, blah...
      G. blah, blah, blah...
      H. blah, blah, blah...
      J. blah, blah, blah...

There are of course some ordinary words like "author," "states," "from," "differs." This question's critical phrases are "common law" and "civil law."

Try three more:

   1. According to the passage, Peters differs from Jefferson in that:
      A. blah, blah, blah...
      B. blah, blah, blah...
      C. blah, blah, blah...
      D. blah, blah, blah...

   2. As discussed in the passage, the integrative movement produced:
      F. blah, blah, blah...
      G. blah, blah, blah...
      H. blah, blah, blah...
      J. blah, blah, blah...

   3. According to the passage, edema and hypoproteinemia:
      A. blah, blah, blah...
      B. blah, blah, blah...
      C. blah, blah, blah...
      D. blah, blah, blah...

- In question 1, the critical words are "Peters" and "Jefferson."

- In question 2, the critical phrase is "integrative movement."

- In question 3, the critical words are "edema" and "hypoproteinemia."

By the way, when you find critical words, don't worry about their meaning. You don't have to know who Peters is or what edema means. Your job at Step 1 is to see that some name, word, or phrase is the focus of a question. Its meaning doesn't matter.

## SOME QUESTIONS DON'T HAVE CRITICAL WORDS

When you follow Step 1, you're going to notice that some questions don't really have any critical words. Look at these three:

1. Among the following assertions, which represents the writer's opinion, and not a fact?
   A. blah, blah, blah...
   B. blah, blah, blah...
   C. blah, blah, blah...
   D. blah, blah, blah...

2. Which of the following conclusions is drawn by the passage?
   F. blah, blah, blah...
   G. blah, blah, blah...
   H. blah, blah, blah...
   J. blah, blah, blah...

3. The author's discussion would best support which of the following statements?
   A. blah, blah, blah...
   B. blah, blah, blah...
   C. blah, blah, blah...
   D. blah, blah, blah...

As you can see, none of these three questions offers any critical words. "Writer," "opinion," "support," and "conclusion" are pretty ordinary. We might find them in lots of different questions. What do you do with these questions when you're pursuing Step 1? You ignore them. Among the ten questions that follow a passage, usually eight or nine will offer you critical words. Those are the questions you're looking for when you follow Step 1.

Take a look at these ten questions. (We've deleted the answer choices completely.) Figure out which five have critical words and which five don't.

1. Among the following assertions, which represents the writer's opinion, and not a fact?

2. As discussed in the passage, Quentin Bell believes that historians and critics:

3. According to the passage, academicism and mannerism:

4. Which of the following conclusions is drawn by the passage?

5. The third paragraph of the passage makes the point that:

6. According to the passage, Renoir differs from Daleur in that:

7. The author's discussion would best support which of the following statements?

8. In lines 33–42, the author implies that:

9. In the author's view the phrase "modern art"
   means:

10. According to the author, subjectivism affected Rodin in
    which of the following ways?

Questions 2, 3, 6, 9, and 10 have critical words: "Quentin Bell," "academicism," "mannerism," "Renoir," "Daleur," "modern art," "subjectivism." On the other hand, questions 1, 4, 5, 7, and 8 are more general. They don't have critical words. If you were to encounter these 10 questions while pursuing Step 1, you'd focus on 2, 3, 6, 9, and 10. You'd ignore 1, 4, 5, 7, and 8.

**Step #2:
Refer Back to the
Passage for the
Critical Words**

Now that you have identified
the critical words in the
question, you can look for them
in the passage.

# STEP 2: SCAN THE *PASSAGE* FOR CRITICAL WORDS

Step 2 of our system should take you about 30 seconds. In Step 2, you *scan* the passage very quickly looking for the same critical words you noticed at Step 1. You don't read the passage, you scan it. That means you pass your eyes over all of it, trying only to spot the critical words. Every time you see a critical word, underline it.

Here's part of a humanities passage followed by five questions. We want you to

- First follow Step 1: Look at the questions and notice the critical words.

- Then follow Step 2: Scan the passage and underline those same critical words wherever you see them.

At Step 2, you should also underline any words or phrases that seem to be very much like the critical words you find in the questions. For instance, if a question uses the phrase "modern art forms," and the phrase "modern styles of art" appears in the passage, you should underline it.

        Rodin was surely a great artist but he was not an
    innovator as was Cezanne; prevailing tides of subjec-
    tivism came over him. Rodin's mission was to reinvest
    sculpture with the integrity it lost when Michelangelo
  5 had died. Rodin succeeded in this mission. His first true
    work, The *Age of Bronze* (1877), marked the beginning
    of the end of academicism, mannerism, and decadence
    that had prevailed since Michelangelo's last sculpture,
    the *Rondanini Pieta*.

 10     Yet it is largely Cezanne, not Rodin, who was artistic
    ancestor to Picasso, Gonzalez, Brancusi, Archipenko,
    Lipchitz, and Laurens, and they are unquestionably
    the first lights in the "new art" of sculpture. This "new
    art," of course, is the sculpture we call "modern." It is
 15 modern because it breaks with tradition and draws little
    on that which preceded it.

When I speak of "modern" sculpture I do not refer
to every sculptor nor even to every highly talented
sculptor of our age. I do not exclude, necessarily, the
20  sculptors of an earlier time. Modern sculpture, so far as
I am concerned, is any that consciously casts tradition
aside and seeks forms more suitable to the senses and
values of its time. Renoir and Daumier are, in this light,
modern sculptors notwithstanding the earlier time at
25  which they worked. Daleur and Carpeaux are not modern, although they belong chronologically to the recent
era. Professor Quentin Bell argues that historians and
critics name as "modern" those sculptors in whom they
happen to be interested and that the term when abused
30  in that way has no historical or artistic significance.
That, I think, is not right. The problem is that Professor
Bell thinks "modern" means "now," when in fact it
means "new."

1. As discussed in the passage, Quentin Bell believes that
   historians and critics:
   A. blah, blah, blah...
   B. blah, blah, blah...
   C. blah, blah, blah...
   D. blah, blah, blah...

2. According to the passage, academicism and mannerism:
   F. blah, blah, blah...
   G. blah, blah, blah...
   H. blah, blah, blah...
   J. blah, blah, blah...

3. According to the passage Renoir differs from Daleur in
   that:
   A. blah, blah, blah...
   B. blah, blah, blah...
   C. blah, blah, blah...
   D. blah, blah, blah...

4. In the author's view, the phrase "modern art" means:
   F. blah, blah, blah...
   G. blah, blah, blah...
   H. blah, blah, blah...
   J. blah, blah, blah...

5. According to the author, subjectivism affected Rodin in
   which of the following ways?
   A. blah, blah, blah...
   B. blah, blah, blah...
   C. blah, blah, blah...
   D. blah, blah, blah...

In the first question, you see the name Quentin Bell (whoever he is). In the
second, you notice the words "academicism" and "mannerism" (whatever they
mean). In question 3 the critical words are "Renoir" and "Daleur," and in question 4 the critical phrase is "modern art." For question 5 you should notice the
words "subjectivism" and "Rodin."

## So Your Underlined Passage Should Look Something Like This

<u>Rodin</u> was surely a great artist, but he was not an innovator as was Cezanne; prevailing tides of <u>subjectivism</u> came over him. Rodin's mission was to reinvest sculpture with the integrity it lost when Michelangelo had died. Rodin succeeded in this mission. His first true work, *The Age of Bronze* (1877), marked the beginning of the end of <u>academicism</u>, <u>mannerism</u>, and decadence that had prevailed since Michelangelo's last sculpture, the *Rondanini Pieta*.

Yet it is largely Cezanne, not <u>Rodin</u>, who was artistic ancestor to Picasso, Gonzalez, Brancusi, Archipenko, Lipchitz, and Laurens, and they are unquestionably the first lights in the "new art" of sculpture. This "<u>new art</u>," of course, is the sculpture we call "<u>modern</u>." It is modern because it breaks with tradition and draws little on that which preceded it.

When I speak of "modern" sculpture I do not refer to every sculptor nor even to every highly talented sculptor of our age. I do not exclude, necessarily, the sculptors of an earlier time. <u>Modern sculpture</u>, so far as I am concerned, is any that consciously casts tradition aside and seeks forms more suitable to the senses and values of its time. <u>Renoir</u> and Daumier are, in this light, modern sculptors notwithstanding the earlier time at which they worked. <u>Daleur</u> and Carpeaux are not modern, although they belong chronologically to the recent era. Professor <u>Quentin Bell</u> argues that historians and critics name as "<u>modern</u>" those sculptors in whom they happen to be interested and that the term when abused in that way has no historical or artistic significance. That, I think, is not right. The problem is that Professor <u>Bell</u> thinks "<u>modern</u>" means "now," when in fact it means "new."

## Let's Do It Again

Here's another short passage followed by four questions. Follow Steps 1 and 2 just as you did before.

Such relatively reliable insights as we have into the nature of Halley's comet's nucleus derive largely from the work done by the Giotto imaging team. Named for the spacecraft from which six key photographs of the
5   comet were taken at distances ranging from 14,430 to 2,730 kilometers, the team forged a single composite photograph under the directorship of H. Use Keler. As the photograph is normally held, north is up and the sun is at the left.

10    Discernibility of detail varies at different points in
      the photograph. The greatest resolution, 100 meters,
      is found in the upper left portion of the image and the
      poorest resolution, 400 meters, is found at the lower
      right. This circumstance and other of the photograph's
15    features largely reflect the "instructions" that were
      given to the Giotto camera, which had been system-
      atically programmed to track the brightest feature in
      its visual field. This, for example, explains why the
      greatest detail in the composite photograph is of the
20    nucleus's uppermost aspect; it was photographed when
      Giotto was closest to the comet.

      The Giotto photographs have allowed investigators
      to conclude that the surface of the nucleus is rough.
      This conclusion emanates from the observation that
25    the border area between light and dark portions of the
      comet is irregular. In addition, the light side reveals
      a large crater and a hill. The most noticeable of the
      comet's features relate to the movement of dust away
      from selected portions of the comet's nucleus toward
30    the sun. The resulting dust jets are brightly colored and
      likely arise from points and places that lack surface
      crust which then would expose the deeper lying ices to
      the sun.

5. According to the passage, the nuclear surface of Halley's
   comet is believed to be:
   A. blah, blah, blah...
   B. blah, blah, blah...
   C. blah, blah, blah...
   D. blah, blah, blah...

6. As described in the passage, Giotto's camera was
   specifically programmed to:
   F. blah, blah, blah...
   G. blah, blah, blah...
   H. blah, blah, blah...
   J. blah, blah, blah...

7. As used in the passage, the word *resolution* (line 11)
   means:
   A. blah, blah, blah...
   B. blah, blah, blah...
   C. blah, blah, blah...
   D. blah, blah, blah...

8. The passage indicates that H. Use Keler:
   F. blah, blah, blah...
   G. blah, blah, blah...
   H. blah, blah, blah...
   J. blah, blah, blah...

   For question 5, the critical phrase is "nuclear surface." For question 6 it's "Giotto's camera," and for question 7 it's "resolution." For question 8 it's "H. Use Keler."

## Your Underlined Passage Should Look Something Like This

Such relatively reliable insights as we have into the nature of <u>Halley's comet's nucleus</u> derive largely from the work done by the <u>Giotto</u> imaging team. Named for the spacecraft from which six key photographs of the comet were taken at distances ranging from 14,430 to 2,730 kilometers, the team forged a single composite photograph under the directorship of <u>H. Use Keler</u>. As the photograph is normally held, north is up and the sun is at the left.

Discernibility of detail varies at different points in the photograph. The greatest <u>resolution</u>, 100 meters, is found in the upper left portion of the image and the poorest <u>resolution</u>, 400 meters, is found at the lower right. This circumstance and other of the photograph's features largely reflect the "instructions" that were given to the <u>Giotto camera</u>, which had been systematically programmed to track the brightest feature in its visual field. This, for example, explains why the greatest detail in the composite photograph is of the nucleus's uppermost aspect; it was photographed when <u>Giotto</u> was closest to the comet.

The <u>Giotto photographs</u> have allowed investigators to conclude that the <u>surface of the nucleus</u> is rough. This conclusion emanates from the observation that the border area between light and dark portions of the comet is irregular. In addition, the light side reveals a large crater and a hill. The most noticeable of the comet's features relate to the movement of dust away from selected portions of the comet's nucleus toward the sun. The resulting dust jets are brightly colored and likely arise from points and places that lack surface crust which then would expose the deeper lying ices to the sun.

## How Steps 1 and 2 Help You

If you were actually to read a passage from beginning to end you'd never know, as you read, which words or lines you're supposed to understand. Furthermore, when you then went to look at questions about Renoir, H. Use Keler, or the Giotto camera, you'd have to start hunting through the passage to find those words and to figure out what they're all about. By following Steps 1 and 2 you help yourself in two important ways:

1. You avoid wasting time trying to read and comprehend the whole passage.

2. You identify those places in the passage likely to provide answers to the questions you're going to be asked. It's *those* portions of the passage that you'll read carefully when the time comes to answer questions.

## Here's What We Mean

Below is a small piece of the sculpture passage with our underlining in it. There's also a question you've seen before, except this time it has answer choices. Read the question carefully, and look at the answer choices. Then take a look back at the sentence and read *it* very carefully. Think about what it means and figure out which answer choice expresses the same thing—in camouflage. That's the right answer.

> Professor <u>Quentin Bell</u> argues that historians and critics name as "<u>modern</u>" those sculptors in whom they happen to be interested and that the term when abused in that way has no historical or artistic significance.

1. As discussed in the passage, Quentin Bell believes that historians and critics:
   A. should be open-minded to new and innovative art forms.
   B. misuse art and fail to understand its history.
   C. are generally uninterested in modern art.
   D. attach the phrase "modern art" to those sculptors that intrigue them.

The correct answer to this question is **D,** and reading the whole passage definitely would *not* help you answer it any more quickly or accurately. The answer is wholly contained in a single sentence. The author says that Professor Quentin Bell (whoever he is) thinks historians and critics give the name "modern" to the sculptors in whom they happen to be interested. Choice D expresses that same thought—in camouflage.

## YOU WON'T *ALWAYS* FIND THE ANSWER IN A SINGLE SENTENCE

When you're looking for an answer, you might have to go to the underlined words and "read around" a little. You might have to read the sentences that appear immediately before and after the one that has your mark. Sometimes, you'll have to read a whole paragraph.

Here again is the short passage about comets. It's followed by two questions you've already seen, except this time they have answer choices. Follow Steps 1 and 2, and then answer the questions.

> Such relatively reliable insights as we have into the nature of <u>Halley's comet's nucleus</u> derive largely from the work done by the <u>Giotto</u> imaging team. Named for the spacecraft from which six key photographs of the
> 5   comet were taken at distances ranging from 14,430 to 2,730 kilometers, the team forged a single composite photograph under the directorship of <u>H. Use Keler</u>. As the photograph is normally held, north is up and the sun is at the left.
>
> 10    Discernibility of detail varies at different points in the photograph. The greatest <u>resolution</u>, 100 meters, is found in the upper left portion of the image and the

poorest <u>resolution</u>, 400 meters, is found at the lower right. This circumstance and other of the photograph's
15 features largely reflect the "instructions" that were given to the <u>Giotto camera</u>, which had been systematically programmed to track the brightest feature in its visual field. This, for example, explains why the greatest detail in the composite photograph is of the
20 <u>nucleus's uppermost aspect</u>; it was photographed when <u>Giotto</u> was closest to the comet.

The <u>Giotto photographs</u> have allowed investigators to conclude that the <u>surface of the nucleus</u> is rough. This conclusion e manates from the observation that
25 the border area between light and dark portions of the comet is irregular. In addition, the light side reveals a large crater and a hill. The most noticeable of the comet's features relate to the movement of dust away from selected portions of the comet's nucleus toward
30 the sun. The resulting dust jets are brightly colored and likely arise from points and places that lack surface crust which then would expose the deeper lying ices to the sun.

1. According to the passage, the nuclear surface of Halley's comet is believed to be:

   A. smooth since the interface of light and dark shows high resolution.
   B. rough, since a visible border area is irregularly shaped.
   C. smooth at some points and rough at others, depending on the relative degrees of light and dark.
   D. undetectable since even the most sophisticated instruments have limitations.

2. As described in the passage, the Giotto camera was specifically programmed to:

   F. send "instructions" to Halley's comet regarding detail and resolution.
   G. identify the portions of the comet that had relatively low light intensity.
   H. detect areas of Halley's comet that bordered on light and dark.
   J. photograph those areas of Halley's comet that gave off the most light.

**Reminder**
Underline key words or phrases that resemble the critical words in the question. If you don't find the answer, read the sentences surrounding the underlined portion of the passage.

## Here's How to Crack It

The first question concerns the "nuclear surface" of Halley's comet. That precise phrase does not appear in the passage, but the phrase "surface of the nucleus" shows up on line 23. That sentence and the one immediately following it give you the answer to the first question.

The <u>Giotto photographs</u> have allowed investigators to conclude that the <u>surface of the nucleus</u> is rough. This conclusion emanates from the observation that the border area between light and dark portions of the comet is irregular.

These two sentences are telling you that Halley's comet has light and dark areas, and that the border between these areas is irregular. When scientists noticed this they concluded that the surface of the nucleus was rough. You don't have to understand *why* that observation led to that conclusion. You just have to realize that these two sentences are telling you it did. Once you realize that, you know that the correct answer is **B**.

The second question refers to "the Giotto camera." So, when we first scanned the passage we underlined the word Giotto everywhere it appeared. Look at the sentence that specifically mentions the "Giotto camera." What does it say?

> This circumstance and other of the photograph's features largely reflect the "instructions" that were given to the Giotto camera, which had been systematically programmed to track the brightest feature in its visual field.

The Giotto camera was systematically programmed to track the brightest feature in its visual field. Among the answer options, **J** is best. "Brightest feature" is camouflage for "areas . . . that gave off the most light."

## STEP 3: SKIM AND SCRIBBLE

Step 3 should take you about 60 seconds. In Step 3, you skim the passage, and in the margin of each paragraph you scribble a few words that describe its main idea. When we say "skim" we mean you should read fast, so fast that you're uncomfortable, and not at all sure you comprehend the passage in detail. (Remember, you're not trying to understand the passage. You're trying to earn a high score on the ACT.) As you speed through each paragraph you should

- direct a little more attention to the first two sentences than to the remainder

- ask yourself: What, basically, is this paragraph about?

Then, in two or three words scribble an answer in the margin.
Here are three paragraphs from a humanities passage. Let's skim and scribble.

> If we were to start fresh in the study of sculpture or any art we might observe that the record is largely filled by works of relatively few great contributors. Next to the influences of these great geniuses, time periods themselves are of little significance. The study of art and art history are properly directed to the achievements of outstanding individual artists, not the particular decade or century in which any may have worked.
>
> Nonetheless, when we study art in historical perspective we select a convenient frame of reference through which diverse styles and talents are to be compared. Hence we write of "movements" and attempt

to understand each artist in terms of the one to which he "belongs." Movements have limited use, but we should not talk of realism, impressionism, cubism, or surrealism as though they genuinely had lives of their own to which the artist was answerable. We regard the movement as the governing force and the artist as its servant. Yet it is well to remember that the movements do not necessarily present themselves in orderly chronological series and the individual artist frequently weaves her way into one and out of another over the course of a single career.

Great artists are not normally confined by the "movements" that others may name for them. Rather, they transcend the conventional structure working now in one style, then in another, and later in a third. Picasso's work, for example, echoes many of the artistic movements, and other artists, too, work their way from one style through another. Indeed, artists are people, and any may decide to alter her style for no more complex a reason than that which makes most people want to "try something new" once in a while.

## Step #3:
## Skim the Passage

As you read the passage, underline key phrases in the passage or jot down notes next to each paragraph. Don't try to memorize information in the passage, just know the lay of the land.

## Paragraph 1

The paragraph seems to be about the fact that individual artists are more important than the time periods in which they work. So, you scribble:

*artist > periods*

That's enough.

## Paragraph 2

The second paragraph has something to do with artistic "movements." What should you scribble?

*movements*

## Paragraph 3

The third paragraph tells us that great artists don't really conform to movements. They vary their styles over time. So, for paragraph 3 you scribble:

*artists switch styles*

Enough said, and enough scribbled.

After practice, skim and scribble should take you about one minute per passage.

## Use Trigger Words

When you're skimming a passage, pay attention to words that *signal a change in direction*. In line 1 of the second paragraph, for instance, we see the word "nonetheless," which means the author is about to criticize, negate, or "take something away" from thoughts previously expressed. "Nonetheless" is what we call a *trigger word*. Trigger words tell you the author is about to "go somewhere," and you should watch where he's going. Sometimes a trigger word means the author is reaching some sort of conclusion ("therefore," "hence" ).

Here are 15 trigger words and/or phrases:

Despite • However, • In spite of • Nonetheless • On the other hand • On the contrary • Yet • Notwithstanding • But • Ironically • Rather • Unfortunately • Therefore • Hence • Consequently

## Look for Trigger Words

What are trigger words? Trigger words are words that signal a change in a sentence. Some of the most common trigger words are *but, although, despite,* and *however.*

An alarm should go off every time you see one of these words. Trigger words will help you figure out what a paragraph is all about. The "nonetheless" at the beginning of paragraph two indicates that the author's going to say something that kind of opposes what he said in the first paragraph. He says there's some purpose in thinking of art in terms of "movements," even though he has already said the individual artist is more important than time periods.

## Try Another Skim and Scribble

Here are four paragraphs from the comet passage. Skim and scribble. See if you can do it in a minute.

On the other hand, the Giotto photographs reveal virtually nothing of the interior of the comet's nucleus or its rotational period. For instance, it is not known, even, whether the interior of the nucleus had a density greater than or less than 1 gram per cubic centimeter, which is the density of water. Hans Rickman has attempted to estimate the comet's density, hoping, with good reason, that this information would ultimately lead to better understanding of the nuclear interior. Rickman recognized that if he could gain estimates of the comet's mass and volume he would be able to derive an estimate of density from the simple physical formulas relating mass, volume, and density: He would divide the volume into the mass and arrive at an estimate.

The comet's overall dimensions were already known to an approximation and on this basis Rickman took the volume as 500–550 cubic kilometers. He then employed a rather ingenious method of estimating the nuclear mass. Rickman considered the fact that the comet was losing gas at all times and that the expulsion produced a thrust. He then reasoned, according to simple law, that mass times the thrust due to expelled gas had to equal the product [rate at which mass was lost by expulsion of gas and dust] and the velocity of the expelled substance. Rickman then derived estimates of these values from the comet's motion and from the rate at which the comet visibly produced water. Rickman arrived at a value of 0.1 to 0.3 grams per cubic centimeter for the density of Halley's nucleus.

Using an analogous technique, R.Z. Sagdeev and colleagues arrived at a value of 0.2 to 1.5 grams per cubic centimeter. Stanton J. Peale, however, wrote that he had little confidence in the estimates of mass and volume that had been used in connection with the density calculations. He believed that little could be said about the nuclear density except that it was approximately equal to 1 gram per cubic centimeter.

Zdenek Sekanina and Stephen M. Larson studied the rotational period by first processing images of 1920 photographs in an attempt to improve the image of spiral dust features. They assumed that the spiral dust characteristics were caused by emission from distinct parts of the nuclear surface and that these areas were visible when rotation brought them into sunlight and were invisible in the dark of the cometary night. On these premises, the pair estimated that Halley has a rotation period of 2.2 days, and some spacecraft data have seemed to confirm the figure. However, Robert L. Millis and David G. Schleicher estimated a rotational period of 7.4 days by resort to filters that allowed them to explore fluorescence of CN, C and $C_2$ emissions and the continuum emission from dust particles. Other investigators have reported additional approximations of Halley's rotational period and the issue remains, for the time being, clouded.

The first paragraph has something to do with the inside of the comet. Maybe it's about density too. So we scribble:

*interior, density*

The second paragraph seems to provide details about what someone named Rickman did to calculate the density of the comet's interior.

*Rickman, details, density*

The third paragraph concerns what other scientists said and did in response to Rickman's work.

*other peop.*

The last paragraph has something to do with calculating the comet's rotational period.

*rotat. per.*

So, that's what we're talking about. It doesn't take long. Steps 1 through 3 together should take, maybe, one and a half to two minutes.

## SUMMARY: STEPS 1, 2, AND 3

- **Step 1—Note Critical Words:** Look quickly at the questions. Notice critical words. Ignore questions that don't have critical words.
  *Approximate Time:* 30 seconds

- **Step 2—Scan and Underline:** Scan the passage and underline critical words.
  *Approximate Time:* 30 Seconds

- **Step 3—Skim and Scribble:** Read the passage at racing speed giving special attention to the first two to three sentences of each paragraph. For each paragraph, scribble in the margin a few words that describe the main subject.
  *Approximate Time:* 60 seconds

## AFTER STEPS 1, 2, AND 3

After you've spent about two minutes completing Steps 1, 2, and 3, the passage will be underlined and scribbled. The next thing you do is go back to the questions.

Here's the full humanities passage about modern sculpture. It's underlined and scribbled, and it's complete with ten questions. Even though we've already completed Steps 1–3 for you, you should run through them again yourself so you're familiar with the underlining and scribbling. After you do that we'll discuss Step 4, which is called "the loop."

*artist>period*

If we were to start fresh in the study of sculpture or any art we might observe that the record is largely filled by works of relatively few great contributors. Next to the influences of these great geniuses, time
5 periods themselves are of little significance. The study of art and art history are properly directed to the achievements of outstanding individual artists, not the particular decade or century in which any may have worked.

*movements*

10 Nonetheless, when we study art in historical perspective we select a convenient frame of reference through which diverse styles and talents are to be compared. Hence we write of "<u>movements</u>" and attempt to understand each artist in terms of the one to which
15 he "belongs." <u>Movements</u> have limited use, but we should not talk of <u>realism</u>, <u>impressionism</u>, <u>cubism</u>, or <u>surrealism</u> as though they genuinely had lives of their own to which the artist was answerable. We regard the movement as the governing force and the artist as
20 its servant. Yet it is well to remember that the movements do not necessarily present themselves in orderly chronological series and the individual artist frequently weaves her way into one and out of another over the course of a single career.

25 Great artists are not normally confined by the "movements" that others may name for them. Rather, they transcend the conventional structure working now in one style, then in another, and later in a third.

*artists switch styles*

Picasso's work, for example, echoes many of the
30 artistic movements, and other artists too, work their way from one style through another. Indeed, artists are people, and any may decide to alter her style for no more complex a reason than that which makes most people want to "try something new" once in a while.

35 In studying modern sculpture one is tempted to begin a history with Auguste Rodin (1840–1917), who

*Rodin and Cezanne*

was a contemporary of Cezanne. Yet the two artists did not, in artistic terms, belong to the same period. Their strategies and objectives differed. Although Rodin
40 and Cezanne was surely a great artist he did not do for sculpture what Cezanne did for painting. In fact, although Cezanne was a painter, he had a more lasting effect on sculpture than did Rodin.

Cezanne's work constitutes a reaction against
45 impressionism and the confusion he thought it created. He searched persistently for the "motif." Cezanne

*Cezanne v. Impressionism*

strived for clarity of form and was able to convert his personal perceptions into concrete, recognizable substance. He is justly considered to have offered the first
50 glimmer of a new art—a new classicism.

Rodin was surely a great artist but he was not an innovator as was Cezanne; prevailing tides of subjec-

*Rodin not innovator; recalled Michelangelo*

tivism came over him. Rodin's mission was to reinvest sculpture with the integrity it lost when Michelangelo
55 had died. Rodin succeeded in this mission. His first true work, *The Age of Bronze* (1877), marked the beginning of the end of academicism, mannerism, and decadence that had prevailed since Michelangelo's last sculpture, the *Rondanini Pieta.*

60 Yet it is largely Cezanne, not Rodin, who was

*Cezanne influenced "modern" sculpture*

artistic ancestor to Picasso, Gonzalez, Brancusi, Archipenko, Lipchitz, and Laurens, and they are unquestionably the first lights in the "new art" of sculpture. This "new art," of course, is the sculpture we call
65 "modern." It is modern because it breaks with tradition and draws little on that which preceded it.

When I speak of "modern" sculpture I do not refer to every sculptor nor even to every highly talented sculptor of our age. I do not exclude, necessarily, the sculptors

*"modern" does not necessarily mean "recent"*

70 of an earlier time. Modern sculpture, so far as I am concerned, is any that consciously casts tradition aside and seeks forms more suitable to the senses and values of its time. Renoir and Daumier are, in this light, modern sculptors notwithstanding the earlier time at which they
75 worked. Daleur and Carpeaux are not modern, although they belong chronologically to the recent era.

Professor Quentin Bell argues that historians and critics name as "modern" those sculptors in whom they happen to be interested and that the term when abused in that way has no historical or artistic significance. That, I think, is not right. The problem is that Professor Bell thinks "modern" means "now," when in fact it means "new."

1. Which of the following conclusions is drawn by the passage?
   A. Cezanne had greater influence on modern sculpture than did Rodin.
   B. Rodin made no significant contribution to modern sculpture.
   C. Daumier should not be considered a modern sculptor.
   D. Carpeaux should be considered a modern sculptor.

2. As discussed in the passage, Quentin Bell believes that historians and critics:
   F. have no appreciation for the value of modern art.
   G. abuse art and its history.
   H. should evaluate works of art on the basis of their merit without regard to the artist's fame.
   J. attach the phrase "modern art" to those sculptors that intrigue them.

3. The author expresses the idea that:
   A. art should never be studied in terms of movements.
   B. true artists are seldom understandable in terms of a single movement.
   C. lesser artists do not usually vary their styles.
   D. great artists are always nonconformists.

4. According to the passage, academicism and mannerism:
   F. were readily visible in Rodin's earliest work.
   G. are partially manifest in the *Rondanini Pieta*.
   H. characterized the work of artists who followed Michelangelo.
   J. were primarily part of the Bronze Age.

5. Among the following assertions, which represents the writer's opinion, and not a fact?
   A. Realism, impressionism, cubism, and surrealism are recognized artistic movements.
   B. Cezanne is said to have had a primary role in creating a new art.
   C. A true modern artist is one who transcends tradition.
   D. Rodin and Cezanne were contemporaries.

6. According to the passage, Renoir differs from Daleur in that:
   F. Daleur had no inspiration and Renoir was tremendously inspired.
   G. Renoir's work was highly innovative and Daleur's was not.
   H. Daleur was a sculptor and Renoir was not.
   J. Renoir revered tradition and Daleur did not.

7. According to the fifth paragraph, Cezanne's work is characterized by:
   A. a return to subjectivism.
   B. a pointless search for form.
   C. excessively personal expressions.
   D. rejection of the impressionistic philosophy.

8. In lines 52–54, the author implies that:
   F. mannerism reflects a lack of integrity.
   G. Rodin disliked the work of Michelangelo.
   H. Rodin embraced the notion of decadence.
   J. Rodin should have resisted the appeal of subjectivism.

9. In the author's view, the phrase "modern sculpture" means sculpture that:
   A. postdates the *Rondanini Pieta*.
   B. is not significantly tied to work that comes before it.
   C. shows no artistic merit.
   D. genuinely interests contemporary critics.

10. According to the author, subjectivism affected Rodin in which of the following ways?
    F. It ended his affiliation with mannerism.
    G. It caused him to lose his artistic integrity.
    H. It limited his ability to innovate.
    J. It caused him to become decadent.

## QUESTIONS THAT POINT

With the passage underlined and scribbled, go back to the questions, but don't go necessarily to question 1. Go first to the questions that point you to an answer. Look at questions 1–10 on the last passage. Questions 2, 4, 6, 7, 8, 9, and 10 point to the answer. Questions 2, 4, 6, 7, 9, and 10 have critical words. For those questions we've already underlined the relevant sections of the passage, and we know where to look.

- Question 7 sends us directly to the relevant paragraph (and also features the critical word "Cezanne").

- Question 8 directs us to the relevant portion of the passage by citing line numbers.

- Questions 1, 3, and 5 don't point anywhere. We'll save them for last.

Now we're ready to answer questions, which means we're ready for the following step.

# STEP 4: THE LOOP

Step 4 should take you about 40 seconds per question.

- Go to the first question that points. Read it.

- Go to the appropriate portion of the passage. (Either you've underlined it or the question sends you there.)

- Read it carefully. Understand it as best you can.

- Go back to the question and look at the answer choices.

## Step #4:
## Practice the Loop

Once you've practiced using these techniques you can put them together and form "the loop." Read the question, go to the passage, underline the appropriate words or phrases that relate to the question, then go to the answer choices. As you read each answer choice watch out for the distracters. If you're stuck, then take another pass through the loop.

Now, suppose something strikes you as correct. Be suspicious. Ask yourself if you're falling for a distortion or a switch, or something too "nice." If you consider those possibilities and still think the answer is right, choose it and go to the next question.

Now, suppose that when you come back to the question nothing strikes you as right. Fine. Try to eliminate answers that are wrong. Look for a distortion, a switch, a statement in the extreme, and eliminate! (In the process the right answer might strike you, in which case you'll choose it and move on.)

If you don't settle on an answer, take a second pass through the loop.

- Go back to the appropriate portion of the passage.

- Read it again. Understand it as best you can.

- Come back to the question.

- Look at the choices that still remain (some were eliminated a few seconds earlier, during your first pass through the loop).

If one of the choices now strikes you as correct, choose it. If nothing strikes you as correct, see if you can eliminate—and then guess among whatever answer choices remain.

## PRACTICE THE LOOP

We'll start with question 2 because question 1 doesn't point.

2. As discussed in the passage, Quentin Bell believes that historians and critics:

   F. have no appreciation for the value of modern art.
   G. abuse art and its history.
   H. should evaluate works of art on the basis of their merit without regard to the artist's fame.
   J. attach the phrase "modern art" to those sculptors that intrigue them.

## Here's How to Crack It

We go to the relevant part of the passage, which we've already underlined.

> Professor <u>Quentin Bell</u> argues that historians and critics name as "<u>modern</u>" those sculptors in whom they happen to be interested and that the term when abused in that way has no historical or artistic significance.

- We read it carefully and try to understand it.

- We go back to the question.

Suppose nothing strikes us as right. Fine. We look for answers that are wrong. Answer choice F is a statement in the extreme ("<u>no</u>" appreciation). We eliminate it!

Choice H is very "nice" and very irrelevant. We eliminate it!

We're left with G and J, and we're not sure which is right.

So we take a second pass through the loop.

- We go back to the relevant part of the passage and read it again.

- We return to the question and try to choose again between G and J.

We're still not sure, so we try to eliminate one of the choices. Answer choice G, we now see, is a distortion. (The author uses the word "abuse," but he doesn't say that anyone abuses art or its history.) We eliminate G. That leaves **J**, so we choose it.

Altogether we've spent 30 to 50 seconds answering question 2.

## WE'RE READY FOR QUESTION 4

Use the loop to answer question 4:

4. According to the passage, academicism and mannerism:
   F. were readily visible in Rodin's first true work.
   G. are partially manifest in the *Rondanini Pieta.*
   H. characterized the work of artists who followed Michelangelo.
   J. were primarily part of the Bronze Age.

## Here's How to Crack It

We go to the pertinent part of the passage:

> <u>Rodin</u> was surely a great artist but he was not an innovator as was Cezanne; prevailing tides of <u>subjectivism</u> came over him. <u>Rodin</u>'s mission was to reinvest sculpture with the integrity it lost when Michelangelo had died. <u>Rodin</u> succeeded in this mission. His first true work, *The Age of Bronze* (1877), marked the beginning of the end of <u>academicism</u>, <u>mannerism</u>, and decadence that had prevailed since Michelangelo's last sculpture, the *Rondanini Pieta.*

- We read it carefully and try to understand it.

- We go back to the question.

We're not sure of the answer, but we realize that choices F and J are distortions, so we eliminate them! We're left with G and H.

Now, we take a second pass through the loop.

- We go back to the relevant part of the passage and read it again.

- We return to the question.

The last sentence tells us that academicism, mannerism, and decadence were around *since Michelangelo produced his last sculpture*. Answer choice H says the same thing—in camouflage. We choose **H** and move on.

## USE THE LOOP TO ANSWER QUESTION 6

6. According to the passage, Renoir differs from Daleur in that:
   F. Daleur had no inspiration and Renoir was tremendously inspired.
   G. Renoir's work was highly innovative and Daleur's was not.
   H. Daleur was a sculptor and Renoir was not.
   J. Renoir revered tradition and Daleur did not.

### Here's How to Crack It

- We read the important part of the passage carefully.

> When I speak of "modern" sculpture I do not refer to every sculptor nor even to every highly talented sculptor of our age. I do not exclude, necessarily, the sculptors of an earlier time. Modern sculpture, so far as I am concerned, is any that consciously casts tradition aside and seeks forms more suitable to the senses and values of its time. Renoir and Daumier are, in this light, modern sculptors notwithstanding the earlier time at which they worked. Daleur and Carpeaux are not modern although they belong chronologically to the recent era.

- We come back to the question.

- F is a statement in the extreme. We eliminate it!

- H is a switch. (The passage tells you that "Renoir and Daumier are modern sculptors." That means Renoir was a sculptor.) We eliminate it!

- We take a second pass.
  The author writes that modern sculpture is any that "casts tradition aside..." Then he writes that Renoir is a modern sculptor, and Daleur is not. That means Renoir casts tradition aside and Daleur does not. Choice G says the same thing in camouflage, so **G** is right. (J is a distortion.)

Now, use the loop to answer questions 7–10. When you're done, you can read on from here, and compare your reasoning to ours.

# Let's See How You Did

7. According to the fifth paragraph, Cezanne's work is characterized by:
   - A. a return to subjectivism.
   - B. a pointless search for form.
   - C. excessively personal expressions.
   - D. rejection of the impressionistic philosophy.

## Here's How to Crack It

We go to paragraph 5:

> <u>Cezanne's</u> work constitutes a reaction against <u>impressionism</u> and the confusion he thought it created. He searched persistently for the "<u>motif</u>." <u>Cezanne</u> strived for clarity of form and was able to convert his personal perceptions into concrete, recognizable substance. He is justly considered to have offered the first glimmer of a new art—a new classicism.

- Go back to the question. Answer choice B is extreme (and ridiculous). Eliminate it! With our eye on A, C, and D, we take a second pass. The first sentence tells us that Cezanne reacted against impressionism. Choice **D** says the same thing—in camouflage.

Question 8: **J** is right.

- F, G, and H are distortions.

Question 9: **B** is right.

- A and D are distortions. C is a statement in the extreme.

Question 10: **H** is right.

- F, G, and J are distortions.

## What If You *Can't* Settle on an Answer?

Simple. You guess. If you've taken two (or maybe three) passes through the loop, and you still can't decide on an answer, look at the choices still remaining, take a guess, and move on. Remember: Having eliminated one or two choices, you've raised the odds that your guess will be right.

## The Questions We Didn't Answer: 1, 3, and 5

We held questions 1, 3, and 5 for last because they don't point. Now it's time to answer them. For questions that don't point, you:

- Use the answer choices to tell you what the question is about.

- Use your scribbles to get you to the right part of the passage.

Here are the answer choices for question 1:

A. Cezanne had greater influence on modern sculpture than did Rodin.
B. Rodin made no significant contribution to modern sculpture.
C. Daumier should not be considered a modern sculptor.
D. Carpeaux should be considered a modern sculptor.

Apparently this question has a lot to do with the phrase *modern sculpture*. For paragraph 8 we scribbled:

*modern does not necessarily mean recent*

So, you go to paragraph 8. From there on, you follow the loop. The correct answer is **A.**

- Answer choice B is extreme.

- Answer choices C and D are both switches.

Let's look at question 3. Here are the answer choices:

A. art should never be studied in terms of movements.
B. true artists are seldom understandable in terms of a single movement.
C. lesser artists do not usually vary their styles.
D. great artists are always nonconformists.

Apparently, the question has something to do with movements and style. It calls our attention to paragraphs 2 and 3 where we scribbled:

*(2) movements*

*(3) artists switch styles*

It turns out that the answer is in paragraph 3. It's **B.**

- Answer choices A and D are extreme.

- Answer choice C is a distortion.

Now, what about question 5? Question 5 is a *Fact vs. Opinion* question, and we're going to discuss it separately in our next section.

# SUMMARY: STEPS 1–4

> **Step 1—Find the Critical Words**
>
> Time: 30 seconds
>
> **Step 2—Scan the Passage for Critical Words**
>
> Time: 30 seconds
>
> **Step 3—Skim and Scribble**
>
> Time: 60 seconds
>
> **Step 4—The Loop**
>
> Time: 40 seconds per question

## SPECIAL QUESTION TYPE: FACT VS. OPINION

When you take the ACT Reading Test, you'll probably have one or two questions that ask you to distinguish between a fact and the author's opinion:

> 5. Which of the following statements is the author's opinion and not a fact?
>    A. blah, blah, blah...
>    B. blah, blah, blah...
>    C. blah, blah, blah...
>    D. blah, blah, blah...

> **Some Question Types Do Not Require That You Go Through the Loop.**
>
> Why? The answer is not found in the passage. These question types are:
> The author's opinion questions and tone questions.

You'll probably be able to answer fact vs. opinion questions without looking at the passage. Just look at the answer choices and remember that in the test writer's mind

- a statement is a "fact" if you can say this about it: It's either true or it isn't.

- a statement is an "opinion" if you can say this about it: People might disagree.

**Fact:** Trees are alive. (Either it's true or it isn't.)

**Opinion:** Trees are beautiful. (People might disagree.)

**Fact:** In order to serve as president of the United States, one must be 35 years old or older. (Either it's true or it isn't.)

**Opinion:** Those with greater political experience make better presidents. (People might disagree.)

**Fact:** Professor George Rosen spent his professional life studying the history of medicine. (Either it's true or it isn't.)

**Opinion:** The history of medicine is at least as important as medicine itself. (People might disagree.)

Look at these five statements. Decide which ones sound like facts, and which sound like opinions.

1. World War II proceeded for several years before the United States sent its troops to engage in combat.

2. The United States would have been better advised to enter World War II in 1939.

3. World War II was the most tragic military conflict in history.

4. With respect to World War II, Germany surrendered to the allies before Japan did.

5. During World War II many of the allied nations experienced domestic shortages in steel and rubber.

The ACT writers would say that statements 1, 4, and 5 represent facts.

- **Statement 1:** The United States did not involve itself in World War II combat until several years after the war had begun.

  *Either it's true or it isn't.*

- **Statement 4:** Germany surrendered before Japan did.

  *Either it's true or it isn't.*

- **Statement 5:** The allied nations experienced shortages.

  *Either it's true or it isn't.*

On the other hand, statements 2 and 3 represent what the ACT writers would call opinions.

- **Statement 2:** Who's to say that the United States should have entered the war earlier? One person might think so. Another might disagree.

  *People might disagree.*

- **Statement 3:** Who's to say which war was most "tragic"? Different people have different ideas about tragedy. One person might think the most tragic war of all was World War II. Another might think it was the American Civil War, and a third might believe that all wars are equally tragic.

  *People might disagree.*

Here are five more statements. Decide which ones sound like facts and which sound like opinions.

6. Painting and drawing are not usually called performing arts.

7. Most professional musicians do not really have genuine musical talent.

8. Comparing a painter to a pianist is like comparing a dining table to a desk.

9. Most people who aspire to be actors are employed part-time in fields outside of acting.

10. There have been very few great actors in the last century.

The ACT writers would say that statements 6 and 9 represent facts.

- **Statement 6:** People don't usually use the term "performing arts" to describe painting and drawing.

  *Either it's true or it isn't.*

- **Statement 9:** Most aspiring actors have jobs outside of the acting field.

  *Either it's true or it isn't.*

The ACT writers would say that statements 7, 8, and 10 represent opinions.

- **Statement 7:** Who's to say that someone does or doesn't have talent?

  *People might disagree.*

- **Statement 8:** Who's to say that these two comparisons are similar?

  *People might disagree.*

- **Statement 10:** Who's to say whether an actor is or isn't "great"?

  *People might disagree.*

Now, let's look at question 5 from the previous section, and decide which of the answer choices represents "opinion."

5. Among the following assertions, which represents the writer's opinion, and not a fact?
   A. Realism, impressionism, cubism, and surrealism are recognized artistic movements.
   B. Cezanne is said to have had a primary role in creating a new art.
   C. A true modern artist is one who transcends tradition.
   D. Rodin and Cezanne were contemporaries.

Choice C is the ACT answer. Who's to say that someone is or is not a "true" modern artist?

## Fact vs. Opinion: Don't Use the Loop

When you're answering a fact vs. opinion question, don't use the loop. Just look for the choice that makes you want to say, "people might disagree."

## SPECIAL QUESTION TYPE: STATE OF MIND QUESTIONS

When you take the ACT, you'll probably get a few questions that ask you to describe an attitude or state of mind. Often, the answer choices have just one word:

1. The author's attitude toward…blah, blah, blah…is best described as:
   A. skeptical.
   B. approving.
   C. concerned.
   D. hopeful.

In a literature passage these questions pertain not to the author, but to some character. Read this final paragraph of a prose fiction passage and look at the question that follows it.

So they parted with a shake of the hand, Jonathan Tinker saying that he believed he should go down to the vessel and sleep aboard, if he could sleep, and murmuring at the last moment the hope of returning the compliment, while the contributor walked homeward, weary to the flesh, but, in spite of his sympathy for Jonathan Tinker, very elated in spirit. The truth is, and however disgraceful to human nature, let the truth be told, he had recurred to his primal satisfaction in the man as calamity capable of being used for such and such literary ends, and, while he pitied him, rejoiced in him as an episode of real life quite as striking and complete as anything in fiction.

1. As final response to his conversation with Jonathan Tinker, the contributor experienced a feeling of:
   A. worry.
   B. amusement.
   C. gratification.
   D. disappointment.

If this kind of item throws you, it's probably because you start thinking about the distracters and lose sight of the question.

## Here's How to Crack It

- Think about the person and the situation about which you're being asked.

- Turn the item into four true/false questions by saying to yourself:

    TRUE/FALSE      "This guy was _____"

and fill in the blank with each of the answer choices. When you hit a statement that's true, you've got the ACT answer.

Let's try it.

- We think about the contributor as he is described in the last paragraph, and we say to ourselves (very quickly):

    TRUE/FALSE      "This guy was <u>worried</u>."

    TRUE/FALSE      "This guy was <u>amused</u>."

    TRUE/FALSE      "This guy was <u>gratified</u>."

    TRUE/FALSE      "This guy was <u>disappointed</u>."

Answer choices A, B, and D yield statements that sound false. There's nothing in the paragraph to suggest that this guy was worried or disappointed, and he's not particularly amused either. (He didn't, for example, "chuckle," or "grin.") The paragraph tells us that the contributor experiences "satisfaction," and that he "rejoices." Answer choice **C** yields a statement that seems true.

Try another one:

> Many decisions of the United States Supreme Court are inconsistent with the precedents by which they are theoretically balanced. It is true that the court has some freedom to overrule its own precedents, but in such cases it is expected to announce, forthrightly, that it has determined a particular precedent to be erroneous, and that such precedent is renounced.
>
> Contrary to what should be so, however, there are a great many occasions on which the Supreme Court does in fact disavow its own precedents without acknowledging that it has done so. Instead, the Court contrives some implausible distinction between the precedent and the case before it, and purports dishonestly to abide by a precedent it has in fact determined to repudiate.

1. In this passage, the author's attitude toward the United States Supreme Court is best described as one of:
   A. criticism.
   B. disbelief.
   C. appreciation.
   D. surprise.

## Here's How to Crack It

- We consider what the author has said about the Supreme Court's attitude toward precedent. She objects to the dishonesty through which the Court sometimes avoids precedent while pretending to honor it.

- We make four true/false questions:

  TRUE/FALSE      "This woman is <u>critical</u>."

  TRUE/FALSE      "This woman is in a state of <u>disbelief</u>."

  TRUE/FALSE      "This woman is <u>appreciative</u>."

  TRUE/FALSE      "This woman is <u>surprised</u>."

The correct answer choice is **A**. The author thinks that if the Supreme Court decides not to abide by a precedent, it should do so honestly. Contrary to what should be so, the author explains, the Court rejects precedents while pretending to honor them. She's making a criticism.

**PART ◆ V**

# How to Beat the ACT Science Reasoning Test

# THE SCIENCE REASONING TEST

Remember that tough biology test for which you had to memorize dozens of facts about photosynthesis? When you sat down to take the test, you either knew the answers or you didn't. Well, that's not the case on the science portion of the ACT. Even though the word "science" appears in the title, this section doesn't resemble the science tests you've had in high school. The ACT Science Reasoning Test presents you with science-based reading passages and requires that you answer questions about them. Sounds just like the Reading Test, doesn't it? That's because it *is* just like the Reading Test. Rather than test your knowledge of science, it's supposed to test your ability to "think about science."

Of course, a little science knowledge doesn't hurt. If a passage is about photosynthesis, you'll undoubtedly do better if you know something about photosynthesis. But remember, the information you need to answer each question is contained within the passage itself. So if science has never been your strength, don't worry. In this chapter, we're going to show you techniques that will help you master scientific reasoning, even if you don't know anything about photosynthesis, bacteria, the periodic table, or quantum mechanics.

## WHAT DOES THE SCIENCE REASONING TEST LOOK LIKE?

The Science Reasoning Test has seven passages, each of which is followed by five to seven questions. The passages cover material drawn from biology, chemistry, physics, and the physical sciences (including geology, astronomy, and meteorology). They vary in organization and difficulty, as well as in the scientific reasoning skills they test.

Sound intimidating? It really isn't—all you need is the ability to answer questions strategically.

You've already developed some of these skills during science lab in school. Others you can borrow from what we've taught you in the ACT Reading section. (If you had any trouble mastering those skills, this is a good time to review them and make them stick.) The only additional skill you'll need is a basic understanding of math to help you read and interpret charts, figures, and graphs.

You'll have 35 minutes to answer 40 questions. That's about five minutes a passage! It's like a car race: You have to move fast but you don't want to crash. In this section, we'll teach you how to do exactly that.

## WHAT ARE THE PASSAGES LIKE?

All of the passages fall within three basic categories.

### 1. Data Representation — 15 questions, 3 passages

These passages provide you with one or more charts, tables, graphs, or illustrations, and are intended to test your ability to understand and interpret the information that's presented. There are three data representation passages per test, and each one has five questions.

### 2. Research Summaries — 18 questions, 3 passages

These passages describe several experiments and their results to see whether you can follow the procedures in each experiment (or experiments) and interpret them. There are three research summaries passages per test, each with six questions.

**The ACT Science Test Format**

7 passages; 40 questions:
35 minutes

**Do You Need to Be a Science Whiz?**

Not at all. This section is more like a Reading Test whose sole subject matter is science. What you *do* need is an understanding of the scientific method and of how to interpret charts, graphs, and tables.

### 3. Conflicting Viewpoints — 7 questions, 1 passage, 2–3 fighting scientists

These passages present (usually) two or three conflicting views on a research hypothesis. Typical topics include: Is there Life on Mars? Where Did the Dinosaurs Go? and What's Fire? Frequently, the fight is over something that has already been resolved (such as *what's fire?*). You will be asked about the conflict and the evidence supporting each view. The ACT writers may also ask you to figure out what kind of evidence might actually resolve the conflict. There will be only one conflicting viewpoints passage per test, and it will have seven questions.

## WHAT ARE THE QUESTIONS LIKE?

The questions test your ability to interpret scientific data evenly and fall into three categories.

### 1. Understanding

These questions test your ability to paraphrase specific parts of the passage. They're like the questions that you see on the Reading Test, and they usually require that you focus on one sentence or paragraph. You might be asked to think about what happened in the passage, and what the underlying assumptions are behind it. Or you may have to look up a value on a chart.

### 2. Analysis

These questions call for a deeper understanding of the information in the passage, "deeper" meaning that you have to consider more than one part of the passage. You'll be required to recognize relationships between different pieces of information in the passage. For instance, you might be asked to put two thoughts together and figure out why something happened, or what's *going* to happen.

### 3. Generalization

These questions require that you see things in perspective ("the bigger picture"). You're asked to understand how events described in the passage may relate to situations not described in the passage. For instance, a passage may describe an experiment and the results. One question might ask you to predict the result if the experiment was performed under different conditions. Or suppose a passage describes an experimental finding. A question might ask you to assess the impact of the finding on the "real world."

## HERE'S OUR STEP-BY-STEP GAME PLAN FOR TACKLING SCIENCE REASONING PASSAGES

We have a step-by-step game plan for reading ACT Science passages and answering questions about them. We'll outline the plan first, then discuss each step in detail.

**Level of Difficulty**

Just like in the Reading Test of the ACT, the passages here are not organized in order of difficulty. So prioritize the passages. Before you read a passage, take a good look at the layout. Can you identify the passage type? Do easy passages right away, more difficult passages later.

## Step 1. Scan the Passage

Before you read the passage, take a quick look at the format. Your first task is to identify the passage type. Is it a charts and graphs, experiments, or fighting scientists passage? Count the questions. Charts and graphs passages always have 5 questions; experiments passages always have 6 questions; fighting scientists passages always have 7 questions. If there are tables, illustrations, or graphs, familiarize yourself with their content. This should only take you about 20 seconds. (Remember, time is limited.) After you have scanned the passage, then you should go back and deal with the introduction.

Since most of the questions have nothing to do with the introduction, you don't want to spend much time on it. What's more, many of the introductions are really complex, giving detailed explanations of stuff they never ask you about! ACT is trying to waste your time with the introductions—don't let 'em.

There are three basic introductions that commonly appear on the test, and each has its own approach.

| | |
|---|---|
| **One long paragraph** | Skim this (fast), and underline key words. Don't try to understand it. |
| **Two equal paragraphs** | Skim them and underline key words. One of them is usually in plain English—read that one. |
| **One long paragraph and one short paragraph** | Skim the long one (ultrafast) and underline key words. Read the short one—it's a clear explanation of what's going on in the passage. |

## Step 2. Look at Each Question and Identify Its Type

Once you've scanned the passage, you should move on to the questions. To which category does each question belong? Identify each as either an understanding, analysis, or generalization question. Why? Because knowing the question type will help you eliminate distracters and zero in on the right answer.

## Step 3. Guesstimate

Some of the questions will require you to do some pretty simple calculations. Sometimes you can come up with the right answer choice by "guesstimating," which means making a rough estimate. (Remember this from our geometry chapter?) This technique works particularly well on problems that require you to interpret graphs.

## Step 4. Use Process of Elimination (POE)

As on all sections of the ACT, you should use POE to eliminate incorrect answer choices. Once you have eliminated a couple of answer choices, you'll be able to spend a little time on the remaining choices and make a pretty good guess.

**Time Management**

Since you must complete seven passages in 35 minutes, you need to budget your time accordingly. Don't forget that you're getting the same number of points for correctly answering easy as well as hard questions. Use the Triage Rule. Don't waste time struggling with a hard question when you can move on and answer an easy question. You can always come back to the question if you have time.

## DON'T FORGET TO PACE YOURSELF

In order to finish the Science Reasoning Test you'll have to move along at a good clip. That means you'll have to answer the questions strategically. Remember the "Triage" rule? Well, it applies to the Science Reasoning Test as well. As always, you should answer the easiest questions first. If you find yourself spending lots of time on a particular question—move on. You can always come back to it later.

Which questions are the easiest? Questions that simply require going to the passage and looking something up tend to be easy. So do questions that ask you to project what will happen based on a trend established in the passage. Questions about assumptions underlying an experiment or hypothesis tend to be most difficult.

## ONE MORE NOTE

Some questions are fairly long themselves. They're like "mini passages" and usually accompany experiments and fighting scientists passages. These take a lot of time to do, so leave them for the end.

Now that we've outlined our general step-by-step strategy, we'll show you how to apply that strategy to the three passage types that you'll see on the ACT Science Reasoning Test.

# 16

# Charts and Graphs

These passages use charts, tables, graphs, diagrams, or illustrations to convey information. Often the figures will have an explanatory key or footnote to help you better understand the information presented in the passage. There will be five questions for each of these passages.

# STEP 1: SCAN THE PASSAGE

You'll notice that the text is pretty skimpy on a charts and graphs passage. (Some passages contain only three sentences.) Since charts, tables, or graphs make up the major part of the passage you'll need to examine them carefully. What does "carefully" mean? It means using some of the skills you've developed in everyday life.

What do you do when you have to take a bus to a place you've never been? You look at a bus map. In order to understand the map, you have to figure out how it's designed, and what the signs and symbols mean. Well, the same rule applies to the graphs, tables, and charts you'll see on the ACT.

## What Is a Variable?

A variable is a quantity ("thing") that has some type of value. There are two types of variables you'll need to know for the ACT: an independent variable and a dependent variable.

## SCANNING A GRAPH: LOOK AT THE VARIABLES AND UNITS

When you see a graph, table, or chart, you should ask yourself two questions:

1. What are the variables? (sunlight? temperature? number of plants?)

2. How are they measured? (in grams? quarts? meters?) Keep in mind that values can also be represented as percentages.

Let's look at an example:

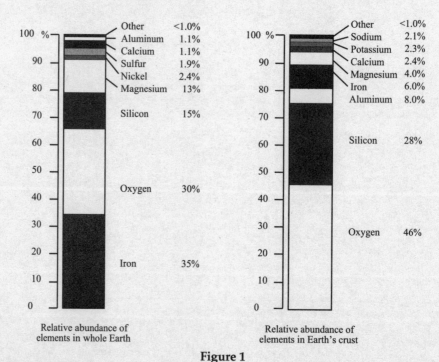

**Figure 1**

Relative abundance by weight of elements in the whole Earth and in the Earth's crust.

We see two bar graphs that describe the composition of the whole Earth compared to the Earth's crust.

1. What are the variables?

2. How are they measured?

Do you see the numbers on either side of the bar graphs? They tell you the values are given in percentages (%). The graph on the left describes the percent (by mass) of an element in the whole Earth. The one on the right describes the percent (by mass) of an element in the Earth's crust.

Now, let's see if you can work with a slightly more complicated graph.

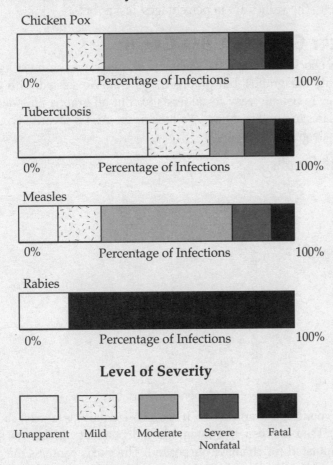

### Infection Severity Incidence for Four Diseases

## FIRST: SCAN THE BAR GRAPHS

1. What are the variables?
   - There are four diseases: chicken pox, tuberculosis, measles, and rabies.
   - Did you notice the small boxes under the bar graphs? They make up a key that gives you more information about the variables. The graph is about diseases, and the key describes levels of severity.
   - Now, how many levels are there?
   - There are five levels: unapparent, mild, moderate, severe (nonfatal), and fatal.

2. How are they measured?
   - The values are in percentages, just as before.

## NOT EVERY GRAPH IS A BAR GRAPH

The ACT is chock full of graphs. There are all types, so you must learn how to read not only bar graphs, but graphs in general. We started with bar graphs because they're usually easy to understand. But all graphs illustrate how one variable relates to another. Now let's look at the ACT's favorite type of graph: the coordinate graph.

### Coordinate Graphs

**What Are the Three Types of Coordinate Graphs?**

- Linear graphs
- Exponential graphs
- Scatter diagrams

Look at the coordinate graph above. It has a horizontal axis (*x*-axis) and a vertical axis (*y*-axis). The *x*-axis usually contains the independent variable, the thing that's being manipulated (or changed purposely). The *y*-axis contains the dependent variable, the thing that is affected when the independent variable is changed.

Now, let's look at what happens when we put some points on the graph.

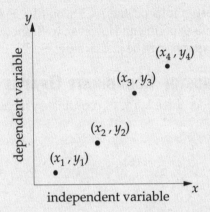

Every point on the graph represents a value for both the independent variable (x-variable) and the dependent variable (y-variable). In other words, each point represents an (x,y) pair. Don't forget that. Whenever you see a point on a graph you should remember that it has both an x-component and a y-component.

Now, let's look at what happens when we take the same graph and indicate that the graph represents an experiment performed by Dr. Frankenstein.

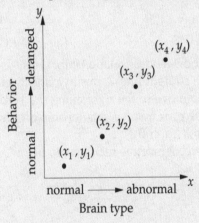

**Dr. Frankenstein's Experiment**

Take a look at the axes. The variables are brain type and behavior. The brain type is an independent variable and is represented along the x-axis. The brain type affects the monster's behavior, which is represented along the y-axis.

When building his monster, Dr. Frankenstein can use the brain of either a normal person or a psychopath. In this experiment $(x_1, y_1)$ represents a normal brain (the independent variable) with a normal behavior (dependent variable). The point $(x_4, y_4)$ represents a psychopath's brain, and the associated tendency to burn down villages.

Let's look, for example, at point $(x_2, y_2)$ on the graph. When the monster is given this brain type $(x_2)$, what type of behavior does he exhibit? Does he behave normally, or does he burn down villages?

Point $(x_2, y_2)$ represents a fairly normal brain, and, consequently, a reasonably well-behaved individual.

Unfortunately, most graphs on the ACT won't be as interesting as the one about Dr. Frankenstein's experiment. However, we'll show you how interpreting even the most boring graphs can be just as easy.

## KNOW THREE KINDS OF COORDINATE GRAPHS

On the ACT, you will see three kinds of coordinate graphs.

### Linear Graphs

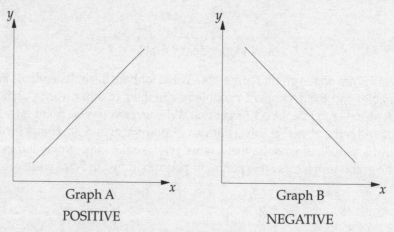

Graph A
POSITIVE

Graph B
NEGATIVE

The graphs above show a linear relationship. Linear is a fancy word meaning that the points follow a straight line. A positive linear relationship occurs when an **increase** in $x$ (as you move to the right along the *x-axis*) leads to an **increase** in $y$ (Graph A). A negative, or inverse, relationship occurs when an **increase** in $x$ leads to a **decrease** in $y$ (Graph B).

Let's see if you can recognize the relationship below.

Does the graph show a positive or a negative linear relationship between temperature and volume?

If you answered positive, you're right. If, for some reason, you forget which graph shows a positive relationship, just remember that positive means that the line is pointing upward to the right.

# Graphs with Curves

Graph C

Another common graph displays a curve, as shown in Graph C. The curve above means that for every increase in $x$, the $y$ values are becoming larger and larger. The changes in $y$ are **exponential** and become greater and greater the more $x$ increases. If a graph is curved, that means that the amount $y$ changes with each change in $x$ is different at different points on the graph. Let's look at another example:

When the wind speed is 40 km/hr, what is the rate of sand movement?

The answer is 0.3. Now, let's see what happens when the wind speed is 50 km/hr. The rate of sand movement increases to 0.6. Did you notice that the rate of sand movement doubled? Now, what happens when the wind speed is 60 km/hr? The rate of sand movement increased a whole lot! As you pick larger values for wind speed, the rate of sand movement will shoot up in value.

## Scatter Diagrams

The ACT writers expect you to understand one more graph. This graph is called a scatter diagram. See the line that runs through the center of the graph? It's called a "best-fit" line. It tells you that if you took the average of all the points on the graph and lined them up, they would form the straight line above. Therefore, the graph tells you two things: (1) what the points would look like if they were averaged and lined up (a line), and (2) how they *really* look on the graph (scattered).

So when you see a graph on the Science Reasoning Test, you should look at the graph and determine what the variables are, how they are measured, and how they are related.

Now that we have tackled scanning graphs, let's see if we can apply the same technique to scanning tables.

## SCANNING A TABLE: LOOK AT THE VARIABLES

Just as we did with graphs, look at the chart to figure out what the variables are. You want to know what's being compared to what. As you read the chart, take the time to understand how these variables are related to each other (don't skimp on this part). Here's an example:

| Number of half-lives expired for radioactive thorium | Remaining fraction of original thorium sample |
|:---:|:---:|
| 0 | 1 |
| 1 | $\frac{1}{2}$ |
| 2 | $\frac{1}{4}$ |
| 3 | $\frac{1}{8}$ |
| 4 | $\frac{1}{16}$ |

This table has something to do with the radioactive element thorium, which has something called a "half-life."

What are the variables? They are

A.  the number of half-lives expired

B.  the remaining fraction of the original thorium sample

As you can see, the more half-lives that expire, the less we have of the original thorium sample.

## SCANNING AN ILLUSTRATION: LOOK AT THE VARIABLES

Instead of a chart or graph, sometimes the ACT writers will give you an illustration. Sometimes these illustrations will have text within the picture, but usually they will not have a specific explanation accompanying them. The ACT writers want to see if you can follow a flow chart or interpret a diagram. Here's an example:

**Know the Three Question Types**
- Understanding
- Analysis
- Generalization

The Cycle of Oxygen Through the Atmosphere

### Figure 2

This figure illustrates the oxygen cycle. Based on this figure, which of the processes releases oxygen into the atmosphere? Look at the arrows associated with each box. The information inside every box is the variable. Which of the boxes has an arrow that shows that oxygen is released into the atmosphere? The box labeled "photosynthesis on land and in surface sea-water produces oxygen."

Now what if the ACT writers ask you what kinds of living organisms produce oxygen? According to this diagram, the answer is algae and plants on land. The direction of the arrow indicates that oxygen is moving from algae and the ground to the atmosphere. All the other arrows are pointing away from the atmosphere.

# STEP 2: IDENTIFY THE QUESTION TYPE

Now that you know how to scan the various charts, graphs, and illustrations, let's go right to the questions. Remember that there are only three basic question types, each addressing a different skill.

## UNDERSTANDING

The majority of these questions test your ability to understand the passages. They want you to explain, describe, and identify some of the basic scientific concepts or assumptions that underlie the information provided in the passage. Other times the ACT writers are looking for a summary of the passage. Usually, you'll need to look at only one portion of a passage to answer the question. This means that the correct answers tend to be specific and refer back to a specific part of the passage. So, for understanding questions, identify the piece of information needed.

Here's an example:

## Passage A

The term *solubility* refers to the amount of a substance (solute) that will dissolve in a given amount of a liquid substance (solvent). The solubility of solids in water varies with temperature. The graph below displays the water solubility curves for six crystalline solids.

1. Which of the following factors affect(s) the degree to which KCl is soluble in water?
   A. Only the quantity of KCl added to 100 grams of water
   B. The temperature of the solution
   C. Only the amount of solvent present in the solution
   D. The weight of KCl

## Here's How to Crack It

This question requires that you understand the variables—what's being compared to what. The variables are

   A. the solution's temperature

   B. solubility, or the mass of solute that will dissolve in 100 ml of water

The passage stated that when we talk about solubility we're talking about the amount of solute that will dissolve in a given amount of a solvent. The question asks you what, according to this graph, affects the solubility of solids in water? Let's look at the variables. The graph shows you that for KCl the solubility varies with the solution's temperature. That's why the answer is **B**.

## TRANSLATING TABLES TO GRAPHS

One more note: Sometimes you will be given a question that asks, "Which of the following graphs would best represent the results in the passage?" If you're given a table, you might have to translate the information into a graph.

Luckily, we've just learned a few things about graphs and tables. Now we have to learn how to read a table and translate this information into a graph. To make a graph, draw both axes and label the axes as $x$ and $y$. Remember, the $x$-axis is the independent variable and the $y$-axis is the dependent variable. After you have drawn your axes, you can begin to plot some points on the graph.

Let's see if we can translate the information in the table about radioactive thorium into a graph.

| Number of half-lives expired for radioactive thorium | Remaining fraction of original thorium sample |
|---|---|
| 0 | 1 |
| 1 | $\frac{1}{2}$ |
| 2 | $\frac{1}{4}$ |
| 3 | $\frac{1}{8}$ |
| 4 | $\frac{1}{16}$ |

The first thing to do is draw your axes.

What is the independent variable? It's the number of expired half-lives. Label your $x$-axis with the numbers 0 through 4. Now, what is the dependent variable? It's the amount of thorium left after each expired half-life. Label the $y$-axis with the numbers $\frac{1}{16}$ to 1. Now you can plot the values on the graph and connect the dots!

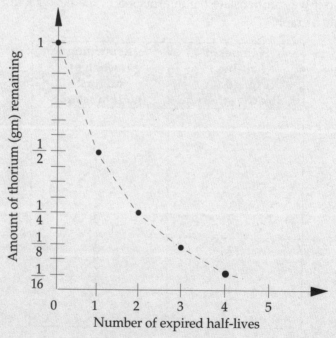

Now, let's see if you can translate a table into a graph.

An investigator conducted a study to determine the relationship between temperature and pH of the enzyme chymotrypsin. Her findings are listed in the table below.

| Temp. (°C) | pH Level |
|:----------:|:--------:|
| 47 | 2 |
| 42 | 5 |
| 37 | 7 |
| 32 | 4 |
| 27 | 3 |

**Chymotrypsin acidity: temperature dependence**

Use the space below to draw a graph that represents the relationship between temperature and pH in this experiment.

## This Is What Your Graph Should Look Like

Did you label your axes? Temperature is the independent variable, and pH is the dependent variable. Now, here's where it can get a little tricky. You should have labeled your x-axis with the units increasing as you move to the right. If you plotted your numbers differently, you probably got the wrong answer. Are you ever going to have to draw a graph on the ACT? No, but you will have to recognize which of the graphs in the answer choices best represents the information in the chart or passage. These questions are fairly easy if you practice how to read the axes, and look at the points (or lines) on the graphs.

## ANALYSIS

For this type of question you're supposed to have a little deeper understanding of the passage. The question will usually require you to look at several pieces of information to get the right answer. Basically, you're being asked to figure out how different pieces of information are related to each other. So for analysis questions:

## Draw on More Than One Piece of Information

Here's an example using the previous passage about solubility. Don't forget to refer to the graph on page 264.

> **2.** How many grams of $NH_4Cl$ can be dissolved in 200 ml of water at 70°C?
>
> **F.** 70 grams
> **G.** 90 grams
> **H.** 140 grams
> **J.** 180 grams

## Here's How to Crack It

The passage tests your ability to interpret the graph. What are the units? Temperature is measured in degrees Celsius and solubility is measured in grams of solute per 100 milliliters of water. You need to identify which line represents $NH_4Cl$ on the graph. Then, follow the curve until you see where it crosses 70°C. You can then look at the y-axis to see how many grams of $NH_4Cl$ can dissolve in water. The answer is 70 grams. But hold it! The question is asking you to determine how many grams of $NH_4Cl$ dissolve in *200* ml of water at 70°C. (This is what makes it an analysis question.) This question requires that you double the number of grams of solute since you're dissolving the solute in double the amount of water. Therefore the correct answer choice is **H**.

## GENERALIZATION

In this type of question, you need to go beyond the information given. You may be presented with a new situation and be asked to apply the concepts provided in the passage. So for generalization questions:

## Step Back and Look at the Big Picture

Here's an example using the same passage about solubility.

 3. Based on the passage, what can you conclude about the relationship between solubility and temperature?
  A. The solubility of a substance has little to do with the concentration of the solvent or the temperature.
  B. Temperature is a dependent variable in the study.
  C. For any given solution, a temperature increase allows for more solute to be dissolved in a solvent.
  D. An increase in temperature will always lead to a decrease in solubility.

## Here's How to Crack It

This is a generalization question, which means you're supposed to look at the "big picture." The ACT test writers want you to make a generalization not just about the six solids on the graph, but about solids in general. What are some of the trends you notice among all the solutes? As the temperature increases, the number of grams that can be dissolved in water increases (more stuff can be added). This means that higher temperatures allow for more solute to be dissolved in water. Therefore **C** is the correct answer. Answer choice A is clearly wrong since solubility and temperature are related (just look at the graph). Is temperature an independent variable or a dependent variable? Well, an independent variable is one you can play around with. Therefore, temperature is the independent variable, so answer choice B is wrong. Answer choice D presents just the opposite and is incorrect—an increase in temperature leads to an increase rather than a decrease in solubility.

# STEP 3: GUESSTIMATING

## INTERPOLATION

Sometimes the ACT writers will give you a graph and ask you to predict the position of an unplotted point. This means that you may have to make a guess about where a point will lie on the graph based on the data you already have. The word for this is **interpolation,** and it's a skill you'll need for analyzing graphs. It's really easy. The values that they want you to guess are within the range of points on the graph. Let's look at the graph below:

**Interpolation**—to estimate values on a graph between two known values.

What if the test writers asked you to predict the value of $y$ if you were given a value $x$ on the graph. Based on the position of the other points (the trend), you would predict the point would be located where the question mark is.

Let's try an example:

If $x$ is 10, what is the value of $y$?

We're not sure! The ACT test writers didn't give you a value of 10 on the x-axis. What should you do? First determine where 10 would lie on the x-axis. This is the first step in **guesstimating.** Remember, guesstimating will help you approximate an answer. Since 10 falls between 5 and 15, you can guesstimate where x and its corresponding y-value lie on the graph. Can you make a guess as to the value of y on the graph? Move across the x-axis to the approximate position of 10, then move up from the x-axis until you reach the line. What is the value of y? It's about 17 or 18. Piece of cake, right?

## LET's DO IT AGAIN

1. Based on the graph above, what is the atmospheric pressure when the temperature is 350˚K?
   A. 2.0 atm
   B. 2.5 atm
   C. 3.0 atm
   D. 3.5 atm

## Here's How to Crack It

Once again, the test writers didn't give a value of 350°K for x. But, you do know that 350°K is half way between 300°K and 400°K. So, what do you do next? Guess-timate. Move across the x-axis until you reach the midpoint between 300°K and 400°K. Then move up until you reach the line. What is the approximate value of y? The answer is 3.0 atm, answer choice **C.**

## EXTRAPOLATION

The ACT writers want to test another skill. Sometimes, they want you to extend the line on a graph.

**Extrapolation**—to project or expand known data into an area not known.

See the dashed line on the picture above? This shows that if you continued the experiment and picked values of $x$ that were outside of the range given by the solid line you would get the dashed line shown above. This is called **extrapolation.** Let's look at an example:

**Estimated $CO_2$ concentration in the atmosphere up to the year 2020.**

What will be the $CO_2$ concentration in the atmosphere in the year 2020?

This is a graph of the concentration of $CO_2$ in the atmosphere since 1860. Notice that the graph gives values of $CO_2$ concentration all the way up to the year 2020. But we're barely in the 21st century! So how did they arrive at these values? They "projected" the $CO_2$ concentration level based on previous trends in the data. Therefore the $CO_2$ concentration will be about 470 parts per million. That's extrapolation. You'll probably need this skill to answer several analysis or generalization questions.

# STEP 4: USE PROCESS OF ELIMINATION

**Use Process of Elimination**

If two answer choices are opposites, start with them first.

Often the ACT writers will give you several answer choices that look a lot alike. Why's that? They are attempting to disguise the correct answer choice. Test writers usually write the question first, then the correct answer, and finally the incorrect answers. Since they don't want the correct answer to be too obvious, they often surround it with several similar (but wrong) answers.

## So How Does This Information Help You?

It means that if you're given a couple of answer choices that look alike, you should always consider them first. This technique works particularly well with answer choices that present opposite trends—one of them is usually correct. Let's look back at question 3, which refers to the solubility passage on page 264.

3. Based on the passage, what can you conclude about the relationship between solubility and temperature?
   A. The solubility of a substance has little to do with the concentration of the solvent or the temperature.
   B. Temperature is a dependent variable in the study.
   C. For any given solution, a temperature increase allows for more solute to be dissolved in a solvent.
   D. An increase in temperature will always lead to a decrease in solubility.

Did you notice that answer choices C and D are opposites? So which answer choices should you consider first? Answer choices C and D.

## PUTTING THE STRATEGY TO WORK

Let's try this strategy on the sample charts and graphs passages.

## Passage I

The kinetic molecular theory provides new insights into the movement of molecules in liquids. It states that molecules are in constant motion and collide with one another. When the temperature of a liquid increases there will be an increase in the movement of molecules and in the average kinetic energy. The figure below depicts the distribution of the kinetic energy of two samples of water at different temperatures (T).

**Distribution of Kinetic Energy for Two Samples of Water**

**Figure 1**

Water has attractive intermolecular forces that keep the molecules together. When enough heat is added to water, it will weaken these forces and allow some molecules to escape the liquid as a gas. The activation energy ($E_a$) is the minimum energy necessary for molecules to escape the liquid and undergo a phase change.

1. Which of the following statements best describes the changes observed in the graph?
   A. The molecules in Sample 2 have, on average, less kinetic energy than those in Sample 1.
   B. The molecules in Sample 1 have, on average, less kinetic energy than those in Sample 2.
   C. An increase in temperature leads to a decrease in kinetic energy.
   D. Water never undergoes a phase change.

2. Assume that water undergoes a phase change to a gas. Which of the following statements would be true?

  F. The attractive intermolecular forces of the escaping molecule(s) are weak.
  G. The average kinetic energy of the water remains the same.
  H. The rate of movement of the gas molecules decreases.
  J. The gas will undergo no further phase changes.

3. Suppose a third sample of water is heated to a higher temperature than Sample 2. It is then found that a greater number of molecules escaped the liquid in Sample 3 than in Sample 2. Would these results be consistent with the results depicted in Figure 1?

  A. Yes, an increase in temperature leads to a decrease in the number of escaping molecules in the liquid.
  B. Yes, as the temperature increases it leads to more molecules escaping the liquid.
  C. No, the temperature reading of Sample 2 would be five times as high as that of the third sample.
  D. No, the average kinetic energy of the water will decrease.

4. It can be inferred from Figure 1 that when a substance undergoes a phase change from a liquid to a gas it will:

  F. evaporate.
  G. condense.
  H. disintegrate.
  J. remain the same.

## Here's How to Crack It

**Question 1:** This is an understanding question on which you can use POE. As you were reading the question, did you notice that answer choices A and B were the same except that the words "Sample 1" and "Sample 2" were switched? The answer choices are opposites, and one of them will probably be correct. Let's try A and B first. We need to compare the average kinetic energies of Sample 1 and Sample 2 at the peaks of their line graphs, or where, for each, the number of molecules in motion is the greatest. Look at the $x$-axis and follow the dotted line of each peak down to the $x$-axis. Sample 1 clearly has a lower kinetic energy. So the answer is B. Even though Sample 1's peak is higher than Sample 2's peak, this reinforces our original observation that Sample 1 has a lower average kinetic energy. Now, let's check the other two choices. Does an increase in temperature lead to a decrease in kinetic energy? No. The passage states that an increase in temperature leads to an increase in kinetic energy. So we can eliminate choice C. Now, let's look at answer choice D. Is it true that water never undergoes a phase change? No, in fact the text accompanying the graph says just the opposite. So we can eliminate answer choice D. The correct answer is **B**, as suspected.

**Question 2:** This is an analysis question since it requires a greater understanding of the passage than does question 1. The question refers to the second paragraph, which mentions phase changes. What happens during a phase change? Two things happen: (1) Increased kinetic energy weakens the attractive intermolecular forces in the water and (2) some molecules escape the liquid as a gas. Now that we have reviewed this information, it's pretty easy to eliminate answer choices G and H. Now, let's look at answer choice J. Did we read anything in the passage that told us about other phase changes? No. This answer choice is beyond the realm of the passage and can be eliminated. So the correct answer choice is **F**, and again we've reached it by using POE.

**Question 3:** This is a generalization question. The ACT writers want to see if you can predict what will happen if you raise the temperature of water higher than that of Sample 2. What answer choices should you eliminate? Decide whether the correct answer should begin with a yes or a no. How do we do that? Just check the graph with the results for Samples 1 and 2. When you increase the temperature will the sample have more or less kinetic energy? It will have more. That means we can rule out answer choice D. We can eliminate C because the temperature reading of Sample 2 is lower than the third sample. Now compare answer choices A and B to see which one is correct. Does an increase in temperature lead to greater or fewer numbers of molecules escaping the liquid? Greater. Thus, the correct answer is choice **B**.

**Question 4:** This is an analysis question. The passage states that when a substance goes from the liquid to the gas phase, it will evaporate. When a substance has reached the temperature at which it undergoes the phase change, it will evaporate. That's how molecules will escape. Therefore, the answer is **F**.

## Passage II

Amphibians are unique organisms that undergo drastic physical changes during the transformation from an immature organism into an adult form. This process, called metamorphosis, begins with the determination of cells at the tadpole stage. A study was conducted using tadpoles to determine the influence of thyroxine (a hormone) on metamorphosis.

**Decrease in tail width in relation to varying levels of thyroxine solutions.**
Figure 2

As shown in the graph on the previous, tadpoles were placed in solutions containing various concentrations of thyroxine.

Increased levels of thyroxine correlated with increased rates of tail reabsorption and the appearance of adult characteristics such as lungs and hind legs.

1. Suppose that a tadpole were immersed in a 0.3 µg/ml solution for 72 hours. What would be the expected approximate decrease in tail width?
   A. 22%
   B. 30%
   C. 41%
   D. 50%

2. Which of the following generalizations about tadpoles is supported by the results of the study?
   F. They will not undergo metamorphosis if they are not given thyroxine.
   G. The metamorphosis process in a normal tadpole takes at least 5 days.
   H. The most rapid disappearance of the tail is associated with the immersion of tadpoles in the most dilute thyroxine solution.
   J. Temperature plays a major role in the metamorphic process.

3. After four days, the tadpoles are checked for development. In which of the following concentrations of thyroxine would the tadpoles be likely to show the LEAST development?
   A. 0.5 µg/ml
   B. 0.2 µg/ml
   C. 0.1 µg/ml
   D. All of the tadpoles would show the same development.

4. Based on the information in the passage, which of the following would be a correct order of the stages of tadpole development?
   F. Tadpole→ adult→ reabsorption of tail→ cell determination
   G. Tadpole→ cell determination→ reabsorption of tail→ adult
   H. Tadpole→ reabsorption of tail→ adult→ cell determination
   J. Cell determination→ tadpole→ adult→ reabsorption of tail

## Here's How to Crack It

**Question 1:** This is an analysis question. Do we see a solution of thyroxine that is 0.3 µg/ml? No. The ACT writers want you to "guesstimate" where 0.3 µg/ml would fall on the table. This value would have to lie somewhere between 0.2 µg/ml and 0.5 µg/ml. The question requires that you make a guess within the values given. What do we call this skill? Interpolation! Now, if we move across the x-axis to the value of 72 hours, and we move up to the range of values between 0.2 µg/ml and 0.5 µg/ml, we see that the y-values range from about 23 percent to 37 percent. The only answer choice that falls in that range is answer choice **B**—30 percent.

**Question 2:** This is a generalization question. Notice that they want to know what is true for tadpoles in general. Let's start with answer choice F. This is a ridiculous answer choice. We know that all normal tadpoles undergo metamorphosis. If you're not sure, take a look at the graph. The control group in the graph represents normal tadpoles. They do have some decrease in tail width, although not a lot, in 120 hours or 5 days. (Notice that you needed to know that 5 days is the same as 120 hours.) Thus, answer choice F is incorrect. You can also rule out answer choice H, since the figure clearly shows that high concentrations of thyroxine solutions lead to the greatest decrease in tail width. The passage doesn't mention anything about temperature, thus answer choice J is out. The correct answer choice is **G.** We see that the control sample shows some reduction in tail size in 120 hours, so it must take longer for the process to be complete.

**Question 3:** This is an understanding question. You must realize that as the tadpole develops, his tail is reabsorbed, or it shrinks. The graph compares percent decrease in tail width to hours. At 96 hours (4 days), the tadpoles showing the lowest percent decrease in tail width would be the least developed. Therefore, the answer must be choice **C,** the tadpoles in 0.1 μg/ml.

**Question 4:** This is also an understanding question. Thyroxine affects the metamorphosis of the tadpole by influencing the process of cell determination from tadpole cells into mature adult cells. You don't have to understand this process—just realize that it occurs between tadpole and adult stages. Begin with answer choices F, G, and H since you need a tadpole to start the process. Using POE, the correct answer choice can only be **G.**

## Passage III

Elements are arranged in the periodic table according to their atomic number, which represents the number of protons in the nucleus. In every neutrally charged atom, the number of electrons equals the number of protons. The table below lists some of the properties of row 2 elements in the periodic table. *Electronegativity* is a measure of the relative strength with which the atoms attract outer electrons. Within a row of the periodic table, the electronegativity tends to increase with increasing atomic number, due to the tighter bonding between protons and electrons. The highest value for electronegativity is 4.0.

| Element | Atomic number | Atomic radius | Electro– negativity | Characteristic |
|---------|---------------|---------------|---------------------|----------------|
| Li | 3 | 1.52 | 1.0 | metal |
| Be | 4 | 1.13 | 1.5 | metal |
| B | 5 | 0.88 | 2.0 | non-metal |
| C | 6 | 0.77 | 2.5 | non-metal |
| N | 7 | 0.70 | 3.0 | non-metal |
| O | 8 | 0.66 | 3.5 | non-metal |
| F | 9 | 0.64 | 4.0 | non-metal |

**Table 1**

1. Which of the following graphs best represents the relationship between atomic number and atomic radius for row 2 elements?

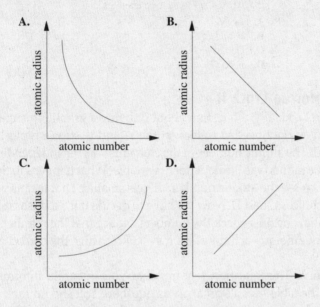

A.

B.

C.

D.

2. What conclusion could be appropriately drawn from the data regarding electronegativity in Table 1?
   F. An element with high electronegativity has an even atomic number.
   G. An element with high electronegativity will be a metal.
   H. An element with high electronegativity will have little tendency to attract outer electrons.
   J. An element with high electronegativity will be a non-metal.

3. What generalization can one make concerning the relationship between two properties of elements?
   A. As the atomic radius decreases, the electronegativity decreases.
   B. As the atomic radius decreases, the electronegativity increases.
   C. All metals have large electronegativity values.
   D. The atomic radius of F is larger than that of N.

4. Which of the following is true regarding the comparative electronegativity of fluorine (F) and lithium (Li)?
   F. The electronegativity of F is greater than Li because F has more electrons in its outer shell.
   G. The electronegativity of F is greater than Li because F electrons are more tightly bound.
   H. The electronegativity of F is greater than Li because F has a greater metallic character.
   J. The electronegativity of Li is greater than F because Li has a greater metallic character.

5. Generally speaking, ionization energy follows the same trends as does electronegativity. Elements with a high electronegativity also have a high ionization energy. Which of the following is a correct order of elements with INCREASING ionization energies?

A. Li, N, F
B. F, N, Li
C. O, N, F
D. F, N, O

## Here's How to Crack It

**Question 1:** Finally, a question about drawing a graph! This question was easy because you only needed to look at the *x*- and *y*-axes (a typical understanding question). The atomic number of the elements was the independent variable, and the atomic radius was the dependent variable. What happens to the atomic radius as you increase the atomic number? It gets smaller. That means we can eliminate answer choices C and D. Now we have to decide if it's a linear relationship or an exponential one. Just check the numbers. Notice that the numbers are decreasing a different amount each time—so it's a curve. Thus, the correct answer is **A**.

**Question 2:** This question requires that you integrate information from two parts of the table—so it's an analysis question. You should look at relationships between electronegativity and one of the other properties of elements. Let's start with answer choices G and J. Why? They are opposites (the switch again), so they can't both be true. If an element has a high electronegativity, is it a metal or a non-metal? It's a non-metal, so eliminate answer choice G. Now we can check the other answer choices. Must an element with a high electronegativity have an even or an odd atomic number? Let's check. If you look at the two highest electronegative elements, O and F, one is even and one is odd. So, is it true that elements with high electronegativity values have even atomic numbers? No. As for answer choice H, we know that elements with high electronegativity pull their outer electrons (the passage defines electronegativity as a measure of that strength). Therefore, we can eliminate answer choice H. The correct answer is **J**.

**Question 3:** This question asks you to make a generalization about trends in the chart, with regard to the bigger picture. Let's take a moment to think about the answer choices. If we want to make generalizations about elements, would an answer choice that refers to specific elements be the correct answer? Probably not. So we can probably scratch answer choice D. But, let's look at answer choice D more closely to be sure. Is the atomic radius of fluorine larger than nitrogen? No. Do all metals have high electronegativity values? No. Now notice that choices A and B state opposite trends. Use the chart to determine which answer choice is correct. As the atomic radius decreases, electronegativity increases. Thus, the correct answer choice is **B**.

**Question 4:** This is an analysis question, since you have to integrate the information on the chart and information in the passage. The first part is easy. Look at the chart to tell you which has a greater electronegativity, Li or F. F, of course! So, we can get rid of J. Now, why is the electronegativity of F greater than that of Li? Well, certainly not because it has a greater metallic character, because the chart tells us it's a non-metal. So, cross out H. Now we have to choose between F and G. The passage says specifically that within a row of the periodic table, the electronegativity tends to increase with increasing atomic number, due to the tighter bonding between protons and electrons. F has a higher atomic number than Li and more electrons than Li, so, F's electrons are more tightly bound than Li's. Therefore, the best answer is **G.**

**Question 5:** This is an analysis question. You must take new information given in the question and apply it to the chart given in the passage. Fortunately, this is very easy. Be careful; the question asks for increasing order of ionization energies. Since it follows the same trend as electronegativity, just find the answer choice that lists elements with increasing electronegativities. The answer can only be choice **A.**

# 17

# Experiments

Experiments passages are easy to spot. They each have six questions. They usually contain an introductory paragraph followed by a number of experiments. Like charts and graphs passages, they may include graphs, tables, illustrations, or charts.

# STEP 1: SCAN THE PASSAGE

## IDENTIFY THE RESEARCH OBJECTIVE

Have you ever heard of the *scientific method*? That's a fancy name for the steps an investigator takes in conducting a study. One of the key steps is to state the objective. The objective is a statement that tells you the purpose of the study. For every experiment described on the ACT, there will always be an objective. Let's look at an example:

> An investigator was interested in observing whether a chemical reaction occurs when compounds are mixed with water. Chemical reactions are known to produce heat. Three compounds were selected to be observed whether, based on the release of heat, a reaction took place. A thermometer was placed in each test tube to record any change in temperature.

| Test Tubes | △ Heat | |
|---|---|---|
| | Yes | No |
| 1. Powdered bleach + $H_2O$ | x | |
| 2. Salt + $H_2O$ | | x |
| 3. Sugar + $H_2O$ | | x |

## How Do You Spot the Objective?

It's easy. The objective is to determine whether heat was released in any of the reactions listed on the table. Notice that the objective tells you exactly what the investigator wants to know: Did a reaction take place?

Where do you usually find the objective of the study? The objective is usually found in the beginning or at the end of the introductory paragraph. Once you find the objective of the study, underline it. Knowing the objective of the study will keep you focused throughout your reading of the passage.

## Your Underlined Passage Should Look Like This:

> An investigator was interested in observing whether a chemical reaction occurs when compounds are mixed with water. Chemical reactions are known to produce heat. Three compounds were selected to be observed whether, based on the release of heat, a reaction took place. A thermometer was placed in each test tube to record any change in temperature.

## Let's Do It Again

> A laboratory experiment was conducted to determine whether the lack of sunlight influences photosynthesis (production of glucose). Eight potted *Salvia* flowers were randomly selected and divided into two groups and labeled Group A and Group B. The plants were then subjected to differing light conditions and examined one week later.

## Group A

> These plants were exposed to sunlight for the duration of the study. At the end of the study these plants were green in appearance and produced glucose.

## Group B

> These plants were kept in the dark. At the end of the study they were yellow in appearance and did not produce glucose.

What is the objective of the study?

## Here's How to Crack It

The objective of the study is to determine whether the lack of sunlight influences photosynthesis in plants.

> <u>A laboratory experiment was conducted to determine whether the lack of sunlight influences photosynthesis (production of glucose).</u> Eight potted *Salvia* flowers were randomly selected and divided into two groups and labeled Group A and Group B. The plants were then subjected to differing light conditions and examined one week later.

So, what should you do once you realize you've been given an experimental reasoning passage? Identify the objective and don't answer the questions until you're sure you understand it. Test takers often make careless mistakes when they read the passage too quickly and lose sight of the objective.

## Follow the Procedure and Identify the Variables

It's a good idea to make notes on each experiment. These notes should highlight the differences between experiments in a passage. (Why else would the ACT writers include two or more experiments if they weren't different?) Often these notes will refer to the procedure in the experiment.

The ACT writers also want to see whether you can identify the variables in the experiments. Generally, there will be two or more variables that are important in the passage, and you're supposed to identify the relationship between them.

So whenever you read an experimental reasoning passage, you should do two things:

1. Follow the procedure.

2. Identify the variables.

**Write, Write, Write!**
Don't forget to take notes on each step within the experiment.

Let's take some notes using the experiment about photosynthesis.

> A laboratory experiment was conducted to determine whether the lack of sunlight influences photosynthesis (production of glucose). Eight potted *Salvia* flowers were randomly selected and divided into two groups and labeled Group A and Group B. The plants were then subjected to differing light conditions and examined one week later.

**Group A**

> These plants were exposed to sunlight for the duration of the study. At the end of the study these plants were green in appearance and produced glucose.

**Group B**

> These plants were kept in the dark. At the end of the study they were yellow in appearance and did not produce glucose.

Look at each of the study groups and follow the procedure.

What happened in Group A? What happened in Group B?

Just refer back to the appropriate sections of the passage. Group A plants were green and made glucose. Group B plants turned yellow and didn't undergo photosynthesis (or make glucose). For experimental reasoning passages on the test, you should scribble a few key words next to each experiment. That way, you'll come away with not only a better understanding of the key points in the paragraph, but you'll also leave out extraneous information.

## Here's What the Scribbles Should Look Like

> A laboratory experiment was conducted to determine whether the lack of sunlight influences photosynthesis (production of glucose). Eight potted *Salvia* flowers were randomly selected and divided into two groups and labeled Group A and Group B. The plants were then subjected differing light conditions and examined one week later.

**Group A**

> These plants were exposed to sunlight for the duration of the study. At the end of the study these plants were green in appearance and produced glucose.
>
> *sun*
> *green*
> *glucose*

**Group B**

> These plants were kept in the dark. At the end of the study they were yellow in appearance and did not produce glucose.
>
> *no sun*
> *yellow*
> *no glucose*

## Study the Results

The results are the conclusion of the study. When you examine the results, make sure that you underline them or scribble some notes in the margin. Once you've completed this step, try to identify any similarities or differences between the results. Do you notice any trends in the data?

For example, let's look at a passage about the effects of gibberellins (a plant hormone) on plants.

Dr. Keller examined the influence of gibberellins (a plant hormone) on a crop of dwarf tomato plants for 180 days.

|  | Amount of gibberellins (ml) | Average height of tomato plants (cm) |
|---|---|---|
| Sample 1 | 0 | 10.0 |
| Sample 2 | 2 | 13.5 |
| Sample 3 | 4 | 15.7 |
| Sample 4 | 6 | 16.0 |
| Sample 5 | 8 | 16.0 |

What was the trend in the experiment?

The average plant height increased with the addition of the hormone until the plants reached a certain height, at which point they grew no further.

## Here's What the Scribbles Should Look Like

Plant height = more with gibb. then leveled off.

What are the variables?

Look at the chart. The variables are the amount of gibberellins and the height of the tomato plants.

Let's read the passage about catalysts and apply the same technique.

An investigator was interested in observing whether a chemical reaction occurs when compounds are mixed with water. Chemical reactions are known to produce heat. Three compounds were selected to be observed whether, based on the release of heat, a reaction took place. A thermometer was placed in each test tube to record any change in temperature.

| Test Tubes | △ Heat | |
|---|---|---|
|  | Yes | No |
| 1. Powdered bleach + $H_2O$ | x |  |
| 2. Salt + $H_2O$ |  | x |
| 3. Sugar + $H_2O$ |  | x |

What was the procedure in this experiment?

The investigator took a bunch of test tubes and filled them with different mixtures to see if a chemical reaction took place.

## Here's What the Scribbles Should Look Like

Powdered bleach + $H_2O$ = Reaction

Salt + $H_2O$ ≠ Reaction

Sugar + $H_2O$ ≠ Reaction

What are the variables?

In this case, all you have to do is to look at the chart. The variables are the reactants and the presence or absence of a reaction. Did you need to take a lot of notes for this experiment? Nope. Why not? The key information was already laid out for you in a simple table.

### So How Do You Scan Experiments Passages?

1. Look for the objective.

2. Follow the procedure and identify the variables.

3. Study the results.

# STEP 2: IDENTIFY THE QUESTION TYPE

You'll see the same categories of questions as those for data representation.

## UNDERSTANDING

The ACT writers want to know whether you understand the experiment. For instance, do you know the variables? (We now know how to tackle those questions.) If you removed one of the variables in the study, would it change the results? What happened in the experiment?

Let's look at an example using the study about gibberellins on page 287.

1. Which of the following graphs would best represent the effect of gibberellins on dwarf tomato plants in the study?

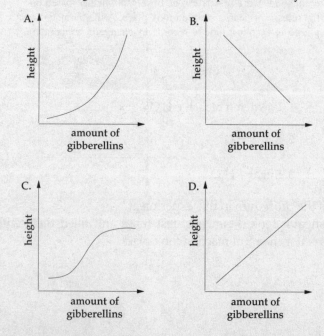

## Here's How to Crack It

Remember our technique on how to translate charts into graphs? Well, we can also use it in this section of the test. Let's go back to the chart.

We can use this information to find the correct graph. The answer choice that illustrates the same trend as the chart is **C**. Look at the numbers in the chart and notice that the height increases up to sample 5 and then it remains constant, as the amount of gibberellins increases further.

## KNOW HOW TO IDENTIFY CONTROLS

The ACT writers will sometimes ask you to identify the control of the study. A control is simply a standard of comparison. What does a control do? It enables the investigator to be certain that the outcome of the study is due to changes in the independent variable and nothing else. So a control is something they don't mess with during the experiment. Let's look at an example.

> **What Is a Control?**
>
> A control is a variable (or group) that remains constant throughout the study.

Say the principal of your school thinks that students who eat breakfast do better on standardized tests than those who don't eat breakfast. He takes a group of ten students from your class and gives them free breakfast every day for a year. When the school year is over he administers the ACT and they all score brilliantly!

Did they do well because they ate breakfast every day? How do you know whether the principal's theory is right? Maybe he just got lucky and picked the best test takers in the class to participate in the study.

The best way to be sure that eating breakfast made a difference in this case is to pick students in the class who *never* eat breakfast and to follow them for a year as well. Have *them* take the ACT and see how they score. What if they do just as well as the group that ate breakfast? Then we'll know that eating breakfast didn't make a difference.

The group that didn't eat breakfast was the control group. They were not "exposed" to the variable of interest—breakfast.

Let's read the photosynthesis experiment again.

> A laboratory experiment was conducted to determine whether the lack of sunlight influences photosynthesis (production of glucose). Eight potted *Salvia* flowers were randomly selected and divided into two groups and labeled Group A and Group B. The plants were then subjected to differing light conditions and examined one week later.

### Group A

> These plants were exposed to sunlight for the duration of the study. At the end of the study these plants were green in appearance and produced glucose.

### Group B

> These plants were kept in the dark. At the end of the study they were yellow in appearance and did not produce glucose.

Which of the plants served as the control(s) in this study?

The plants in group A served as controls. Why? Because these plants were exposed to sunlight throughout the study. The experimental group was subjected to the factor being investigated—no sunlight. Here's another example using the gibberellin experiment.

Dr. Keller examined the influence of gibberellins (a plant hormone) on a crop of dwarf tomato plants for 180 days.

| | Amount of gibberellins (ml) | Average height of tomato plants (cm) |
|---|---|---|
| Sample 1 | 0 | 10.0 |
| Sample 2 | 2 | 13.5 |
| Sample 3 | 4 | 15.7 |
| Sample 4 | 6 | 16.0 |
| Sample 5 | 8 | 16.0 |

1. Which of the following samples served as the control(s) in the study?
   A. Sample 1
   B. Sample 2
   C. Sample 4
   D. Samples 1 and 2

## Here's How to Crack It

Let's find the control in this study. A control in this case is something that is *not* exposed to the hormone. In this case, the control is the first sample. The first measure of the sample was collected *before* the hormone was added to the crop (the chart tells you that the amount of gibberellins found in sample 1 plants is 0). So the correct answer is **A**.

## ASSUMPTIONS

**What Is an Assumption?**

Assumptions are facts or statements that are taken for granted.

Another common understanding question on the Science Reasoning Test asks you to identify the assumption in the argument.

What is an assumption? An assumption is a sort of simple logic that everyone takes for granted. Suppose I say,

*Brenda's car is in the driveway; now I can stop by and see her.*

What is the assumption in this statement? The assumption is

*Brenda is home when her car is in the driveway.*

Yet, Brenda could be at a neighbor's house or out of town. For the ACT, an assumption is an unwritten belief that, if *false*, would make the conclusion of the study invalid.

Here's an assumption question that refers to the passage on photosynthesis.

2. Which of the following was assumed in the design of the experiment?
   F. Each plant requires the same amount of water.
   G. The plants are genetically identical.
   H. The plants are naturally green all season.
   J. The plants will be exposed to sunlight.

## Here's How to Crack It

Think about it for a moment. What are some of the things you would have to assume about the study in order for the results to be acceptable? A major assumption is that the plants are genetically identical. If they weren't, then the findings could be invalid. For example, if a bunch of different plants were used, the experimenter couldn't be sure if the differences in the results were due to the lack of sunlight or to the variety of the plants themselves. So, the answer to this question is **G**.

## ANALYSIS

Remember the *analysis* questions that came with charts and graphs passages? They required you to integrate two or more pieces of information. Well, that's how it works on experiments questions as well. The only difference is that they may also ask you to compare the results of the data with the ideas presented in the passage. Here are some of the types of questions they may ask:

Can you think of another way to test the same relationship between the independent and dependent variables?

If the experiment were repeated many times and gave different results, what would that mean in terms of the conclusion of the study?

Let's look at an example that refers to the passage on photosynthesis.

3. Suppose the Group B plants were placed in the dark for only 2 days and continued to produce glucose. What would these results mean in terms of the objective of the study?
   A. Plants require sunlight to produce glucose.
   B. Plants are able to make glucose under any conditions.
   C. Photosynthesis occurs in all plants.
   D. Photosynthesis is not completely inhibited by the lack of sunlight for 2 days.

## Here's How to Crack It

The ACT writers want to see if you can relate these new results to the original ones. The Group B plants did not undergo photosynthesis if they were placed in the dark for one week. However, the plants did undergo photosynthesis if they were put in the dark for 2 days. This must mean that 2 days wasn't enough time to halt photosynthesis. The correct answer choice is therefore **D**.

## GENERALIZATION

Sometimes you'll be asked how the knowledge gained from the experiment might be applied to new situations. As usual, we're supposed to look at the "bigger picture." Here are some sample questions:

> Given the results of the study, can we predict the outcome of some future experiments?
>
> How do these results influence our understanding of the world?

Let's look at a generalization question that refers to the passage about gibberellins.

> 4. Suppose 20 mls of gibberellins was given to a similar crop of tomato plants for 180 days. What would happen to the height of these plants relative to the height of the plants in the initial experiment?
>    F. The new plants would be taller than the plants in the experiment.
>    G. The new plants would be shorter than the plants in the experiment.
>    H. The new plants would die.
>    J. The new plants would have the same height as Samples 4 and 5 in the experiment.

### Here's How to Crack It

Let's look back at the experiment and review the results. The tomato plants grew when the hormone was added, but eventually leveled off. What would happen if we added even more hormone to the plants? Based on the results of the experiment, their height should remain the same. The correct answer is **J**.

# PUTTING THE STRATEGY TO WORK

Let's try this strategy on some sample experiments passages. For practice, write down the objective and the type of question before you work out the answer.

## Passage I

It has been observed that plants exhibit phototropism (bending toward light) when placed in the presence of a light source. The actual part of the plant that bends toward the light source is not the tip of the plant but rather a region farther down the stem. Four flowering plants were exposed to sunlight in order to determine the site of light detection and the response of these plants.

*Experiment 1*

When light struck Plant 1 from the side, a region a few millimeters down from the tip bent as it grew until the tip pointed directly toward the light source.

*Experiment 2*

Plant 2 was also placed in the presence of sunlight, but the tip of the plant was covered with a dark cap. The plant failed to bend toward the light source.

*Experiment 3*

Plant 3 was exposed to the same conditions as Plant 2 except that a clear cap replaced the dark cap. This plant bent toward the light source.

*Experiment 4*

When a flexible dark collar was placed around the bending region of Plant 4, the plant still bent toward the light source.

OBJECTIVES:

1. The results of Experiments 1 and 2 indicate that:
   A. the plant requires both sunlight and nutrition in order to bend.
   B. the tip of the plant detects the light source.
   C. the light-proof cap assists the plant in its bending action.
   D. it is the amount of sunlight that causes the bending of the plant.

QUESTION TYPE: _____

2. Which of the following plant(s) served as the control(s) in the experiment?
   F. Plant 1 only
   G. Plant 3 only
   H. Plants 1 and 3 only
   J. Plants 2 and 3 only

QUESTION TYPE: _____

3. Based on the results of Experiments 1–4, it can be concluded that:
   A. the strength of the sun's rays correlated with the bending of the plant.
   B. flowering plants are unaffected by sunlight.
   C. the tip of the plant must transmit information about light direction to the lower bending region.
   D. flowering plants respond to light quite differently than non-flowering plants.

QUESTION TYPE: _____

**4.** Suppose the tip of the flowering plant is cut off in the presence of a light source, and a new tip does not grow. What will be the response of the plant?

   **F.** The plant will not bend toward the light.
   **G.** The plant will exhibit phototropism.
   **H.** The plant will die.
   **J.** The plant will produce flowers.

QUESTION TYPE: _____

## Here's How to Crack It

**Question 1:** This is an understanding question, and it directs your attention to Experiments 1 and 2. In Experiment 1, the plant bends when exposed to sunlight. In Experiment 2, the light-proof cap inhibits the influence of sunlight in such a way that prevents the bending of the plant. Clearly, the cap prevented sunlight from having any effect. So we can eliminate C. The passage doesn't give any information on the amount of sunlight (D) or the influence of nutrition (A). The only answer that correctly addresses the effect of the cap on the plant tip is answer choice **B**. It was the tip of the plant that was covered by the cap and therefore the tip of the plant must somehow perceive sunlight.

**Question 2:** Here is an understanding question about the control of the study. The control sample is Plant 1. Nothing was done to this plant. Plants 2, 3, and 4 were all manipulated to some degree to determine the influence of sunlight on phototropism. Plant 1 is left as is in the sunlight. Therefore the answer is **F**.

**Question 3:** This is an analysis question that requires more than one piece of information, so you need to look at the results of all of the experiments. Did you notice that when the tip was covered, the plant didn't bend? Actually, it's not the tip that bends but a region farther down from the tip. That means there must be some sort of communication between the tip of the plant and that region in order for this response to take place. Therefore the answer is **C**. Answer choice B is incorrect because plants *do* respond to sunlight—they bend. The passage does not give any information about differences between flowering plants and non-flowering plants (D) or the strength of the sun's rays (A).

**Question 4:** This is a generalization question. Did you notice that the question begins with the word "suppose"? That's a hint that you're supposed to predict the outcome of a similar study. You already know that the initial communication for phototropism occurs in the tip of the plant. If the tip is cut off, the most likely reaction would be that the plant will no longer be able to send information to the lower bending region, and therefore the plant will not bend. If you followed all the results of the study, then this should have been a logical follow-up based on the results. The answer to this question is choice **F**.

# Passage II

*Stratification* (the horizontal layering of particles) causes settling sediments to form distinct rock formations that contain different types of fossils. Breaks in the sequence of layers may be due to erosion by wind or water. A geologist studied the bedding of different rock formations in an area in order to establish the stratigraphic succession of rock formations and their fossil assemblage.

## Study 1

On her expedition the geologist found rock formations with the order and content shown below.

| Rock | Fossil assemblage |
| --- | --- |
| 1. Limestone | all kinds of marine animal fossils |
| 2. Black shale | small marine animal fossils only |
| 3. Coal | plant fossils |

## Study 2

The geologist examined the rock formation in another location 10 miles away and discovered rock formations with the order and content shown below.

| Rock | Fossil assemblage |
| --- | --- |
| 1. Black shale | small marine animal fossils |
| 2. Coal | plant fossils |
| 3. Sandstone | rare vertebrate bones |

## Study 3

At a third site 20 miles away the geologist discovered another rock sequence.

| Rock | Fossil assemblage |
| --- | --- |
| 1. Limestone | all kinds of marine animal fossils |
| 2. Coal | plant fossils |
| 3. Sandstone | rare vertebrate bones |

The following table gives the types of fossilized organisms normally found in a variety of rock formations.

| Rock | Types of fossilized organisms |
| --- | --- |
| 1. Sandstone | ancient fish skeletons and shark teeth |
| 2. Coal | tree stumps, ferns, twigs, green algae |
| 3. Black shale | snails, clams, oysters, and periwinkles |
| 4. Limestone | annelids, sponges, clams, and radiolarians |

1. Which of the following findings would NOT be consistent with the types of fossils normally found in the black shale formation?
   A. Periwinkles
   B. Clams
   C. Oysters
   D. Sponges

2. Based on the information presented in the studies, it could be inferred that the remains of ancient pine needles would be found in which of the following types of rocks?
   F. Limestone
   G. Black shale
   H. Coal
   J. Sandstone

3. Given the sequence of rock formation in Studies 1 and 2, what might have been the ordered sequence of rock formations in the area at one time?
   A. Limestone, coal, black shale, and sandstone
   B. Limestone, black shale, coal, and sandstone
   C. Coal, sandstone, black shale, and limestone
   D. Black shale, limestone, black shale, and coal

4. The sequence of rock formations in Study 3 is similar but not identical to the sequence of rock formations in Studies 1 and 2. Which of the following factors could be responsible for differences among the three sites?
   F. Weathering
   G. Extreme heat
   H. A mild rainstorm
   J. Cohesion

## Here's How to Crack It

**Question 1:** This is an understanding question. You need to find the types of fossilized organisms that are found in the black shale layer. You should therefore look at the table. What types of fossilized organisms are found in the black shale layer? They are snails, clams, oysters, and periwinkles. You can eliminate any of these answer choices since you're looking for the wrong answer choice. The only one that is not found in this layer is sponges. So the answer is **D**.

**Question 2:** This is an analysis question. Pine needles are not mentioned in any of the studies, but if you look at the data in each study, you will notice that plant fossils occur in only one kind of rock: coal. Thus the correct answer is **H**.

**Question 3:** This is an analysis question. You're supposed to observe the results of Studies 1 and 2 and figure out the correct sequence of the rock formations. Did you notice that the layers of Studies 1 and 2 overlap? The ordering of the layers must have been limestone, black shale, coal, and sandstone. The only answer choice with the correct sequence is **B**.

**Question 4:** This is an understanding question. The test writers want you to read the passage that mentions that the rock formations can be altered by various types of erosions. Which of the answer choices is an example of erosion?

The correct answer is the term "weathering," which refers to the break-up of rock formations by physical or chemical means. Answer choice J is ridiculous because it has nothing to do with the passage. In addition, a mild rainstorm or extreme heat would not be sufficient to wear away rock formations. So the correct answer is choice F.

## Passage III

Consider a massless spring hanging vertically from a stationary wooden block. When a mass is attached to the spring it causes the spring to vibrate. This is an example of simple harmonic motion in which a force leads to the displacement of the spring.

The equation for Hooke's spring law is $F = -kx$. The force (F) is proportional to the displacement ($x$) where $k$ is called the proportionality constant pertaining to a given spring. The negative sign signifies that the force exerted by the spring is in the opposite direction of the displacement. Several trials were done to observe the relationship between force and the displacement of an object. The results are tabulated in the chart below.

| Trial | Mass (gm) | $k$ | $x$ (cm) | F (lb) |
|-------|-----------|-----|----------|--------|
| 1 | 2 | 2.0 | 4 | 8 |
| 2 | 3 | 2.0 | 6 | 12 |
| 3 | 4 | 2.0 | 8 | 16 |
| 4 | 5 | 2.0 | 10 | 20 |

**Table 1**

OBJECTIVES:

1. From the trials above, it can be concluded that the displacement of an object depends on the:
   A. length of the spring.
   B. force according to Hooke's Law.
   C. density of air.
   D. height of the wooden block.

QUESTION TYPE: _____

2. If a downward force of 9 lbs. were placed on the mass, the approximate displacement would be:

   F. 2.5 cm.
   G. 3.0 cm.
   H. 4.5 cm.
   J. 18.0 cm.

QUESTION TYPE: _____

3. Based on the results of the study, it appears that $k$:

   A. increases as the force increases.
   B. is a constant in the experiment.
   C. leads to a decrease in force.
   D. leads to an increase in force.

QUESTION TYPE: _____

## Here's How to Crack It

**Question 1:** This is an understanding question. You can use the table to help you answer this question. Displacement changes according to what other variable? Force. As force changes, the displacement also changes. You could have looked at the formula $F = -kx$, which shows that force is related to displacement $(x)$. None of the other factors listed will affect the displacement. So, the answer to this question is **B**.

**Question 2:** This analysis question requires you to predict the displacement that would result from a hypothesized value of force. This is an example of interpolation. We're looking for a value that is going to fall within the range of values provided. What do we do? Guesstimate using the chart. The displacement from a force of 8 lbs. is 4 and from 10 lbs. would be 5. The only answer choice in that range is H, 4.5, and **H** is the correct answer.

**Question 3:** This is an analysis question. What function does $k$ serve in this study? Look at the table. It's a constant. How can you tell? Because the value of $k$ remains the same throughout the trials. So, the correct answer is **B**.

# 18

# Fighting Scientists

The third type of passage is called "fighting scientists." Each of these passages typically presents two or three conflicting views on a scientific phenomenon.

Think of it as a debate. Each debater proposes a hypothesis and then supports that hypothesis with facts, opinions, and assumptions. The ACT writers want you to evaluate and compare the arguments made by each debater. As far as they're concerned, it doesn't matter which hypothesis is correct. (They don't care who wins the debate.) They only want you to understand each of the viewpoints.

So don't choose sides. Your goal is to analyze the arguments based on the information provided in the passage. Even if you know something about the topic, your answers should come from the passage and nothing else.

# STEP 1: IDENTIFY THE DISAGREEMENT

Your first task when you see a fighting scientists passage is to identify the disagreement. You will be given two or more essays, each one expressing a particular point of view.

Because the arguments are going to conflict, you're going to have to learn how to pick out the points in each argument that make it different from the others. So as you read each argument, look for its main point. This is particularly important because it helps make the argument less confusing. Let's look at an example:

## Passage A

> Is the Earth the center of the solar system? Here are two conflicting views.
>
> *Hypothesis 1*
>
> The Earth is the center of our solar system and all celestial bodies revolve around it. When we look up at the sky, we see that the sun rises from the East and sets in the West. The idea of a moving Earth is absurd. If the Earth is a revolving planet, why don't we feel its motion? These phenomena, which are obvious to even a child, must prove that the Earth is a stationary body.
>
> *Hypothesis 2*
>
> The sun is the center of our solar system. The only reason we perceive the sun as moving is because of the Earth's rotation on its axis. Mathematical calculations by astronomers have shown that the Earth is not a stationary body and that it makes a complete revolution around the sun every 365 days. In addition, it is the Earth's gravitational force that does not allow us to perceive the Earth's motion.

What are the two opinions in this passage?

The main point of each argument appeared in the first sentence of each paragraph, and in this case each was clearly stated. The best way to remember the main point of the argument is to underline the sentence that states it.

## Your Underlined Version Should Look Like This

*Hypothesis 1*

<u>The Earth is the center of our solar system and all celestial bodies revolve around it.</u> When we look up at the sky, we see that the sun rises from the East and sets in the West. The idea of a moving Earth is absurd. If the Earth is a revolving planet, why don't we feel its motion? These phenomena, which are obvious to even a child, must prove that the Earth is a stationary body.

*Hypothesis 2*

<u>The sun is the center of our solar system.</u> The only reason we perceive the sun as moving is because of the Earth's rotation on its axis. Mathematical calculations by astronomers have shown that the Earth is not a stationary body and that it makes a complete revolution around the sun every 365 days. In addition, it is the Earth's gravitational force that does not allow us to perceive the Earth's motion.

Some of the scientific theories you'll read about in this section of the ACT were disproved a long time ago. That doesn't matter. For the ACT, it's the arguments that count. You may already know that the Earth isn't the center of our solar system. But it's still possible to evaluate, scientifically, the argument.

Now that we know how an ACT fighting scientists passage is set up, let's look at another example and try to find the main point of each argument:

## Passage B

Why did dinosaurs become extinct? Here are two opinions.

*Hypothesis 1*

About 65 million years ago the dinosaurs, the largest land animals, became extinct. Although no prevailing theory exists that explains their disappearance, the most logical explanation is that dramatic changes in sea level and climate destroyed their habitat. About the same time that dinosaurs died off, many other life forms, both on land and in the sea, became extinct. The shallow seas dried up and were suddenly empty. Since dinosaurs were quite heavy, it is believed that the only way they could have supported their weight was by using the buoyancy of water in swamps and lakes. Thus, the lack of water limited their mobility and their ability to acquire food. These enormous creatures therefore became extinct as a result of their inability to adapt to the harsh conditions that limited their natural habitat.

*Hypothesis 2*

For many years scientists have speculated about the cause of the extinction of the dinosaurs. Fossil records confirm that dinosaurs as well as other life forms were suddenly wiped out. The most natural cause of extinction is the inability of an organism to adapt to environmental changes. Yet, the extinction of all life forms is unlikely. Chemical analysis of clay found from this era attributes the sweeping extinction of dinosaurs to the collision of a huge meteorite with the Earth.

These fossil records confirm the presence of a high concentration of iridium, a rare heavy metal, which is abundant in meteorites. It is believed that a meteorite hit the Earth and created a huge crater, threw up dust that clouded the sun for several months. This event first led to the destruction of plant life and eventually all other life forms, including the dinosaurs.

Can you identify the disagreement in the passage?
What is the main point of Hypothesis 1?
What is the main point of Hypothesis 2?
According to Hypothesis 1, the extinction of dinosaurs was caused by changes in sea level and climate. According to Hypothesis 2, the extinction of dinosaurs was caused by dust from a meteorite collision.

If you didn't come up with the right answer, look at the underlined portions of the passages below.

*Hypothesis 1*

About 65 million years ago the dinosaurs, the largest land animals, became extinct. Although no prevailing theory exists that explains their disappearance, the most logical explanation is that dramatic changes in sea level and climate destroyed their habitat. About the same time that dinosaurs died off, many other life forms, both on land and in the sea, became extinct. The shallow seas dried up and were suddenly empty. Since dinosaurs were quite heavy, it is believed that the only way they could have supported their weight was by using the buoyancy of water in swamps and lakes. Thus, the lack of water limited their mobility and their ability to acquire food. These enormous creatures therefore became extinct as a result of their inability to adapt to the harsh conditions that limited their natural habitat.

*Hypothesis 2*

For many years scientists have speculated about the cause of the extinction of the dinosaurs. Fossil records confirm that dinosaurs as well as other life forms were suddenly wiped out. The most natural cause of extinction is the inability of an organism to adapt to environmental changes. Yet, the extinction of all life forms is unlikely. Chemical analysis of clay found from this era attributes the sweeping extinction of dinosaurs to the collision of a huge meteorite with the Earth. These fossil records confirm the presence of a high concentration of iridium, a rare heavy metal, which is abundant in meteorites. It is believed that a meteorite hit the Earth and created a huge crater, which threw up dust that clouded the sun for several months. This event first led to the destruction of plant life and eventually all other life forms, including the dinosaurs.

Did you notice that the main point of Hypothesis 1 could be found in two places? That's because in that case the last sentence was a summary of the main point.

## IDENTIFY THE QUESTION TYPE

Now that you understand how to evaluate arguments, you need to know which kinds of questions follow them.

## Understanding

The ACT writers are looking to see if you're able to understand and explain the arguments as well as the scientific concepts behind them. These types of questions test your ability to draw conclusions based on each of the arguments. Whenever you see an understanding question, stick to our general rule: The answer is contained in one portion of the passage.

Let's try an example using the passage about dinosaurs on pages 301–302.

> **1.** The two hypotheses are alike in that they both suggest that dinosaurs:
>
>     I.   were hit by meteorites.
>    II.  became extinct due to the limitations on their habitat.
>   III.  became extinct due to some external force other than predation.
>
>   **A.** I only
>   **B.** II only
>   **C.** III only
>   **D.** I and III only

## Here's How to Crack It

We're looking for a statement that agrees with both theories. The best way to tackle this question is to eliminate answer choices that only support one of the theories. Let's start with statement I. Does the statement that dinosaurs were hit by meteorites support both theories? No. In fact, it doesn't support either of them! The passage didn't state that the meteorite hit the dinosaurs; it stated that a meteorite hit the Earth and threw up a cloud of dust. So we can cancel choices A and D. (Both contain statement I.) Statement II says that dinosaurs became extinct because they were limited by their habitat. Hypothesis 1 agrees with this statement but not Hypothesis 2. So, we can get rid of answer choice B. Now let's check statement III. Do both hypotheses state that dinosaurs became extinct because of some external force? Yes. So the correct answer choice is **C**.

## HOW TO TACKLE ASSUMPTION QUESTIONS

Another question that comes up a lot concerns the assumption of the argument. Remember what assumptions are? We just covered them in the experiments section. Let's look back at the example we used under experiments.

*Brenda's car is in the driveway; now I can stop by and see her.*

What's the assumption in this sentence again? The assumption is

*Brenda is home when her car is in the driveway.*

That's right. An assumption is an unwritten belief that, if false, would make the conclusion invalid. Remember, assumptions are those points we take for granted. When it comes to alternative viewpoints passages, the underlying assumption is used to support the argument. If the assumption is proved false, then the argument will be weakened.

Here's an example concerning the dinosaur passage:

2. To accept Hypothesis 1, one must assume that:
   F. dinosaurs were primarily plant-eaters.
   G. all dinosaurs were large and thus depended on water for movement.
   H. the dinosaurs died because they were unable to drink the sea water.
   J. a meteor hit the Earth approximately 65 million years ago.

## Here's How to Crack It

First, let's review what Hypothesis 1 stated. It said that the dinosaurs died off because they were unable to thrive in their natural habitat. We need an answer choice that states something we take for granted about this theory. If dinosaurs were limited because of their size, then we must assume that all dinosaurs were huge. Only if all dinosaurs were huge would the lack of water in the swamps and seas limit their movement. That's the assumption. The correct answer is therefore **G.** Answer choice J supports Hypothesis 2 so it should be eliminated immediately. Do dinosaurs have to eat plants? No. So get rid of F. Was the problem that dinosaurs were unable to drink the sea water? No, the passage said they needed water for movement, not for drinking, so H is out. Remember, stick to the scope of the passage.

## ANALYSIS

These questions involve the integration of information from both (or all) arguments. For instance, they may ask you to identify a strength or weakness in the argument of one of the scientists. How do you do that? You want to find a statement or an assumption that, if invalid, would make the hypothesis wrong.

There are two ways to weaken an argument. One way is to find a shaky point in the argument of the scientist. Let's go back to the passage about the Earth being the center of the solar system. One shaky point might be that just because the sun looks like it revolves around the Earth doesn't mean it actually does. The other way to weaken this argument is to use information from the "opposing camp"—the other scientist. For instance, let's go back to the passage about the Earth being the center of the solar system. You could say that there is mathematical evidence to prove that the Earth does revolve around the sun. Where did we get this point? From the other scientist.

Here's an example using the dinosaur passage:

> **3.** Which of the following discoveries would best support Hypothesis 2?
>
>    **A.** The existence of radioactive substances in the soil.
>
>    **B.** The presence of other rare metals common to meteorites in the clay beds of the ocean from that period.
>
>    **C.** Fossil records of land-dwelling reptiles that roamed the Earth for an additional 10 million years.
>
>    **D.** Evidence of dramatic changes in sea level 65 million years ago.

## Here's How to Crack It

This question tests your ability to recognize trends in the argument. What type of evidence would support Hypothesis 2? Any evidence that shows that dinosaurs were wiped out as a result of the impact of a meteorite. Would the presence of radioactive substances in the soil support Hypothesis 2? It could only support the passage if the radioactive elements were from meteorites (like iridium). Answer choice A did not specify that. Would the fact that some land-dwelling reptiles survived past this period support Hypothesis 2? No, so answer choice C doesn't give us additional information to support Hypothesis 2. We can also get rid of answer choice D because it supports Hypothesis 1. What about answer choice B? What if other rare metals that are known to be found in meteorites were discovered? Would this support Hypothesis 2? Yes. The correct answer choice is **B.**

### GENERALIZATION

This type of question requires that you make predictions based on the information provided. This time, the test writers may give you new information such as the discovery of a fossil, or the results of a new experiment, and ask how this information influences the conclusions of the two hypotheses. Here again they are asking you to look at the "big picture."

Let's look at an example using the dinosaur passage again:

> **5.** Suppose a geologist discovered that the bones of dinosaurs contained traces of radioactive iridium. How would this evidence influence the two hypotheses?
>
>    **A.** It would support both hypotheses.
>
>    **B.** It would support Hypothesis 1 and weaken Hypothesis 2.
>
>    **C.** It would support Hypothesis 2 and weaken Hypothesis 1.
>
>    **D.** It would not support Hypothesis 1 or Hypothesis 2.

## Here's How to Crack It

Did you notice that this question starts with the word "suppose?" This tells you that this is probably a generalization question. Now, which of the hypotheses would be supported if a geologist found fossil bones that contained traces of radioactive iridium? Hypothesis 2 of course! The passage states that radioactive iridium is abundant in meteorites. If dinosaurs were exposed to the dust of meteorites, their bones would contain this metal. The correct answer is **C.** Which answer choices were you supposed to begin with? Answer choices B and C. Why? Because these answer choices present opposite trends.

# PUTTING THE STRATEGY TO WORK

Let's try this strategy on these sample fighting scientists passages. For practice, write down what type of question it is before you work out the answer.

## Passage 1

How did the continents take on their current shape? Two differing views are presented below.

*Scientist 1*

According to a theory based on plate tectonics, the land surface of the Earth once comprised a single continent, termed *Pangaea,* which was surrounded by a single vast ocean. Pangaea broke apart because the surfaces of the Earth floated on massive plates above the deeper mantle of the ocean's basin. Horizontal movement of the plates began to split up the land about 137 million years ago during the Jurassic period. The continents and the ocean basins moved along convection currents in the mantle resulting in a continuous degeneration of the Earth's physical features. The movement of these rigid plates produced zones of tectonic activity along their margins such as earthquakes, volcanoes, and mountain formations. Fossil records as well as geological evidence show similarities between widely displaced continents. For instance, the coastlines of South America and Africa contain similar rock formations and appear to fit together like a jigsaw puzzle.

*Scientist 2*

The continents and the ocean basins of the Earth are permanent, fixed features of the planet. The hypothesis of plate tectonics is flawed because there is insufficient evidence to support it. The force of gravity is stronger than any known tangential force that can act on the Earth's crust. The layers of crust that support the continents and ocean basins are strong enough to preserve the Earth's physical features and are too strong to permit horizontal drift. Tectonic activity has always been present but the hypothesis of plate tectonics only explains such activity in one late period of ancient history. In addition, it is not clear what kind of force could allow the continents, composed largely of granite, to move through areas of dense, iron-rich rock that comprise the ocean basins. Any geological evidence that supports such a theory may be due to the existence of similar conditions on different continents.

1. Which of the following statements is the most inconsistent with the beliefs of Scientist 1?
   A. Continents were once part of a large land mass.
   B. Continents split up and drifted apart.
   C. Ocean basins have not changed for millions of years.
   D. Geological evidence shows similarities between widely displaced continents.

QUESTION TYPE: _____

2. Scientist 1 studied the fossils along the coast of South America and Africa and found identical fernlike plants on rocks of the same age. What claim could Scientist 2 make to refute the findings of Scientist 1?
   F. The dating and comparison of plant fossils is an exact science.
   G. The ferns floated from the shore of one continent to the other.
   H. The ferns were extremely large.
   J. The ferns thrive in tropical regions.

QUESTION TYPE: _____

3. A new zone of tectonic activity has been discovered in the large land mass of Eurasia. This zone shows geological evidence of having been active for several thousand years. Which scientist is supported by this finding and why?
   A. Scientist 1, because it proves that tectonic activity occurs on the planet.
   B. Scientist 1, because it shows that Pangaea and Eurasia are the same land mass.
   C. Scientist 2, because it proves that tectonic activity occurs in land masses and not solely in the ocean basin and along coastlines.
   D. Scientist 2, because it shows that the continents are made out of granite.

QUESTION TYPE: _____

4. Both Scientist 1 and Scientist 2 are experts in plate tectonics. To what discipline of science do these scientists belong?
   F. Physics
   G. Geology
   H. Biology
   J. Chemistry

QUESTION TYPE: _____

5. Which of the following claims would be supported by both scientists?

    I.   Tectonic activity has always been a factor in the geology of land masses.

    II.  The continents and the ocean basins are fixed features of the planet.

    III. Continental drift occurred in the Jurassic period.

    **A.** I only
    **B.** II only
    **C.** I and II only
    **D.** II and III only

QUESTION TYPE: _____

## Here's How to Crack It

**Question 1:** This is an understanding question. What are the beliefs of Scientist 1? His main point is that Pangaea (one continent) existed 137 million years ago. Now, let's start by looking at each of the answer choices. Were the continents once part of one large land mass? Yes. We read that in the passage. What about choice B? Did the continents break up and drift apart? Definitely. Does the statement that the ocean basins remained fixed agree with the theory? No. If so, how would the continents drift apart? So answer choice C is inconsistent. Answer choice D is not inconsistent with the theory of Scientist 1. So the correct answer choice is **C**.

**Question 2:** This is an analysis question. Scientist 2 needs to come up with a statement that would disprove the other scientist's argument. How can he do that? By stating a point that weakens the argument. Let's look at which answer choice does that best. Answer choice F states that the techniques used to date and compare fossils are accurate. This statement supports the opinion of Scientist 1. What about the statement that ferns floated from one continent to the other? Would that weaken the argument? Most definitely! Then the rock would contain the same plants! Answer choice H supports Scientist 1 because extremely large ferns would have a hard time floating thousands of miles across the ocean. You can eliminate answer choice J, because it doesn't support either scientist. You can only infer that these ferns grow well in Africa and South America. The answer is **G**.

**Question 3:** This is an analysis question and it's kind of tricky. Either scientist could use this information to support his theory if he could come up with a valid reason. Answer choice A says that Scientist 1 is supported because the finding shows tectonic activity. But we already knew about that and besides, that's a point on which the scientists agree. So eliminate choice A. Answer choice D also gives us information that was already stated in Scientist 2's statement, so this choice is weak. Choice B is ridiculous because neither scientist believes that Pangaea exists today, so cross it out. At this point, answer choice C is looking pretty good. Scientist 2 could soundly reason that tectonic activity in a solid land mass demonstrates that this geological phenomenon does not lead to continental drift. The best answer choice is **C**.

**Question 4:** This is an understanding question. The passage tells us about the formation of land masses, tectonic plates, and other geological evidence, namely fossils. You must be able to add this together and determine that the scientists know something about geology. So, only answer **G** can be the correct answer.

**Question 5:** This is an understanding question. You must know what each scientist supports. Let's go through the choices one by one. Statement I is supported by both scientists because both believe that tectonic activity exists and changes geological formations. (Scientist 1 thinks it's more important than does Scientist 2, but that doesn't matter here.) So, statement I is correct and we're down to choices A and C. Let's keep checking. Only Scientist 2 supports statement II and only Scientist 1 supports statement III. Therefore, **A** must be the correct answer choice.

# Passage II

How did life on Earth originate? Two differing views are presented.

*Hypothesis 1*

In 1953 a graduate student attempted to recreate the conditions of primeval Earth in a sealed glass apparatus that he filled with methane, ammonia, hydrogen, and water. Sparks were released into the glass to simulate lightning, and heat was applied to the water. The result was the formation of organic compounds, known as amino acids, which are the building blocks of proteins. Since that time, others have shown how DNA may have been synthesized under various conditions as well. RNA, which is DNA's partner in the translation of genetic information into protein products, has been found to have the ability to reproduce itself under certain conditions. Thus, the origins of life are to be found in the "primordial soup" of the ancient Earth that provided conditions for the simplest forms of organic matter to form and develop increasingly sophisticated means of organization. With the ability of compounds to make copies of themselves comes the opportunity for evolution by the mechanisms of heredity and mutation.

*Hypothesis 2*

Previous assumptions about the makeup of the "primordial soup" are inaccurate. It is not at all clear that methane and ammonia were present on the primeval Earth or that conditions were as favorable as in the graduate student's experiment. The ability of RNA to reproduce itself is also limited to particular conditions that the primeval Earth is unlikely to have provided. There is a possibility that, given enough time, random events could alone have resulted in the development of entire single-celled organisms, but some have likened that possibility to the chance that a tornado whirling through a junkyard could result in the formation of a 747 jetliner. During much of the time when the "primordial soup" was to have existed, the Earth was a regular target of meteors that kept oceans boiling and the atmosphere inhospitable to organic development. Clearly much more research is needed before this theory can be widely accepted.

1. Which of the following statements about the conditions on primeval Earth could be used to support Hypothesis 2?
   A. Atmospheric conditions were too unstable to support the gases essential to the theories of the "primordial soup."
   B. Organic molecules were able to thrive under primeval Earth conditions.
   C. The origin of life began in the "primordial soup."
   D. The atmosphere contained methane, ammonia, hydrogen, and water.

QUESTION TYPE: _____

2. To accept Hypothesis 1, one must assume that:
   F. the Earth was bombarded by meteors during that time period.
   G. the conditions in the glass were analogous to the conditions on primeval Earth.
   H. proteins are the building blocks of amino acids.
   J. the Earth lacked hydrogen in the atmosphere.

QUESTION TYPE: _____

3. Which of the following shows how, according to Hypothesis 1, the building blocks of life were formed?
   A. Methane + Ammonia + Hydrogen + Water → Primordial Soup → Amino Acids
   B. Meteors → Primordial Soup → Amino Acids.
   C. Amino Acids → Primordial Soup → DNA → Methane + Ammonia + Hydrogen + Water
   D. Primordial Soup → proteins → Amino Acids

QUESTION TYPE: _____

## Here's How to Crack It

**Question 1:** This is an analysis question because we're asked to find an answer that supports the argument. What's the main point of Hypothesis 2? The debater believes that the chance of RNA reproducing as the graduate student described is extremely small. Look for an answer choice that supports this argument. Answer choice A states that conditions in the atmosphere were too unstable to support the necessary gases. Does this statement support Hypothesis 2? Yes. How? Because it weakens Hypothesis 1. So answer choice **A** is correct. Answer choices B, C, and D are wrong because they support Hypothesis 1.

**Question 2:** This is an understanding question, and we're looking for an assumption in the argument. What does Scientist 1 believe? That the experiment shows how the first organic compounds were made. Is answer choice F an assumption in this argument? No, it refers to Hypothesis 2. What about answer choice G? Yes. The scientist assumed that the experiment mimicked the conditions of primeval Earth. So, **G** is correct. Answer choice H states that proteins are the building blocks of amino acids. That's wrong, as stated in Hypothesis 1. Amino acids are the building blocks of proteins. So get rid of H. Answer choice J is incorrect because the Earth had to have hydrogen in order to form organic compounds.

**Question 3:** This is an understanding question. What does Hypothesis 1 say about amino acids? The passage tells us that amino acids are the building blocks of life, so let's start with the answer choices that list amino acids last. We can quickly eliminate C. We can also eliminate B, because the meteor theory was part of Hypothesis 2, not 1. And we're down to choices A and D. We can also find in the passage that amino acids are the building blocks of proteins, so amino acids should be before protein in the list. So, by POE and understanding the passage, we arrive at the correct answer, **A.**

## Passage III

Will the Earth experience another ice age?

*Hypothesis 1*

Scientists have long speculated whether glaciation will ever take place again. Given that glaciation is an unusual event, it is highly unlikely that such a phenomenon will ever repeat itself. Glaciation usually takes place under periods of extremely cool temperatures. However, it appears that the temperature on the Earth has been milder and more stable than at any other period. In fact, it would take a 5°C drop in the average surface temperature in order for glaciation to occur. In addition, there would have to be a significant increase in precipitation.

*Hypothesis 2*

Although the Earth has not experienced glaciation in a long time, the event, no matter how rare, can occur if the right conditions are met. Two factors that are critical to the growth of glaciers are precipitation and temperature. There are a number of areas, specifically land masses in the polar regions, that are currently cold enough to produce glaciers, but do not have sufficient snowfall to develop glacier systems. However, if enough events occur simultaneously, they can bring on an ice age. For instance, if there is an increase in the level of snowfall in the winter in these polar regions, this could eventually lead to glaciation. On the other hand, the level of pollution in the atmosphere is also sufficient to gradually cool the earth. Under these conditions it is quite clear that glaciation is only a matter of the right combination of events at the right time.

1. Which of the following discoveries would most clearly favor Hypothesis 2?
   A. Canada has more snowfall this year than any other year.
   B. When snow falls, it sticks to the ground.
   C. The more pollution in the air, the more the temperature drops.
   D. The Earth's bodies of waters are becoming more polluted.

QUESTION TYPE: _____

2. Which of the following statements is the strongest argument a supporter of Hypothesis 2 would use to counter Hypothesis 1?
   F. The temperature around polar regions fluctuates.
   G. The precipitation rate has been increasing in the Swiss Alps.
   H. Just because ideal conditions are rare does not mean they will not occur in the future.
   J. The temperature in the North pole has gone up 2°C.

QUESTION TYPE: _____

3. If Hypothesis 2 is correct and glaciation can take place in the future, what regions would be most affected?
   I.   Heavily polluted regions
   II.  Polar regions
   III. Humid regions

   A. I only
   B. II only
   C. I and II only
   D. II and III only

QUESTION TYPE: _____

4. According to Hypothesis 2, what conditions could cause glaciation?
   A. Low levels of pollution leading to high precipitation
   B. High levels of pollution leading to a blanketing effect that blocks out the sun and decreases the temperature dramatically
   C. High levels of pollution leading to low precipitation
   D. A major snowstorm for three days in Chicago

QUESTION TYPE: _____

## Here's How to Crack It

**Question 1:** This is an analysis question. We are looking for an answer choice that supports Hypothesis 2. Hypothesis 2 states that an increase in precipitation or an increase in pollution would lead to a significant drop in temperature. Answer choice A says that there is more snow in Canada this year, but we don't know if that's enough snow for glaciation. So we can eliminate it. Let's look at B. If snow didn't stick to the ground, would there be an ice age? Answer choice B is silly; eliminate it. What about answer choice C? If there is a drop in temperature for every increase in the pollution rate, could that lead to glaciation? Yes. Let's look at answer choice D. If the water became more polluted would that necessarily lead to the next ice age? We're not sure. The passage states that pollution in the air, not necessarily water, leads to a decrease in temperature. So the correct answer is **C**.

**Question 2:** This is an analysis question. For this question we're looking for an answer choice that could disprove Hypothesis 1. What is the main point of Hypothesis 1? The debater says that it is highly unlikely that the Earth will experience another ice age. Why? Because he believes that the necessary conditions will not be met in the future. What is the best way to disprove this point? Just indicate that the conditions could change in the future and then the chance for glaciation could increase. Which answer choice states that? Answer choice H. Now let's look at answer choice F. A fluctuation in temperature would not necessarily mean that the temperature was low enough for glaciation to occur. We therefore can eliminate this choice. Even if there was more snowfall in the Swiss Alps, we are not given an indication of how long it lasted. So you can get rid of answer choice G. Now, if the temperature went up 5°C in the North pole, it would be warmer, not colder, so answer choice J is out. So the correct answer choice is **H**.

**Question 3:** What type of question is this? It's an understanding question because you are being asked to identify the regions in which glaciation would take place. Let's start with statement II, since it appears in the most answer choices. Based on the passage, would glaciation take place in polar regions? The passage tells us that polar regions would be one of the first locations in which glaciation would take place. Now that you can eliminate answer choices that don't include statement II, you can eliminate answer choice A. What about heavily polluted regions? Yes, the passage refers to the other possible cause of a temperature drop—pollution. Now, according to the passage, does humidity have anything to do with glaciation? No. So answer choice is **C** is correct.

**Question 4:** This is also an understanding question. There are two conditions that are critical to glaciation: temperature and precipitation. Answer choice A is incorrect because pollution doesn't cause precipitation. Answer choice B sounds good since it states that pollution leads to a major drop in temperature (it has one of the conditions). What about answer choice C? You can eliminate C since it states that pollution leads to low precipitation levels. Answer choice D is ridiculous: As unpleasant as it may be, a Chicago snowstorm would not cause glaciation! The answer is **B**.

# SUMMARY

1. There are three types of passages on the ACT Science Reasoning Test. They are charts and graphs, experiments, and fighting scientists.

2. For the Science Reasoning Test, you should always scan the passage first.

3. If you're given a charts and graphs passage, you should focus on the graphs, tables, and charts. If you're given an experiments passage, you should look for the objective, identify the variables, and study the results. If you're given a fighting scientists passage, identify the disagreement.

4. Once you have glanced at the passage, go directly to the questions.

5. Your next task is to identify the question type. If it is an understanding question, the answer is supposed to be in a specific portion of the passage. If it is an analysis question, you'll need to draw upon larger portions of the passage and integrate them. If it is a generalization question, you're supposed to look at the big picture and relate the results to the real world.

6. An understanding question may ask you to find the control of the study. Look for the variable (the thing) that has not been manipulated or exposed: That's the control!

7. An understanding question may also ask you to find the assumption of an argument. The assumption is an underlying point in the experiment or argument. Look for an answer choice with a statement that is taken for granted in the study.

8. Guesstimate to help you approximate values on a graph or figure. This will save you a lot of time that could be better spent on other questions.

9. Use Process of Elimination (POE) to eliminate ridiculous answer choices.

# PART ◆ VI

# The Princeton Review Assessment (PRA)

Most colleges require that you submit either an ACT or SAT score with your transcript. However, you may find it difficult to determine which test will best represent your abilities. The Princeton Review Assessment (PRA) is a single three-and-a-half-hour test that will give you an idea of how you will perform on *both* exams so that you can make an educated decision about which test to take.

It is important that you take the PRA as if it were a real ACT or SAT.

- Find a quiet spot to take the exam, preferably at a desk or table where you can sit up straight.

- Tell your family that you have important business to attend to and should not be interrupted.

- Disconnect any phones within earshot. You can talk with your friends after the test.

- Use a timer. Do not give yourself more than the indicated amount of time on any section. Extra time will invalidate your scores.

The best results will be obtained if you take the entire exam in one sitting with a five-minute break between the third and fourth sections. The answers and a guide for scoring are printed on the pages following the exam. There is also a sheet for recording your answers immediately following the test. You should remove it from the book and use it while taking the test. Take some time after you finish to read about what your score means.

Good luck!

**GO ON TO THE NEXT PAGE.**

## LANGUAGE SKILLS

*30 Minutes–55 Questions*

**DIRECTIONS:** In the five passages that follow, certain words and phrases are underlined and numbered. In the right-hand column, you will find alternatives for each underlined part. You are to choose the one that best expresses the idea, makes the statement appropriate for standard written English, or is worded most consistently with the style and tone of the passage as a whole. If you think the original version is best, choose "NO CHANGE."

You will also find questions about a section of the passage, or the passage as a whole. These questions do not refer to

an underlined portion of the passage, but rather are identified by a number or numbers in a box.

For each question, choose the alternative you consider best and blacken the corresponding oval on your answer sheet. Read each passage through once before you begin to answer the questions that accompany it. You cannot determine most answers without first reading several sentences beyond the question. Be sure that you have read far enough ahead each time you choose an alternative.

### PASSAGE I

### Animal Migration

It seems inconceivable to us <u>when some animals</u>
                                          <sub>1</sub>
travel thousands of miles during their life cycles.

1. **A.** NO CHANGE
   **B.** whereby
   **C.** that
   **D.** if

<u>For understanding</u> why they do it, we need only look
       <sub>2</sub>
at the changing seasons in the North. As summer fades

into fall, which in turn fades into winter, we turn on our

furnaces and take our warm coats out of storage

<u>because it is cold.</u> We eat less fresh food. If our winter
       <sub>3</sub>

2. **F.** NO CHANGE
   **G.** To understand
   **H.** As understanding
   **J.** If we understand

3. **A.** NO CHANGE
   **B.** as if it was cold
   **C.** because it was cold
   **D.** OMIT the underlined portion.

food is <u>fresh, it has</u> probably been shipped from a warmer
           <sub>4</sub>
climate.

4. **F.** NO CHANGE
   **G.** fresh. They have
   **H.** fresh; it has
   **J.** fresh. It has

Wild animals, <u>nevertheless,</u> have not developed the
                    <sub>5</sub>
sophisticated technologies necessary for the

5. **A.** NO CHANGE
   **B.** however
   **C.** although
   **D.** despite this

<u>adaptations and adjustments that we employ and utilize.</u>
                              <sub>6</sub>
In order to endure the harsher seasons, some change their

coats like us. Others, though, are not able to adapt to the

fluctuating temperatures. They follow the warm weather

south (or north, if they live south of the Equator). These

6. **F.** NO CHANGE
   **G.** adaptations and adjustments that we employed
         and utilized.
   **H.** adaptations and adjustments that we are
         employing.
   **J.** adaptations we employ.

**GO ON TO THE NEXT PAGE.**

migratory creatures, a group that encompasses birds,
                                    ⎯⎯⎯⎯⎯⎯⎯
                                         7
whales, fish, insects, and quadrupedal mammals, have

bodies adapted to the demands of long seasonal journeys.

Why do they travel so very far?  This is something

of a mystery, especially since some creatures must

traverse inhospitable areas during the trip to they're
                                              ⎯⎯⎯⎯
                                                8
seasonal homes. For example, certain sea birds must

cross oceans to get to their winter nesting grounds.

During its migration from equatorial Africa to northern

Europe, the white stork crossed the Sahara Desert and
                        ⎯⎯⎯⎯⎯⎯
                            9
the Mediterranean Sea. Although the exact cause for such

journeys is impossible to determine. Scientists speculate
                          ⎯⎯⎯⎯⎯⎯⎯⎯⎯⎯⎯⎯⎯⎯⎯
                                  10
that continental drift has pulled traditional

seasonal grounds far apart and that instinct
                     ⎯⎯⎯⎯
                      11

having precluded a change in territorial preference.
⎯⎯⎯⎯⎯⎯
  12

7. A. NO CHANGE
   B. encompasses: birds
   C. encompasses, birds
   D. encompass birds

8. F. NO CHANGE
   G. their
   H. it's
   J. its

9. A. NO CHANGE
   B. having crossed
   C. crosses
   D. had crossed

10. F. NO CHANGE
    G. determine—scientists
    H. determine; scientists
    J. determine, scientists

11. A. NO CHANGE
    B. apart and,
    C. apart: and
    D. apart; and

12. F. NO CHANGE
    G. had precluded
    H. was precluding
    J. has precluded

---

Item 13 poses a question about Passage I
as a whole.

---

13. Which of the following best describes the tone and
    purpose of this essay?

    A. The tone is ironic; the purpose is to point out
       the similarities between people and animals.
    B. The tone is objective; the purpose is to discuss
       some possible reasons for migration in animals.
    C. The tone is critical; the purpose is to condemn
       animals for being unable to adapt to the
       seasons.
    D. The tone is humorous; the purpose is to present
       an amusing anecdote.

**GO ON TO THE NEXT PAGE.**

**Passage II**

### The Dada Movement

[1]

Max Ernst, in the Dada movement, was a German
$\overline{\phantom{xx}14\phantom{xx}}$
artist and a leading figure.

However, Ernst cut up photographs, engravings, and
$\overline{15}$
illustrations, and recombined the images in collage form.

The featured objects thereby assumed new, sometimes

multiple, identities.

[2]

Horrified by trench warfare, a lasting imprint was left
$\overline{\phantom{xx}16\phantom{xx}}$
on the generation of European intellectuals who came of

age during World War I.  Painters, sculptors, and people

who wrote turned their expressions of protest into works
$\overline{17}$
of art and gave their movement the

nonsensical and meaningless name Dada. Dada
$\overline{\phantom{xx}18\phantom{xx}}$
condemned the existing cultural institutions and

advocated the liberation of artistic form.

14. **F.** NO CHANGE
    **G.** In the Dada movement, a leading figure and a German artist, was Max Ernst.
    **H.** Max Ernst was a German artist and a leading figure in the Dada movement.
    **J.** A German artist and a leading figure in the Dada movement was Max Ernst.

15. **A.** NO CHANGE
    **B.** As a consequence,
    **C.** Despite the fact,
    **D.** OMIT the underlined portion.

16. **F.** NO CHANGE
    **G.** Horrified, trench warfare left a lasting imprint
    **H.** The horror of trench warfare left a lasting imprint
    **J.** A lasting imprint left by trench warfare

17. **A.** NO CHANGE
    **B.** writers
    **C.** writing people
    **D.** OMIT the underlined portion.

18. **F.** NO CHANGE
    **G.** nonsensical, and meaningless
    **H.** nonsensical and absurd
    **J.** nonsensical

**GO ON TO THE NEXT PAGE.**

[3]

Max Ernst is best known for contributing to this
19
period was the development of the frottage technique.


Ernst lay down paper over raised surfaces, rubbed a pencil
20
over the paper, then isolated images in the haphazard

design that resulted. These images were then

to be translated to paintings. The desolate landscapes
21


portrayed in many of Ernsts' later works suggest the
22
destruction of a depraved society.

[4]

The Dada movement had lost much of their impetus
23
by the early 1920s. At that time, Ernst moved to Paris

where another artistic movement, surrealism, was in

its formative stages. Surrealists sought to capture the

images produced by free association of the unconscious

mind. They combined these images in incongruous ways,

creating effects that were sometimes humorous, although

sometimes frightening.

19. **A.** NO CHANGE
    **B.** Max Ernst's best-known contribution
    **C.** Max Ernsts' best-known contribution
    **D.** Max Ernst is best known for his contribution

20. **F.** NO CHANGE
    **G.** placed down
    **H.** placed
    **J.** placed and lay

21. **A.** NO CHANGE
    **B.** translated into paintings.
    **C.** translated into becoming paintings.
    **D.** being translated into paintings.

22. **F.** NO CHANGE
    **G.** Ernsts' later work
    **H.** the later work of Ernst's
    **J.** Ernst's later works

23. **A.** NO CHANGE
    **B.** its
    **C.** the movement's
    **D.** the movements'

Item 24 poses a question about Passage II
as a whole.

24. Which of the following sequences of paragraphs will
make the essay most logical?

**F.** NO CHANGE
**G.** 4, 2, 1, 3
**H.** 2, 1, 3, 4
**J.** 2, 3, 4, 1

**GO ON TO THE NEXT PAGE.**

**PASSAGE III**

### Ella Fitzgerald

Jazz singer, Ella Fitzgerald, was born in 1918 in
                                              25

Newport News, Virginia. She took part in a performance
                                              26
on amateur night at the Apollo Theatre in New York when

she caught the eye and ear of band leader Chick Webb,

who hired her immediately. Fitzgerald performed with

Webb's band until his death in 1935, at which time she

took over the group. Two years later, she left

to pursue a career as a soloist.
   27

[1] She flawlessly interpreted the works of such

musical legends as Jerome Kern, Cole Porter, and George

Gershwin, who are very famous.  [2] She sang a broad
          28
spectrum of music, ranging from slow and sultry to

upbeat and swinging.   [3] Nicknamed "The First Lady of

Song," Ella Fitzgerald had a long and illustrious career.

[4] Her contribution to the world of
        29

music, and indeed to society as a whole, was

great. [30]

25. A. NO CHANGE
    B. singer: Ella Fitzgerald,
    C. singer Ella Fitzgerald
    D. singer Ella Fitzgerald,

26. F. NO CHANGE
    G. was performing
    H. has been performing
    J. is performing

27. A. NO CHANGE
    B. having pursued
    C. only to pursue
    D. and pursuing

28. F. NO CHANGE
    G. all of who are famous
    H. all famous
    J. OMIT the underlined portion.

29. A. NO CHANGE
    B. contributions
    C. contributing
    D. having contributed

30. For the sake of unity and coherence, Sentence 3
    should be placed

    F. where it is now.
    G. after Sentence 1.
    H. (It should be omitted.)
    J. before Sentence 1.

**GO ON TO THE NEXT PAGE.**

Fitzgerald helped <u>pave</u> the way for other black
        31

singers and brought jazz to a larger audience. <u>Her singing</u>
                                                      32
facilitated the integration of blacks and whites, at

least within the confines of the music hall. <u>Either blacks</u>
                                                 33
<u>or whites</u> flocked to hear her sing,

<u>united under a brief time</u> by the magic of her sound.
        34

31. **A.** NO CHANGE
    **B.** the paving of
    **C.** paving
    **D.** OMIT the underlined portion.

32. **F.** NO CHANGE
    **G.** Since her singing
    **H.** Since Fitzgerald's singing
    **J.** That her singing

33. **A.** NO CHANGE
    **B.** All blacks and whites
    **C.** Both blacks and whites
    **D.** Because blacks and whites

34. **F.** NO CHANGE
    **G.** united for a brief time
    **H.** united—for a brief time
    **J.** united, for a brief time

---

Item 35 poses a question about Passage III
as a whole.

---

35. Suppose that a newspaper editor had assigned the
    writer to describe an instance of racial unity in the
    arts. Does the essay successfully fulfill the assign-
    ment?

    **A.** No, because its main focus is on the career of
          Ella Fitzgerald.
    **B.** Yes, because Fitzgerald sang works by white
          composers.
    **C.** Yes, because blacks and whites alike went to
          see Fitzgerald sing.
    **D.** No, because very few people listen to jazz.

**GO ON TO THE NEXT PAGE.**

**PASSAGE IV**

### The Change to Agriculture

Approximately ten thousand years ago, a radical change took place in the way people lived, significantly altering their lives. They abandoned the traditional methods of hunting and gathering their food, which required an arduous migration to seasonal grounds. Instead, they domesticated the plants and animals they
37

needed to survive.
38

The shift to domestication and a sedentary lifestyle
39

wrought great change. A given area of land could now support more people than were ever before possible.
40

Moreover, agriculture necessitated the storage of seed stock, the division of labor, and allocating land.
41

As each region became more specialized in what they
42

produced, the need for greater trade and communication intensified. The population in each area became situated around natural, centrally located points, which developed
43

into the first cities. It became necessary to organize the

**36. F.** NO CHANGE
**G.** to alter their lives
**H.** which significantly altered their lives
**J.** OMIT the underlined portion.

**37. A.** NO CHANGE
**B.** Nevertheless,
**C.** However,
**D.** Even so,

**38. F.** NO CHANGE
**G.** surviving.
**H.** for surviving.
**J.** to have survived.

**39. A.** NO CHANGE
**B.** from
**C.** of
**D.** for

**40. F.** NO CHANGE
**G.** than was
**H.** than they were
**J.** than it were

**41. A.** NO CHANGE
**B.** to allocate
**C.** allocated
**D.** the allocation of

**42. F.** NO CHANGE
**G.** it produced. The need
**H.** they produced. The need
**J.** it produced, the need

**43. A.** NO CHANGE
**B.** points: which
**C.** points: which,
**D.** points; which

**GO ON TO THE NEXT PAGE.**

increasingly complex and complicated economic
                    44

relationships and develop a structure capable to deal
                                              45
with the many societal changes. Thus, centrally

located authority developed, giving rise to the first real

governments.

44. F.  NO CHANGE
    G.  complex, and complicated
    H.  complex but complicated
    J.  complex

45. A.  NO CHANGE
    B.  of dealing
    C.  to have dealt
    D.  OMIT the underlined portion.

---

**PASSAGE V**

### Who Was Dracula?

[1] Many legends, such as those of Bluebeard and
King Arthur, are based on real people and events. [2] One
of the most striking examples of a legendary character
who is based on real people is Count Dracula. [3] Many
                   46
people believe that Dracula is a fictional character

invented by Bram Stoker, the nineteenth century writer,

and that tales of vampires in turn derive from Stoker's
                                    47
popular story. [4] In actuality, though, Stoker based his

character on Prince Vlad IV, a Transylvanian resistance

fighter also known as "Vlad the Impaler."

[5] Vlad had been living in the fifteenth century, when
     48
Transylvania was under constant attack. [6] He united

armies to fight the invaders, who were notorious for their

cruelty and barbarity, for which they were famous.
                       49
[7] Vlad earned his nickname by outdoing his enemies

at their own game; when he captured them alive, he

would impale them on stakes and watch them die slow,

excruciating deaths. [8] The Prince's cruelty was not

limited to foes, however. [9] When soldiers deserted his

army or failed to meet his

46. F.  NO CHANGE
    G.  on real people was
    H.  on a real person was
    J.  on a real person is

47. A.  NO CHANGE
    B.  were deriving
    C.  are deriving from
    D.  being derived from

48. F.  NO CHANGE
    G.  Vlad, living
    H.  Vlad lived
    J.  Vlad, who lived

49. A.  NO CHANGE
    B.  and which made them famous
    C.  which they were famous for
    D.  OMIT the underlined portion.

**GO ON TO THE NEXT PAGE.**

military standards received the same treatment.
                      50
[10] Hundreds of thousands of people died while Vlad

calmly went about his everyday business. 51

50. **F.** NO CHANGE
    **G.** standards receiving the same treatment.
    **H.** standards, they received the same treatment.
    **J.** standards, received the same treatment.

51. The writer has been told that the first paragraph needs to be broken into two. Where would be the best place to split the paragraph?

    **A.** between Sentences 3 and 4
    **B.** between Sentences 4 and 5
    **C.** between Sentences 5 and 6
    **D.** between Sentences 8 and 9

It is not surprising that Vlad's legend lived long after

his death. Nor is it surprising that in the retelling, several
          52
details were changed and exaggerated. For example, the

stakes upon which Vlad impaled his victims became, in

popular legend, the only weapon that could kill a vampire.

Similarly, Vlad's bloodthirsty nature was also likewise
                                              53
transformed into a central

52. **F.** NO CHANGE
    **G.** death. Or is it surprising
    **H.** death, nor is it surprising
    **J.** death, or is it surprising

53. **A.** NO CHANGE
    **B.** also
    **C.** likewise
    **D.** OMIT the underlined portion.

feature of vampire lore—by the vampire's grisly habit
                      54
of sucking his victim's blood. The enduring legend of

Dracula is one of countless examples of the merging of

fact and fiction.

54. **F.** NO CHANGE
    **G.** lore: the vampire's
    **H.** lore as evidenced by the vampire's
    **J.** lore: as evidenced by the vampire's

Item 55 poses a question about Passage V
as a whole.

55. Which of the following sentences most effectively summarizes the conclusion drawn by the essay as a whole?
    **A.** Vlad the Impaler was very famous.
    **B.** Dracula is an example of a fictional character who is based on an actual historical figure.
    **C.** Vlad the Impaler was also known as Count Dracula.
    **D.** History often repeats itself.

# STOP

IF YOU FINISH BEFORE TIME IS CALLED, YOU MAY CHECK YOUR WORK ON THIS SECTION ONLY.
DO NOT WORK ON ANY OTHER SECTION IN THE TEST.

**NO TEST MATERIAL ON THIS PAGE**

**Time—45 Minutes**
**35 Questions**

In this section solve each problem, using any available space on the page for scratchwork. Then decide which is the best of the choices given and fill in the corresponding oval on the answer sheet.

<u>Notes:</u>

Figures that accompany problems in this test are intended to provide information useful in solving the problems. They are drawn as accurately as possible EXCEPT when it is stated in a specific problem that the figure is not drawn to scale. All figures lie in a plane unless otherwise indicated.

## Reference Information

$A = \pi r^2$
$C = 2\pi r$

$A = \ell w$

$A = \frac{1}{2} bh$

$V = \ell wh$

$V = \pi r^2 h$

$c^2 = a^2 + b^2$

Special Right Triangles

The number of degrees of arc in a circle is 360.
The measure in degrees of a straight angle is 180.
The sum of the measures in degrees of the angles of a triangle is 180.

## Directions for Quantitative Comparison Questions

<u>Questions 1–15</u> each consist of two quantities in boxes, one in Column A and one in Column B. You are to compare the two quantities and on the answer sheet fill in oval

A if the quantity in Column A is greater;
B if the quantity in Column B is greater;
C if the two quantities are equal;
D if the relationship cannot be determined from the information given.

**AN E RESPONSE WILL NOT BE SCORED.**

<u>Notes:</u>

1. In some questions, information is given about one or both of the quantities to be compared. In such cases, the given information is centered above the two columns and is not boxed.
2. In a given question, a symbol that appears in both columns represents the same thing in Column A as it does in Column B.
3. Letters such as $x$, $n$, and $k$ stand for real numbers .

**EXAMPLES**

| <u>Column A</u> | <u>Column B</u> | <u>Answers</u> |

E1 | $5^2$ | 20 | ●ⒷⒸⒹⒺ

150° $x°$

E2 | $x$ | 30 | ⒶⒷ●ⒹⒺ

E3 | $r + 1$ | $s - 1$ | ⒶⒷⒸ●Ⓔ

Column A | Column B

Column A | Column B

$$61x = 743$$
$$62y = 743$$

**1** | $x$ | $y$

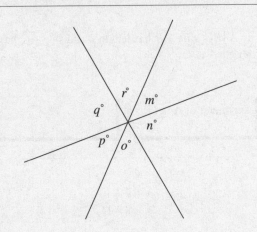

Three lines intersect at a point.

**2** | $m + o + q$ | $n + p + r$

**3** | $(2a + 3b) - (3a + 2b)$ | $(a - b)$

$T$ is the set of integers from 1 to 80, inclusive.

**4** | The number of integers in T that are closer to 25 than to 35 | The number of integers in $T$ that are closer to 35 than to 25

**5** | $4\sqrt{3}$ | $\sqrt{50}$

**GO ON TO THE NEXT PAGE** →

<u>Column A</u>          <u>Column B</u>

Car 1 costs $p$ dollars and Car 2 costs $q$ dollars more than Car 1.

**6**

| $p - q$ | $q - p$ |

$ab = 20$ and $bc = 15$

**7**

| $\dfrac{12}{a}$ | $\dfrac{9}{c}$ |

<u>Column A</u>          <u>Column B</u>

In $\triangle ABC$, side $\overline{AB}$ has length 3 and side $\overline{AC}$ has length 4.

**8**

| Perimeter of $\triangle ABC$ | 12 |

$x + y = 10$
$x - y = 11$

**9**

| $y$ | $-1$ |

**10**

| $2^{19} - 2^{18}$ | $2^{18}$ |

**GO ON TO THE NEXT PAGE**

## Directions for Student-Produced Response Questions

Each of the remaining 7 questions (11–17) requires you to solve the problem and enter your answer by marking the ovals in the special grid, as shown in the examples below.

Answer: $\frac{7}{12}$ or 7/12

Write answer → in boxes.

← Fraction line

Grid in → result.

Answer: 2.5

← Decimal point

Answer: 201
Either position is correct

Note: You may start your answers in any column, space permitting. Columns not needed should be left blank.

- Mark no more than one oval in any column.

- Because the answer sheet will be machine-scored, **you will receive credit only if the ovals are filled in correctly.**

- Although not required, it is suggested that you write your answer in the boxes at the top of the columns to help you fill in the ovals accurately.

- Some problems may have more than one correct answer. In such cases, grid only one answer.

- No question has a negative answer.

- **Mixed numbers** such as $2\frac{1}{2}$ must be gridded as 2.5 or 5/2. (If ⊡ is gridded, it will be interpreted as $\frac{21}{2}$, not $2\frac{1}{2}$.)

- **Decimal Accuracy:** If you obtain a decimal answer, **enter the most accurate value the grid will accommodate.** For example, if you obtain an answer such as 0.6666 . . . , you should record the result as .666 or .667. **Less accurate values such as .66 or .67 are not acceptable.**

Acceptable ways to grid $\frac{2}{3}$ = .6666 . . .

---

**11**   If $\dfrac{x + 2x + 3x}{2} = 6$, then $x =$

**12**   There are 24 fish in an aquarium. If $\dfrac{1}{8}$ of them are tetras and $\dfrac{2}{3}$ of the remaining fish are guppies, how many guppies are in the aquarium?

**GO ON TO THE NEXT PAGE** ➡

**13** When $n$ is divided by 5, the remainder is 4. When $n$ is divided by 4, the remainder is 3.
If $0 < n < 100$, what is one possible value of $n$?

**14** If $x^2 = 16$ and $y^2 = 4$, what is the greatest possible value of $(x - y)^2$?

**15** Segment $AB$ is perpendicular to segment $CD$. Segment $AB$ and segment $CD$ bisect each other at point $x$. If $AB = 6$ and $CD = 8$, what is the length of $BD$?

**16** At a certain high school, 30 students study French, 40 study Spanish, and 25 study neither. If there are 80 students in the school, how many study both French and Spanish?

**17** In the figure above, if $AE = 1$, what is the sum of the area of $\triangle ABC$ and the area of $\triangle CDE$?

**GO ON TO THE NEXT PAGE**

For questions 18–35 solve each problem, using any available space on the page for scratchwork. Then decide which is the best of the choices given and fill in the corresponding oval on the answer sheet.

Notes:

Figures that accompany problems in this test are intended to provide information useful in solving the problems. They are drawn as accurately as possible EXCEPT when it is stated in a specific problem that the figure is not drawn to scale. All figures lie in a plane unless otherwise indicated.

**18** If $8 + x = 12$, then $4 - x =$

(A) $-8$
(B) $-4$
(C) $0$
(D) $4$
(E) $8$

**19** $\dfrac{1}{5} + \dfrac{2}{25} + \dfrac{3}{50} =$

(A) 0.170
(B) 0.240
(C) 0.320
(D) 0.340
(E) 0.463

**20** What number is exactly in the middle of the set of consecutive whole numbers from 20 to 100, inclusive?

(A) 40
(B) 50
(C) 55
(D) 60
(E) 80

**21** What are the coordinates of $B$ if $\overline{AOB}$ is a straight line and the measure of $\overline{BO}$ is equal to the measure of $\overline{AO}$ ?

(A) $(-x, -y)$
(B) $(-x, y)$
(C) $(x, -y)$
(D) $(x, y)$
(E) $(y, -x)$

**22** An hour long call to Smithtown from Jonestown at the normal day rate costs $12.50. If Bill calls at night and talks for one hour, how much does he pay if the company gives a 40% discount for night calls?

(A) $5.00
(B) $7.50
(C) $12.10
(D) $12.90
(E) $17.50

**GO ON TO THE NEXT PAGE**

**23** Ann scored 82, 85, 92, and 95 on her first 4 tests. What grade must she get on her other test to earn an average (arithmetic mean) of 90 for all 5 tests?

(A) 88
(B) 89
(C) 92
(D) 95
(E) 96

**24** Jill has twice as many sand dollars as Carla. After Jill gives Carla 8 sand dollars, Jill still has 6 more sand dollars than Carla. How many sand dollars did Carla have originally?

(A) 14
(B) 16
(C) 18
(D) 20
(E) 22

$x°$  $(x-40)°$

Note: Figure not drawn to scale

**25** In the figure above, $x =$

(A) 70
(B) 110
(C) 130
(D) 135
(E) 140

**26** A 30-inch by 40-inch rectangular kitchen counter is to be completely covered with 1-inch square tiles, which cannot overlap one another and cannot overhang the counter. If white tiles are to cover the center of the counter, and red tiles are to form a 1-inch wide border along the edges of the counter, how many red tiles will be used?

(A) 70
(B) 136
(C) 140
(D) 142
(E) 144

**27** At Clinton College, 50% of the students have radios. Of the students who have radios, 30% have televisions. What percentage of the students at Clinton College have both a radio and a television?

(A) 15
(B) 20
(C) 25
(D) 40
(E) 80

**GO ON TO THE NEXT PAGE**

**28** If a car's odometer reads 73,333 miles, what is the LEAST number of miles the car must travel before four digits on the odometer are identical again?

(A)     99
(B)    444
(C)    666
(D)  1,111
(E)  4,444

**29** $\dfrac{1}{10^{100}} - \dfrac{1}{10^{99}}$

(A) $\dfrac{-9}{10^{100}}$  (B) $\dfrac{-1}{10^{100}}$  (C) $\dfrac{1}{10^{100}}$

(D) $\dfrac{1}{10}$  (E) $\dfrac{9}{10}$

**30** The figure above is made of 3 concentric semi-circles. What is the area of the shaded region?

(A) $3\pi$

(B) $\dfrac{9}{2}\pi$

(C) $6\pi$

(D) $7\pi$

(E) $9\pi$

**31** If, for all real numbers $p$ and $q$, $p \oslash q = 3pq - (p + 2q)$, which of the following must be true?

  I. $q \oslash q = 3q(q - 1)$
 II. $0 \oslash q = 0$
III. $q \oslash q = 2q$

(A) I only
(B) II only
(C) II and III only
(D) I and III only
(E) I, II, and III

**32** In the figure above, what is the sum of the degree measures of the marked angles?

(A) 180
(B) 270
(C) 360
(D) 540
(E) It cannot be determined from the information given.

**GO ON TO THE NEXT PAGE**

**33** If twice the length of the shortest leg of a right triangle is equal to $\frac{3}{2}$ the length of the other leg, what is the ratio of the length of the longer leg to the length of the hypotenuse of the triangle?

(A) $\frac{1}{2}$

(B) $\frac{2}{3}$

(C) $\frac{4}{5}$

(D) $1$

(E) $\frac{3}{2}$

**35** Jim's recipe for cranberry-grape juice calls for 4 cups of grape juice for every 7 cups of cranberry juice. He wants to make 132 ounces of cranberry-grape juice, but realizes that he is short by exactly 4 cups of cranberry juice. How many ounces of cranberry juice does he have? (1 cup = 8 ounces)

(A) 32
(B) 52
(C) 56
(D) 84
(E) 132

Note: Figure not drawn to scale

**34** On the straight line in the figure above, if $P$ is the midpoint of $\overline{BC}$ and $Q$ is the midpoint of $\overline{AD}$, what is the length of $\overline{PQ}$?

(A) $5\frac{5}{8}$   (B) $2\frac{1}{2}$   (C) $2$   (D) $1$   (E) $\frac{1}{2}$

# S T O P
IF YOU FINISH BEFORE TIME IS CALLED, YOU MAY CHECK YOUR WORK ON THIS SECTION ONLY. DO NOT WORK ON ANY OTHER SECTION IN THE TEST.

**NO TEST MATERIAL ON THIS PAGE**

## MATHEMATICS TEST

*30 Minutes—27 Questions*

**DIRECTIONS:** Solve each problem, choose the correct answer, and then darken the corresponding oval on your answer sheet.

Do not linger over problems that take too much time. Solve as many as you can; then return to the others in the time you have left for this test.

Note: Unless otherwise stated, all of the following should be assumed:

1. Illustrative figures are NOT necessarily drawn to scale.
2. Geometric figures lie in a plane.
3. The word *line* indicates a straight line.
4. The word *average* indicates arithmetic mean.

---

**DO YOUR FIGURING HERE.**

1. In the figure above, the measure of ∠*A* is 80°. If the measure of ∠*B* is half the measure of ∠*A*, what is the measure of ∠*C*?

   A. 40°
   B. 60°
   C. 80°
   D. 100°
   E. 120°

2. A plumber charges $75 for the first thirty minutes of each house call plus $2 for each additional minute that she works. The plumber charges Adam $113 for her time. For what amount of time, in minutes, did the plumber work?

   F. 38
   G. 44
   H. 49
   J. 59
   K. 64

**GO ON TO THE NEXT PAGE.**

3. $\sqrt{64 + 36} = ?$

    A.    10
    B.    14
    C.    28
    D.    48
    E.    100

4. $4.326 \div 0.2 = ?$

    F.    0.2163
    G.    2.163
    H.    21.63
    J.    216.3
    K.  2,163.0

5. If $x = -2$, then $3x^2 - 5x - 6 = ?$

    A.    $-30$
    B.    $-8$
    C.    $-4$
    D.    10
    E.    16

6. In the figure above, $D$, $B$, and $E$ are collinear.
What is the measure of $\angle p$?

    F.    $20°$
    G.    $35°$
    H.    $50°$
    J.    $60°$
    K.    $70°$

**GO ON TO THE NEXT PAGE.**

7. A rectangular garden is surrounded by a 60 foot long fence. One side of the garden is 6 feet longer than the other. Which of the following equations could be used to find $s$, the shorter side, of the garden?

    A. $8s + s = 60$
    B. $4s = 60 + 12$
    C. $s(s + 6) = 60$
    D. $2(s - 6) + 2s = 60$
    E. $2(s + 6) + 2s = 60$

**DO YOUR FIGURING HERE.**

8. Property tax is 8% of the assessed value of a house. How much would the property tax be on a house with an assessed value of $80,000?

    F. $100
    G. $640
    H. $1,000
    J. $6,400
    K. $10,000

9. For all $x$, $(10x^4 - x^2 + 2x - 8) - (3x^4 + 3x^3 + 2x + 8) = ?$

    A. $7x^4 - 3x^3 - x^2 - 16$
    B. $7x^4 - 4x^2 - 16$
    C. $7x^4 + 3x^3 - x^2 + 4x$
    D. $7x^4 + 2x^2 + 4x$
    E. $13x^4 - 3x^3 - x^2 + 4x$

10. If $\sqrt[N]{48} = 2\sqrt[N]{3}$, then $N = ?$

    F. 1
    G. 2
    H. 3
    J. 4
    K. 5

**GO ON TO THE NEXT PAGE.**

11. Which of the following is the sum of both solutions to the equation $x^2 - 2x - 8 = 0$?

   A. $-6$
   B. $-4$
   C. $-2$
   D. $2$
   E. $6$

12. After $N$ chocolate bars are divided equally among 6 children, 3 bars remain. How many would remain if $(N + 4)$ chocolate bars were divided equally among the 6 children?

   F. $0$
   G. $1$
   H. $2$
   J. $3$
   K. $4$

13. For all $y \neq 3$, $\dfrac{y^2 - 9}{3y - 9} = ?$

   A. $y$

   B. $\dfrac{y + 1}{8}$

   C. $y + 1$

   D. $\dfrac{y}{3}$

   E. $\dfrac{y + 3}{3}$

**GO ON TO THE NEXT PAGE.**

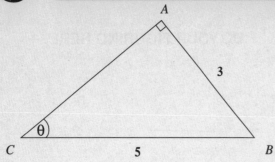

**14.** In the figure above, ∠A is a right angle. $\overline{AB}$ is 3 units long and $\overline{BC}$ is 5 units long. If the measure of ∠C is θ, what is the value of cos θ?

F. $\dfrac{3}{5}$

G. $\dfrac{3}{4}$

H. $\dfrac{4}{5}$

J. $\dfrac{5}{4}$

K. $\dfrac{5}{3}$

**15.** The hypotenuse of an isosceles right triangle has a length of 20 units. What is the length of one of the legs of the triangle?

A. 10

B. $10\sqrt{2}$

C. $10\sqrt{3}$

D. 20

E. $20\sqrt{2}$

**16.** What is the *y*-intercept of the line determined by the equation $5x + 2 = 7y - 3$?

F. −1

G. $-\dfrac{1}{7}$

H. $\dfrac{1}{7}$

J. $\dfrac{5}{7}$

K. 5

**GO ON TO THE NEXT PAGE.**

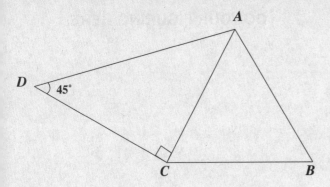

**DO YOUR FIGURING HERE.**

**17.** In the figure above, ΔABC is an equilateral triangle with $\overline{BC}$ 7 units long. If ∠DCA is a right angle and ∠D measures 45°, what is the length of $\overline{AD}$, in units?

A.  7
B.  $7\sqrt{2}$
C.  14
D.  $14\sqrt{2}$
E.  It cannot be determined from the information given.

**18.** What graph would be created if the equation $x^2 + y^2 = 12$ were graphed in the standard $(x, y)$ coordinate plane?

F.  Circle
G.  Ellipse
H.  Parabola
J.  Straight line
K.  2 rays forming a "V"

**19.** The formula for calculating sales tax is $S = Ar$, where $S$ is the sales tax, A is the cost of the product, and $r$ is the local sales-tax rate. If the cost of a television was $400 and the sales tax was $24, what was the local sales-tax rate?

A.    .60%
B.   1.67%
C.   6.00%
D.  16.67%
E.  60.00%

**GO ON TO THE NEXT PAGE.**

**20.** Grace tried to compute the average of her 5 test scores. She mistakenly divided the correct total ($T$) of her scores by 6 and her result was 14 less than what it should have been. Which of the following equations would determine the value of $T$?

DO YOUR FIGURING HERE.

**F.** $5T + 14 = 6T$

**G.** $\dfrac{T}{6} = \dfrac{(T-14)}{5}$

**H.** $\dfrac{T}{6} - 14 = \dfrac{T}{5}$

**J.** $\dfrac{(T-14)}{6} = \dfrac{T}{5}$

**K.** $\dfrac{T}{6} + 14 = \dfrac{T}{5}$

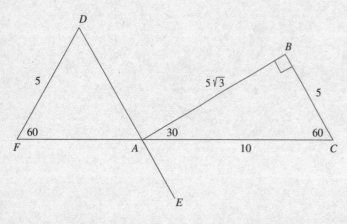

**21.** In the figure above, $\angle B$ is a right angle, $\overline{BC}$ is parallel to $\overline{DE}$, and $\angle C$ and $\angle F$ both measure 60°. If $\overline{BC}$ and $\overline{DF}$ both measure 5 units, what is the sine of $\angle C$?

**A.** $\dfrac{1}{2}$

**B.** $\dfrac{\sqrt{3}}{2}$

**C.** 5

**D.** 30°

**E.** 60°

GO ON TO THE NEXT PAGE.

**22.** Which of the following represents the solution to the inequality $x^2 - 9x + 8 < 0$?

**DO YOUR FIGURING HERE.**

   **F.** $-8 < x < -1$

   **G.** $-\dfrac{1}{8} < x < 1$

   **H.** $1 < x < 8$

   **J.** $x < 8$ or $x > 1$

   **K.** $x < -1$ or $x > 8$

**23.** In the figure above, the measure of $\angle A$ is $30°$ and the measure of $\angle B$ is $60°$. If $\overline{AC}$ is 6 units long, what is the measure of $\overline{BC}$, in units?

   **A.** 3

   **B.** $2\sqrt{3}$

   **C.** $3\sqrt{3}$

   **D.** 6

   **E.** $6\sqrt{3}$

**24.** A line in the standard $(x, y)$ coordinate plane has the same slope as the line $12 = 3y - 7x$. If the line passes through the point $(3, 6)$, what is its $y$-intercept?

   **F.** $-3$

   **G.** $-\dfrac{7}{3}$

   **H.** $-1$

   **J.** $1$

   **K.** $\dfrac{7}{3}$

**GO ON TO THE NEXT PAGE.**

**25.** In the figure above, ∠A and ∠ADC are right angles, the length of $\overline{AD}$ is 7 units, the length of $\overline{AB}$ is 10 units, and the length of $\overline{DC}$ is 6 units. What is the area, in square units, of △DCB?

    **A.**   21

    **B.**   24

    **C.**   $3\sqrt{149}$

    **D.**   42

    **E.**   210

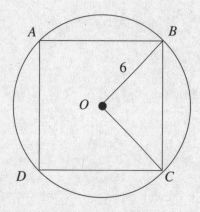

**26.** In the figure above, *ABCD* is a square inscribed in the circle centered at *O*. If $\overline{OB}$ is 6 units long, how many units long is minor arc *BC*?

    **F.**   $\dfrac{3}{2}\pi$

    **G.**   $3\pi$

    **H.**   $6\pi$

    **J.**   $12\pi$

    **K.**   $36\pi$

**GO ON TO THE NEXT PAGE.**

**27.** At what point $(x,y)$ do the two lines with equations $y = 2x - 2$ and $7x - 3y = 11$ intersect?

A. $(5,8)$

B. $(8,5)$

C. $\left(\dfrac{5}{8}, -1\right)$

D. $\left(\dfrac{5}{8}, 1\right)$

E. $\left(\dfrac{25}{16}, \dfrac{9}{8}\right)$

**END OF TEST 3**
**STOP! DO NOT TURN THE PAGE UNTIL TOLD TO DO SO.**
**DO NOT RETURN TO THE PREVIOUS TEST.**

**Time — 45 Minutes**
**46 Questions**

For each question in this section, select the best answer from among the choices given and fill in the corresponding oval on the answer sheet.

Each sentence below has one or two blanks, each blank indicating that something has been omitted. Beneath the sentence are five words or sets of words labeled A through E. Choose the word or set of words that, when inserted in the sentence, <u>best</u> fits the meaning of the sentence as a whole.

Example:

Medieval kingdoms did not become constitutional republics overnight; on the contrary, the change was ----.

(A) unpopular
(B) unexpected
(C) advantageous
(D) sufficient
(E) gradual   

**1** There is no place in today's active society for idle and dependent ---- who would like nothing more than to sit back and leave all the tasks and responsibilities to more energetic souls.

(A) introverts
(B) athletes
(C) sluggards
(D) vertebrates
(E) cowards

**2** Although our excuses for arriving late to the party seemed ---- enough, it was obvious to everyone that our disappointed hostess did not believe us.

(A) rigid
(B) far-fetched
(C) plausible
(D) mature
(E) obtuse

**3** Despite the efforts of family and friends to enliven him, Wilson remained ---- in his ----.

(A) vulnerable. .unease
(B) content. .anger
(C) mired. .depression
(D) obdurate. .zest
(E) steadfast. .enjoyment

**4** Certain animal behaviors, such as mating rituals, seem to be ----, and therefore ---- external factors such as climate changes, food supply, or the presence of other animals of the same species.

(A) learned. .immune to
(B) innate. .unaffected by
(C) intricate. .belong to
(D) specific. .confused with
(E) memorized. .controlled by

**5** While many of today's critics busy themselves ---- the death of classical music, composers the world over are producing exciting, often brilliant work that due to its lack of ---- appeal, goes unnoticed by the established critical community.

(A) ignoring. .popular
(B) proclaiming. .mainstream
(C) enjoying. .borderline
(D) mourning. .cryptic
(E) avoiding. .musical

**6** The new nation is attempting to ---- its present and its past, to mix age-old traditions with ---- political realities.

(A) compare. .unknown
(B) reconcile. .contemporary
(C) understand. .fundamental
(D) denounce. .modern
(E) dislodge. .uncertain

**7** Paradoxically, much social etiquette involves inverting traditional virtues and vices: tact, for instance, inevitably entails ----, whereas what is commonly condemned as a lack of tact is nothing more than ----.

(A) politeness. .curiosity
(B) humility. .humor
(C) generosity. .beneficence
(D) lying. .honesty
(E) ingenuity. .prying

**GO ON TO THE NEXT PAGE**

**8** Despite a marked increase in efforts to stem the tide of unwanted domestic animals that are born every day, and despite ---- evidence of a slower birthrate, the sheer number of animals has risen so sharply in recent years that even the most committed of animal advocates is ---- of ever solving the problem.

(A) depressing. .hopeful
(B) disheartening. .lessening
(C) overwhelming. .confident
(D) encouraging. .despairing
(E) ambiguous. .unsure

**9** A truly ---- writer, Shakespeare has something to say to all people of whatever time, culture, or race.

(A) celebrated
(B) catholic
(C) soporific
(D) experienced
(E) artful

**10** Modern evolutionary biologists have shifted from ---- mirroring Darwin's ideas to actually ---- elaborate innovative theories that call into question the very foundations of Darwinian evolution.

(A) knowingly. .inscribing
(B) utterly. .defoliating
(C) overtly. .implementing
(D) naturally. .selecting
(E) merely. .formulating

**11** Only when one actually visits the ancient ruins of marvelous bygone civilizations does one truly appreciate the sad ---- of human greatness.

(A) perspicacity
(B) magnitude
(C) artistry
(D) transience
(E) quiescence

**GO ON TO THE NEXT PAGE**

Each question below consists of a related pair of words or phrases, followed by five pairs of words or phrases labeled A through E. Select the pair that <u>best</u> expresses a relationship similar to that expressed in the original pair.

Example:

CRUMB : BREAD ::
(A) ounce : unit
(B) splinter : wood
(C) water : bucket
(D) twine : rope
(E) cream : butter

Ⓐ ● Ⓒ Ⓓ Ⓔ

**12** LABORATORY : SCIENTIST ::
(A) hospital : patient
(B) desktop : writer
(C) apartment : tenant
(D) ladder : painter
(E) classroom : teacher

**13** CLIMAX : DRAMA ::
(A) plateau : land
(B) tension : scene
(C) peak : mountain
(D) suspense : movie
(E) tragedy : theatre

**14** THERMOMETER : TEMPERATURE ::
(A) radio : news
(B) Fahrenheit : degrees
(C) scale : weight
(D) hourglass : sand
(E) barometer : rain

**15** ALLOY : METALS ::
(A) carat : gold
(B) compound : elements
(C) atom : chemicals
(D) germ : disease
(E) tree : blossom

**16** PHARMACIST : PRESCRIPTION ::
(A) chef : order
(B) seamstress : stocking
(C) juror : defense
(D) driver : auto
(E) disciplinarian : prohibition

**17** IRASCIBLE : PROVOKE ::
(A) angry : violate
(B) desirable : tempt
(C) sad : fury
(D) intolerant : initiate
(E) docile : lead

**18** INVALUABLE : ASSESS ::
(A) incorrigible : lie
(B) important : enjoy
(C) insatiable : satisfy
(D) innovative : change
(E) indescribable : appreciate

**19** VOLATILE : VAPORIZED ::
(A) oily : dried
(B) combustible : smoked
(C) concave : curved
(D) diverse : concentrated
(E) malleable : molded

**20** FOMENT : AGITATION ::
(A) ossify : fission
(B) contain : division
(C) cohere : remission
(D) disperse : separation
(E) view : magnification

**21** ORDER : CHAOS ::
(A) anarchy : power
(B) distaste : enmity
(C) sadness : fury
(D) diffidence : confidence
(E) dilemma : confusion

**22** APOCRYPHAL : AUTHENTICITY ::
(A) casual : attire
(B) unique : precedent
(C) destruction : bomb
(D) lucid : truth
(E) catastrophic : power

**23** PERSPICACITY : DISCERNING ::
(A) ravishing : attractive
(B) infatuation : distasteful
(C) perspiration : moist
(D) pursuing : desisting
(E) graceful : dancing

**GO ON TO THE NEXT PAGE** ➡

**NO TEST MATERIAL ON THIS PAGE**

GO ON TO THE NEXT PAGE

Each passage below is followed by questions based on its content. Answer the questions on the basis of what is <u>stated</u> or <u>implied</u> in the passage and in any introductory material that may be provided.

*Questions 24–28 are based on the following passage.*

*The following passage describes a conversation between a young student and his private tutor.*

What Morgan said at last was said suddenly, irrelevantly, when the moment came, in the middle of a lesson, and consisted of the apparently unfeeling words: "You ought to *filer*, you know—you really ought."

*Line*
*(5)*     Pemberton stared. He had learnt enough French slang from Morgan to know that to *filer* meant to go away. "Why should I do that?"

Morgan pulled a Greek dictionary toward him, to look up a word, instead of asking it of Pemberton. "You can't
*(10)* go on like this, you know."

"Like what, my boy?"

"You know they don't pay you up," said Morgan, blushing and turning his leaves.

"Don't pay me?" Pemberton stared again and feigned
*(15)* amazement. "What on earth put that into your head?"

"It has been there a long time," the boy replied, continuing his search.

Pemberton was silent, then he went on: "I say, what are you hunting for? Your parents pay me beautifully."

*(20)*     "I'm hunting for the Greek for transparent fiction," Morgan dropped.

"Find that rather for gross impertinence, and disabuse your mind. What do I want of money?"

"Oh, that's another question!"

*(25)*     Pemberton hesitated—he was drawn in different ways. The severely correct thing would have been to tell the boy that such a matter was none of his business and bid him go on with his lines. But they were really too intimate for that; it was not the way he was in the
*(30)* habit of treating him; there had been no reason it should be. On the other hand Morgan had quite lighted on the truth—he really shouldn't be able to keep it up much longer; therefore why not let him know one's real motive for forsaking him? At the same time it wasn't decent
*(35)* to abuse to one's pupil the family of one's pupil; it was better to misrepresent than to do that. So in reply to Morgan's last exclamation he just declared, to dismiss the subject, that he had received several payments.

**24** Morgan tells Pemberton to *filer* (line 4) because he:

(A) doesn't think Pemberton will understand him.
(B) seeks a better tutor.
(C) wishes to be left alone.
(D) is concerned with Pemberton's interests.
(E) plans to abandon his parents also.

**25** When Morgan says, "I'm hunting for the Greek for transparent fiction," (line 20) his attitude is most likely one of:

(A) pointed sarcasm.
(B) probing intelligence.
(C) supreme indifference.
(D) benign negligence.
(E) casual regard.

GO ON TO THE NEXT PAGE →

**26** According to the passage Pemberton may be forced to forsake Morgan because he:

(A) fears an unpleasant confrontation with Morgan's parents.

(B) can no longer tolerate Morgan's gross impertinences.

(C) refuses to apologize for verbally abusing his employers.

(D) is not receiving due payments for his tutoring.

(E) disapproves of Morgan's incessant use of slang.

**27** According to the passage, Pemberton chooses "to misrepresent" (line 36) because he:

(A) believes it is discourteous to criticize Morgan's parents.

(B) is obligated to protect Morgan from painful discoveries.

(C) intends to demonstrate his authority over Morgan.

(D) wishes to conceal his duplicity from Morgan and his parents.

(E) hopes it will successfully instruct Morgan in the ways of the world.

**28** It can be inferred from the passage that Pemberton is least likely to be which of the following?

(A) respectful
(B) erudite
(C) selfish
(D) anxious
(E) evasive

**GO ON TO THE NEXT PAGE**

*Questions 29–33 are based on the following passage.*

*This passage discusses a number of theories on the subject of dreaming, many of which challenge established notions of the scientific community.*

The phenomenon of dreaming has long fascinated philosophers and scientists. The ancients believed that dreams were messages from the gods or portents of
*Line* one's future. Nineteenth and twentieth century scientists
(5) have sought rational explanations—the first such effort to receive wide acceptance was Sigmund Freud's psychoanalytic theory. Freud called dreams "the royal road to the unconscious," by which he meant that dreams lead the way to a realm of mental functioning where
(10) our fantasies, emotional conflicts, repressed memories, and infantile impulses find expression. Through condensation, displacement, and symbol formation, troubling and fantastic thoughts evade the vigilant censor that keeps us largely unaware of them in our waking
(15) moments.

Recently, however, cognitive psychologists have challenged Freud's ideas. They point out that cats in laboratory experiments have been repeatedly shown to dream. So, in fact, have all other mammals except
(20) one: the anteater, which has a tiny brain. In addition, newborn infants spend half the day dreaming. These organisms do not have unconscious conflicts of the type Freud described, but during sleep they show obvious signs of dreaming. For example, when humans dream,
(25) their eyes dart around. This period of sleep, called Rapid Eye Movement (REM) sleep, is one of the most reliable signs that a person is dreaming and also is part of the sleeping pattern of almost all mammals. It happens at regular intervals: every hour and a half for
(30) a human, for instance, or every twelve minutes for a rat. Some researchers have even linked acetylcholine, a neurotransmitter in the brain, to dreaming. All of this research suggests that the cause of dreaming is physiological, rather than emotional.

(35) Others have proposed different alternatives. They suggest that the brain functions in some ways like an enormous computer, and that REM sleep is a way of "dumping" unwanted data that could otherwise overload the system. With 50 billion neurons and ten times that
(40) many glial cells wiring them all together, the brain is capable of taking on huge amounts of information. But like a computer, it has a finite capacity for storing information, and REM sleep may be a way that the brain "clears out" unusable data in order to free itself to attend
(45) new tasks during waking hours.

**29** The passage primarily concerns:

(A) Sigmund Freud's psychoanalytic theories.
(B) the effect of dreams on the personality.
(C) the attempts of psychologists to explain dreaming.
(D) the role of REM sleep in dreaming.
(E) the similarities of computers to the brain.

**30** "Condensation, displacement, and symbol formation" (lines 12–13) are probably:

(A) an attempt by Freud to make his theories sound more scientific than they in fact were.
(B) terms that Freud used to explain the process by which feelings find expression in dreams.
(C) universally accepted explanations for the fantastic images that occur during dreaming.
(D) simplistic attempts to account for a complex process.
(E) repressed material that is found in the unconscious.

**31** The two new theories outlined in the passage challenge Freud's belief that:

(A) dreams must be primarily understood as an attempt to come to terms with unconscious material.
(B) we dream in order to find out about ourselves.
(C) dreams originate in a specific area of the brain.
(D) researchers have discovered the place in the brain where repressed memories are stored.
(E) the conscious mind represses unpleasant thoughts.

**GO ON TO THE NEXT PAGE** ⟩

**32** The author would most likely argue that the reason an anteater does not dream is that:

(A) it lacks the type of unconscious conflict Freud describes.

(B) neurotransmitters other than acetyl-choline have been found in anteaters' brains.

(C) its brain is not complex enough to support the mechanisms that cause dreams.

(D) anteaters' REM sleep differs from that of humans or rats.

(E) its glial cells outnumber its neurons ten to one.

**33** The author's attitude toward Sigmund Freud's theories could best be described as:

(A) skeptical

(B) emotional

(C) envious

(D) indifferent

(E) admiration

**GO ON TO THE NEXT PAGE**

Each passage below is followed by questions based on its content. Answer the questions on the basis of what is <u>stated</u> or <u>implied</u> in the passage and in any introductory material that may be provided.

*Questions 34–46 are based on the following passages.*

*In passage 1, the author presents his view of the early years of the silent film industry. In passage 2, the author draws on her experiences as a mime to generalize about her art. (A mime is a performer who, without speaking, entertains through gesture, facial expression, and movement.)*

## Passage 1

Talk to those people who first saw films when they were silent, and they will tell you the experience was magic. The silent film had extraordinary powers to draw
Line members of an audience into the story, and an equally
(5) potent capacity to make their imaginations work. It required the audience to become engaged—to supply voices and sound effects. The audience was the final, creative contributor to the process of making a film.

The finest films of the silent era depended on two
(10) elements that we can seldom provide today—a large and receptive audience and a well-orchestrated score. For the audience, the fusion of picture and live music added up to more than the sum of the respective parts.

The one word that sums up the attitude of the silent
(15) filmmakers is *enthusiasm*, conveyed most strongly before formulas took shape and when there was more room for experimentation. This enthusiastic uncertainty often resulted in such accidental discoveries as new camera or editing techniques. Some films experimented
(20) with players; the 1915 film *Regeneration*, for example, by using real gangsters and streetwalkers, provided startling local color. Other films, particularly those of Thomas Ince, provided tragic endings as often as films by other companies supplied happy ones.

(25) Unfortunately, the vast majority of silent films survive today in inferior prints that no longer reflect the care that the original technicians put into them. The modern versions of silent films may appear jerky and flickery, but the vast picture palaces did not attract four to six
(30) thousand people a night by giving them eyestrain. A silent film depended on its visuals; as soon as you degrade those, you lose elements that go far beyond the image on the surface. The acting in silents was often very subtle, very restrained, despite legends to the
(35) contrary.

## Passage 2

Mime opens up a new world to the beholder, but it does so insidiously, not by purposely injecting points of interest in the manner of a tour guide. Audiences are not unlike visitors to a foreign land who discover that the
(40) modes, manners, and thoughts of its inhabitants are not meaningless oddities, but are sensible in context.

I remember once when an audience seemed perplexed at what I was doing. At first, I tried to gain a more immediate response by using slight exaggerations. I soon
(45) realized that these actions had nothing to do with the audience's understanding of the character. What I had believed to be a failure of the audience to respond in the manner I expected was, in fact, only their concentration on what I was doing; they were enjoying a gradual
(50) awakening—a slow transference of their understanding from their own time and place to one that appeared so unexpectedly before their eyes. This was evidenced by their growing response to succeeding numbers.

Mime is an elusive art, as its expression is entirely
(55) dependent on the ability of the performer to imagine a character and to re-create that character for each performance. As a mime, I am a physical medium, the instrument upon which the figures of my imagination play their dance of life. The individuals in my
(60) audience also have responsibilities—they must be alert collaborators. They cannot sit back, mindlessly complacent, and wait to have their emotions titillated by mesmeric musical sounds or visual rhythms or acrobatic feats, or by words that tell them what to
(65) think. Mime is an art that, paradoxically, appeals both to those who respond instinctively to entertainment and to those whose appreciation is more analytical and complex. Between these extremes lie those audiences conditioned to resist any collaboration with what is
(70) played before them; and these the mime must seduce despite themselves. There is only one way to attack those reluctant minds—take them unaware! They will be delighted at an unexpected pleasure.

**GO ON TO THE NEXT PAGE** →

**34** Lines 12–15 of passage 1 indicate that:

(A) music was the most important element of silent films.
(B) silent films rely on a combination of music and image in affecting an audience.
(C) the importance of music in silent film has been overestimated.
(D) live music compensated for the poor quality of silent film images.
(E) no film can succeed without a receptive audience.

**35** The "formulas" mentioned in line 16 of the passage most probably refer to:

(A) movie theaters.
(B) use of real characters.
(C) standardized film techniques.
(D) the fusion of disparate elements.
(E) contemporary events.

**36** The author uses the phrase *enthusiastic uncertainty* in line 17 to suggest that the filmmakers were:

(A) excited to be experimenting in an undefined area.
(B) delighted at the opportunity to study new acting formulas.
(C) optimistic in spite of the obstacles that faced them.
(D) eager to challenge existing conventions.
(E) eager to please but unsure of what the public wanted.

**37** The author uses the phrase *by giving... eye strain* (line 30) in order to:

(A) indicate his disgust with the incompetence of early film technicians.
(B) suggest that audiences today perceive silent films incorrectly.
(C) convey his regret about the decline of the old picture palaces.
(D) highlight the pitfalls of the silent movie era.
(E) argue for the superiority of modern film technology over that of silent movies.

**38** The word *legends* in line 34 most nearly means:

(A) arguments
(B) symbolism
(C) propaganda
(D) movie stars
(E) misconceptions

**39** The last sentence of passage 1 implies that:

(A) the stars of silent movies have been criticized for overacting.
(B) many silent film actors became legends in their own time.
(C) silent film techniques should be studied by filmmakers today.
(D) visual effects defined the silent film.
(E) many silent films that exist today are of poor quality.

**40** The word *restrained* (line 34) most nearly means:

(A) sincere
(B) dramatic
(C) understated
(D) inexpressive
(E) consistent

**41** The author mentions the incident in lines 42–53 in order to imply that:

(A) the audience's lack of response was a positive sign and reflected their captivated interest in the performance.
(B) she was forced to resort to stereotypes in order to reach an audience that was otherwise unattainable.
(C) exaggeration is an essential part of mime because it allows the forums used to be fully expressed.
(D) her audience, though not initially appearing knowledgeable, had a good understanding of the subtlety of mime.
(E) although vocalization is not necessary in mime, it is sometimes helpful for slower audiences.

**GO ON TO THE NEXT PAGE**

**42** Lines 42–53 indicate that the author of passage 2 and the silent filmmakers of passage 1 were similar because:

(A) neither used many props.
(B) both conveyed universal truths by using sophisticated technology.
(C) for both, trial and error was a part of the learning process.
(D) both used visual effects and dialogue.
(E) both had a loyal following.

**43** The sentence *As a . . . life* (lines 57–59) suggests that the author of passage 2 feels mimes:

(A) cannot control the way audiences interpret their characters.
(B) must suspend their own identities in order to successfully portray their characters.
(C) have to resist outside attempts to define their acting style.
(D) should focus on important events in the lives of specific characters.
(E) know the limitations of performances that do not incorporate either music or speech.

**44** Which of the following pieces of information makes mime and silent film seem less similar?

(A) Vaudeville and theatrical presentations were also popular forms of entertainment during the silent film era.
(B) Silent films presented both fictional drama and factual information.
(C) Silent film sometimes relied on captions to convey dialogue to the audience.
(D) Musicians working in movie theaters were usually employed for long periods of time.
(E) Many of the characters in silent films gained wide popularity among moviegoers.

**45** Passages 1 and 2 are similar in that both are mainly concerned with:

(A) the use of special effects.
(B) differences among dramatic styles.
(C) the visual aspects of performance.
(D) the suspension of disbelief in audiences.
(E) nostalgia for a bygone era.

**46** Which of the following is an element that figures in the success of the dramatic arts described in both passages?

(A) A successful combination of different dramatic styles
(B) The exaggeration of certain aspects of a character
(C) The incorporation of current events in the narrative
(D) High audience attendance
(E) The active participation of the audience

# STOP

IF YOU FINISH BEFORE TIME IS CALLED, YOU MAY CHECK YOUR WORK ON THIS SECTION ONLY.
DO NOT WORK ON ANY OTHER SECTION IN THE TEST.

**NO TEST MATERIAL ON THIS PAGE**

## SCIENCE REASONING TEST

*30 Minutes—34 Questions*

**DIRECTIONS:** There are six passages in the following section. Each passage is followed by several questions. After reading a passage, choose the best answer to each question and blacken the corresponding oval on your answer sheet. You may refer to the passages as often as necessary.

### Passage I

Four different strains of bacteria were raised in petri dishes at different temperatures (10°, 20°, 30°, & 40°C). Four sets of experiments were conducted. At each temperature, each strain was placed in a separate petri dish in a lighted chamber. They were each taken out of the chamber after one hour and the number of living organisms in each dish was counted, using approximation techniques. The results are shown in Figure 1.

A researcher also used these data to approximate the growth rates of these bacteria strains within each tested temperature. *Growth rate* represents the percentage increase in the total number of organisms in the experimental dish. Table 1 shows the growth rates, during the test period of one hour, for each strain at 40°C.

During this experiment, the only *limiting factor* was food supply. So, the total growth of these bacteria populations was limited by the available food supply. If a population uses up its food supply, the growth rate declines and the organisms die. In this experiment some test strains used up all of the petri dish medium (their food supply) within the test period of 1 hour.

Note: Each petri dish began with approximately 1,000 organisms.

**Table 1**

| Strain 1 | Strain 2 | Strain 3 | Strain 4 |
|----------|----------|----------|----------|
| 400% | 650% | 800% | 0% |

**Growth rate at 40°C**

**Figure 1**

Temperature in °C

**GO ON TO THE NEXT PAGE.**

1. Given the test conditions of the experiment, which temperature produces the maximum growth in Strain 1?

    A. 30°C
    B. 35°C
    C. 40°C
    D. It cannot be determined from the information given.

2. If Strain 1 was kept at 40° C for a period of time longer than one hour and all other test conditions remained constant, what would you expect to find?

    F. More organisms than the total in the initial trial at 40°C
    G. Fewer organisms than the total in the initial trial at 40°C
    H. Approximately the same total number of organisms as in the initial trial at 40°C
    J. Approximately the same total number of organisms as in the initial trial at 10°C

3. At which temperatures do Strains 2 and 3 exhibit the same <u>growth</u> <u>rate</u>?

    A. 10°C
    B. Between 10°C and 20°C
    C. 20°C
    D. Between 20°C and 30°C

4. Some bacteria are sensitive to light and will not grow in a lighted environment. Of the strains used in this experiment, which types of bacteria are NOT light-sensitive?

    F. Strain 3 only
    G. Strain 4 only
    H. Strains 1, 2, and 3 only
    J. Strains 2, 3, and 4 only

5. Which test strains show signs of being affected by a limiting factor present in this experiment?

    A. Strain 1 only
    B. Strain 4 only
    C. Strains 1 and 2 only
    D. Strains 1, 2, 3, and 4

6. To clarify the bacteria's dependence on food supply, the researcher continued these experiments using petri dishes large enough to contain an unlimited supply of food. Given these conditions, how many organisms of Strain 3 bacteria would exist after one hour at 40°C?

    F. 4,000
    G. 8,000
    H. 10,000
    J. 16,000

**GO ON TO THE NEXT PAGE.**

**Passage II**

In the full electromagnetic spectrum, waves vary greatly in length and frequency. Radio waves, which can measure up to many miles, are approximately 10 million times longer than visible light rays, which are 10 million times longer than gamma rays. How we use waves are indicative of these characteristics. For instance, television, AM/FM broadcasts, and short-wave signals are types of radio waves that can travel long distances.

Visible light rays are composed of several waves at different wavelengths. White light can be refracted through a prism to display the different color components of the light. Each color band represents a distinct wavelength. Figure 1 below depicts the wavelengths (cm) and frequencies (cycles/second) of some common waves.

Figure 1

7. Vitamin D can be collected from rays with a wavelength of $1 \times 10^{-6}$ cm. These rays could be:

A. radio waves.
B. visible light rays.
C. ultraviolet rays.
D. gamma rays.

8. A short-wave radio emits waves of a wavelength $5 \times 10^4$ cm. Express this term in meters.

F. 400 m
G. 500 m
H. 40,000 m
J. 50,000 m

9. Which of the following is a correct sequence of waves in order of increasing frequency?

A. Cosmic rays, gamma rays, infrared
B. Infrared, ultraviolet, visible light
C. Yellow, orange, and red light
D. Radio waves, visible light, x-rays

10. Wavelength, frequency, and velocity are interrelated characteristics of an electromagnetic wave. According to Figure 1, as wavelength increases, at a constant velocity, the frequency of a wave would:

F. decrease.
G. increase.
H. increase by a factor of 2.
J. be unchanged.

11. When a prism refracts white light, the longest component rays are refracted the least, while the rays with the shortest wavelengths are refracted the most. In the visible light spectrum, which color is refracted the LEAST?

A. Ultraviolet
B. Blue
C. Red
D. White

**GO ON TO THE NEXT PAGE.**

## Passage III

The complex behavior of the poor-sighted, three-spined male stickleback fish has been studied extensively as a model of species behavior in courtship and mating. After a male has migrated to a suitable spot, he builds a spawning nest of sand and sediment. In courting, he performs a special "zigzag" dance. The female then follows the male to the nest where she spawns and he fertilizes the spawned eggs. Also, male sticklebacks have been shown to exhibit territorial behaviors. A biologist performed three experiments to learn more about the behavior of the stickleback.

### Experiment 1

Tank 1 and Tank 2 are set up with identical conditions and one male stickleback is placed in each tank. Both fish build nests in their respective tanks. The male from Tank 1 is removed from his tank and is replaced with an egg-laden female; the male from Tank 2 is removed from his tank and is introduced into Tank 1. In Tank 1, the male does not perform the zigzag dance and no spawning occurs. The male retreats to a corner of the tank.

### Experiment 2

A male stickleback in an aquarium builds his nest. A fat, round male is introduced into the environment. The original male performs the zigzag dance and attempts to lead the round male to the nest. The round male refuses and begins to flap his fins and swim in circles. The first male then begins to flap his fins, circle his nest, and occasionally prod the other fish to a far corner of the tank.

### Experiment 3

A small, flat-shaped female is introduced into a tank where a male has built a nest. The male circles the female a few times, then retreats to a corner of the tank.

12. The experimental data would support the hypothesis that the purpose of the male stickleback's mating dance is to:

   F. keep away other male sticklebacks.
   G. lure and entice the female to the nest.
   H. fertilize the eggs.
   J. establish territorial rights.

13. Based on observations from the experiments to the left, which factor initially stimulates the male to do the zigzag dance?

   A. The physical environment
   B. The number of fish in the tank
   C. The sex of the fish
   D. The shape of the fish

14. Which experiment supports the hypothesis that the male exhibits territorial behavior?

   F. 2 only
   G. 3 only
   H. 2 and 3 only
   J. 1, 2, and 3

15. To further investigate the territorial behavior of the stickleback, the biologist should vary which of the following factors in Experiment 2?

   A. The temperature of the water
   B. The sediment and sand in the tank
   C. The fatness of the male fish
   D. The size of the tank

16. To clarify the results of Experiment 1, the biologist should set up which of the following test situations?

   F. Return the original male stickleback to Tank 1 and observe its behavior with the female fish.
   G. Maintain the positions of the male sticklebacks and add another egg-laden female to Tank 1.
   H. Place both male sticklebacks in Tank 2.
   J. Repeat the experiment using a different species of fish.

17. A male stickleback has been established in an aquarium and has built a nest. If one egg-laden female and several flat-shaped male sticklebacks are placed in the tank, one would most likely observe:

   A. all the males performing the zigzag dance.
   B. only the male that was originally in the tank performing the zigzag dance.
   C. all the males circling the female.
   D. the female retreating to a corner.

**GO ON TO THE NEXT PAGE.**

## Passage IV

Photosynthesis is a biological process in which light energy is converted to chemical bond energy. This essential process takes place on the primary level of the food chain and provides most of the food energy available to living organisms. Also, photosynthesis is the source for most of the oxygen in the Earth's atmosphere. Photosynthesis takes place in two distinctive stages called the "light" reactions and the "dark" reactions.

### Light reactions:

These reactions are also known as the photochemical reactions. Plants and some types of microorganisms contain specialized organelles called chloroplasts. In the chloroplasts, light energy is absorbed by the pigment chlorophyll. Some of this energy is used to convert water molecules into hydrogen ions and oxygen gas. The oxygen gas is released into the atmosphere through specialized openings on the plant's leaves. Some of the light energy is used to produce molecules of ATP.

### Dark reactions:

These reactions, also called "carbon-fixing" reactions, are not dependent on light. During the dark reactions, the hydrogen ions produced in the light reactions and carbon dioxide from the atmosphere pass through a series of chemical changes to form the simple sugar glucose and other compounds, including water. This glucose can be either consumed immediately or stored for later use. To test the effect of various environmental factors on the process of photosynthesis, a student observed the growth of plants over a period of time. The conditions and the results are described in Table 1. All plants were watered on a regular basis.

### Table 1

| Plant | Conditions | Results |
|-------|------------|---------|
| 1 | Sunlight | Normal growth Green |
| 2 | Darkness | Plant sickly Yellow |
| 3 | Sunlight Cut off all the leaves, but left the flowers intact. | Plant dead Brown |
| 4 | Sunlight Cut off all the flowers, but left the leaves intact. | Normal growth Green |
| 5 | Sunlight Entire plant covered with plastic wrap. | Normal growth Green Condensed water on the plastic wrap. |

18. Which word equation represents the process of photosynthesis?

   F. Sunlight + Carbon Dioxide + Water → Glucose + Oxygen + Water
   G. Glucose + Sunlight → Alcohol + Carbon Dioxide
   H. Oxygen + Sunlight + Water → Sugar + Carbon Dioxide + Water
   J. Glucose + Sunlight + Oxygen → Carbon Dioxide + Water

19. According to the passage, oxygen gas is produced in which of the following processes?

   A. Carbon-fixing reactions only
   B. Photochemical reactions only
   C. Chlorophyll-fixing reactions
   D. Both the photochemical and carbon-fixing reactions

20. Which of the following substances undergoes a transformation during the dark reactions of photosynthesis?

   I. Chlorophyll
   II. Hydrogen Ions
   III. Carbon Dioxide

   F. I only
   G. III only
   H. I and III only
   J. II and III only

21. Which of the plants represents the control for the experiments?

   A. 1 only
   B. 1 and 2 only
   C. All of the plants
   D. None of the plants

**GO ON TO THE NEXT PAGE.**

22. What hypothesis is supported by a comparison of the changes in Plant 1 and Plant 2?

    F. Darkness is a necessary factor in photosynthesis.
    G. The researcher neglected to water Plant 2.
    H. Plant respiration occurs only in sunlight.
    J. Chloroplasts can function only in sunlight.

23. Which of the following hypotheses is supported by the comparison of changes in Plant 3 and Plant 4?

    A. Chloroplasts are found in leaves, not flowers.
    B. Chloroplasts are found in flowers, not leaves.
    C. Oxygen is an essential requirement for photosynthesis.
    D. No chemical reactions occur in the stems.

24. Based on the information in the passage, what caused the condensation of water to occur inside the plastic wrap in Plant 5?

    F. Temperature differences between the environment inside the plastic wrap and outside the plastic wrap
    G. Trapped water vapor in the air surrounding the plant
    H. Water given off by the plant not used as a by-product of photosynthesis
    J. Excess water not used in the synthesis of glucose in the carbon fixation reactions

**GO ON TO THE NEXT PAGE.**

## Passage V

Social insects live in colonies and the survival of the colony is dependent on all of its members working together to obtain food, to secure safe home sites, and to continue the reproductive cycle of the species. All species of termites exhibit this social behavior. Biologists have observed that certain members of a termite colony, called soldiers, patrol the area surrounding a colony and, if alarmed, they alert other soldier termites to the danger. At this time, the soldier termite exhibits synchronous, convulsive movements and it may strike its head against wood or other nest materials. Though the convulsive movements are inaudible to human ears, the head-striking can be heard by man as a rustling or cracking sound. Two divergent theories exist concerning what kind of information is exchanged by these motions.

### Hypothesis 1

Termites have highly specialized appendages that enable them to receive vibrations sent through the air. The convulsive movements of an alarmed soldier termite create "sound waves," which are perceivable to other termites but not to humans. This method is used to communicate with nearby termites. When a soldier termite strikes its head against wood, it creates a louder sound message, which provides a warning to distant termites. The rate of these movements indicate how near the danger is to the colony—the closer the source, the more convulsions or head-strikes occur within a certain time period.

### Hypothesis 2

Termites are known to have highly developed sensory organs for smell. This theory supposes that the convulsive motions of a soldier termite do not emit sound messages, but instead accompany the release of pheromones, or scent. The characteristic scent of the soldier termite serves as a warning to members of the colony. Head-striking is a ritual that does not, by itself, carry any information about the danger or its distance from the colony.

25. In order to support Hypothesis 2, what must be assumed?

    A. Termites do not have well-developed sensory organs for sight.
    B. All termites can release different types of scents in order to send the colony different messages.
    C. Termites cannot perceive sources of danger that are more than 500 feet from the colony.
    D. The soldier termite scent is sufficient to alert the colony that a danger is present.

26. These hypotheses are similar because they both suggest that termites:

    I. use a symbolic language to communicate information to the other members of the colony.
    II. require exact information about a danger source in order to respond to a warning.
    III. are social insects that work together within a colony.

    F. I only
    G. II only
    H. III only
    J. II and III only

27. Which of the following observations would support Hypothesis 2?

    A. Soldier termites strike their heads against wood or other nest materials when food is found, but no danger is present.
    B. All types of termites, not just soldier termites, convulse and strike their heads when a danger source is present.
    C. Termites respond more quickly to danger signals when no wind is present.
    D. Termites respond more quickly to danger signals during the daylight hours.

**GO ON TO THE NEXT PAGE.**

**28.** Using a device that emits a high-pitched sound, a biologist determined the frequency of sound that triggers the soldier termites' danger mechanisms. These devices were placed at different distances from the colony. Data were collected to compare the rate of a soldier termite's convulsions to the distance the danger was from the colony. All experiments were performed on calm days and the sound devices were placed on flat land in a straight line from the colony. A significant variation in convulsion rates was reported in different soldiers reacting to a sound source at an equal distance. Furthermore, each soldier seemed to exhibit a uniform number of convulsions, regardless of the distance the sound source was placed from the colony. Which of the following explanations for this behavior was NOT investigated in this study?

   **I.** Wind may affect a soldier termite's perception of the distance of a danger source.
  **II.** The convulsion rate does not convey information about the distance of a danger source.
 **III.** Experienced soldiers can more accurately determine the distance of a danger source than can a novice soldier.

  **F.** I only
  **G.** II only
  **H.** I and II only
  **J.** I and III only

**29.** Which of these discoveries would NOT support Hypothesis 1?

  **A.** When a soldier termite's scent has been removed, it can still effectively warn a colony of danger.
  **B.** Termites have a range of hearing that is exactly the same as humans.
  **C.** If a termite loses its specialized appendages, it is forced out of the soldier position by other members of the colony.
  **D.** On a windy day, a soldier termite cannot as accurately warn the colony of danger as it can on a calm day.

**GO ON TO THE NEXT PAGE.**

**Passage VI**

Ionization energy is the amount of energy needed to take one electron from the outer shell of an elemental atom. Ionization energies are measured by removing successive electrons from the shells of an atom. The energy needed to withdraw the first electron is termed the first ionization energy, and each successive stage of electron withdrawal—named the second or third ionization energy, accordingly—requires more energy than the stage preceding it. Yet, an atom just beginning a new shell or subshell will have a smaller first ionization energy than the atom preceding it.

**Figure 1**

Figure 1 shows the first ionization energies (Kcal/mole of atoms) of the first fifty-three elements on the periodic table. Each of the first five periods is represented by a line connecting the elements of that period. The first period, containing only hydrogen, is represented by a dot. The noble gases are excluded.

If an element has a low first ionization energy, the atom is likely to form a positive cation, while an element with a high first ionization energy is less likely to lose an electron and more likely to form a negative anion. Also, metals tend to have lower first ionization energies and tend to give away electrons, forming positive cations. Figure 2 shows an expanded graph of Group IA to give a clearer representation of the trend down a group on the periodic table.

**Figure 2**

**30.** Some cations and anions will form ionic bonds with each other. Which of the following pairs of atoms could form a cation and an anion pair, respectively?

F. Na and Mg
G. Na and K
H. Br and I
J. Li and F

**31.** As a general trend, the lower the first ionization energy, the more metallic character the element exhibits. According to Figure 1, which three elements are the MOST metallic?

A. Na, K, Rb
B. Li, Na, Al
C. In, Ga, Sr
D. F, Cl, O

**32.** Comparing the first ionization energies of Mg and Al, what is a possible explanation for their different values?

F. Mg > Al because Mg contains more electrons than Al.
G. Mg > Al because Mg is more metallic and more energy is required to remove its outermost electron.
H. Mg > Al because Al represents a new subshell and less energy is required to remove its outermost electron.
J. Al > Mg because each successive ionization stage requires more energy.

**GO ON TO THE NEXT PAGE.**

**33.** Using Figure 2, predict the approximate first ionization energy for Cesium (Cs), element #55 (Group IA, Period 6)?

A.   55
B.   90
C.   160
D.   280

**34.** Hydrogen (H), element #1, has a high first ionization energy compared to Lithium (Li), element #3, though they both have only one electron in their outermost shell. What is a possible explanation for this phenomenon?

F.   Hydrogen is heavier than lithium.
G.   Hydrogen has fewer shells than lithium and its nucleus exerts a greater comparative force on its one electron.
H.   In a vacuum, hydrogen and lithium would have the same first ionization energy.
J.   Hydrogen is an anomaly and it is usually not included in first ionization energy charts.

**END OF TEST 5**
**STOP! DO NOT TURN THE PAGE UNTIL TOLD TO DO SO.**
**DO NOT RETURN TO THE PREVIOUS TEST.**

## READING

*30 Minutes—36 Questions*

**DIRECTIONS:** There are four passages in this test. Each passage is followed by several questions. After reading a passage, choose the best answer to each question and blacken the corresponding oval on your answer sheet. You may refer to the passages as often as necessary.

### Passage I

Karenin was not overjoyed by the move to Switzerland. Karenin hated change. Dog time cannot be plotted along a straight line; it does not move on and on, from one thing to the next. It moves in a circle
5 like the hands of a clock, which they too, unwilling to dash madly ahead—turn round and round the face, day in and day out following the same path. In Prague, when Tomas and Tereza brought a new chair or moved a flower pot, Karenin would look on in displeasure. It
10 disturbed his sense of time. It was as though they were trying to dupe the hands of the clock by changing the numbers on its face.

Nonetheless, he soon managed to reestablish the old order and old rituals in the Zurich flat. As in Prague,
15 he would jump up on the bed and welcome them to the day, accompany Tereza on her morning shopping jaunt, and make certain he got the other walks coming to him as well.

He was the timepiece of their lives. In periods
20 of despair, she would remind herself she had to hold on because of him, because he was weaker than she, weaker perhaps even than Dubcek and their abandoned homeland.

One day when they came back from a walk, the
25 phone was ringing. She picked up the receiver and asked who it was.

It was a woman's voice, and Tereza felt there was a hint of derision in it. When she said that Tomas wasn't there and she didn't know when he'd be back,
30 the woman on the other end of the line started laughing and, without saying good-bye, hung up.

Tereza knew it did not mean a thing. It could have been a nurse from the hospital, a patient, a secretary, anyone. But still she was upset and unable to concentrate
35 on anything. It was then that she realized she had lost the last bit of strength she had had at home; she was absolutely incapable of tolerating this absolutely insignificant incident.

Being in a foreign country means walking a
40 tightrope high above the ground without the net afforded a person by the country where he has his family, colleagues, and friends, and where he can easily say what he has to say in a language he has known from childhood. In Prague she was dependent on Tomas only
45 when it came to the heart; here she was dependent on him for everything. What would happen to her here if he abandoned her? Would she have to live her whole life in fear of losing him?

She told herself: Their acquaintance had been
50 based on an error from the start. The copy of *Anna Karenina* under her arm amounted to false papers; it had given Tomas the wrong idea. In spite of their love, they had made each other's life a hell. The fact that they loved each other was merely proof that the fault
55 lay not in themselves, in their behavior or inconstancy of feeling, but rather in their incompatibility; he was strong and she was weak. She was like Dubcek, who made a thirty-second pause in the middle of a sentence; she was like her country, which stuttered, gasped for
60 breath, could not speak.

But when the strong were too weak to hurt the weak, the weak had to be strong enough to leave.

And having told herself all this, she pressed her face against Karenin's furry head and said, "Sorry,
65 Karenin. It looks as though you're going to have to move again."

**1.** From the information in the passage, it can be inferred that:

   **A.** Tomas now lives in Prague.
   **B.** Tomas and Tereza want to move to Zurich.
   **C.** Tomas wants to move to Prague.
   **D.** Tomas and Tereza used to live in Prague.

**GO ON TO THE NEXT PAGE.**

**2.** According to the passage, it can be inferred that Karenin jumps in Tereza's bed (line 15) in order to:

   **F.** let Tereza know it is time to go shopping.

   **G.** let Tereza know he is hungry.

   **H.** reestablish his old routines.

   **J.** express his happiness.

**3.** Tereza believed that her copy of *Anna Karenina:*

   **A.** made her see she had to move from Switzerland.

   **B.** gave Tomas a false impression of her.

   **C.** indicated her weakness.

   **D.** symbolized her love.

**4.** Karenin is displeased about the move because:

   **F.** it disturbed his sense of time.

   **G.** he doesn't like the new place.

   **H.** he is unable to understand the change.

   **J.** he prefers to move in a circle.

**5.** In lines 39–44, an analogy is drawn between being in a foreign country and walking a tightrope in order to:

   **A.** show how difficult it is for Tereza.

   **B.** emphasize that Tereza's love for Tomas was in danger.

   **C.** show the precarious political situation.

   **D.** show how important it is to have friends.

**6.** In the passage, Tereza's state of mind can best be described as:

   **F.** despairing.

   **G.** calm.

   **H.** frantic.

   **J.** jealous.

**7.** Dubcek (line 57) is mentioned as an example of:

   **A.** a powerful ruler.

   **B.** an enemy of the state.

   **C.** a weak figure.

   **D.** a political refugee.

**8.** Tereza believed that the difficulty with her relationship with Tomas was that:

   **F.** they did not truly love each other.

   **G.** Tomas was too dependent.

   **H.** her feelings were constantly changing.

   **J.** he was strong while she was weak.

**9.** The author probably uses Karenin to symbolize:

   **A.** Tomas's love for Tereza.

   **B.** the recent move to Zurich.

   **C.** feelings of strength.

   **D.** continuity amidst change.

**GO ON TO THE NEXT PAGE.**

**Passage II**

In the 1740s, gold mines were discovered in what was then eastern Hungary, and is now northwestern Rumania. The usual avid search uncovered more veins of gold elsewhere in Hungary, but sometimes
5 the quantity of gold obtained from such veins was disappointingly small. Hungarian mineralogists naturally got to work in order to find out what was wrong.

One of them, Anton von Rupprecht, analyzed ore
10 from a gold mine in 1782 and found that a non-gold impurity accounted for the gold that was not obtained. Studying this impurity, Rupprecht found it had some properties that resembled those of antimony, an element well known to the chemists of the day. Judging from
15 its appearance, therefore, he concluded that antimony was what he had.

In 1784, another Hungarian mineralogist, Franz Joseph Muller (1740–1825), studied Rupprecht's ore and decided that the metal impurity was not antimony
20 because it did not have some of that metal's properties. He began to wonder if he had a completely new element, but didn't dare commit himself to that. In 1796, he sent samples to the German chemist Martin Heinrich Klaproth (1743–1817), a leading authority, telling him
25 of his suspicions that he had a new element and asking him to check the matter.

Klaproth gave it all the necessary tests and, by 1798, was able to report it as a new element. He carefully, as was proper, gave Muller credit for the discovery, and
30 supplied it with a name. He called it "tellurium," from the Latin word for "earth."

Tellurium is a very rare element, less than half as common in the earth's crust as gold is. However, it is commonly associated with gold in ores, and since
35 few things are as assiduously searched for as gold, tellurium is found more often than one would expect from its rareness.

Tellurium is (as was eventually understood) one of the sulfur family of elements, and the Swedish chemist
40 Jons Jakob Berzelius (1779–1848) was not surprised, therefore, when, in 1817, he found tellurium in the sulfuric acid being prepared in a certain factory. At least he found an impurity that looked like tellurium so that he took it for granted that was what it was.

45 Working with the supposed tellurium, he found that some of its properties were not like those of tellurium. By February, 1818, he realized that he had still another new element on his hands, one that strongly resembled tellurium... he called it
50 "selenium."

In the periodic table, selenium falls between sulfur and tellurium. Selenium is not exactly a common element, but it is more common than either tellurium or gold. Selenium is, in fact, nearly as
55 common as silver.

Selenium and tellurium were not particularly important elements for nearly a century after their discovery. Then, in 1873, there came a peculiar and completely unexpected finding. Willoughby Smith
60 found that selenium would conduct an electric current with much greater ease when it is exposed to light than when it is in the dark. This was the first discovery ever made of something that was eventually called "the photoelectric effect"; that is, the effect of light upon
65 electrical phenomena.

10. Rupprecht found that:

F. gold is impure.
G. a non-gold impurity accounted for the little gold obtained.
H. antimony is an element just like gold.
J. the impurity was not antimony.

11. The credited discoverer of tellurium is:

A. Klaproth.
B. Rupprecht.
C. Berzelius.
D. Muller.

12. Based on the information in the passage, which of the following is a hypothesis rather than a fact?

F. Selenium falls between sulfur and tellurium in the periodic table.
G. Tellurium's being found with gold is due to the special bonding between them.
H. Selenium conducts an electric current.
J. Tellurium is often found because of its closeness to gold.

13. It can be inferred that silver is:

A. slightly more common than selenium.
B. slightly less common than gold.
C. as common as sulfur.
D. as common as tellurium.

**GO ON TO THE NEXT PAGE.**

**14.** Based on the information in the passage, the periodic table (line 51) is most likely:

   **F.** a list of new elements.
   **G.** a listing of all elements.
   **H.** a description of selenium, sulfur, and tellurium.
   **J.** a list of the properties of common elements.

**15.** Selenium and tellurium:

   **A.** have no important applications.
   **B.** were ignored until 1873.
   **C.** were not utilized practically until well after their discovery.
   **D.** are equally important in terms of practical applications.

**16.** It can be inferred from the passage that all of the following are elements EXCEPT:

   **F.** sulfuric acid.
   **G.** antimony.
   **H.** selenium.
   **J.** gold.

**17.** Which event most contributed to the discovery of selenium?

   **A.** The discovery of tellurium in gold ore
   **B.** The analysis of sulfuric acid
   **C.** The discovery of the photoelectric effect
   **D.** The discovery that tellurium is similar to sulfur

**18.** Given the information on the photoelectric effect (lines 58–64), which of the following can be inferred?

   **F.** Electricity and light are the same thing.
   **G.** Electricity is usually the result of light.
   **H.** Electricity and light are related phenomena.
   **J.** Electricity has little effect on light.

**GO ON TO THE NEXT PAGE.**

**Passage III**

Every school child is taught that Robert Fulton was the first American to build and operate a steamboat on New York waters. When his *Clermont* sauntered four miles per hour upstream on the Hudson River in 1807,
5  Fulton opened up new possibilities in transportation, marketing, and city building. What is not often taught about Fulton is that he had a monopoly enforced by the state. The New York legislature gave Fulton the privilege of carrying *all* steamboat traffic in New York
10 for thirty years. It was this monopoly that Thomas Gibbons, a New Jersey steamboat man, tried to crack when he hired young Cornelius Vanderbilt in 1817 to run steamboats in New York by charging less than the monopoly rates.

15 Vanderbilt was a classic market entrepreneur, and he was intrigued by the challenge of breaking the Fulton monopoly. On the mast of Gibbon's ship Vanderbilt hoisted a flag that read: "New Jersey must be free." For sixty days in 1817, Vanderbilt defied capture as he
20 raced passengers cheaply from Elizabeth, New Jersey, to New York City. He became a popular figure on the Atlantic as he lowered the fares and eluded the law. Finally, in 1824, in the landmark case of *Gibbons v. Ogden,* the Supreme Court struck down the Fulton
25 monopoly. Chief Justice John Marshall ruled that only the federal government, not the states, could regulate interstate commerce. This extremely popular decision opened the waters of America to complete competition. A jubilant Vanderbilt was greeted in
30 New Brunswick, New Jersey, by cannon salutes fired by "citizens desirous of testifying in a public manner their good will." Ecstatic New Yorkers immediately launched two steamboats named for John Marshall. On the Ohio River, steamboat traffic doubled in the
35 first year after *Gibbons v. Ogden* and quadrupled after the second year.

The triumph of market entrepreneurs in steamboating led to improvements in technology. As one man observed, "The boat builders, freed from
40 the domination of the Fulton-Livingston interests, were quick to develop new ideas that before had no encouragement from capital." These new ideas included tubular boilers to replace the heavy and expensive copper boilers Fulton used. Cordwood for
45 fuel was also a major cost for Fulton, but innovators soon found that anthracite coal worked well under the new tubular boilers, so "the expense of fuel was down one-half."

The real value of removing the Fulton monopoly
50 was that the costs of steamboating dropped. Passenger traffic, for example, from New York City to Albany immediately dropped from seven to three dollars after *Gibbons v. Ogden.* Fulton's group couldn't meet the new rates and soon went bankrupt. Gibbons and
55 Vanderbilt, meanwhile, adopted the new technology, cut their costs, and earned $40,000 profit each year during the late 1820s.

With such an open environment for market entrepreneurs, Vanderbilt decided to quit his pleasant
60 association with Gibbons, buy the two steamboats, and go into business for himself. During the 1830s, Vanderbilt would establish trade routes all over the Northeast. He offered fast and reliable service at low rates. He first tried the New York to Philadelphia route
65 and forced the "standard" three-dollar fare down to one dollar. On the New Brunswick to New York City run, Vanderbilt charged six cents a trip and provided free meals. As *Niles' Register* said, the "times must be hard indeed when a traveller who wishes to save
70 money cannot afford to walk."

19. According to the passage, Vanderbilt was a "market entrepreneur" (line 15) because he:

    A. broke the Fulton monopoly.
    B. ran a successful steamship company.
    C. operated the cheapest steamship line on the Hudson.
    D. believed in the free market as opposed to a state enforced monopoly.

20. The phrase "New Jersey must be free" (line 18) meant that:

    F. there should be no fares on the Hudson line.
    G. the New Jersey market should be open to competition.
    H. Fulton's line should be dismantled.
    J. the government should regulate the steamship industry.

21. The Supreme Court's decision in *Gibbons v. Ogden* had all of the following effects EXCEPT:

    A. it struck down the Fulton monopoly.
    B. it led to cheaper fares.
    C. it enabled Fulton to expand.
    D. it opened America's waterways to competition.

**GO ON TO THE NEXT PAGE.**

**22.** It can be inferred that Fulton's business faltered while Gibbons's and Vanderbilt's business flourished because:

- **F.** Fulton didn't adopt the new technology.
- **G.** Gibbons and Vanderbilt took over Fulton's state-enforced monopoly.
- **H.** Fulton was less popular than Vanderbilt.
- **J.** steamship travel on the Hudson, Fulton's primary route, decreased.

**23.** After *Gibbons v. Ogden,* steamboat travel most probably increased because of:

- **A.** larger steamships.
- **B.** more efficient technology.
- **C.** reduced fares.
- **D.** a population explosion.

**24.** Gibbons and Vanderbilt were:

- **F.** competitors.
- **G.** employer and employee.
- **H.** equal partners.
- **J.** legal experts.

**25.** According to the passage, Vanderbilt was able to expand all over the Northeast because:

- **A.** demand was very high there for steamship transportation.
- **B.** Gibbons's monopoly was broken.
- **C.** there were very few rival steamship lines.
- **D.** he offered cheap and efficient service.

**26.** It can be inferred from the passage that:

- **F.** Fulton was essentially dishonest.
- **G.** everything that children are usually taught about Fulton is wrong.
- **H.** school children learn only part of Fulton's story.
- **J.** fulton does not deserve to be honored.

**27.** The author's tone toward Vanderbilt is one of:

- **A.** admiration.
- **B.** glorification.
- **C.** understanding.
- **D.** empathy.

**GO ON TO THE NEXT PAGE.**

## Passage IV

We know today that the traditions of tribal art are more complex and less "primitive" than its discoverers believed; we have even seen that the imitation of nature is by no means excluded from its aims. But the style of
[5] these ritualistic objects could still serve as a common focus for that search for expressiveness, structure, and simplicity that the new movements had inherited from the experiments of the three lonely rebels: Van Gogh, Cezanne, and Gauguin.

[10] The experiments of Expressionism are, perhaps, the easiest to explain in words. The term itself may not be happily chosen, for we know that we are all expressing ourselves in everything we do or leave undone, but the word became a convenient label because of its easily
[15] remembered contrast to Impressionism, and as a label it is quite useful. In one of his letters, Van Gogh had explained how he set about painting the portrait of a friend who was very dear to him. The conventional likeness was only the first stage. Having painted a
[20] "correct" portrait, he proceeded to change the colors and the setting: "I exaggerate the fair color of the hair, I take orange, chrome, lemon color, and behind the head I do not paint the trivial wall of the room but the Infinite. I make a simple background out of the most intense and
[25] richest blue the palette will yield. The blond luminous head stands out against this strong blue background mysteriously like a star in the azure. Alas, my dear friend, the public will see nothing but caricature in this exaggeration, but what does that matter to us?"

[30] Van Gogh was right in saying that the method he had chosen could be compared to that of the caricaturist. Caricature had always been "expressionist," for the caricaturist plays with the likeness of his victim, and distorts it to express just what he feels about his fellow
[35] man. As long as these distortions of nature sailed under the flag of humor nobody seemed to find them difficult to understand. Humorous art was a field in which everything was permitted, because people did not approach it with the prejudices they reserved for "Art
[40] with a capital A." But the idea of a serious caricature, of an art that deliberately changed the appearance of things not to express a sense of superiority, but maybe love, or admiration, or fear, proved indeed a stumbling block as Van Gogh had predicted. Yet there is nothing
[45] inconsistent about it. It is the sober truth that our feelings about things do color the way in which we see them and, even more, the forms that we remember. Everyone must have experienced how different the same place may look when we are happy and when
[50] we are sad.

What upset the public about the Expressionist art was, perhaps, not so much the fact that nature had been distorted as that the result led away from beauty. That the caricaturist may show up the ugliness of man was
[55] granted—it was his job. But that men who claimed to be serious artists should forget that if they must change the appearance of things they should idealize them, rather than make them ugly, was strongly resented. But an Expressionist might have retorted that a shout of
[60] anguish is not beautiful, and that it would be insincere to look only at the pleasing side of life. For the Expressionists felt so strongly about human suffering, poverty, violence, and passion, that they were inclined to think that the insistence on harmony and beauty were
[65] only born out of a refusal to be honest. The art of the classical masters, of a Raphael or Correggio, seemed to them insincere and hypocritical. They wanted to face the stark facts of our existence, and to express their compassion for the disinherited and the ugly. It became
[70] almost a point of honor with them to avoid anything that smelt of pettiness and polish, and to shock the "bourgeois" out of his real or imagined complacency.

**28.** The term "correct" in line 20 means:

**F.** critically acclaimed.
**G.** traditionally accepted.
**H.** objectively beautiful.
**J.** simple and trivial.

**29.** Van Gogh, Cezanne, and Gauguin all:

**A.** used the same methods of distortion.
**B.** began their careers as caricaturists.
**C.** experimented with new styles of expression.
**D.** were concerned with educating people about the "new" art.

**30.** It can be inferred from the passage that people found it easier to accept distortions in humorous art for all of the following reasons EXCEPT:

**F.** people had fewer preconceptions toward it.
**G.** people didn't take it seriously.
**H.** they thought of the distortions as deliberate attempts at humor.
**J.** they accepted the distortions as expressions of love, admiration, and fear.

**GO ON TO THE NEXT PAGE.**

**31.** What was the Expressionist position regarding beauty in art?

   **A.** There was essentially no such thing as true beauty.
   **B.** It resulted from conformity and fear of change.
   **C.** It was totally unnecessary.
   **D.** It stemmed from dishonesty.

**32.** Expressionism was essentially a(n):

   **F.** close association of radical artists.
   **G.** new style whose sole purpose was to shock people.
   **H.** artistic movement founded on a more expressive style.
   **J.** fundamental revolution in art.

**33.** The author quotes Van Gogh's description of his painting (lines 21–29) in order to:

   **A.** show how the Expressionist style differed from conventional painting.
   **B.** show that Van Gogh was essentially a caricaturist.
   **C.** give the reader a feel for a typical Expressionist work.
   **D.** demonstrate Van Gogh's importance to the new movement.

**34.** The author implies that the art of Raphael and Correggio:

   **F.** was similar to that of the Expressionists.
   **G.** used caricature to show the darker side of the human condition.
   **H.** was characterized by an insistence on harmony and beauty.
   **J.** expressed compassion for the disinherited and the ugly.

**35.** It can be inferred that the Expressionists:

   **A.** were lonely people.
   **B.** were motivated by a desire to change for the sake of changing.
   **C.** were not immediately accepted by the public.
   **D.** were appreciative of the influence of caricatures on their work.

**36.** The author believes that:

   **F.** Expressionism is a more advanced style of art than conventional painting.
   **G.** caricatures are not serious art.
   **H.** Expressionism was responsible for an eventual decrease in the importance of beauty in twentieth-century art.
   **J.** Expressionism shares characteristics with the art of caricature.

**END OF TEST 6**
**STOP! DO NOT TURN THE PAGE UNTIL TOLD TO DO SO.**
**DO NOT RETURN TO THE PREVIOUS TEST.**

The Princeton Review

# PRINCETON REVIEW ASSESSMENT
# ANSWER SHEET

Use a No. 2 pencil only. Be sure each mark is dark and completely fills the intended oval. Completely erase any errors or stray marks.

Start with number 1 for each new section. If a section has fewer questions than answer spaces, leave the extra answer spaces blank.

**SECTION 1**

| 1 ⊂A⊃ ⊂B⊃ ⊂C⊃ ⊂D⊃ ⊂E⊃ | 16 ⊂F⊃ ⊂G⊃ ⊂H⊃ ⊂J⊃ ⊂K⊃ | 31 ⊂A⊃ ⊂B⊃ ⊂C⊃ ⊂D⊃ ⊂E⊃ | 46 ⊂F⊃ ⊂G⊃ ⊂H⊃ ⊂J⊃ ⊂K⊃ |
| 2 ⊂F⊃ ⊂G⊃ ⊂H⊃ ⊂J⊃ ⊂K⊃ | 17 ⊂A⊃ ⊂B⊃ ⊂C⊃ ⊂D⊃ ⊂E⊃ | 32 ⊂F⊃ ⊂G⊃ ⊂H⊃ ⊂J⊃ ⊂K⊃ | 47 ⊂A⊃ ⊂B⊃ ⊂C⊃ ⊂D⊃ ⊂E⊃ |
| 3 ⊂A⊃ ⊂B⊃ ⊂C⊃ ⊂D⊃ ⊂E⊃ | 18 ⊂F⊃ ⊂G⊃ ⊂H⊃ ⊂J⊃ ⊂K⊃ | 33 ⊂A⊃ ⊂B⊃ ⊂C⊃ ⊂D⊃ ⊂E⊃ | 48 ⊂F⊃ ⊂G⊃ ⊂H⊃ ⊂J⊃ ⊂K⊃ |
| 4 ⊂F⊃ ⊂G⊃ ⊂H⊃ ⊂J⊃ ⊂K⊃ | 19 ⊂A⊃ ⊂B⊃ ⊂C⊃ ⊂D⊃ ⊂E⊃ | 34 ⊂F⊃ ⊂G⊃ ⊂H⊃ ⊂J⊃ ⊂K⊃ | 49 ⊂A⊃ ⊂B⊃ ⊂C⊃ ⊂D⊃ ⊂E⊃ |
| 5 ⊂A⊃ ⊂B⊃ ⊂C⊃ ⊂D⊃ ⊂E⊃ | 20 ⊂F⊃ ⊂G⊃ ⊂H⊃ ⊂J⊃ ⊂K⊃ | 35 ⊂A⊃ ⊂B⊃ ⊂C⊃ ⊂D⊃ ⊂E⊃ | 50 ⊂F⊃ ⊂G⊃ ⊂H⊃ ⊂J⊃ ⊂K⊃ |
| 6 ⊂F⊃ ⊂G⊃ ⊂H⊃ ⊂J⊃ ⊂K⊃ | 21 ⊂A⊃ ⊂B⊃ ⊂C⊃ ⊂D⊃ ⊂E⊃ | 36 ⊂F⊃ ⊂G⊃ ⊂H⊃ ⊂J⊃ ⊂K⊃ | 51 ⊂A⊃ ⊂B⊃ ⊂C⊃ ⊂D⊃ ⊂E⊃ |
| 7 ⊂A⊃ ⊂B⊃ ⊂C⊃ ⊂D⊃ ⊂E⊃ | 22 ⊂F⊃ ⊂G⊃ ⊂H⊃ ⊂J⊃ ⊂K⊃ | 37 ⊂A⊃ ⊂B⊃ ⊂C⊃ ⊂D⊃ ⊂E⊃ | 52 ⊂F⊃ ⊂G⊃ ⊂H⊃ ⊂J⊃ ⊂K⊃ |
| 8 ⊂F⊃ ⊂G⊃ ⊂H⊃ ⊂J⊃ ⊂K⊃ | 23 ⊂A⊃ ⊂B⊃ ⊂C⊃ ⊂D⊃ ⊂E⊃ | 38 ⊂F⊃ ⊂G⊃ ⊂H⊃ ⊂J⊃ ⊂K⊃ | 53 ⊂A⊃ ⊂B⊃ ⊂C⊃ ⊂D⊃ ⊂E⊃ |
| 9 ⊂A⊃ ⊂B⊃ ⊂C⊃ ⊂D⊃ ⊂E⊃ | 24 ⊂F⊃ ⊂G⊃ ⊂H⊃ ⊂J⊃ ⊂K⊃ | 39 ⊂A⊃ ⊂B⊃ ⊂C⊃ ⊂D⊃ ⊂E⊃ | 54 ⊂F⊃ ⊂G⊃ ⊂H⊃ ⊂J⊃ ⊂K⊃ |
| 10 ⊂F⊃ ⊂G⊃ ⊂H⊃ ⊂J⊃ ⊂K⊃ | 25 ⊂A⊃ ⊂B⊃ ⊂C⊃ ⊂D⊃ ⊂E⊃ | 40 ⊂F⊃ ⊂G⊃ ⊂H⊃ ⊂J⊃ ⊂K⊃ | 55 ⊂A⊃ ⊂B⊃ ⊂C⊃ ⊂D⊃ ⊂E⊃ |
| 11 ⊂A⊃ ⊂B⊃ ⊂C⊃ ⊂D⊃ ⊂E⊃ | 26 ⊂F⊃ ⊂G⊃ ⊂H⊃ ⊂J⊃ ⊂K⊃ | 41 ⊂A⊃ ⊂B⊃ ⊂C⊃ ⊂D⊃ ⊂E⊃ | 56 ⊂F⊃ ⊂G⊃ ⊂H⊃ ⊂J⊃ ⊂K⊃ |
| 12 ⊂F⊃ ⊂G⊃ ⊂H⊃ ⊂J⊃ ⊂K⊃ | 27 ⊂A⊃ ⊂B⊃ ⊂C⊃ ⊂D⊃ ⊂E⊃ | 42 ⊂F⊃ ⊂G⊃ ⊂H⊃ ⊂J⊃ ⊂K⊃ | 57 ⊂A⊃ ⊂B⊃ ⊂C⊃ ⊂D⊃ ⊂E⊃ |
| 13 ⊂A⊃ ⊂B⊃ ⊂C⊃ ⊂D⊃ ⊂E⊃ | 28 ⊂F⊃ ⊂G⊃ ⊂H⊃ ⊂J⊃ ⊂K⊃ | 43 ⊂A⊃ ⊂B⊃ ⊂C⊃ ⊂D⊃ ⊂E⊃ | 58 ⊂F⊃ ⊂G⊃ ⊂H⊃ ⊂J⊃ ⊂K⊃ |
| 14 ⊂F⊃ ⊂G⊃ ⊂H⊃ ⊂J⊃ ⊂K⊃ | 29 ⊂A⊃ ⊂B⊃ ⊂C⊃ ⊂D⊃ ⊂E⊃ | 44 ⊂F⊃ ⊂G⊃ ⊂H⊃ ⊂J⊃ ⊂K⊃ | 59 ⊂A⊃ ⊂B⊃ ⊂C⊃ ⊂D⊃ ⊂E⊃ |
| 15 ⊂A⊃ ⊂B⊃ ⊂C⊃ ⊂D⊃ ⊂E⊃ | 30 ⊂F⊃ ⊂G⊃ ⊂H⊃ ⊂J⊃ ⊂K⊃ | 45 ⊂A⊃ ⊂B⊃ ⊂C⊃ ⊂D⊃ ⊂E⊃ | 60 ⊂F⊃ ⊂G⊃ ⊂H⊃ ⊂J⊃ ⊂K⊃ |

**SECTION 2**

| 1 ⊂A⊃ ⊂B⊃ ⊂C⊃ ⊂D⊃ ⊂E⊃ |
| 2 ⊂A⊃ ⊂B⊃ ⊂C⊃ ⊂D⊃ ⊂E⊃ |
| 3 ⊂A⊃ ⊂B⊃ ⊂C⊃ ⊂D⊃ ⊂E⊃ |
| 4 ⊂A⊃ ⊂B⊃ ⊂C⊃ ⊂D⊃ ⊂E⊃ |
| 5 ⊂A⊃ ⊂B⊃ ⊂C⊃ ⊂D⊃ ⊂E⊃ |
| 6 ⊂A⊃ ⊂B⊃ ⊂C⊃ ⊂D⊃ ⊂E⊃ |
| 7 ⊂A⊃ ⊂B⊃ ⊂C⊃ ⊂D⊃ ⊂E⊃ |
| 8 ⊂A⊃ ⊂B⊃ ⊂C⊃ ⊂D⊃ ⊂E⊃ |
| 9 ⊂A⊃ ⊂B⊃ ⊂C⊃ ⊂D⊃ ⊂E⊃ |
| 10 ⊂A⊃ ⊂B⊃ ⊂C⊃ ⊂D⊃ ⊂E⊃ |

Grid-in questions 11, 12, 13, 14, 15, 16, 17 each contain four columns with:
⊂/⊃ ⊂/⊃ (fraction bars)
⊂•⊃ ⊂•⊃ ⊂•⊃ ⊂•⊃ (decimal points)
⊂0⊃ ⊂1⊃ ⊂2⊃ ⊂3⊃ ⊂4⊃ ⊂5⊃ ⊂6⊃ ⊂7⊃ ⊂8⊃ ⊂9⊃

| 18 ⊂A⊃ ⊂B⊃ ⊂C⊃ ⊂D⊃ ⊂E⊃ | 23 ⊂A⊃ ⊂B⊃ ⊂C⊃ ⊂D⊃ ⊂E⊃ | 28 ⊂A⊃ ⊂B⊃ ⊂C⊃ ⊂D⊃ ⊂E⊃ | 33 ⊂A⊃ ⊂B⊃ ⊂C⊃ ⊂D⊃ ⊂E⊃ |
| 19 ⊂A⊃ ⊂B⊃ ⊂C⊃ ⊂D⊃ ⊂E⊃ | 24 ⊂A⊃ ⊂B⊃ ⊂C⊃ ⊂D⊃ ⊂E⊃ | 29 ⊂A⊃ ⊂B⊃ ⊂C⊃ ⊂D⊃ ⊂E⊃ | 34 ⊂A⊃ ⊂B⊃ ⊂C⊃ ⊂D⊃ ⊂E⊃ |
| 20 ⊂A⊃ ⊂B⊃ ⊂C⊃ ⊂D⊃ ⊂E⊃ | 25 ⊂A⊃ ⊂B⊃ ⊂C⊃ ⊂D⊃ ⊂E⊃ | 30 ⊂A⊃ ⊂B⊃ ⊂C⊃ ⊂D⊃ ⊂E⊃ | 35 ⊂A⊃ ⊂B⊃ ⊂C⊃ ⊂D⊃ ⊂E⊃ |
| 21 ⊂A⊃ ⊂B⊃ ⊂C⊃ ⊂D⊃ ⊂E⊃ | 26 ⊂A⊃ ⊂B⊃ ⊂C⊃ ⊂D⊃ ⊂E⊃ | 31 ⊂A⊃ ⊂B⊃ ⊂C⊃ ⊂D⊃ ⊂E⊃ | 36 ⊂A⊃ ⊂B⊃ ⊂C⊃ ⊂D⊃ ⊂E⊃ |
| 22 ⊂A⊃ ⊂B⊃ ⊂C⊃ ⊂D⊃ ⊂E⊃ | 27 ⊂A⊃ ⊂B⊃ ⊂C⊃ ⊂D⊃ ⊂E⊃ | 32 ⊂A⊃ ⊂B⊃ ⊂C⊃ ⊂D⊃ ⊂E⊃ | 37 ⊂A⊃ ⊂B⊃ ⊂C⊃ ⊂D⊃ ⊂E⊃ |

BE SURE TO ERASE ANY ERRORS OR STRAY MARKS COMPLETELY.

Start with number 1 for each new section. If a section has fewer questions than answer spaces, leave the extra answer spaces blank.

## SECTION 3

| 1 cAɔ cBɔ cCɔ cDɔ cEɔ | 8 cFɔ cGɔ cHɔ cJɔ cKɔ | 15 cAɔ cBɔ cCɔ cDɔ cEɔ | 22 cFɔ cGɔ cHɔ cJɔ cK |
| 2 cFɔ cGɔ cHɔ cJɔ cKɔ | 9 cAɔ cBɔ cCɔ cDɔ cEɔ | 16 cFɔ cGɔ cHɔ cJɔ cKɔ | 23 cAɔ cBɔ cCɔ cDɔ cE |
| 3 cAɔ cBɔ cCɔ cDɔ cEɔ | 10 cFɔ cGɔ cHɔ cJɔ cKɔ | 17 cAɔ cBɔ cCɔ cDɔ cEɔ | 24 cFɔ cGɔ cHɔ cJɔ cK |
| 4 cFɔ cGɔ cHɔ cJɔ cKɔ | 11 cAɔ cBɔ cCɔ cDɔ cEɔ | 18 cFɔ cGɔ cHɔ cJɔ cKɔ | 25 cAɔ cBɔ cCɔ cDɔ cE |
| 5 cAɔ cBɔ cCɔ cDɔ cEɔ | 12 cFɔ cGɔ cHɔ cJɔ cKɔ | 19 cAɔ cBɔ cCɔ cDɔ cEɔ | 26 cFɔ cGɔ cHɔ cJɔ cK |
| 6 cFɔ cGɔ cHɔ cJɔ cKɔ | 13 cAɔ cBɔ cCɔ cDɔ cEɔ | 20 cFɔ cGɔ cHɔ cJɔ cKɔ | 27 cAɔ cBɔ cCɔ cDɔ cE |
| 7 cAɔ cBɔ cCɔ cDɔ cEɔ | 14 cFɔ cGɔ cHɔ cJɔ cKɔ | 21 cAɔ cBɔ cCɔ cDɔ cEɔ | 28 cFɔ cGɔ cHɔ cJɔ cK |

## SECTION 4

| 1 cAɔ cBɔ cCɔ cDɔ cEɔ | 16 cAɔ cBɔ cCɔ cDɔ cEɔ | 31 cAɔ cBɔ cCɔ cDɔ cEɔ | 46 cAɔ cBɔ cCɔ cDɔ cE |
| 2 cAɔ cBɔ cCɔ cDɔ cEɔ | 17 cAɔ cBɔ cCɔ cDɔ cEɔ | 32 cAɔ cBɔ cCɔ cDɔ cEɔ | 47 cAɔ cBɔ cCɔ cDɔ cE |
| 3 cAɔ cBɔ cCɔ cDɔ cEɔ | 18 cAɔ cBɔ cCɔ cDɔ cEɔ | 33 cAɔ cBɔ cCɔ cDɔ cEɔ | 48 cAɔ cBɔ cCɔ cDɔ cE |
| 4 cAɔ cBɔ cCɔ cDɔ cEɔ | 19 cAɔ cBɔ cCɔ cDɔ cEɔ | 34 cAɔ cBɔ cCɔ cDɔ cEɔ | 49 cAɔ cBɔ cCɔ cDɔ cE |
| 5 cAɔ cBɔ cCɔ cDɔ cEɔ | 20 cAɔ cBɔ cCɔ cDɔ cEɔ | 35 cAɔ cBɔ cCɔ cDɔ cEɔ | 50 cAɔ cBɔ cCɔ cDɔ cE |
| 6 cAɔ cBɔ cCɔ cDɔ cEɔ | 21 cAɔ cBɔ cCɔ cDɔ cEɔ | 36 cAɔ cBɔ cCɔ cDɔ cEɔ | 51 cAɔ cBɔ cCɔ cDɔ cE |
| 7 cAɔ cBɔ cCɔ cDɔ cEɔ | 22 cAɔ cBɔ cCɔ cDɔ cEɔ | 37 cAɔ cBɔ cCɔ cDɔ cEɔ | 52 cAɔ cBɔ cCɔ cDɔ cE |
| 8 cAɔ cBɔ cCɔ cDɔ cEɔ | 23 cAɔ cBɔ cCɔ cDɔ cEɔ | 38 cAɔ cBɔ cCɔ cDɔ cEɔ | 53 cAɔ cBɔ cCɔ cDɔ cE |
| 9 cAɔ cBɔ cCɔ cDɔ cEɔ | 24 cAɔ cBɔ cCɔ cDɔ cEɔ | 39 cAɔ cBɔ cCɔ cDɔ cEɔ | 54 cAɔ cBɔ cCɔ cDɔ cE |
| 10 cAɔ cBɔ cCɔ cDɔ cEɔ | 25 cAɔ cBɔ cCɔ cDɔ cEɔ | 40 cAɔ cBɔ cCɔ cDɔ cEɔ | 55 cAɔ cBɔ cCɔ cDɔ cE |
| 11 cAɔ cBɔ cCɔ cDɔ cEɔ | 26 cAɔ cBɔ cCɔ cDɔ cEɔ | 41 cAɔ cBɔ cCɔ cDɔ cEɔ | 56 cAɔ cBɔ cCɔ cDɔ cE |
| 12 cAɔ cBɔ cCɔ cDɔ cEɔ | 27 cAɔ cBɔ cCɔ cDɔ cEɔ | 42 cAɔ cBɔ cCɔ cDɔ cEɔ | 57 cAɔ cBɔ cCɔ cDɔ cE |
| 13 cAɔ cBɔ cCɔ cDɔ cEɔ | 28 cAɔ cBɔ cCɔ cDɔ cEɔ | 43 cAɔ cBɔ cCɔ cDɔ cEɔ | 58 cAɔ cBɔ cCɔ cDɔ cE |
| 14 cAɔ cBɔ cCɔ cDɔ cEɔ | 29 cAɔ cBɔ cCɔ cDɔ cEɔ | 44 cAɔ cBɔ cCɔ cDɔ cEɔ | 59 cAɔ cBɔ cCɔ cDɔ cE |
| 15 cAɔ cBɔ cCɔ cDɔ cEɔ | 30 cAɔ cBɔ cCɔ cDɔ cEɔ | 45 cAɔ cBɔ cCɔ cDɔ cEɔ | 60 cAɔ cBɔ cCɔ cDɔ cE |

## SECTION 5

| 1 cAɔ cBɔ cCɔ cDɔ cEɔ | 16 cFɔ cGɔ cHɔ cJɔ cKɔ | 31 cAɔ cBɔ cCɔ cDɔ cEɔ | 46 cFɔ cGɔ cHɔ cJɔ cK |
| 2 cFɔ cGɔ cHɔ cJɔ cKɔ | 17 cAɔ cBɔ cCɔ cDɔ cEɔ | 32 cFɔ cGɔ cHɔ cJɔ cKɔ | 47 cAɔ cBɔ cCɔ cDɔ cE |
| 3 cAɔ cBɔ cCɔ cDɔ cEɔ | 18 cFɔ cGɔ cHɔ cJɔ cKɔ | 33 cAɔ cBɔ cCɔ cDɔ cEɔ | 48 cFɔ cGɔ cHɔ cJɔ cK |
| 4 cFɔ cGɔ cHɔ cJɔ cKɔ | 19 cAɔ cBɔ cCɔ cDɔ cEɔ | 34 cFɔ cGɔ cHɔ cJɔ cKɔ | 49 cAɔ cBɔ cCɔ cDɔ cE |
| 5 cAɔ cBɔ cCɔ cDɔ cEɔ | 20 cFɔ cGɔ cHɔ cJɔ cKɔ | 35 cAɔ cBɔ cCɔ cDɔ cEɔ | 50 cFɔ cGɔ cHɔ cJɔ cK |
| 6 cFɔ cGɔ cHɔ cJɔ cKɔ | 21 cAɔ cBɔ cCɔ cDɔ cEɔ | 36 cFɔ cGɔ cHɔ cJɔ cKɔ | 51 cAɔ cBɔ cCɔ cDɔ cE |
| 7 cAɔ cBɔ cCɔ cDɔ cEɔ | 22 cFɔ cGɔ cHɔ cJɔ cKɔ | 37 cAɔ cBɔ cCɔ cDɔ cEɔ | 52 cFɔ cGɔ cHɔ cJɔ cK |
| 8 cFɔ cGɔ cHɔ cJɔ cKɔ | 23 cAɔ cBɔ cCɔ cDɔ cEɔ | 38 cFɔ cGɔ cHɔ cJɔ cKɔ | 53 cAɔ cBɔ cCɔ cDɔ cE |
| 9 cAɔ cBɔ cCɔ cDɔ cEɔ | 24 cFɔ cGɔ cHɔ cJɔ cKɔ | 39 cAɔ cBɔ cCɔ cDɔ cEɔ | 54 cFɔ cGɔ cHɔ cJɔ cK |
| 10 cFɔ cGɔ cHɔ cJɔ cKɔ | 25 cAɔ cBɔ cCɔ cDɔ cEɔ | 40 cFɔ cGɔ cHɔ cJɔ cKɔ | 55 cAɔ cBɔ cCɔ cDɔ cE |
| 11 cAɔ cBɔ cCɔ cDɔ cEɔ | 26 cFɔ cGɔ cHɔ cJɔ cKɔ | 41 cAɔ cBɔ cCɔ cDɔ cEɔ | 56 cFɔ cGɔ cHɔ cJɔ cK |
| 12 cFɔ cGɔ cHɔ cJɔ cKɔ | 27 cAɔ cBɔ cCɔ cDɔ cEɔ | 42 cFɔ cGɔ cHɔ cJɔ cKɔ | 57 cAɔ cBɔ cCɔ cDɔ cE |
| 13 cAɔ cBɔ cCɔ cDɔ cEɔ | 28 cFɔ cGɔ cHɔ cJɔ cKɔ | 43 cAɔ cBɔ cCɔ cDɔ cEɔ | 58 cFɔ cGɔ cHɔ cJɔ cK |
| 14 cFɔ cGɔ cHɔ cJɔ cKɔ | 29 cAɔ cBɔ cCɔ cDɔ cEɔ | 44 cFɔ cGɔ cHɔ cJɔ cKɔ | 59 cAɔ cBɔ cCɔ cDɔ cE |
| 15 cAɔ cBɔ cCɔ cDɔ cEɔ | 30 cFɔ cGɔ cHɔ cJɔ cKɔ | 45 cAɔ cBɔ cCɔ cDɔ cEɔ | 60 cFɔ cGɔ cHɔ cJɔ cK |

## SECTION 6

| 1 cAɔ cBɔ cCɔ cDɔ cEɔ | 16 cFɔ cGɔ cHɔ cJɔ cKɔ | 31 cAɔ cBɔ cCɔ cDɔ cEɔ | 46 cFɔ cGɔ cHɔ cJɔ cK |
| 2 cFɔ cGɔ cHɔ cJɔ cKɔ | 17 cAɔ cBɔ cCɔ cDɔ cEɔ | 32 cFɔ cGɔ cHɔ cJɔ cKɔ | 47 cAɔ cBɔ cCɔ cDɔ cE |
| 3 cAɔ cBɔ cCɔ cDɔ cEɔ | 18 cFɔ cGɔ cHɔ cJɔ cKɔ | 33 cAɔ cBɔ cCɔ cDɔ cEɔ | 48 cFɔ cGɔ cHɔ cJɔ cK |
| 4 cFɔ cGɔ cHɔ cJɔ cKɔ | 19 cAɔ cBɔ cCɔ cDɔ cEɔ | 34 cFɔ cGɔ cHɔ cJɔ cKɔ | 49 cAɔ cBɔ cCɔ cDɔ cE |
| 5 cAɔ cBɔ cCɔ cDɔ cEɔ | 20 cFɔ cGɔ cHɔ cJɔ cKɔ | 35 cAɔ cBɔ cCɔ cDɔ cEɔ | 50 cFɔ cGɔ cHɔ cJɔ cK |
| 6 cFɔ cGɔ cHɔ cJɔ cKɔ | 21 cAɔ cBɔ cCɔ cDɔ cEɔ | 36 cFɔ cGɔ cHɔ cJɔ cKɔ | 51 cAɔ cBɔ cCɔ cDɔ cE |
| 7 cAɔ cBɔ cCɔ cDɔ cEɔ | 22 cFɔ cGɔ cHɔ cJɔ cKɔ | 37 cAɔ cBɔ cCɔ cDɔ cEɔ | 52 cFɔ cGɔ cHɔ cJɔ cK |
| 8 cFɔ cGɔ cHɔ cJɔ cKɔ | 23 cAɔ cBɔ cCɔ cDɔ cEɔ | 38 cFɔ cGɔ cHɔ cJɔ cKɔ | 53 cAɔ cBɔ cCɔ cDɔ cE |
| 9 cAɔ cBɔ cCɔ cDɔ cEɔ | 24 cFɔ cGɔ cHɔ cJɔ cKɔ | 39 cAɔ cBɔ cCɔ cDɔ cEɔ | 54 cFɔ cGɔ cHɔ cJɔ cK |
| 10 cFɔ cGɔ cHɔ cJɔ cKɔ | 25 cAɔ cBɔ cCɔ cDɔ cEɔ | 40 cFɔ cGɔ cHɔ cJɔ cKɔ | 55 cAɔ cBɔ cCɔ cDɔ cE |
| 11 cAɔ cBɔ cCɔ cDɔ cEɔ | 26 cFɔ cGɔ cHɔ cJɔ cKɔ | 41 cAɔ cBɔ cCɔ cDɔ cEɔ | 56 cFɔ cGɔ cHɔ cJɔ cK |
| 12 cFɔ cGɔ cHɔ cJɔ cKɔ | 27 cAɔ cBɔ cCɔ cDɔ cEɔ | 42 cFɔ cGɔ cHɔ cJɔ cKɔ | 57 cAɔ cBɔ cCɔ cDɔ cE |
| 13 cAɔ cBɔ cCɔ cDɔ cEɔ | 28 cFɔ cGɔ cHɔ cJɔ cKɔ | 43 cAɔ cBɔ cCɔ cDɔ cEɔ | 58 cFɔ cGɔ cHɔ cJɔ cK |
| 14 cFɔ cGɔ cHɔ cJɔ cKɔ | 29 cAɔ cBɔ cCɔ cDɔ cEɔ | 44 cFɔ cGɔ cHɔ cJɔ cKɔ | 59 cAɔ cBɔ cCɔ cDɔ cE |
| 15 cAɔ cBɔ cCɔ cDɔ cEɔ | 30 cFɔ cGɔ cHɔ cJɔ cKɔ | 45 cAɔ cBɔ cCɔ cDɔ cEɔ | 60 cFɔ cGɔ cHɔ cJɔ cK |

BE SURE TO ERASE ANY ERRORS OR STRAY MARKS COMPLETELY.

# 19

# How to Score the PRA

## STEP A

Count the number of correct answers for Section 1 and record the number in the space provided for your raw score on the Score Conversion Worksheet on the next page. Repeat for each section of the test.

## STEP B

On Section 2, questions 1–10, subtract a third of a point from your raw score for every question that you answered incorrectly. Do not deduct points for those questions you left blank. On Section 2, questions 18–35, deduct a quarter of a point for every wrong answer. Again, do not deduct points for those questions you left blank. On Section 4, deduct a quarter of a point for any question you answered incorrectly. And, you guessed it: Do not deduct points for those questions you left blank.

## STEP C

Some questions count toward both of your scores. We call these Crossover Points. You'll notice that on your answer key, Sections 2, 3, and 6 have two columns, and selected questions in each have asterisks. If you get one of those questions right, give yourself an ACT point and an SAT point. Then add those points to their respective raw scores. Crossover Points on Section 2 count toward Section 3 and vice versa and Crossover Points on Section 6 count toward your score on Section 4. (Don't bother deducting anything for wrong answers.)

## STEP D

Using the score conversion charts on pages 385–386, convert your raw scores on each section to scaled scores. Then compute your composite ACT score by averaging the four subject scores: Add them up and divide by four. To calculate the range of your SAT scores, add the lowest number from Math to the lowest number from Verbal and the highest number from Math to the highest number from Verbal. Let's see how Joe B. did on his PRA:

| ACT | | SAT | |
|---|---|---|---|
| Language Skills: | 20–26 | Math: | 390–450 |
| Math: | 23–29 | Verbal: | 520–580 |
| Science: | 14–20 | | |
| Reading: | 25–31 | | |

So, by adding 20 + 23 + 14 + 25 and dividing the sum (82) by four and rounding up, he gets a low score of 21. When he adds 26 + 29 + 20 + 31, he gets 106, which averages out to 27. So, his ACT range is 21–27. By adding 390 + 520 and 450 + 580, he gets an SAT range of 910–1,030.

## ESTIMATED ACT SCORE

| PRA Section | Raw Score | ACT Score |
|---|---|---|
| SECTION 1 | _____ / (55) | converts to _____ - _____ |
| SECTION 3 | _____ / (27) | |
| CROSSOVER POINTS | + _____ / (8) | |
| TOTAL | _____ / (35) | converts to _____ - _____ |
| SECTION 5 | _____ / (34) | converts to _____ - _____ |
| SECTION 6 | _____ / (36) | converts to _____ - _____ |

**TOTAL (add ACT scores):** _____ - _____

**Composite ACT score (divide total by 4):** _____ - _____

## ESTIMATED SAT SCORE

| PRA Section | Raw Score | SAT Score |
|---|---|---|

**SECTION 2: Math**
Number Right: _____ / (35)
Number Wrong:

Questions 1–10 divided by 3 − _____

Questions 18–35 divided by 4 − _____

CROSSOVER POINTS + _____ / (12)

TOTAL _____ / (47) converts to _____ - _____

**SECTION 4: Verbal**
Number Right _____ / (46)

Number Wrong divided by 4 −

CROSSOVER POINTS + _____ / (7)

TOTAL _____ / (53) converts to _____ - _____

**Combined SAT Score (add scores):** _____ - _____

# CORRECT ANSWERS FOR PRINCETON REVIEW ASSESSMENT

| Section 1 ACT Language Skills | Section 2 SAT Math | | Section 3 ACT Math | | Section 4 SAT Verbal | Section 5 ACT Science | Section 6 ACT Reading | |
|---|---|---|---|---|---|---|---|---|
| | SAT | ACT | ACT | SAT | | | ACT | SAT |
| 1. C | 1. A ___ | | 1. B ___ | * | 1. C | 1. A | 1. D ___ | |
| 2. G | 2. C ___ | | 2. H ___ | | 2. C | 2. G | 2. H ___ | |
| 3. D | 3. D ___ | | 3. A ___ | | 3. C | 3. A | 3. B ___ | |
| 4. F | 4. B ___ | | 4. H ___ | | 4. B | 4. H | 4. F ___ | |
| 5. B | 5. B ___ | | 5. E ___ | * | 5. B | 5. C | 5. A ___ | * |
| 6. J | 6. D ___ | | 6. K ___ | * | 6. B | 6. G | 6. F ___ | |
| 7. A | 7. C ___ | | 7. E ___ | | 7. D | 7. C | 7. C ___ | |
| 8. G | 8. D ___ | | 8. J ___ | * | 8. D | 8. G | 8. J ___ | |
| 9. C | 9. A ___ | | 9. A ___ | | 9. B | 9. D | 9. D ___ | |
| 10. J | 10. C ___ | | 10. J ___ | | 10. E | 10. F | 10. G ___ | * |
| 11. A | 11. 2 ___ | | 11. D ___ | | 11. D | 11. C | 11. D ___ | |
| 12. J | 12. 14 ___ | | 12. G ___ | * | 12. E | 12. G | 12. G ___ | |
| 13. B | 13. 19, 39, 59, 79 | | 13. E ___ | * | 13. C | 13. D | 13. A ___ | |
| 14. H | or 99 ___ | | 14. H ___ | | 14. C | 14. J | 14. G ___ | |
| 15. D | 14. 36 ___ | | 15. B ___ | | 15. B | 15. C | 15. C ___ | |
| 16. H | 15. 5 ___ | | 16. J ___ | | 16. A | 16. F | 16. F ___ | |
| 17. B | 16. 15 ___ | | 17. B ___ | | 17. E | 17. B | 17. B ___ | |
| 18. J | 17. .5 ___ | | 18. F ___ | | 18. C | 18. F | 18. H ___ | |
| 19. B | 18. C ___ | * | 19. C ___ | * | 19. E | 19. B | 19. D ___ | * |
| 20. H | 19. D ___ | * | 20. K ___ | * | 20. D | 20. J | 20. G ___ | |
| 21. B | 20. D ___ | | 21. B ___ | | 21. D | 21. A | 21. C ___ | * |
| 22. J | 21. A ___ | * | 22. H ___ | * | 22. C | 22. J | 22. F ___ | |
| 23. B | 22. B ___ | * | 23. B ___ | * | 23. A | 23. A | 23. C ___ | * |
| 24. H | 23. E ___ | * | 24. H ___ | | 24. D | 24. H | 24. G ___ | |
| 25. C | 24. E ___ | | 25. A ___ | * | 25. A | 25. D | 25. D ___ | |
| 26. G | 25. B ___ | | 26. G ___ | * | 26. D | 26. H | 26. H ___ | |
| 27. A | 26. B ___ | | 27. A ___ | | 27. A | 27. A | 27. A ___ | |
| 28. J | 27. A ___ | * | | | 28. C | 28. J | 28. G ___ | |
| 29. A | 28. B ___ | | | | 29. C | 29. B | 29. C ___ | |
| 30. J | 29. A ___ | | | | 30. B | 30. J | 30. J ___ | * |
| 31. A | 30. A ___ | * | *If you got this question right, add a crossover point to your raw score on Section 2 of the PRA. | | 31. A | 31. A | 31. D ___ | |
| 32. F | 31. A ___ | | | | 32. C | 32. H | 32. H ___ | |
| 33. C | 32. C ___ | | | | 33. A | 33. B | 33. A ___ | * |
| 34. G | 33. C ___ | | | | 34. B | 34. G | 34. H ___ | |
| 35. A | 34. D ___ | * | | | 35. C | | 35. C ___ | |
| 36. J | 35. B ___ | | | | 36. A | | 36. J ___ | |
| 37. A | | | | | 37. B | | | |
| 38. F | | | | | 38. E | | | |
| 39. A | | | | | 39. A | | | |
| 40. G | | | | | 40. C | | | |
| 41. D | *If you got this question right, add a crossover point to your raw score on Section 3 of the PRA. | | | | 41. A | | *If you got this question right, add a crossover point to your raw score on Section 4 of the PRA. | |
| 42. J | | | | | 42. C | | | |
| 43. A | | | | | 43. B | | | |
| 44. J | | | | | 44. C | | | |
| 45. B | | | | | 45. C | | | |
| 46. J | | | | | 46. E | | | |
| 47. A | | | | | | | | |
| 48. H | | | | | | | | |
| 49. D | | | | | | | | |
| 50. H | | | | | | | | |
| 51. B | | | | | | | | |
| 52. H | | | | | | | | |
| 53. D | | | | | | | | |
| 54. G | | | | | | | | |
| 55. B | | | | | | | | |

| Number Correct ___ /(55) | Number Correct ___ /(47) | Number Correct ___ /(35) | Number Correct ___ /(53) | Number Correct ___ /(34) | Number Correct ___ /(36) |
|---|---|---|---|---|---|

## ESTIMATED ACT SCALE SCORE

| Section 1 ACT Language Skills | | Section 3 (and 2) ACT Math | | Section 5 ACT Science | | Section 6 ACT Reading | |
|---|---|---|---|---|---|---|---|
| Raw Score | ACT Score | Raw Score | ACT Score | Raw Score | ACT Score | Raw Score | ACT Score |
| 55 | 30 – 36 | 35 | 30 – 36 | 34 | 30 – 36 | 36 | 30 – 36 |
| 54 | 30 – 36 | 34 | 30 – 36 | 33 | 30 – 36 | 35 | 30 – 36 |
| 53 | 30 – 36 | 33 | 30 – 36 | 32 | 30 – 36 | 34 | 30 – 36 |
| 52 | 29 – 35 | 32 | 29 – 34 | 31 | 29 – 35 | 33 | 30 – 36 |
| 51 | 28 – 34 | 31 | 27 – 33 | 30 | 27 – 33 | 32 | 29 – 35 |
| 50 | 27 – 33 | 30 | 26 – 32 | 29 | 26 – 33 | 31 | 28 – 34 |
| 49 | 26 – 32 | 29 | 26 – 32 | 28 | 24 – 30 | 30 | 27 – 33 |
| 48 | 25 – 31 | 28 | 25 – 31 | 27 | 23 – 29 | 29 | 26 – 32 |
| 47 | 24 – 30 | 27 | 24 – 30 | 26 | 23 – 29 | 28 | 25 – 31 |
| 46 | 23 – 29 | 26 | 24 – 30 | 25 | 22 – 28 | 27 | 24 – 30 |
| 45 | 23 – 29 | 25 | 23 – 29 | 24 | 21 – 27 | 26 | 23 – 29 |
| 44 | 22 – 28 | 24 | 22 – 28 | 23 | 20 – 26 | 25 | 22 – 28 |
| 43 | 21 – 27 | 23 | 21 – 27 | 22 | 19 – 25 | 24 | 21 – 27 |
| 42 | 21 – 27 | 22 | 20 – 26 | 21 | 18 – 24 | 23 | 20 – 26 |
| 41 | 20 – 26 | 21 | 19 – 25 | 20 | 17 – 23 | 22 | 19 – 25 |
| 40 | 20 – 26 | 20 | 18 – 24 | 19 | 17 – 23 | 21 | 18 – 24 |
| 39 | 19 – 25 | 19 | 17 – 23 | 18 | 16 – 22 | 20 | 17 – 23 |
| 38 | 19 – 25 | 18 | 17 – 23 | 17 | 16 – 22 | 19 | 16 – 22 |
| 37 | 18 – 24 | 17 | 16 – 22 | 16 | 15 – 21 | 18 | 15 – 21 |
| 36 | 18 – 24 | 16 | 16 – 22 | 15 | 14 – 20 | 17 | 14 – 20 |
| 35 | 17 – 23 | 15 | 15 – 21 | 14 | 13 – 19 | 16 | 13 – 19 |
| 34 | 16 – 22 | 14 | 14 – 20 | 13 | 12 – 18 | 15 | 12 – 18 |
| 33 | 16 – 22 | 13 | 14 – 20 | 12 | 12 – 18 | 14 | 11 – 17 |
| 32 | 16 – 22 | 12 | 13 – 19 | 11 | 11 – 17 | 13 | 11 – 17 |
| 31 | 15 – 21 | 11 | 13 – 19 | 10 | 11 – 17 | 12 | 10 – 16 |
| 30 | 15 – 21 | 10 | 12 – 18 | 9 | 10 – 16 | 11 | 9 – 15 |
| 29 | 14 – 20 | 9 | 11 – 17 | 8 | 9 – 15 | 10 | 8 – 14 |
| 28 | 14 – 20 | 8 | 10 – 16 | 7 | 8 – 14 | 9 | 7 – 13 |
| 27 | 13 – 19 | 7 | 9 – 15 | 6 | 7 – 13 | 8 | 6 – 12 |
| 26 | 13 – 19 | 6 | 8 – 14 | 5 | 6 – 12 | 7 | 5 – 11 |
| 25 | 12 – 18 | 5 | 7 – 13 | 4 | 5 – 11 | 6 | 4 – 10 |
| 24 | 12 – 18 | 4 | 6 – 12 | 3 | 4 – 10 | 5 | 3 – 9 |
| 23 | 11 – 17 | 3 | 5 – 11 | 2 | 3 – 9 | 4 | 2 – 8 |
| 22 | 11 – 17 | 2 | 2 – 8 | 1 | 0 – 6 | 3 | 1 – 7 |
| 21 | 11 – 17 | 1 | 1 – 7 | 0 | 0 – 6 | 2 | 0 – 6 |
| 20 | 10 – 16 | 0 | 0 – 6 | | | 1 | 0 – 6 |
| 19 | 10 – 16 | | | | | 0 | 0 – 6 |
| 18 | 10 – 16 | | | | | | |
| 17 | 9 – 15 | | | | | | |
| 16 | 9 – 15 | | | | | | |
| 15 | 8 – 14 | | | | | | |
| 14 | 7 – 13 | | | | | | |
| 13 | 7 – 13 | | | | | | |
| 12 | 6 – 12 | | | | | | |
| 11 | 6 – 12 | | | | | | |
| 10 | 6 – 12 | | | | | | |
| 9 | 5 – 11 | | | | | | |
| 8 | 4 – 10 | | | | | | |
| 7 | 4 – 10 | | | | | | |
| 6 | 3 – 9 | | | | | | |
| 5 | 2 – 8 | | | | | | |
| 4 | 2 – 8 | | | | | | |
| 3 | 1 – 7 | | | | | | |
| 2 | 0 – 6 | | | | | | |
| 1 | 0 – 6 | | | | | | |
| 0 | 0 – 6 | | | | | | |

# ESTIMATED SAT SCALE SCORE

| Section 2 (and 3) SAT Math | | Section 4 (and 6) SAT Verbal | |
| --- | --- | --- | --- |
| Raw Score | SAT Score | Raw Score | SAT Score |
| 47 | 740 – 800 | 53 | 740 – 800 |
| 46 | 740 – 800 | 52 | 740 – 800 |
| 45 | 730 – 790 | 51 | 730 – 790 |
| 44 | 730 – 790 | 50 | 730 – 790 |
| 43 | 730 – 790 | 49 | 720 – 780 |
| 42 | 720 – 780 | 48 | 710 – 770 |
| 41 | 710 – 770 | 47 | 690 – 750 |
| 40 | 690 – 750 | 46 | 680 – 740 |
| 39 | 690 – 750 | 45 | 650 – 710 |
| 38 | 680 – 740 | 44 | 640 – 700 |
| 37 | 670 – 730 | 43 | 620 – 680 |
| 36 | 650 – 710 | 42 | 620 – 670 |
| 35 | 630 – 690 | 41 | 600 – 660 |
| 34 | 610 – 670 | 40 | 590 – 650 |
| 33 | 600 – 660 | 39 | 580 – 640 |
| 32 | 590 – 650 | 38 | 570 – 630 |
| 31 | 580 – 640 | 37 | 550 – 610 |
| 30 | 550 – 610 | 36 | 540 – 600 |
| 29 | 530 – 590 | 35 | 520 – 580 |
| 28 | 520 – 580 | 34 | 510 – 570 |
| 27 | 500 – 560 | 33 | 500 – 560 |
| 26 | 480 – 540 | 32 | 490 – 550 |
| 25 | 460 – 520 | 31 | 480 – 540 |
| 24 | 440 – 500 | 30 | 470 – 530 |
| 23 | 430 – 490 | 29 | 460 – 520 |
| 22 | 410 – 470 | 28 | 450 – 510 |
| 21 | 400 – 460 | 27 | 440 – 500 |
| 20 | 390 – 450 | 26 | 430 – 490 |
| 19 | 380 – 440 | 25 | 420 – 480 |
| 18 | 370 – 430 | 24 | 410 – 470 |
| 17 | 360 – 420 | 23 | 390 – 450 |
| 16 | 340 – 400 | 22 | 380 – 440 |
| 15 | 330 – 390 | 21 | 370 – 430 |
| 14 | 310 – 370 | 20 | 360 – 420 |
| 13 | 300 – 360 | 19 | 350 – 410 |
| 12 | 270 – 330 | 18 | 340 – 400 |
| 11 | 260 – 320 | 17 | 330 – 390 |
| 10 | 250 – 310 | 16 | 320 – 380 |
| 9 | 240 – 300 | 15 | 310 – 370 |
| 8 | 230 – 290 | 14 | 290 – 350 |
| 7 | 210 – 270 | 13 | 280 – 340 |
| 6 | 200 – 260 | 12 | 270 – 330 |
| 5 | 200 – 260 | 11 | 240 – 300 |
| 4 | 200 – 260 | 10 | 200 – 260 |
| 3 | 200 – 260 | 9 | 200 – 260 |
| 2 | 200 – 260 | 8 | 200 – 260 |
| 1 | 200 – 260 | 7 | 200 – 260 |
| 0 | 200 – 260 | 6 | 200 – 260 |
| | | 5 | 200 – 260 |
| | | 4 | 200 – 260 |
| | | 3 | 200 – 260 |
| | | 2 | 200 – 260 |
| | | 1 | 200 – 260 |

# 20

# Using the PRA

Take some time before deciding which admissions test is right for you. The chart on the next page will help you compare your scores on the ACT and the SAT.

Most schools will accept either score; others accept only one or the other. The best way to determine which schools take which scores is to look at an up-to-date college guide such as The Princeton Review's *The Best 345 Colleges*. What is the average score on each test of incoming freshmen at the schools you are considering? How do your scores stack up against their scores?

A warning: While this is a good way to decide which test to take, it is a lousy way to pick a school. Colleges print average test scores: Many of their students scored lower. Colleges consider your grades and your extracurricular record along with your scores (as a rule of thumb, the smaller the school, the more time they spend reading your application). Don't drop a school from your list simply because your SAT score was 100 points below its average.

Your scores will change in fits and starts. Good preparation should increase your scores on either test, but in different ways. The ACT is more straightforward and relies a little more on actual knowledge of subject matter. The SAT, on the other hand, is pretty much a test of how well you take the SAT. The best way to prepare is to practice on real tests, available from the Educational Testing Service (for the SAT) and ACT (for the ACT).

As you might have guessed, we at The Princeton Review believe that there is no better way to prepare for these tests than by taking a good course. But you already have all the tools you need at your disposal. Get copies of old tests and practice, practice, practice. Review concepts that you haven't used for a while. Use the information in this book to brush up on what you need to know to do well on the ACT. The Question-by-Question Breakdown at the end of this chapter will help you home in on your weaknesses (what to learn) and your strengths (what to practice).

If you decide that the SAT is the test for you, get ready to beef up your vocabulary. About half of your SAT Verbal score is based entirely on your knowledge of words. So, start looking up words that you don't know. Make flash cards. Keep lists of unfamiliar words. Most important of all: Read more! By the way, we also publish *Cracking the SAT*.

Time and again, we hear from former students who laugh at how anxious they once were about the college admissions process. Take it seriously, do your homework, but relax. Wherever you go to school, you'll find kids getting a great education and kids goofing off, kids enjoying themselves and kids hating every minute of the day. Do your best, but don't let any person (or any standardized test) make you crazy.

Good luck!

# THE PRA CHART

**Directions:** Follow these steps to help you decide which admissions test (ACT or SAT) better represents you.

I. Add your SAT Math and Verbal scores. Since they are estimates, you should estimate. For example, if your SAT Math score is in the 500–540 range and your SAT Verbal score is in the 450–510 range, your total would be about 520 + 480 = 1,000.

II. Find your combined SAT score on the bottom line of the chart. Draw a vertical line up from that point.

III. Find your ACT score on the left side of the chart (e.g., go to 25 if your projected score is between 22 and 27). Draw a horizontal line across from that point.

IV. Look at the point where the two lines intersect. If it's in the white area, your scores on the two tests are about the same. If it's in the light grey area, your SAT score is stronger. If it's in the dark grey area, your ACT score is stronger.

# QUESTION-BY-QUESTION BREAKDOWN

Each category refers to certain questions on the test. This breakdown helps you analyze your weak areas. Take a close look at each question in the category where you feel you need improvement. Try to identify the problem. Difficult vocabulary? Look up the words you don't know. Too tough a concept? Have a friend or teacher help, or refer back to the appropriate chapter in this book. Carelessness? The final analysis you have to do yourself.

| **ACT English** | **Section 1 Questions** |
|---|---|
| Punctuation | 4, 7, 8, 10, 11, 19, 22, 23, 25, 34, 43, 44, 48, 52, 54 |
| Grammar | 9, 12, 20, 21, 26, 27, 38, 40, 41, 47 |
| Sentence Structure | 2, 3, 6, 14, 16, 18, 28, 32, 33, 36, 45, 46, 49, 50 |
| Diction/Style | 1, 5, 15, 17, 29, 31, 37, 39, 53 |
| Logic/Organization | 13, 24, 30, 35, 42, 51, 55 |

| **SAT Math** | **Section 2 Questions** |
|---|---|
| Fractions/Ratios | 12, 19, 35 |
| Percent/Decimals | 22, 27 |
| Averages | 23 |
| Arithmetic Operations | 4, 5, 10, 14, 16, 20, 29 |
| Algebra Basics | 1, 18 |
| Algebra Manipulation | 3, 6, 7, 9, 11, 24, 31 |
| Angles/Lengths | 2, 15, 21, 25, 32, 33, 34 |
| Area/Perimeter/Volume | 8, 17, 26, 30 |
| Abstract Math | 13, 28 |

| **ACT Math** | **Section 3 Questions** |
|---|---|
| Fractions/Ratios | |
| Percent/Decimals | 4, 8 |
| Averages | |
| Arithmetic Operations | 2, 3 |
| Algebra Basics | 5, 12, 19 |
| Algebra Manipulation | 7, 9, 10, 11, 13, 20 |
| Intermediate Algebra | 22 |
| Angles/Lengths | 1, 6, 15, 17, 23 |
| Area/Perimeter/Volume | 25, 26 |
| Graphs and Trig | 14, 16, 18, 21, 24, 27 |

**SAT Verbal**

**Section 4 Questions**

Sentence Completion: 1–11

Analogies: 12–23

Reading Comprehension:

- ■ Line reference 24, 27, 30, 34, 35, 36, 37
- ■ Tone 25, 28, 33, 43
- ■ Specifics 26, 32, 39, 46
- ■ General Idea 29, 31, 41, 42, 44, 45
- ■ Vocabulary in Context 38, 40

**ACT Science** | **Section 5 Questions**
--- | ---
Biology | 1, 2, 3, 4, 5, 6, 12, 13, 14, 15, 16, 17, 18, 19, 20, 21, 22, 23, 24, 25, 26, 27, 28, 29
Physics | 7, 8, 9, 10, 11
Chemistry | 30, 31, 32, 33, 34

**ACT Reading** | **Section 6 Questions**
--- | ---
Prose Fiction | 1, 2, 3, 4, 5, 6, 7, 8, 9
Natural Science | 10, 11, 12, 13, 14, 15, 16, 17, 18
Social Science | 19, 20, 21, 22, 23, 24, 25, 26, 27
Humanities | 28, 29, 30, 31, 32, 33, 34, 35, 36

# PART VII

# The Princeton Review ACT Practice Exam and Explanations

# 21

# ACT Practice Exam

# ENGLISH TEST
### 45 Minutes—75 Questions

**DIRECTIONS:** In the passages that follow, certain words and phrases are underlined and numbered. In the right-hand column, you will find alternatives for the underlined part. You should choose the one that best expresses the idea, is worded most consistently with the tone and style of the passage, or makes the sentence conform to the rules of standard written English. If you think the original version is best, choose "NO CHANGE." You will also find questions about a section of the passage, or about the passage as a whole. These questions do not refer to an underlined portion of the passage, but are instead identified by a number in a box.

## PASSAGE I

### Lindbergh's Journey

On May 20, 1927, Charles Lindbergh, a twenty-five-year-old from the Midwest, embarked on a journey. Destined to become the first successful flight from New York to Paris. Flying in his single-engine plane, it was *The Spirit of St. Louis*, Lindbergh took off from Roosevelt Field in Long Island at 7:24 A.M. and did not touch down in France until thirty-three and a half hours later.

Lindbergh's flight was unique in several respects that it was unlike any previous flights. First, Lindbergh flew without a co-pilot, an extremely risky undertaking despite the duration of the flight and the exhaustion that would be an inevitable threat to a solo pilot. Second, Lindbergh's flight was four hundred miles longer than any that had come before it. A French attempt to fly the same route shortly before had ended in the death of the two pilots when his plane crashed before reaching its destination.

1. **A.** NO CHANGE
   **B.** embarked, on a journey destined
   **C.** embarked on a journey destined
   **D.** embarked. On a journey destined

2. **F.** NO CHANGE
   **G.** plane,
   **H.** plane, being
   **J.** plane. This was

3. **A.** NO CHANGE
   **B.** respects, and unlike flights previous to it.
   **C.** differences from flights that came before.
   **D.** respects.

4. **F.** NO CHANGE
   **G.** except for
   **H.** given
   **J.** regardless of

5. **A.** NO CHANGE
   **B.** that would inevitably threaten
   **C.** in an inevitably threatening regard to
   **D.** however inevitable the threat of

6. **F.** NO CHANGE
   **G.** they're
   **H.** their
   **J.** there

**GO ON TO THE NEXT PAGE.**

It was therefore not surprising that Lindbergh's success was met with such a trickle of joy and admiration. When Lindbergh landed in Paris, nearly thirty-four hours after leaving New York, the crowd descended on him, carrying the exhausted pilot on their shoulders for half an hour. Finally, he was whisked off to the American Embassy, where he can get some well-deserved sleep.

When he got back to the United States, the uproar only has grown. Thousands of songs and poems were written for him, and throngs made up of American admirers fol-lowed him everywhere he went. Every day brought more fan letters, even though proposals of marriage from female devotees. Lindbergh became, and to some extent still becoming, the quintessential American hero. Indeed, who could typify the American ideal better than one who beat the odds, challenged the laws of nature, and showed the world that we as a country are capable of anything, even flight?

**7. A.** NO CHANGE
   **B.** an outpouring
   **C.** an undercurrent
   **D.** a murmur

**8. F.** NO CHANGE
   **G.** him: to carry
   **H.** him; carrying
   **J.** him. And carried

**9. A.** NO CHANGE
   **B.** will
   **C.** might
   **D.** was able to

**10. F.** NO CHANGE
   **G.** growed.
   **H.** grew.
   **J.** had been growing.

**11. A.** NO CHANGE
   **B.** consisting of admirers from the United States
   **C.** of admiring, Americans
   **D.** of admirers

**12. F.** NO CHANGE
   **G.** letters—even
   **H.** letters, despite
   **J.** OMIT the underlined portion.

**13. A.** NO CHANGE
   **B.** has already become,
   **C.** remains,
   **D.** remain,

**14. F.** NO CHANGE
   **G.** challenged the natural odds as well as the laws
   **H.** beat the odds, and challenged the laws of nature
   **J.** beat upon the most challenging laws of nature,

**15.** Which of the following would best convey the idea that Lindbergh is emblematic of the hope and pride of America?
   **A.** NO CHANGE
   **B.** a plane could indeed be aerodynamically sound?
   **C.** America was a land of great economic power?
   **D.** Charles Lindbergh was a truly extraordinary pilot?

**GO ON TO THE NEXT PAGE.**

**PASSAGE II**

### The War of the Worlds

In 1938, CBS Radio hired the young Orson Welles to

direct a sophisticated but deft weekly drama series to go
                              ___
                               16
opposite *Chase and Sanborn Radio Hour*, a particularly

popular show on the rival station, NBC. ☐17 CBS hoped

to draw on highbrow viewers who were more interested

in serious literary material, than in the songs and jokes
_____
            18

that dominated *Chase and Sanborn*. Welles was so rising
                                    _____
                                            19
a promising stage director that he seemed like the perfect
_____
              19
person for the job.

The first episode of the series was to be an adaptation of

H.G. Wells' *The War of the Worlds*, the story of a Martian

invading of Earth. Rather than tell the story in traditional radio
_____
   20

play format, however, he decided to present it as an unfolding
                       __
                       21
news story, complete with actors playing radio

---

**16.** The author would like to convey the idea that CBS wanted Orson Welles' series to appeal to a wide range of listeners. Which of the following would best accomplish this?
   **F.** NO CHANGE
   **G.** accessible
   **H.** youthful
   **J.** wordy

**17.** The author would like to insert a sentence to give a sense of the popularity of *Chase and Sanborn Radio Hour*. If all of the following are true, which would best accomplish this?
   **A.** *Chase and Sanborn* starred the well-known ventriloquist Edgar Bergan and his hilariously insolent dummy, Charlie McCarthy.
   **B.** *Chase and Sanborn*, like many radio shows of its era, was a variety show, and may be seen as the prototype for the many television variety shows of the 1970s.
   **C.** Although *Chase and Sanborn* was enjoyed by many, others felt that its vapid subject matter did little to enrich the minds of its listeners.
   **D.** *Chase and Sanborn* had such a large and devoted audience that most sponsors refused to advertise on any show that broadcast at the same time.

**18. F.** NO CHANGE
   **G.** serious, literary material, than
   **H.** serious literary, material than
   **J.** serious literary material than

**19. A.** NO CHANGE
   **B.** Welles was a rising, promising stage director,
   **C.** Welles, a rising stage director of great promise,
   **D.** On the promising rise as a stage director, Welles

**20. F.** NO CHANGE
   **G.** invasion
   **H.** invades
   **J.** invaded

**21. A.** NO CHANGE
   **B.** they
   **C.** he then
   **D.** Orson Welles

**GO ON TO THE NEXT PAGE.**

reporters "stunned" by the horrific events unfolding before their eyes. The director, realizing that some might mistake the program for a real newscast, made sure that the program started with a disclaimer; he assured listeners that the program to come
____
22
was a work of fiction.

It did not occur to him, however, that a great number of people would tune in after the broadcast started. Many of them,
____
23

assuming that what they were hearing was genuine on-the-scene coverage, panicked; they were very frightened. The broad-
____
24

cast lasted only an hour, but by the time it ended, much of the
____
25
country was convinced that the United States had been largely overtaken by Martians (this simultaneous fear of and fascination
____
26
with extraterrestrials is present in many cultures).
____
26

In retrospect, it seems strange that so many could have been fooled by what surely could not have been all that
____
27
convincing a radio play. One cannot help but wonder why people did not question why all of the other radio stations

**22. F.** NO CHANGE
    **G.** disclaimer he
    **H.** disclaimer, he
    **J.** disclaimer of which

**23. A.** NO CHANGE
    **B.** has been started.
    **C.** was start.
    **D.** is starting.

**24.** If all of the choices below are true, which of them best uses specific detail to convey the panic that the broadcast of *The War of the Worlds* caused?
    **F.** NO CHANGE
    **G.** the highways were clogged with cars full of people seeking escape, and train stations were crowded with mobs willing to buy a ticket to anywhere far away.
    **H.** many felt that they had never encountered anything as terrifying in their lives and fully believed that what they were hearing was the absolute truth.
    **J.** they did not stop to think that what they were hearing might be fiction, instead leaping to the unlikely conclusion that an interplanetary invasion was indeed going on.

**25. A.** NO CHANGE
    **B.** hour, by
    **C.** hour by
    **D.** hour but, by

**26. F.** NO CHANGE
    **G.** Martians. This simultaneous fear of and fascination with Martians exists in many cultures.
    **H.** Martians, who continue to frighten and fascinate people of various cultures.
    **J.** Martians.

**27. A.** NO CHANGE
    **B.** fooled at
    **C.** foolish by
    **D.** foolhardy in

**GO ON TO THE NEXT PAGE.**

continued to play their normal programs; while a disaster of
28

28. F. NO CHANGE
    G. programs while
    H. program's while
    J. programs' while

global proportions was
29

29. A. NO CHANGE
    B. is
    C. will be
    D. had become

underway. 30

30. The author would like to end the passage with a sentence that places the response to *The War of the Worlds* in a larger context of other stories of alien invasion. Assuming that all of the information in the following sentences is true, which of the following, if inserted at this point, would best accomplish this?
    F. During that period, people relied on radio to tell them about news stories as they were occurring; newspapers did not report on such events until hours after the fact.
    G. Perhaps they assumed that the invasion had happened so suddenly that none of the other stations were even aware of it, and were learning about it along with the listeners.
    H. However, humans have always been inclined to believe in unearthly forces; the response to *The War of the Worlds* is no more absurd than the responses to many equally unlikely rumors in the past, and, doubtless, in the future.
    J. Certainly there were those who immediately recognized it for what it was, and turned the dial back to the *Chase and Sanborn Radio Hour*, aware that *The War of the Worlds* was entirely fictional.

**GO ON TO THE NEXT PAGE.**

**PASSAGE III**

### Our Family Has Chemistry

[1]

There was always one big difference between my twin

brother and I. He was good at subjects such as English and his-
 ⎯⎯
  31

tory, while I was better at math and science. We were always
 ⎯⎯⎯⎯⎯⎯⎯⎯
 32

thoughtful; he would be a professor and I would be a doctor.
 ⎯⎯⎯⎯⎯⎯
 32

Because of this, I never felt particularly competitive with him and

was unconcerned when we accepted offers from the same college.

However, once we started, we would find that things did not
 ⎯⎯⎯⎯⎯⎯⎯⎯⎯
 33

work out quite as I would expect. Continuing to pursue his high
 ⎯⎯⎯⎯⎯⎯⎯
 34

school passions, he immediately joined the editorial board of the

school's literary magazine and convinced a professor to let him

into a graduate-level poetry seminar. 35

[2]

I would never believe it if he hadn't told me himself, but all
 ⎯⎯⎯⎯⎯⎯
 36

of a sudden, my brother wanted to be a doctor, too. I can't say

**31. A.** NO CHANGE
**B.** and me.
**C.** and me were.
**D.** and I had.

**32. F.** NO CHANGE
**G.** Thoughtful as we were,
**H.** I always thought that
**J.** Although we were thoughtful,

**33. A.** NO CHANGE
**B.** he found
**C.** one had found
**D.** I found

**34. F.** NO CHANGE
**G.** had expected.
**H.** was expecting.
**J.** expect.

**35.** Which of the following sentences, if added here, would best link this paragraph to the one that follows?
**A.** My brother had been editor of our high school's literary magazine, and also a frequent contributor, so he was well qualified for both of these things.
**B.** This was, however, the least of my problems.
**C.** However, he also signed up for biology and chemistry, the very same pre-med classes that I was taking.
**D.** I flipped right by the English courses in the catalog, opting instead for biology and chemistry.

**36. F.** NO CHANGE
**G.** of believed
**H.** believed
**J.** have believed

**GO ON TO THE NEXT PAGE.**

that I was too happy about the situation, and I told him so. It was fine if he wanted to "make a difference" and "help humanity," but as far as I was concerned, he could find his own way to do it. [37]

Not surprisingly, he didn't see things that way; the next day, he was sitting beside me in the front row of the lecture hall, waiting for biology class to begin.

[3]

I wasn't too worried; I thought that a few days of lectures
                  ‾‾‾‾‾‾‾
                    38
on stoichiometry and the Krebs cycle would be enough to send him running back to the English department for good. However, as the weeks passed, this did not happen. I found that while we were struggling to maintain a B+ average, my brother was
‾‾‾‾‾‾‾‾‾
    39
getting straight A's. To make matters worse, he seemed to be enjoying himself.

[4]

[1] Determined to outdo him, I was thrown into my work.
                                 ‾‾‾‾‾‾‾‾‾‾‾
                                     40

[2] I went to the library every night, smuggling in big cups of

coffee, to keep me awake, and stayed until closing time.
‾‾‾‾‾‾‾‾‾‾‾‾‾‾‾‾‾‾‾‾‾‾‾‾
          41

[3] Including my brother, I soon had a grade point average as
    ‾‾‾‾‾‾‾‾‾‾‾‾‾‾‾‾‾‾‾‾‾‾‾‾‾‾‾‾‾‾‾‾‾‾‾‾‾‾‾‾‾‾‾
                          42
high as any pre-med. [4] I didn't stop there.
‾‾‾‾‾‾‾‾‾‾‾‾‾‾‾‾‾‾
       42

37. The two sets of quotation marks in this sentence serve to:
    I. show that the writer's brother was justified in his decision to become a doctor.
    II. present some of the phrases used during the writer's discussion with his brother.
    III. suggest that the writer was slightly skeptical of his brother's reasoning.
    A. II only
    B. I and II only
    C. II and III only
    D. I, II, and III

38. F. NO CHANGE
    G. worried, but
    H. worried,
    J. worried however much

39. A. NO CHANGE
    B. he was
    C. I was
    D. they were

40. F. NO CHANGE
    G. threw it
    H. threw myself
    J. was throwing everything

41. A. NO CHANGE
    B. coffee, to keep me awake
    C. coffee to keep me awake,
    D. coffee to keep me awake

42. F. NO CHANGE
    G. None of the grade point averages of my brother and all of the other pre-meds were soon higher than mine.
    H. My grade point average was soon at least as high as my brother's grade point average, and also the grade point averages of the other pre-meds.
    J. Soon no other pre-med, including my brother, had a grade point average higher than mine.

**GO ON TO THE NEXT PAGE.**

[5] I took a summer job working in a professor's chemistry lab, set on getting a letter of recommendation more impressive than any that my brother could get. [6] At first, I thought only of impressing the professor, but soon I realized that I not only enjoyed the work, but also had a real feel for it. [7] By the end of the summer, I decided to apply to graduate school in chemistry instead of medical school. 43

43. The writer would like to divide the final paragraph into two shorter paragraphs. The most logical way to accomplish this would be to start a new paragraph beginning with:
A. Sentence 3.
B. Sentence 4.
C. Sentence 6.
D. Sentence 7.

Question 44 asks about the preceding passage as a whole.

44. The writer wishes to add a sentence at the end of the essay that will demonstrate a sense of perspective gained by the experience described in the essay. Which of the following would accomplish this most effectively?
F. We are both very happy in our chosen fields and have become much closer than we were in college.
G. Although at the time there seemed to be nothing positive about my brother's becoming a pre-med, it ultimately led me into a career that was perfect for me.
H. Had I become a doctor, I probably would have chosen to become a surgeon; however, my brother hopes to become a pediatrician.
J. I often wonder what would have happened had I gotten a job at a biology lab rather than a chemistry lab that summer.

**GO ON TO THE NEXT PAGE.**

## PASSAGE IV

### A Year in Ireland

[1]

We had just touched down in Shannon airport in Dublin, Ireland. Left our native Chicago many hours before, and
45
although we were exhausted, we were all charged with the

excitement, that comes from embarking on a great adventure.
46

Being as everyone had a thick accent, we could barely under-
47
stand them as they tried to direct us where we should claim our
47
baggage.
47

[2]

I was six years old, and my parents, sister, and I were
48

spending a year in Ireland. It all started, nonetheless, when my
49
parents received a grant to work at Trinity College. The next

thing I knew, we were subletting our apartment, packing all of

our clothes into big duffel bags, and convincing my grandfather

to take care of our cat.  Finally, we piled everything into the car
50

and drove off. Watching our house and then our neighborhood
51
disappear in the distance, my apprehension grew.
51

**45. A.** NO CHANGE
   **B.** Having left
   **C.** We had left
   **D.** We left

**46. F.** NO CHANGE
   **G.** excitement that comes from embarking,
   **H.** excitement, that comes from embarking,
   **J.** excitement that comes from embarking

**47. A.** NO CHANGE
   **B.** Having thick accents, those who tried to help us claim our baggage were hard for us to understand.
   **C.** Everyone had such thick accents that we could barely understand their directions to the baggage claim area.
   **D.** Directions to the baggage claim area were barely understandable because of everyone's thick accents.

**48. F.** NO CHANGE
   **G.** old. And
   **H.** old
   **J.** old,

**49. A.** NO CHANGE
   **B.** started, in addition,
   **C.** started, despite this,
   **D.** started

**50. F.** NO CHANGE
   **G.** Because of this,
   **H.** Beforehand,
   **J.** Yet,

**51. A.** NO CHANGE
   **B.** In the distance, my apprehension grew as I watched our house and then our neighborhood disappear.
   **C.** Our house and then our neighborhood disappeared as I watched apprehensively in the distance.
   **D.** My apprehension grew as I watched our house and then our neighborhood disappear in the distance.

**GO ON TO THE NEXT PAGE.**

[3]

Even after we arrived and got settled in, I remained uneasy. Everything was different, from the shape of the milk cartons to the characters in the comic books.

[4]

These may seem like trivial things, but to a first grader,
52
they were very important. A week after we arrived, I told my mother that it was time for us to go home. We could buy our plane tickets that night and the next day could be the one when
53
we would leave.
53

54 My mother smiled sympathetically and promised me that I would get used to it.

[5]

This, in fact, turned out to be true. A few days later, I started school, and immediately achieved celebrity status. There were no other Americans in class P–1 as the first grade, was called, and
55
only three other foreigners in the whole school. During recess, I would hold court on the playground, teaching everyone my own version of American history and culture.

52. F. NO CHANGE
G. (Do NOT combine paragraphs 3 and 4) Seeming
H. (Combine paragraphs 3 and 4) Seeming
J. (Combine paragraphs 3 and 4) These may seem

53. A. NO CHANGE
B. a departure tomorrow.
C. leave the next day.
D. the following day would be the day of our departure.

54. The writer wants to include a detail to show that she was serious about her suggestion to her mother. Assuming all are true, which of the following sentences, if inserted at this point, would best accomplish this?
F. I showed her my little red suitcase, which I had already neatly packed with all of my dolls, books, and stuffed animals.
G. I then reminded her that Father would be home very soon and that she should start his supper right away.
H. My sister didn't mind it there, but since she was only two years old, she didn't know any better.
J. I didn't know whether it would be possible to get plane tickets on such short notice; our tickets to Ireland came in the mail only two weeks before we left.

55. A. NO CHANGE
B. P-1, as the first grade was called,
C. P-1, as the first grade was called
D. P-1 as the first grade was called,

**GO ON TO THE NEXT PAGE.**

[6]

56  As I walked with my family through O'Hare airport

in Chicago, I was glad to be home, but <u>one at a time,</u> a little
                                                        57
sad to go back to being just like everyone else. Soon, however,

something happened that made me smile. A little boy overheard

me talking to my father in the Irish lilt that I had unconsciously

picked up over the course of the year. He immediately turned to

his mother and said, "Wow, look at that! There's a kid over there

from Ireland."

56. The author wishes to add a sentence at the beginning of Paragraph 6 in order to provide a graceful transition and convey the passage of time. Which of the following sentences best accomplishes this?
   F. The flight back was a little bumpy, but the plane landed safely.
   G. The year flew by, and it was soon time to return home.
   H. Air travel can be exhausting, especially for a family with children.
   J. I ended up having a wonderful time in Ireland.

57. A. NO CHANGE
   B. from time to time,
   C. at the same time,
   D. all in good time,

---

**Questions 58 and 59 ask about the preceding passage as a whole.**

---

58. This essay was written in response to an assignment to describe the personal relationships among the writer's family. Does it successfully do so?
   F. Yes, because it describes how the writer's family responded to a difficult year.
   G. Yes, because it mentions a conversation between the writer and her mother.
   H. No, because it focuses mostly on the writer's response to a series of events.
   J. No, because it does not explain how the writer's parents met.

59. The writer is deciding where to include the following sentence in the essay, in order to emphasize her eventual adjustment to life in Ireland.

   Soon, Dublin was like a second home to me.

   The best place to insert this sentence would be:
   A. at the beginning of Paragraph 4.
   B. at the beginning of Paragraph 5.
   C. at the end of Paragraph 5.
   D. at the end of Paragraph 6.

**GO ON TO THE NEXT PAGE.**

**PASSAGE V**

### Wait Just a Minute . . .

I crept in for my first shift as a waiter without a
 ___
 60

care in the world. Everyone told me that waiting tables

was much harder than it looked, and I knew that they
                                   ___
                                   61

were just exaggerating. After all, if you're a college

graduate and you've already spent two nights training,

how much trouble must I have working at a place called
                  ___
                  62

Harry's Burritos? Besides, I reasoned, it was a Tuesday
                           ___
                           63

night, which was sure to be slow.

I changed into my uniform and immediately got my

first customers, a father, with two little boys. I brought
_____
        64

over some chips and salsa, and before I could even take the

family's order, the older boy started to pelt his little brother

with tortilla chips. The younger boy, who was probably
                                 _____
                                        65

about the same age as my little sister, got so upset that he
_____
              65

spilled his water all over the table. The boys' father apol-

ogized for there behavior, but I assured him that it was all
         ___
         66

right. I cleaned up the mess, and within ten minutes, they

were all happily digging into their burritos. I silently con-

gratulated myself, thinking that I was obviously a natural.

60. Which of the following best conveys the way the writer
    entered the restaurant?
    F. NO CHANGE
    G. trudged
    H. skipped
    J. staggered

61. A. NO CHANGE
    B. but
    C. while
    D. so

62. F. NO CHANGE
    G. could I
    H. could you
    J. can one

63. A. NO CHANGE
    B. for many reasons,
    C. within reason,
    D. being reasonable,

64. F. NO CHANGE
    G. customers: a father
    H. customers; a father
    J. customers. A father,

65. A. NO CHANGE
    B. boy was about the same age as my little sister. He
    C. boy (about the same age as my younger sister)
    D. boy

66. F. NO CHANGE
    G. they're
    H. their
    J. his

**GO ON TO THE NEXT PAGE.**

Then came the seven o'clock rush. All of a sudden, five of my six tables were full. I was running around like a crazy man, barely able to remember whose order I had taken. The manager seated a couple at my last empty table and whispered that they were friends of the owner. I nodded, but with one group needing its check, another demanding

about its nachos, and a third complaining that the vegetarian

tacos had beef in them, so I didn't have time to lavish attention on anyone.

[1] Before I knew it, half an hour had passed, and I hadn't even brought the owner's friends their margaritas. [2] I grabbed the drinks and ran toward their table, but the manager stopped me in my path. [3] She wanted to know what was going on. [4] I admitted that I had not been completely truthful. [5] She asked me whether I really had three years of experience waiting tables, as I had indicated on my application. [6] However, I had no choice. [7] Since no one would hire an inexperienced waiter, no waiter could get a first job without lying. [8] She found my argument less than compelling, and by eight-fifteen, I was unemployed. 72

67. A. NO CHANGE
    B. man so
    C. man, then
    D. man, but

68. F. NO CHANGE
    G. one group needed their check,
    H. the check was what one group was needing,
    J. checking one group,

69. A. NO CHANGE
    B. of
    C. for
    D. OMIT the underlined portion.

70. F. NO CHANGE
    G. them, I
    H. them, and I
    J. them. I

71. A. NO CHANGE
    B. years, of experience,
    C. years of experience,
    D. years, of experience

72. In order to make the final paragraph easier to understand, the writer should reverse the order of which two sentences?
    F. Sentence 1 and Sentence 2
    G. Sentence 3 and Sentence 4
    H. Sentence 4 and Sentence 5
    J. Sentence 7 and Sentence 8

**GO ON TO THE NEXT PAGE.**

Questions 73–75 ask about the preceding passage as a whole.

**73.** Assuming each is true, which of the following sentences, if added at the end of the final paragraph, would be most consistent with the writer's tone in the rest of the essay?
   **A.** She was wholly justified in her actions; except in cases when a life is at stake, dishonesty is never justifiable.
   **B.** I had never been treated with so little care or respect, and I told her so.
   **C.** My brilliant career as a waiter was officially over, only three hours after it had begun.
   **D.** I had to fight back the tears as I walked to the bus stop, but I soon started to put things in perspective.

**74.** The writer has written the following sentence and is considering adding it to the essay.

   Harry's Burritos is a moderately priced Mexican restaurant on Manhattan's Upper West Side.

Should this sentence be included in the essay, and if so, where?
   **F.** Yes, at the beginning of the first paragraph, because it helps the reader to envision the setting in which the events described take place.
   **G.** Yes, at the end of the first paragraph, because it explains why the writer is not nervous before his first shift.
   **H.** No, because the readers should be expected to be familiar with Harry's Burritos.
   **J.** No, because the location and cost of the restaurant are not central to the events that the writer describes.

**75.** This essay was a response to an assignment to write a description of an employment experience. Does it fulfill the assignment successfully?
   **A.** Yes, because it describes the writer's experience with a job that he held briefly.
   **B.** Yes, because restaurant work is similar to office work in many ways.
   **C.** No, because the writer was not successful in the job that he describes.
   **D.** No, because it does not describe the application process in sufficient detail.

**END OF TEST 1**

**STOP! DO NOT TURN THE PAGE UNTIL TOLD TO DO SO.**

## MATHEMATICS TEST

*60 Minutes—60 Questions*

**DIRECTIONS:** Solve each problem, choose the correct answer, and then fill in the corresponding oval on your answer document.

You are permitted to use a calculator on this test.

Note: Unless otherwise stated, all of the following should be assumed:

1. Figures are NOT necessarily drawn to scale.
2. Geometric figures lie in a plane.
3. The word *line* indicates a straight line.
4. The word *average* indicates arithmetic mean.

---

1. If $4x + 2 = 20$, then $x = ?$
   A. 4.5
   B. 6.0
   C. 9.0
   D. 12.5
   E. 18.0

2. On a real number line, what is the distance, in coordinate units, between points $M$ and $N$ if point $M$ has coordinate 9 and point $N$ has coordinate $-5$ ?
   F. 2
   G. 4
   H. 7
   J. 12
   K. 14

3. Each week, a store sells $x$ hats and $y$ shirts. If the store makes $5 for each hat and $10 for each shirt, which of the following expressions shows the total amount of money, in dollars, that the store makes each week?
   A. $10x + 5y$
   B. $5x + 10y$
   C. $15(x + y)$
   D. $50(x + y)$
   E. $15xy$

4. Consider the following two logical statements:

   If $x$ is greater than 5, then $y$ is equal to 4.
   $y$ is not equal to 4.

   If these statements are both true, then it follows that:
   F. $x$ is greater than 5.
   G. $x$ is equal to 4.
   H. $y$ is not equal to 5.
   J. $x$ is equal to 5.
   K. $x$ is not greater than 5.

**DO YOUR FIGURING HERE.**

**GO ON TO THE NEXT PAGE.**

**DO YOUR FIGURING HERE.**

5. On Monday, Alice bought a bag of marbles. On Tuesday, she gave $\frac{2}{3}$ of her marbles to a friend. On Wednesday, she gave away $\frac{1}{3}$ of her remaining marbles. If she then had 8 marbles left, how many marbles did she buy originally?
   A. 36
   B. 30
   C. 24
   D. 18
   E. 12

6. If $a = 4y + 2z$ and $b = z - y$, then what is the value of $a + b$?
   F. $5y + 3z$
   G. $5y - 3z$
   H. $3y + 3z$
   J. $3y - 3z$
   K. $3y + z$

7. Susan recorded the number of customers visiting her bookstore each day for five days, as shown in the table below. What was the average number of customers for these five days?

   | Day | Number of Customers |
   | --- | --- |
   | Monday | 56 |
   | Tuesday | 47 |
   | Wednesday | 43 |
   | Thursday | 55 |
   | Friday | 64 |

   A. 48
   B. 50
   C. 53
   D. 55
   E. 56

8. If $x = -2$, then $x^2 + 3x + 15 = $ ?
   F. 19
   G. 13
   H. 11
   J. 7
   K. 5

9. By the end of the year, the population of Greenville is expected to increase 8% from its current population of 45,000. If this prediction is accurate, what would be its new population at the end of the year?
   A. 48,600
   B. 48,000
   C. 46,400
   D. 45,800
   E. 41,400

**GO ON TO THE NEXT PAGE.**

**10.** In the figure below, points $A$, $B$, $C$, and $D$ are collinear, points $B$, $F$, and $I$ are collinear, and $\overline{CD}$ is parallel to $\overline{EG}$. What is the measure of $x$ ?

**F.** 20
**G.** 30
**H.** 45
**J.** 50
**K.** 65

**11.** For all real values of $x$, $y$, and $z$, the expression $(x + y)(x + z) = ?$
**A.** $2x + x(y + z) + yz$
**B.** $x^2 + x(y + z) + yz$
**C.** $x^2 + yz + xz$
**D.** $x(x + y + z)$
**E.** $x(yz + xz)$

**12.** The lengths of the sides of a triangle are 4, 6, and 10 inches. How many inches long is the longest side of a similar triangle that has a perimeter of 40 inches?
**F.** 16
**G.** 20
**H.** 24
**J.** 36
**K.** 30

**13.** $|2 - 4| \times |-2| = ?$
**A.** $-4$
**B.** $-2$
**C.** 2
**D.** 4
**E.** 8

**14.** John needs to pick his clothes for the day. He can choose from 6 different shirts, 4 different pairs of pants, and 8 different pairs of socks. If an outfit consists of 1 shirt, 1 pair of pants, and 1 pair of socks, how many different outfits could he choose?
**F.** 18
**G.** 48
**H.** 64
**J.** 96
**K.** 192

**DO YOUR FIGURING HERE.**

**GO ON TO THE NEXT PAGE.**

**DO YOUR FIGURING HERE.**

15. A formula for the volume of a cylinder with radius $r$ and height $h$ is $V = \pi r^2 h$. What is the volume, to the nearest cubic inch, of a cylindrical can with a radius of 3 inches and a height of 5 inches?
    A. 707
    B. 444
    C. 236
    D. 188
    E. 141

16. Which of the following functions will have the greatest value if $x = -10$ ?
    F. $f(x) = x^2 - 2x$
    G. $f(x) = x^2 + 2x$
    H. $f(x) = -x^2$
    J. $f(x) = x^3 - x^2$
    K. $f(x) = x^0$

17. If 50 is 20 percent of $x$, then $x = $ ?
    A. 10
    B. 100
    C. 250
    D. 1000
    E. 2500

18. The cost of a long-distance phone call is 15 cents for the first minute, and then 3 cents per minute for every additional minute. How many cents would a 24-minute phone call cost?
    F. 42
    G. 45
    H. 72
    J. 84
    K. 87

19. What is the slope of the line that passes through the points $(-1,3)$ and $(1,2)$ ?

    A. $-\dfrac{1}{3}$

    B. $-\dfrac{1}{2}$

    C. $\dfrac{1}{2}$

    D. 1

    E. 2

20. In the standard $(x,y)$ coordinate plane, how many times does the graph of $y = (x + 1)(x^2 + 5)$ intersect the $x$-axis?
    F. 6
    G. 4
    H. 3
    J. 2
    K. 1

**GO ON TO THE NEXT PAGE.**

**DO YOUR FIGURING HERE.**

21. Which of the following is a simplified equivalent of $\dfrac{3x + 9y}{6z}$ ?

    A. $\dfrac{12xy}{z}$

    B. $\dfrac{6xy}{z}$

    C. $\dfrac{3x + 3y}{2z}$

    D. $\dfrac{2x + 3y}{z}$

    E. $\dfrac{x + 3y}{2z}$

22. Quadrilateral *BCDE* has vertices $(-4,-2)$, $(-4,3)$, $(1,-2)$, and $(1,3)$ in the standard $(x,y)$ coordinate plane. Suppose *BCDE* is translated 5 units to the left and 1 unit up, forming quadrilateral *B'C'D'E'*. Which of the following shows the coordinates of *B'C'D'E'* ?

    F. $(-9,-1)$, $(-9,4)$, $(-4,-1)$, $(-4,4)$
    G. $(-5,3)$, $(-5,8)$, $(0,3)$, $(0,8)$
    H. $(-4,-1)$, $(-4,4)$, $(1,-1)$, $(1,4)$
    J. $(-3,-7)$, $(-3,-2)$, $(2,-7)$, $(2,-2)$
    K. $(1,-3)$, $(1,2)$, $(6,-3)$, $(6,2)$

23. What is the slope of the line that is perpendicular to the line with equation $2y = 10 - 3x$ ?

    A. $-\dfrac{2}{3}$

    B. $\dfrac{2}{3}$

    C. $\dfrac{3}{2}$

    D. $2$

    E. $3$

24. If $x^2 + 4x = 12$, what are all possible values of $x$ ?
    F. $-6$ and 2 only
    G. $-2$ and 6 only
    H. 3 and 4 only
    J. 4 only
    K. 6 only

**GO ON TO THE NEXT PAGE.**

**DO YOUR FIGURING HERE.**

25. A certain lemonade mix requires $3\frac{1}{2}$ cups of lemon juice to make 4 quarts of lemonade. How many cups of lemon juice would be required to make 10 quarts of lemonade?

   A. $4\frac{1}{2}$

   B. $6\frac{2}{3}$

   C. 8

   D. $8\frac{3}{4}$

   E. $9\frac{1}{2}$

26. What is the length, in inches, of the hypotenuse of a right triangle with legs measuring 12 inches and 16 inches?

   F. 18

   G. 20

   H. 28

   J. $\sqrt{28}$

   K. $\sqrt{90}$

27. Which of the following is a polynomial factor of $8x^2 + 22x - 6$ ?
   A. $(4x - 3)$
   B. $(4x + 3)$
   C. $(8x - 2)$
   D. $(8x + 3)$
   E. $(8x + 6)$

28. Which of the following is the graph of the solution set for $2(3x + 4) < 20$ ?

**GO ON TO THE NEXT PAGE.**

**29.** If, for all $x$, $(x^{a+1})^3 = x^9$, then $a = ?$

    **A.** 2

    **B.** 3

    **C.** 4

    **D.** 5

    **E.** 6

**DO YOUR FIGURING HERE.**

**30.** What is the cosine of $\angle C$ in $\triangle ABC$ below?

    **F.** $\dfrac{2}{3}$

    **G.** $\dfrac{3}{2}$

    **H.** $\dfrac{\sqrt{13}}{3}$

    **J.** $\dfrac{\sqrt{5}}{3}$

    **K.** $\dfrac{\sqrt{5}}{2}$

**31.** Which of the following equations has $x$ varying directly as the cube of $y$ and inversely as the square of $z$ ?

    **A.** $x = \dfrac{z^2}{y^3}$

    **B.** $x = \dfrac{y^3}{z^2}$

    **C.** $x = \dfrac{\sqrt{z}}{\sqrt[3]{y}}$

    **D.** $y = \dfrac{x^2}{z^3}$

    **E.** $z = \dfrac{x^2}{y^3}$

**GO ON TO THE NEXT PAGE.**

**32.** In the complex numbers, where $i^2 = -1$, what is the value of $3i^2 + i^4$ ?

   **F.** −2

   **G.** −1

   **H.** 0

   **J.** 1

   **K.** 2

**33.** In the figure below, $\overline{BD}$ is the altitude of equilateral triangle $\triangle ABC$. If $\overline{BD}$ is 8 units long, what is the perimeter of $\triangle ABC$?

(Note: An altitude of a triangle is perpendicular to the opposite side.)

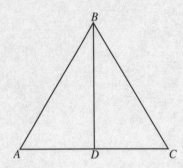

   **A.** 12

   **B.** $8\sqrt{3}$

   **C.** 16

   **D.** 24

   **E.** $16\sqrt{3}$

**34.** A triangle has sides of length 4 inches and 7.5 inches. Which of the following CANNOT be the length of the third side?

   **F.** 3.5 inches

   **G.** 4.0 inches

   **H.** 5.0 inches

   **J.** 5.5 inches

   **K.** 9.5 inches

**35.** In the right triangle below, if $\overline{AC}$ bisects $\angle A$, then what is the measure of $\angle BCA$ ?

   **A.** 75°

   **B.** 80°

   **C.** 85°

   **D.** 90°

   **E.** 95°

**GO ON TO THE NEXT PAGE.**

**36.** The line $y = \dfrac{1}{2}x - 2$ passes through which one of the following points?

   **F.** (0,2)
   **G.** (1,3)
   **H.** (2,4)
   **J.** (2,–1)
   **K.** (1,–3)

**37.** In the figure below, $\overleftrightarrow{BD}$ and $\overleftrightarrow{AE}$ are parallel and crossed by two transversals. The points of intersection and some lengths are shown. What is the length of $AE$?

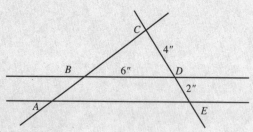

   **A.** 8 inches
   **B.** 9 inches
   **C.** 9.5 inches
   **D.** 10 inches
   **E.** 12 inches

**38.** In the right triangle below, how long is side $\overline{AC}$?

   **F.** $17 - 8$
   **G.** $17^2 - 8^2$
   **H.** $17^2 + 8^2$
   **J.** $\sqrt{17 - 8}$
   **K.** $\sqrt{17^2 - 8^2}$

**GO ON TO THE NEXT PAGE.**

**DO YOUR FIGURING HERE.**

39. A circle in the standard $(x,y)$ coordinate plane has its center at $(-4,3)$ and a radius of 5 units. Which of the following equations represents this circle?

A. $(x-4)^2 + (y+3)^2 = \sqrt{5}$
B. $(x+4)^2 + (y-3)^2 = 5$
C. $(x-4)^2 + (y+3)^2 = 5$
D. $(x+4)^2 + (y-3)^2 = 25$
E. $(x-4)^2 + (y+3)^2 = 25$

40. If $\tan\theta = \dfrac{9}{40}$ and $\sin\theta = \dfrac{9}{41}$ then $\cos\theta = ?$

F. $\dfrac{41}{9}$

G. $\dfrac{41}{40}$

H. $\dfrac{40}{41}$

J. $\dfrac{9}{39}$

K. $\dfrac{1}{9}$

41. What is the perimeter, in feet (ft), of the figure below?

A. 50
B. 56
C. 62
D. 74
E. 96

42. For what value of $b$ would the graph of the following system of equations be a single line in the standard $(x,y)$ coordinate plane?

$$3x + 4y = 15$$
$$9x + 12y = 5b$$

F. 3
G. 5
H. 7
J. 9
K. 11

**GO ON TO THE NEXT PAGE.**

**43.** In the figure below, triangles *ABC* and *ACD* are right triangles. If triangle *ABC* is isosceles, and if $\overline{CD}$ is 6 inches long, how many inches long is $\overline{BC}$?

**A.** 6

**B.** $6\sqrt{3}$

**C.** 12

**D.** $12\sqrt{2}$

**E.** 24

**44.** A certain rectangle has a length that is two feet less than 4 times its width. If the area of the rectangle is 240 square feet, how many feet wide is the rectangle?

**F.** 2

**G.** 5

**H.** 6

**J.** 7

**K.** 8

**45.** The $(x,y)$ coordinates of the center of a circle are $(-1,2)$. If the $(x,y)$ coordinates of one endpoint of a certain diameter of the circle are $(-6,5)$, what are the $(x,y)$ coordinates of the other endpoint of the diameter?

**A.** $(-11,8)$

**B.** $(-7,7)$

**C.** $(0,-2)$

**D.** $(3,0)$

**E.** $(4,-1)$

**46.** If $x - y = -4$ and $x + y = -3$, then $x^2 - y^2 = $ ?

   **F.** −7

   **G.** −3

   **H.** 7

   **J.** 9

   **K.** 12

**47.** A circle is inscribed in a square, as shown in the figure below. If the square measures 10 feet on a side, which of the following expressions gives the area of the shaded region in square feet?

   **A.** $10^2 - 10\pi$

   **B.** $10^2 - 5^2\pi$

   **C.** $10 - 5\pi$

   **D.** $5^2 - 5^2\pi$

   **E.** $5^2 - 10\pi$

**48.** The figure below shows an isosceles trapezoid. What is its area in square centimeters (cm)?

   **F.** 338

   **G.** 312

   **H.** 273

   **J.** 252

   **K.** 192

**GO ON TO THE NEXT PAGE.**

**49.** Miko is walking to a bus stop on the other side of a rectangular pool. She walks 20 feet west, then turns and walks 70 feet north, then turns and walks 60 feet west, then turns and walks 10 feet south to the bus stop. If she had been able to walk in a straight line from her starting point to the bus stop, approximately how many feet shorter would her path have been?

A. 20
B. 47
C. 60
D. 71
E. 88

**50.** If $\log_x 64 = 2$, then $x = ?$

F. 2
G. 4
H. 8
J. 16
K. $64^2$

**51.** If $x$ is a real number, and the value of $\dfrac{x}{x^2 - 7}$ is undefined, then what is the value of $x^3 - 7x$ ?

A. 0
B. 1
C. –1
D. Undefined
E. Cannot be determined from the given information

**52.** Bob can drive 3 miles in $n$ minutes. At this rate, how many minutes will it take him to drive 14 miles?

F. $42n$

G. $\dfrac{3n}{14}$

H. $\dfrac{14n}{3}$

J. $\dfrac{3}{14n}$

K. $\dfrac{14}{3n}$

**GO ON TO THE NEXT PAGE.**

**53.** In the standard $(x,y)$ coordinate plane, which of the following shows the graph of the points that satisfy the inequality $|x| \geq 5$ ?

A.

B.

C.

D.

E.

GO ON TO THE NEXT PAGE.

**DO YOUR FIGURING HERE.**

54. Which of the following calculations will yield an odd integer for any integer $x$ ?

    F.   $x^2$
    G.   $3x^2$
    H.   $2x^2 + 1$
    J.   $3x^2 + 1$
    K.   $5x^2$

55. If the equation $x^2 - 12x + k = 0$ has only one solution for $x$, what is the value of $k$ ?

    A.   1
    B.   6
    C.   12
    D.   36
    E.   48

56. In the figure below, $AE = \dfrac{1}{2} BE$. What is the area of parallelogram $ABCD$ ?

    F.   7

    G.   14

    H.   $7\sqrt{5}$

    J.   $14\sqrt{5}$

    K.   28

57. From point $A$, the top of a pole can be seen at a 29° angle of ascent.  If the distance from point $A$ to the base of the pole is 40 feet, which of the following expresses the height of the pole in feet?

    A.   40 tan 29°

    B.   40 sin 29°

    C.   $\dfrac{40}{\tan 29°}$

    D.   $\dfrac{40}{\sin 29°}$

    E.   $\dfrac{40}{\cos 29°}$

**GO ON TO THE NEXT PAGE.**

58. What is the maximum value of $y = -1 + 4(\sin 2x)$ ?

    F. 3
    G. 4
    H. 5
    J. 6
    K. 7

59. The average of a set of 6 integers is 65. If a seventh number is added to the set, the average of the set increases to 66. What is the seventh number?

    A. 66
    B. 67
    C. 70
    D. 72
    E. 78

60. Jamie's sock drawer contains 10 black socks, 8 red socks, 8 white socks, and 2 yellow socks. She reaches in to pull out one sock at random. She pulls out a black sock and does not put it back. If she reaches back in the drawer to pull out another sock at random, what is the probability that she will pull out another black sock?

    F. $\dfrac{1}{9}$

    G. $\dfrac{9}{28}$

    H. $\dfrac{1}{3}$

    J. $\dfrac{5}{14}$

**END OF TEST 2**

**STOP! DO NOT TURN THE PAGE UNTIL TOLD TO DO SO.**

**DO NOT RETURN TO THE PREVIOUS TEST.**

# Reading Test

*35 Minutes—40 Questions*

**DIRECTIONS:** There are four passages in this test. Each passage is followed by several questions. After reading each passage, choose the best answer to each question and fill in the corresponding oval on your answer document. You may refer to the passages as needed.

---

**Passage I**

**PROSE FICTION:** This passage is taken from *The Heart Is a Lonely Hunter*, by Carson McCullers (© 1940 and 1967 by Carson McCullers).

The sun woke Mick early, although she had stayed out mighty late the night before. It was too hot even to drink coffee for breakfast, so she had ice water with syrup in it and cold biscuits. She messed around the kitchen for a while and then

5  went out on the front porch to read the funnies. She had thought maybe Mister Singer would be reading the paper on the porch like he did most Sunday mornings. But Mister Singer was not there, and later on her Dad said he came in very late the night before and had company in his room. She waited for Mister

10  Singer a long time. All the other boarders came down except him. Finally she went back in the kitchen and took Ralph out of his high chair and put a clean dress on him and wiped off his face. Then when Bubber got home from Sunday School she was ready to take the kids out. She let Bubber ride in the wagon with

15  Ralph because he was barefooted and the hot sidewalk burned his feet. She pulled the wagon for about eight blocks until they came to the big, new house that was being built. The ladder was still propped against the edge of the roof, and she screwed up nerve and began to climb.

20  "You mind Ralph," she called back to Bubber. "Mind the gnats don't sit on his eyelids."

Five minutes later Mick stood up and held herself very straight. She spread out her arms like wings. This was the place where everybody wanted to stand. The very top. But if you lost

25  your grip and rolled off the edge it would kill you. All around were the roofs of other houses and the green tops of trees. On the other side of town were the church steeples and the smokestacks from the mills. The sky was bright blue and hot as fire. The sun made everything on the ground either dizzy white or black.

30  She wanted to sing. All the songs she knew pushed up toward her throat, but there was no sound. One big boy who had got to the highest part of the roof last week let out a yell and then started hollering out a speech he had learned at High School—"Friends, Romans, Countrymen, Lend me your ears!"

35  There was something about getting to the very top that gave you a wild feeling and made you want to yell or sing or raise up your arms and fly.

She felt the soles of her tennis shoes slipping, and eased herself down so that she straddled the peak of the roof. The house

40  was almost finished. It would be one of the largest buildings in the neighborhood—two stories, with very high ceilings and the steepest roof of any house she had ever seen. But soon the work would all be finished. The carpenters would leave and the kids would have to find another place to play.

45  She was by herself. No one was around and it was quiet and she could think for a while. She took from the pocket of her shorts the package of cigarettes she had bought the night before. She breathed in the smoke slowly. The cigarette gave her a drunk feeling so that her head seemed heavy and loose on her shoulders, but she had to finish it.

50

M.K. —That was what she would have written on everything when she was seventeen years old and very famous. She would ride back home in a red-and-white Packard automobile with her initials on the doors. She would have M.K. written in

55  red on her handkerchiefs and underclothes. Maybe she would be a great inventor. She would invent tiny little radios the size of a green pea that people could carry around and stick in their ears. Also flying machines people could fasten on their backs like knapsacks and go zipping all over the world. After that she

60  would be the first one to make a large tunnel through the world to China, and people could go down in big balloons. Those were the first things she would invent. They were already planned.

When Mick had finished half of the cigarette she smashed it dead and flipped the butt down the slant of the roof. Then she

65  leaned forward so that her head rested on her arms and began to hum to herself.

**1.** As it is used in lines 18–19, the phrase *screwed up* most nearly means:
   A. lost.
   B. made a mistake.
   C. examined.
   D. gathered.

**GO ON TO THE NEXT PAGE.**

2. If the passage describes a typical Sunday, Mick then spends part of her Sundays:
   F. learning grammar from Mr. Singer.
   G. cooking breakfast for her family.
   H. going to Sunday School.
   J. caring for her younger brothers.

3. Mick believes that the other children in the neighborhood:
   A. did not want to play with her.
   B. also liked to climb on the roof.
   C. thought that Mick was crazy for climbing on rooftops.
   D. had more housework to do than she did.

4. The name of Mick's father is:
   F. Ralph.
   G. Bubber.
   H. Mr. Singer.
   J. not mentioned in the passage.

5. It can be reasonably be inferred that one of the reasons that Mick enjoyed being on the roof was that:
   A. she could enjoy some time alone.
   B. her friends did not believe that she could do it and she liked proving them wrong.
   C. she felt very athletic while climbing.
   D. she knew that she was the only one who could climb that high.

6. It is suggested that no sound came out of Mick's throat (line 31) because she:
   F. did not think she has a good singing voice.
   G. could not express all of what she was feeling.
   H. was afraid of heights.
   J. did not want to scare her brothers by yelling too loudly.

7. It can be inferred from the passage that Mister Singer is:
   A. Mick's father.
   B. a boarder at Mick's house.
   C. a schoolteacher.
   D. a journalist.

8. All of the following are included in the list of things Mick would like to invent EXCEPT:
   F. a miniature radio.
   G. a small flying machine.
   H. a big balloon.
   J. a tunnel through the earth.

9. The house that Mick climbs onto is:
   A. three stories tall.
   B. on a hill.
   C. unfinished.
   D. owned by a celebrity.

10. According to the passage, it can reasonably be inferred that Mick spent a great deal of time wishing:
    F. to be famous.
    G. to have children.
    H. to get good grades in school.
    J. to spend more time with her mother.

**GO ON TO THE NEXT PAGE.**

## Passage II

**SOCIAL SCIENCE:** This passage, which discusses how news is reported in the age of television, is taken from a book by Neil Postman.

"Now...this" is commonly used on radio and television newscasts to indicate that what one has just heard or seen has no relevance to what one is about to hear or see, or possibly to anything one is ever likely to hear or see. The phrase is a
5  means of acknowledging the fact that the world as mapped by the speeded-up electronic media has no order or meaning and is not to be taken seriously. There is no murder so brutal, no earthquake so devastating, no political blunder so costly—for that matter, no ball score so tantalizing or weather report so threatening—that
10 it cannot be erased from our minds by a newscaster saying, "Now...this." The newscaster means that you have thought long enough on the previous matter (approximately forty-five seconds), that you must not be morbidly preoccupied with it (let us say, for ninety seconds), and that you must now give your
15 attention to another fragment of news or a commercial.

Television did not invent the "Now...this" world view. As I have tried to show, it is the offspring of the intercourse between telegraphy and photography. But it is through television that it has been nurtured and brought to a perverse maturity. For on
20 television, nearly every half hour is a discrete event, separated in content, context, and emotional texture from what precedes and follows it. In part because television sells its time in seconds and minutes, in part because television must use images rather than words, in part because its audience can move freely to and
25 from the television set, programs are structured so that almost each eight-minute segment may stand as a complete event in itself. Viewers are rarely required to carry over any thought or feeling from one parcel of time to another.

Of course, in television's presentation of the "news of the
30 day," we may see the "Now...this" mode of discourse in its bold-est and most embarrassing form. For there, we are presented not only with fragmented news but news without context, without consequences, without value, and therefore without essential seriousness; that is to say, news as pure entertainment.

35 Consider, for example, how you would proceed if you were given the opportunity to produce a television news show for any station concerned to attract the largest possible audience. You would, first, choose a cast of players, each of whom has a face that is both "likable" and "credible." Those who apply would,
40 in fact, submit to you their eight-by-ten glossies, from which you would eliminate those whose countenances are not suitable for nightly display. This means that you will exclude women who are not beautiful or who are over the age of fifty, men who are bald, all people who are overweight or whose noses are too
45 long or whose eyes are too close together. You will try, in other words, to assemble a cast of talking hair-do's. At the very least, you will want those whose faces would not be unwelcome on a magazine cover.

Christine Craft has just such a face, and so she applied for a
50 co-anchor position on KMBC-TV in Kansas City. According to a lawyer who represented her in a sexism suit she later brought against the station, the management of KMBC-TV "loved Christine's look." She was accordingly hired in January 1981. She was fired in August 1981 because research indicated that her
55 appearance "hampered viewer acceptance." What exactly does "hampered viewer acceptance" mean? And what does it have to do with the news? Hampered viewer acceptance means the same thing for television news as it does for any television show: Viewers do not like looking at the performer. It also means that
60 viewers do not believe the performer, that she lacks credibility. In the case of a theatrical performance, we have a sense of what that implies: The actor does not persuade the audience that he or she is the character being portrayed. But what does lack of credibility imply in the case of a news show? What character
65 is a co-anchor playing? And how do we decide that the perfor-mance lacks verisimilitude? Does the audience believe that the newscaster is lying, that what is reported did not in fact happen, that something important is being concealed?

It is frightening to think that this may be so, that the percep-
70 tion of the truth of a report rests heavily on the acceptability of the newscaster. In the ancient world, there was a tradition of banishing or killing the bearer of bad tidings. Does the television news show restore, in a curious form, this tradition?

11. The author of this passage can most reasonably be described as:
   A. a detective who tries to find evidence proving that a tele-vision network is not guilty of misleading the public.
   B. a television executive who discusses important factors for a successful news program.
   C. a critic who warns his readers about the effects that television has had on the reporting of news.
   D. a journalism teacher who wishes to show his students how to write interesting television news stories.

12. As it is used in line 5, the word *mapped* most nearly means:
   F. obscured.
   G. explored.
   H. destroyed.
   J. defined.

**GO ON TO THE NEXT PAGE.**

13. It can reasonably be inferred that the author would most likely agree with which of the following statements?
  A. News stories are more interesting when they are presented on live television than when they are recorded.
  B. The short amount of time given to news stories on television reduces the value of the facts reported.
  C. Television has done a good job of bringing families together by creating programs that the entire family can watch.
  D. Television news reporters should also write news stories for magazines and newspapers.

14. In the fifth paragraph (lines 49–68) the author offers details about Christine Craft in order to:
  F. illustrate the importance of the appearance of the newscaster on television.
  G. show that television gets its nature from both telegraphy and photography.
  H. support a claim about sexism in America.
  J. present the story of a friend and her experiences in television journalism.

15. It can most reasonably be inferred that the author believes that:
  A. well-trained actors are better than newscasters at delivering news on television.
  B. television is not well suited to a serious presentation of the news.
  C. newspapers will likely disappear in a few years if people continue to get their news from television.
  D. the presentation of the news has not fundamentally changed since ancient times.

16. According to the passage, television has become a medium whose main goal is:
  F. to report the facts in an unbiased manner.
  G. to help television reporters become famous.
  H. to inform the public of important new products.
  J. to entertain viewers.

17. The author's reference to "talking hair-do's" (line 46) is a reference to:
  A. people whose faces are pleasing to viewers.
  B. the advertising of hair care products on television.
  C. animated cartoon characters.
  D. the amount of money spent to make television personalities look good.

18. According to the author, the phrase "Now...this" indicates that the next topic:
  F. will be more important than the previous topic.
  G. will receive less time than the previous topic.
  H. will have no connection to the previous topic.
  J. will begin a new eight-minute segment of news.

19. According to the passage, television viewers' perceptions of whether a story is true or false depends largely on the:
  A. appearance of the person reporting the news.
  B. reputation of the television network.
  C. references cited during the news story.
  D. commentary provided by those being interviewed.

20. Which of the following is NOT cited as having an impact on the presentation of television news?
  F. Airtime is a very valuable commodity for television stations.
  G. People are not expected to remain attentive to the television for more than a short period of time.
  H. Television relies more on images than on words to transmit its message.
  J. Television sets are relatively expensive, and not everyone can afford them.

**GO ON TO THE NEXT PAGE.**

## Passage III

HUMANITIES: This passage is taken from THE CENTURY by Peter Jennings (© 1998 by ABC Television Network Group).

The show was grandly titled "The International Exhibition of Modern Art," but the dynamite, as the *New Yorker* later commented, was in the word "modern." And while the new painting and sculpture declared itself with the confidence that comes
5  with a revolution, there were many in the New York crowd and in even larger gatherings that greeted the show when it moved on to Boston and Chicago (where art students burned Matisse and Brancusi in effigy) who would have nothing of it. One of America's more distinguished artists, Kenyon Cox, a longtime
10  holdout against the trends that seemed to be undermining the traditional image, saw in the show nothing less than the "total destruction of the art of painting," and on this he could find only one bit of good news: that the Americans represented here seemed to him to have resisted the "depth of badness [at-
15  tained] by the French and the Germans." Indeed, many of those attending the show looked upon the works before them as the perverse fantasies of the foreigner; Ellis Island art they called it. And no less a chauvinist than Teddy Roosevelt himself, fresh from his unsuccessful 1912 attempt to reenter the White House
20  with the backing of a third party (Roosevelt and his handpicked Republican successor, William Howard Taft, had had a falling-out), was said to have stomped about the opening, waving his arms and declaring in a loud voice his disapproval of all but the American entries, even as he gave praise to the show's general
25  spirit, in particular in the way that it tolerated no "simpering, self-satisfied conventionality."

The star image of the exhibition was most certainly Duchamp's *Nude Descending a Staircase* (or, as Roosevelt called it, "a naked man going downstairs"), a painting so abstract it
30  defied its own title, which, of course, was the point. As critic Robert Hughes has pointed out, the nude had a long and distinguished history with painting, where she (and, more rarely, he) was usually portrayed in a blissful state of recline; by contrast, Duchamp's nude, to the degree that it looked at all like what it
35  was supposed to be, was a nude on the move (indeed, the painting had the quality of a photographic motion study), a metaphor for the change that it heralded. Still, most people saw something else entirely—"an explosion in a shingle factory," "an earthquake on the subway," "a staircase descending a nude"—jokes all, uttered
40  even as the jokesters themselves stood in long lines, necks craning, to see the object of their ridicule. The modern era might be abhorrent, absurd, unnatural, but oh to get a glimpse of it!

Roosevelt said Duchamp's Nude reminded him of a Navaho rug he stood upon while shaving each morning in his bathroom.
45  And indeed, to the degree that Roosevelt, Cox, and others saw any merit to modern abstractions like Duchamp's, it was as decoration, fancy wallpaper. But the fact that these artists attached meaning to their creations, that they saw themselves as articulating an ideology, an "ism" of the new, and one that quite
50  blatantly intended to disassemble the world as men and women had known it, was simply too bold and raw for mainstream temperaments. This modern art was, as its name suggested, something different—art as cause—and the condemnation brought upon it by Roosevelt and others was a denunciation of
55  the new work's politics. After all, when before had reasonable men discovered in painting, as they did here, "the chatter of anarchistic monkeys" or "the harbinger of universal anarchy"?

Anticipating a reluctant audience, the organizers of the Armory Show had included an editorial in the exhibition catalog
60  urging viewers to greet the new art with an open mind. "Art," it read, "is a sign of life. There can be no life without change, as there can be no development without change. To be afraid of what is different is to be afraid of life..." Then, perhaps with Roosevelt's legendary machismo in mind, they added a challenge
65  to contemporary pretensions to the rugged life, concluding with the statement that their exhibition was a proclamation "against cowardice."

21. The author mentions a "photographic motion study" (line 36) in order to emphasize what quality of Duchamp's Nude?
    **A.** The different interpretations of the painting
    **B.** The painting's photographic realism
    **C.** The painting's inappropriate subject matter
    **D.** The movement implied in the painting

22. According to the passage, which of the following was an artist?
    I. Brancusi
    II. Cox
    III. Hughes

    **F.** I only
    **G.** I and II only
    **H.** II and III only
    **J.** I, II, and III

**GO ON TO THE NEXT PAGE.**

**23.** The first paragraph states that certain early critics of modern art:

   **A.** viewed modern art as completely unimportant and ignored it entirely.
   **B.** believed that modern artists were harming the art of painting.
   **C.** thought that modern art was interesting, but not very beautiful.
   **D.** preferred the work of European modernists to those of the Americans.

**24.** It can be inferred from the author's reference to "an explosion" and "an earthquake" (line 38) that Duchamp's Nude:

   **F.** did not look like an ordinary painting of a nude person.
   **G.** depicted many different of natural disasters.
   **H.** was painted during a time of great social upheaval and unrest.
   **J.** was so disturbing to viewers that people did not want to look at it.

**25.** As it is used in line 42, the word *abhorrent* most nearly means:

   **A.** colorful.
   **B.** flimsy.
   **C.** awful.
   **D.** tiresome.

**26.** It can be reasonably concluded from the passage that the most important characteristic of "modern" art was that it was:

   **F.** beautiful.
   **G.** expensive.
   **H.** political.
   **J.** recent.

**27.** Which of the following best describes Roosevelt's reaction to modern art?

   **A.** He wholeheartedly approved of it.
   **B.** He largely approved of it, except for the pieces that he thought were too disorganized.
   **C.** He largely disapproved of it, though he thought that certain pieces had some merit.
   **D.** He disapproved of all of it.

**28.** It can reasonably be inferred that the use of the words "Ellis Island" (line 17) indicated that:

   **F.** many of the modern artists were from countries outside the United States.
   **G.** the exhibition took place on Ellis Island.
   **H.** the exhibition showed many paintings of Ellis Island.
   **J.** many of the pieces were dedicated to the idea of freedom in the United States.

**29.** It can be inferred from the last paragraph that the organizers of the Armory Show:

   **A.** needed a great deal of financial support to put on the exhibition.
   **B.** tried hard to please the American public.
   **C.** were immigrants from Europe.
   **D.** expected that the exhibition would be controversial.

**30.** According to the passage, some of the supporters of modern art believed that modern art represented:

   **F.** a return to the themes of classical painting.
   **G.** the expansion of traditional American tastes into the rest of the world.
   **H.** a force for change and progress in the world of art.
   **J.** an attempt to depict the world as precisely as in a photograph.

**GO ON TO THE NEXT PAGE.**

## Passage IV

**NATURAL SCIENCE:** This passage is adapted from a text on the history of science.

Small beginnings can have great endings—sometimes. As a case in point, note what came of the small, original effort of a self-trained back-country Quaker youth named John Dalton, who along towards the close of the eighteenth century became
[5] interested in the weather, and was led to construct and use a crude water-gauge to test the amount of the rainfall. But this was only a beginning. The simple rain-gauge pointed the way to the most important generalization of the nineteenth century in a field of science with which, to the casual observer, it might seem
[10] to have no alliance whatever. The wonderful theory of atoms, on which the whole gigantic structure of modern chemistry is founded, was the logical outgrowth of those early studies in meteorology.

The way it happened was this: From studying the rain-
[15] fall, Dalton turned naturally to the complementary process of evaporation. He was soon led to believe that vapor exists in the atmosphere as an independent gas. But since two bodies cannot occupy the same space at the same time, this implies that the various atmospheric gases are really composed of discrete
[20] particles. These ultimate particles are so small that we cannot see them—cannot, indeed, more than vaguely imagine them—yet each particle of vapor, for example, is just as much a portion of water as if it were a drop out of the ocean. But, again, water is a compound substance, for it may be separated, as Cavendish
[25] has shown, into the two elementary substances hydrogen and oxygen. Hence the atom of water must be composed of two lesser atoms joined together. Imagine an atom of hydrogen and one of oxygen. Unite them, and we have an atom of water; sever them, and the water no longer exists; but whether united or separate the
[30] atoms of hydrogen and of oxygen remain hydrogen and oxygen and nothing else. Differently mixed together or united, atoms produce different gross substances, but the elementary atoms never change their chemical nature—their distinct personality.

It was about the year 1803 that Dalton first gained a full
[35] grasp of the conception of the chemical atom. At once he saw that the hypothesis, if true, furnished a marvelous key to secrets of matter hitherto insoluble—questions relating to the relative proportions of the atoms themselves. It is known, for example, that a certain bulk of hydrogen gas unites with a certain bulk
[40] of oxygen gas to form water. If it is true that this combination consists essentially of the union of atoms one with another (each single atom of hydrogen united to a single atom of oxygen), then the relative weights of the original masses of hydrogen and of oxygen must be also the relative weights of each of their respec-
[45] tive atoms. If one pound of hydrogen unites with five and one-half pounds of oxygen (as, according to Dalton's experiments, it did), then the weight of the oxygen atom must be five and one-half times that of the hydrogen atom. Other compounds may plainly be tested in the same way. Dalton made numerous tests
[50] before he published his theory. He found that hydrogen enters into compounds in smaller proportions than any other element known to him, and so, for convenience, determined to take the weight of the hydrogen atom as unity. The atomic weight of

oxygen then becomes (as given in Dalton's first table of 1803)
[55] 5.5; that of water (hydrogen plus oxygen) being of course 6.5. The atomic weights of about a score of substances are given in Dalton's first paper, which was read before the Literary and Philosophical Society of Manchester, October 21, 1803.

During these same years the rising authority of the French
[60] chemical world, Joseph Louis Gay-Lussac, was conducting experiments with gases. In 1809, the next year after the publication of the first volume of Dalton's New System of Chemical Philosophy, Gay-Lussac published the results of his observations, and among other things brought out the remarkable fact
[65] that gases, under the same conditions as to temperature and pressure, combine always in definite numerical proportions as to volume. Exactly two volumes of hydrogen, for example, combine with one volume of oxygen to form water.

The true explanation of Gay-Lussac's law of combination
[70] by volumes was thought out almost immediately by an Italian savant, Amadeo Avogadro, and expressed in terms of the atomic theory. The fact must be, said Avogadro, that under similar physical conditions every form of gas contains exactly the same number of ultimate particles in a given volume. Each
[75] of these ultimate physical particles may be composed of two or more atoms (as in the case of water vapor), but such a compound atom conducts itself as if it were a simple and indivisible atom, as regards the amount of space that separates it from its fellows under given conditions of pressure and temperature. The
[80] compound atom, composed of two or more elementary atoms, Avogadro proposed to distinguish, for purposes of convenience, by the name *molecule*.

The other and even more noted advocate of the atomic theory was Johan Jakob Berzelius. This great Swedish chemist at
[85] once set to work to put the atomic theory to such tests as might be applied in the laboratory. He was an analyst of the utmost skill, and for years he devoted himself to the determination of the combining weights, "equivalents" or "proportions," of the different elements. These determinations, in so far as they were accurately
[90] made, were simple expressions of empirical facts, independent of any theory; but gradually it became more and more plain that these facts all harmonized with the atomic theory of Dalton. So by common consent the proportionate combining weights of the elements came to be known as atomic weights—the name
[95] Dalton had given them from the first. Berzelius proposed to improve upon Dalton's method of notation by using the initial of the Latin name of the element represented—O for oxygen, H for hydrogen, and so on—a numerical coefficient to follow the letter as an indication of the number of atoms present in
[100] any given compound. This simple system soon gained general acceptance, and with slight modifications it is still universally employed. Every student now is aware that $H_2O$ is the chemical way of expressing the union of two atoms of hydrogen with one of oxygen to form a molecule of water.

**GO ON TO THE NEXT PAGE.**

**31.** In the first paragraph, the author discusses Dalton's instrument for measuring rainfall in order to show that:
  A. meteorology is more important than chemistry.
  B. water is an important chemical compound found in many more complex substances.
  C. some scientific discoveries arise unexpectedly from simple observations.
  D. many scientists in the 18th century had little or no formal training in the scientific method.

**32.** The scientist who is credited with the modern chemical notation in which water is expressed as $H_2O$ is:
  F. Berzelius.
  G. Dalton.
  H. Avogadro.
  J. Gay-Lussac.

**33.** The author's attitude toward the work of Dalton is best characterized as one of:
  A. scholarly detachment.
  B. restrained criticism.
  C. admiring interest.
  D. scientific indifference.

**34.** The passage states that Gay-Lussac was:
  F. English.
  G. French.
  H. Swedish.
  J. Italian.

**35.** The author credits Avogadro with:
  A. discovering the law that explains the observations of Gay-Lussac.
  B. measuring the atomic weight of oxygen.
  C. showing that some substances were combinations of more basic elements.
  D. realizing that hydrogen was the lightest atom.

**36.** In the final paragraph, the author states that Berzelius:
  F. disproved Dalton's version of atomic theory and replaced it with his own.
  G. was an important influence on the work of Avogadro and Gay-Lussac.
  H. found more evidence that supported Dalton's work.
  J. was the first to show that water can be divided into oxygen and hydrogen.

**37.** The passage states that Dalton believed that the weight of an atom of oxygen is:
  A. about twice the weight of an atom of hydrogen.
  B. between five and six times the weight of an atom of hydrogen.
  C. between six and seven times the weight of an atom of hydrogen.
  D. slightly more than the weight of a molecule of water.

**38.** As described in the passage, the works of Gay-Lussac concerned the:
  F. weight of gases.
  G. volume of gases.
  H. transformation of liquids into gases.
  J. number of electrons in an atom.

**39.** Which of the following assumptions made by Dalton led to a flaw in his atomic theory?
  A. All atoms have the same volume.
  B. All atoms have the same weight.
  C. Two atoms can occupy the same space at the same time.
  D. Atoms combine only in pairs.

**40.** The passage associates the origin of the word *molecule* with:
  F. Dalton.
  G. Avogadro.
  H. Cavendish.
  J. Gay-Lussac.

**END OF TEST 3**

**STOP! DO NOT TURN THE PAGE UNTIL TOLD TO DO SO.**

**DO NOT RETURN TO A PREVIOUS TEST.**

# SCIENCE REASONING TEST

*35 Minutes—40 Questions*

**DIRECTIONS:** There are seven passages in this test. Each passage is followed by several questions. After reading a passage, choice the best answer to each question and fill in the corresponding oval on your answer document. You may refer to the passages as often as necessary.

You are NOT permitted to use a calculator on this test.

## Passage I

It is well known that applying a force to both ends of a bar will cause the bar to compress or to expand, depending on whether the force pushes or pulls the bar. The *stress* on the bar is defined to be the ratio of the force on the bar to the cross-sectional area, and the *strain* on the bar is the fractional change in length. As long as the force is not too strong, stress is directly proportional to strain, and the constant of proportionality is called *Young's modulus*. If the force on the bar exceeds the yield strength of the material, however, permanent deformation will occur, and the bar will not resume its original shape upon removal of the force. In the experiments below, a scientist investigated these properties.

### Experiment 1

Aluminum has a Young's modulus of $70 \times 10^9$ newtons per square meter ($N/m^2$). Using a 2-meter-long bar of cross-sectional area 1 square meter ($m^2$), a scientist applied different forces to the bar and noted the various changes in length. The bar returned to its original shape after the forces were removed in all trials except the final one. The results are shown in Table 1.

Table 1

| Applied Force ($10^6$ N) | Change in Length (mm) |
|---|---|
| 50 | 1.4 |
| 100 | 2.8 |
| 200 | 5.6 |
| 400 | 11.2 |

### Experiment 2

The effect of length expansion or compression can be seen in many materials. The scientist performed another experiment in order to determine to what extent a bar made out of each of the materials tested would stretch. The bars under consideration were each 2 meters long with a cross-sectional area of 1 $m^2$, and compressive forces of $100 \times 10^6$ N were applied to each end before the data was recorded. The results are shown in Table 2.

Table 2

| Material | Young's Modulus ($10^9$ N/m$^2$) | Change in Length (mm) |
|---|---|---|
| Steel | 200 | 1.0 |
| Concrete | 30 | 6.6 |
| Wood | 13 | 15.4 |
| Polystyrene | 2 | 66.7 |

### Experiment 3

Finally, the scientist investigated how different aluminum bars stretched when a force of $100 \times 10^6$ N was applied to both ends of the bars. The results are shown in Table 3.

Table 3

| Length of Bar (m) | Cross-Sectional Area (m$^2$) | Change in Length (mm) |
|---|---|---|
| 1.0 | 2.0 | 0.7 |
| 1.0 | 4.0 | 0.4 |
| 1.0 | 8.0 | 0.2 |
| 2.0 | 2.0 | 1.4 |
| 4.0 | 2.0 | 2.8 |
| 8.0 | 4.0 | 2.8 |
| 16.0 | 4.0 | 5.6 |

**GO ON TO THE NEXT PAGE.**

1. According to the data in the experiments, when both the length and cross-sectional area of an aluminum bar are doubled, the change in length:
   A. quadruples.
   B. doubles.
   C. remains the same.
   D. halves.

2. Based on the information in the passage, one can conclude that the yield strength of aluminum is approximately:
   F. $75 \times 10^6$N.
   G. $125 \times 10^6$N.
   H. $175 \times 10^6$N.
   J. $300 \times 10^6$N.

3. The Young's modulus of glass is $65 \times 10^9$ N/m². A 2-meter-long glass bar with a cross-sectional area of 1 m² with a force of $100 \times 10^6$ N applied to both ends would experience a change in length of:
   A. 3.2 mm.
   B. 7.3 mm.
   C. 30.8 mm.
   D. 133.4 mm.

4. Given the results of the experiments, all of the following would be expected to increase the change in the length of a bar EXCEPT:
   F. increasing the applied force.
   G. increasing the cross-sectional area.
   H. increasing the length of the bar.
   J. decreasing the Young's modulus.

5. The scientist suspected that the temperature of the bar may have an effect on the change in length. Which of the following, if true, would best support that hypothesis?
   A. As the temperature of a material changes, so does its Young's modulus.
   B. As the temperature of a material changes, the material becomes less dense.
   C. The Young's modulus of a given material is independent of temperature.
   D. The Young's modulus of steel is greater than that of aluminum.

6. Based on the data in the passage, if a force of $100 \times 10^6$ N were applied to an aluminum bar 32 meters long with a cross-sectional area of 4.0 m², the change in the length of the bar would most nearly be:
   F. 2.8 mm.
   G. 5.6 mm.
   H. 11.2 mm.
   J. 22.4 mm.

**GO ON TO THE NEXT PAGE.**

### Passage II

A capacitor is a device that stores electromagnetic energy in the form of electric potential energy. The measure of how much energy a capacitor can store is called the *capacitance*, which can (in principle) be determined merely from knowing the geometry of a given capacitor (that is, its shape, the distance between its plates, etc.).

Three common types of capacitor geometries consist of two parallel plates, two coaxial cylinders, and two concentric spherical shells. Another common practice with capacitors is the insertion of a *dielectric*, a material that separates the plates of the capacitor. In the experiments below, scientists set up a potential difference of 9 volts between the plates of different parallel-plate capacitors and measured the capacitance in each case. The results are shown in Table 1.

Table 1

| Distance between plates (mm) | Area of plates (m²) | Capacitance (pF) | Dielectric material | Dielectric constant of material |
|---|---|---|---|---|
| 5 | 0.5 | 3.11 | Paper | 3.5 |
| 10 | 0.5 | 1.57 | Paper | 3.5 |
| 15 | 0.5 | 1.02 | Paper | 3.5 |
| 15 | 1.0 | 2.07 | Paper | 3.5 |
| 15 | 2.0 | 4.13 | Paper | 3.5 |
| 10 | 0.5 | 3.09 | Porcelain | 6.9 |
| 10 | 1.0 | 6.17 | Porcelain | 6.9 |
| 20 | 2.0 | 6.17 | Porcelain | 6.9 |
| 15 | 0.5 | 3.50 | Silicon | 12 |
| 20 | 1.0 | 5.30 | Silicon | 12 |
| 30 | 1.0 | 3.51 | Silicon | 12 |

7. According to the data in Table 1, doubling the distance between the plates:
   A. doubles the area of the plates.
   B. halves the area of the plates.
   C. doubles the capacitance.
   D. halves the capacitance.

8. The dielectric constant of ruby mica is approximately the same as that of porcelain. A parallel plate capacitor with a ruby mica dielectric with a distance of 20 mm between the plates with area 2 m² would have a capacitance of approximately:
   F. 3 pF.
   G. 6 pF.
   H. 12 pF.
   J. 24 pF.

9. One of the essential traits of a capacitor is that the plates do not touch. Thus, one benefit of adding a dielectric to a capacitor is that:
   A. the dielectric increases the electric field strength within the capacitor.
   B. the dielectric changes the geometry of the capacitor.
   C. the dielectric makes the capacitor a better conductor of electricity.
   D. the dielectric provides a practical means of separating the plates.

10. According to the data in Table 1, doubling both the area of the plates and the distance between the plates:
    F. quadruples the capacitance.
    G. halves the capacitance.
    H. has no effect on the capacitance.
    J. doubles the capacitance.

11. According to the data in Table 1, the capacitance of a parallel plate capacitor with a paper dielectric and a separation of 15 mm between plates of area 1.5 m² would most nearly be:
    A. 1 pF.
    B. 2 pF.
    C. 3 pF.
    D. 6 pF.

**GO ON TO THE NEXT PAGE.**

## Passage III

Cell division occurs in four stages: gap 1 (G1), synthesis (S), gap 2 (G2), and mitosis (M). Interphase prepares the cell for division and comprises the G1, S, and G2 phases. The physical division of two cells from one cell occurs during mitosis.

Figure 1 represents the amount of time a typical cell spends in each of the four phases of the cell cycle.

Figure 1

In mammalian cells, cell division is controlled by a class of proteins called cyclins. Figure 2 graphically represents cyclin levels during the cell cycle.

Figure 2

**12.** A certain mammalian cell, the fibroblast, takes 24 hours to divide. How many hours would such a cell be expected to spend in mitosis?
   F.   3.6
   G.   6.0
   H.   8.4
   J.   12.0

**13.** Which of the following conclusions can be made regarding the entry of a mammalian cell into mitosis?
   A.  Cyclin A must be at its maximum level.
   B.  Cyclin B must be decreasing.
   C.  Cyclin D must be increasing.
   D.  Cyclin E must be increasing.

**14.** Suppose that a researcher is adding cyclins to mammalian cells in order to study their effects on the cell cycle. The cyclin that is LEAST likely to have an effect on any phase of the cell cycle is:
   F.  Cyclin A.
   G.  Cyclin B.
   H.  Cyclin D.
   J.  Cyclin E.

**15.** Which cyclin(s) is (are) most likely to initiate the cell cycle in mammalian cells?
     I.  Cyclin A
    II.  Cyclin B
   III.  Cyclin E
   A.  I only
   B.  II only
   C.  III only
   D.  I and II only

**16.** Which of the following processes is most likely to be triggered by an increase in Cyclin A ?
   F.  DNA synthesis
   G.  Protein synthesis
   H.  Cell growth
   J.  Cell division

**GO ON TO THE NEXT PAGE.**

**Passage IV**

An enzyme is a biological catalyst that uses a substrate to make a product. The enzyme converts the substrate to the product at a certain rate, V, measured in reactions per second. The rate of the reaction is a measure of the efficiency of the enzyme. The maximum rate of the reaction, $V_{max}$, is independent of the amount of substrate. The substrate concentration at which $V = \frac{1}{2} V_{max}$ is known as the $K_m$. A typical reaction rate graph is shown in Figure 1.

Figure 1

Monoamine oxidase inhibitors (MAOI) are a class of drugs designed for use as anti-depressants. Because a similar enzyme is present in the heart, patients taking these drugs may experience potentially fatal drug and food interactions. Scientists are interested in designing a drug that will effectively inhibit the enzyme found in the brain (bMAO) while minimizing the drug's action on the heart enzyme (hMAO).

*Experiment 1*

Brain tissue was homogenized and the protein fraction was obtained and purified. Drug X was added in increasing concentrations to bMAO and the reaction rate was measured. The trials were performed using 10 μg/mL of the enzyme. The results are shown in Figure 2.

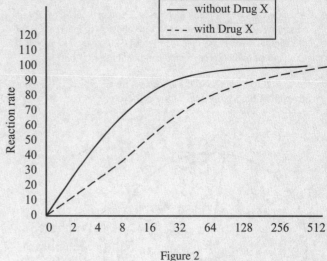

Figure 2

*Experiment 2*

Heart tissue from the same experimental animal was homogenized and the protein fraction was obtained and purified. Drug X was added in increasing concentrations to hMAO and the reaction rate was measured. The trials were performed using 10 μg/mL of the enzyme. The results are shown in Figure 3.

Figure 3

**GO ON TO THE NEXT PAGE.**

17. In Experiment 1, what is the approximate $K_m$ for bMAO following treatment by Drug X ?
    A. 5
    B. 20
    C. 50
    D. 100

18. What is the effect of Drug X on the maximum reaction rate of hMAO ?
    F. Drug X increases the maximum reaction rate.
    G. Drug X decreases the maximum reaction rate.
    H. Drug X increases the maximum reaction rate at low concentrations but decreases it at higher concentrations.
    J. Drug X has no effect on the maximum reaction rate.

19. An important difference between Experiments 1 and 2 is that they:
    A. measured different parameters.
    B. used tissue from different animals.
    C. tested different drugs.
    D. used different enzymes.

20. Which of the following conclusions is most consistent with the results of Experiment 1?
    F. Drug X decreases the $K_m$ but increases $V_{max}$.
    G. Drug X increases the $K_m$ but decreases $V_{max}$.
    H. Drug X increases the $K_m$ but does not affect $V_{max}$.
    J. Drug X does not affect the $K_m$ but increases $V_{max}$.

21. Based on the results of both experiments, Drug X suppresses:
    A. both hMAO and bMAO, but suppresses hMAO more effectively.
    B. both hMAO and bMAO, but suppresses bMAO more effectively.
    C. hMAO but has no effect on bMAO.
    D. bMAO but has no effect on hMAO.

22. For both experiments, what controlled variable was kept constant?
    F. Total enzyme concentration
    G. Reaction rate
    H. Substrate concentration
    J. Tissue homogenation

**GO ON TO THE NEXT PAGE.**

**Passage V**

The possibility that there may be—or may once have been—life on Mars has been debated intensely for over a hundred years. Most of these arguments have focused on whether there was ever enough liquid water on Mars to sustain life. Three scientists present their theories concerning Martian life.

*Scientist 1*

Water is essential for the survival of all known forms of life. There is water on Mars today, in the polar ice caps and the atmosphere. While pools of liquid water may not last long in the frigid climate, they can form under the proper conditions. Salty water has a lower freezing point than pure water, and the soil on Mars contains many salts. Therefore, it is possible that isolated pockets of salty water can be found near the planet's surface. Bacteria found in deserts on Earth can live in extremely salty water, surviving in suspended animation when the water dries up. It is possible that similar bacteria could be living on present-day Mars.

*Scientist 2*

Two of the arguments against life on Mars are that the atmosphere is too thin and the temperature is too low to support life. Water and carbon dioxide released by past volcanic eruptions could have formed a thick atmosphere, thereby creating a greenhouse effect and warming the planet. Instruments sent to Mars since the late 1990s have sent back pictures of stream gullies and layers of sediment, proof that liquid had once flowed on the surface. In one location, the lowlands have a very smooth surface. The surrounding highlands have a rougher surface, forming a well-defined coastline between the two regions and indicating that an ocean once existed there. Life on Earth began in the ocean; there is no reason to believe that life did not form in a similar fashion on Mars.

The thick Martian atmosphere, which also would have protected the planet from harmful ultraviolet radiation, has long since disappeared. Any forms of Martian life—even those lying dormant—would have died out billions of years ago.

*Scientist 3*

The gullies on Mars may be the result of some form of liquid, but there is no reason to assume that it was water. It is much more likely that the gullies were formed by liquid carbon dioxide, which forms at very low temperatures; bursting from under the ground, it could have carved paths into the planet's surface before vaporizing. Alternately, these gorges could have been formed by volcanic activity or high winds. Also, the supposed ocean coastline is merely the result of expansion of the planet's crust. Although water plays an important part in the shaping of the Earth's landscape, this does not mean that similar-looking structures on Mars necessarily were formed by water.

More importantly, the lack of oxygen in the thin Martian atmosphere means that Mars has no protection against the intense ultraviolet radiation from the Sun. Whether water is present or not, the current conditions on the surface of Mars make it impossible for any kind of life to survive.

23. A major difference between the theories of Scientists 1 and 2 is that Scientist 1 believes that life on Mars:
   A. is possible only in salty water, whereas Scientist 2 believes that it began in pure water.
   B. is currently in a state of suspended animation, whereas Scientist 2 believes that it is dormant.
   C. began deep in the ocean, whereas Scientist 2 believes that it began on the planet's surface.
   D. may still exist, whereas Scientist 2 believes that it could have existed only in the distant past.

24. A planetary magnetic field helps to protect the planet's atmosphere from solar wind, which can cause the atmosphere to erode and eventually disappear. Mars has an extremely weak magnetic field. How would this information affect the theory of Scientist 2?
   F. It would strengthen the theory by suggesting that the sediment layers on Mars were caused by strong winds.
   G. It would strengthen the theory by raising the possibility that the Martian atmosphere was once thicker.
   H. It would weaken the theory by challenging the assumption that a greenhouse effect could have existed on Mars.
   J. It would weaken the theory by offering an alternate explanation for the disappearance of the Martian ocean.

25. Scientist 3 mentions all of the following as possible causes of Martian stream gullies EXCEPT:
   A. wind.
   B. volcanoes.
   C. crust deformation.
   D. carbon dioxide.

26. Which of the following, if true, could best defend Scientist 1's theory against criticism voiced by Scientist 3?
   F. Olivine, a mineral that is easily eroded by water, is present in many locations on the Martian surface.
   G. The Martian atmospheric pressure is currently too low to allow pure water to remain in a liquid state.
   H. Liquid water can collect about a meter below the Martian surface, out of the range of ultraviolet radiation.
   J. Martian volcanic rock, almost 2 percent water when formed, currently contains about a hundredth of that amount.

**GO ON TO THE NEXT PAGE.**

**27.** A 4-billion-year-old Martian meteorite called ALH84001 was discovered in Antarctica in 1984. It contained microscopic crystals of *magnetite*, a compound formed by certain bacteria on Earth. The alignment of the magnetite crystals suggests that they were created by living organisms, and many researchers agree that the meteorite could not have been contaminated by Earth bacteria before its discovery. This discovery supports the theory (theories) of which scientist(s)?

    I.  Scientist 1
   II.  Scientist 2
  III.  Scientist 3

**A.** II only
**B.** I and II only
**C.** I and III only
**D.** II and III only

**28.** Scientists 2 and 3 agree that high levels of which of the following would prevent life from developing on a planet?
**F.** Ultraviolet radiation
**G.** Volcanic activity
**H.** Salt concentration
**J.** Atmospheric pressure

**29.** Which of the following statements would be most consistent with the theory of Scientist 3 ?
**A.** The dried-up ocean bed on Mars may contain dormant bacteria.
**B.** The crust of Mars is more geologically active than the crust of Earth.
**C.** Life on Mars will most likely be found near the polar ice caps.
**D.** There is no evidence that Mars ever had a warm climate.

**GO ON TO THE NEXT PAGE.**

### Passage VI

The graph below illustrates the changes that occur in lung volume during respiration. *Total lung capacity* (TLC) is the largest volume of air that the lung can hold and is constant for each individual. However, only a portion of this volume is used for maximal respiration, such as during exercise. An even smaller volume is used for resting respiration, such as while reading. The *vital capacity* (VC) represents maximal respiration and *tidal volume* (TV) represents resting respiration.

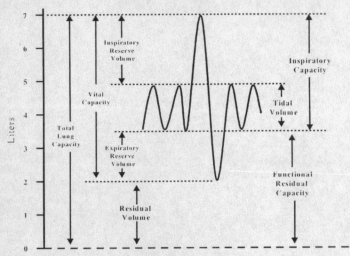

* These volumes are theoretical values calculated for a healthy 75 kilogram man

Figure 1

Forced expiratory volume (FEV) is the maximum volume of air that can be exhaled in one second following maximal inhalation, forced vital capacity (FVC). Most patients with lung (or *pulmonary*) disease demonstrate a diminished forced vital capacity. The FEV/ FVC ratio is used clinically to differentiate between *restrictive* and *obstructive* lung disease. Restrictive lung diseases result from a stiffening of lung tissue while obstructive diseases result from fluid or mucus in the lung. The FEV/ FVC ratio for a healthy individual is 0.8. The FEV/ FVC ratio for a patient with restrictive lung disease is normal or elevated while patients with obstructive lung disease demonstrate a reduced FEV/ FVC ratio. A physician tabulated the following data from four of his patients.

Table 1

|  | Patient 1 | Patient 2 | Patient 3 | Patient 4 |
|---|---|---|---|---|
| FEV | 1.58 | 2.57 | 1.91 | 2.27 |
| FVC | 2.63 | 3.16 | 2.41 | 2.54 |

30. Based on the information given in Figure 1, what is the volume, in liters, of air exchanged at rest?
    F. 0.1
    G. 1.5
    H. 3.0
    J. 5.5

31. Patients with restrictive lung diseases, such as emphysema, demonstrate an FEV/ FVC ratio that is 0.8 or higher. The best explanation for this finding is that:
    A. these patients do not have pulmonary disease.
    B. both FEV and FVC are increased proportionally, resulting in a ratio that is normal or elevated.
    C. both FEV and FVC are reduced, resulting in a ratio that is normal or elevated.
    D. emphysema reduces FEV but not FVC.

32. Patients with obstructive lung diseases, such as asthma, demonstrate a reduced FEV/ FVC ratio. Which patient has lung volumes consistent with obstructive lung disease?
    F. Patient 1
    G. Patient 2
    H. Patient 3
    J. Patient 4

33. Based on the information in Figure 1, which of the following conclusions can be made about pulmonary volumes?
    A. Increasing residual volume will reduce vital capacity.
    B. Decreasing tidal volume will increase vital capacity.
    C. Any change in vital capacity will proportionally affect total lung volume.
    D. The sum of the inspiratory reserve volume and the tidal volume equals the vital capacity.

**GO ON TO THE NEXT PAGE.**

**34.** Pneumonia is commonly caused by a viral infection and results in a build-up of fluid within the lungs. If a patient with emphysema (a restrictive pulmonary disease) acquires pneumonia while in the hospital, which of the following is most likely to occur?

**F.** The FEV/ FVC ratio will increase because both emphysema and pneumonia will increase the ratio.

**G.** The FEV/ FVC ratio will decrease because both emphysema and pneumonia will decrease the ratio.

**H.** The FEV/ FVC ratio will be unaffected because pneumonia will not affect respiration.

**J.** The FEV/ FVC ratio will decrease because pneumonia will decrease the ratio.

**GO ON TO THE NEXT PAGE.**

## Passage VII

An *electromagnetic wave* (or EM wave) is a wave that has oscillating electric and magnetic fields that vary over time and space. The electric and magnetic fields are perpendicular both to each other and to the direction of propagation of the wave. Light is an EM wave, and one can generalize its behavior in most cases to that of all other EM waves. A normal beam of light is made up of a large number of waves emitted by the atoms or molecules of the light source. Each atom produces a randomly directed electric field, and the resulting beam is considered to be *unpolarized*. However, with the use of a *polarizing filter*, it is possible to pick out the components of the electric field pointing in a particular direction. This direction is called the *axis of polarization* of the filter. A beam of light is called *polarized* if the electric field always vibrates in the same direction at a particular point. In the experiments below, scientists investigated various properties of polarized and unpolarized light.

### Experiment 1

The scientists used a laser emitting unpolarized light. The light was directed toward a polarization filter with an axis of polarization pointing straight up, and then through another whose axis of polarization varied. The scientists chose to describe the axis of the second filter by examining the angle between its axis and the axis of the first filter. The intensity of the original beam was 8 W/m$^2$ (Watts per square meter). Their results are shown in Table 1.

Table 1

| Angle between axis of first and second filters (degrees) | Intensity of emerging beam (W/m$^2$) |
|---|---|
| 0 | 4.00 |
| 15 | 3.73 |
| 30 | 2.99 |
| 45 | 2.01 |
| 60 | 1.00 |
| 75 | 0.27 |
| 90 | 0.00 |

### Experiment 2

The scientists repeated the experimental setup of Experiment 1 but used a source of polarized light polarized in the same direction as the axis of the first polarization filter (straight up). The intensity of the original beam was still 8 W/m$^2$. The results are shown in Table 2.

Table 2

| Angle between axis of first and second filters (degrees) | Intensity of emerging beam (W/m$^2$) |
|---|---|
| 0 | 8.00 |
| 15 | 7.46 |
| 30 | 6.01 |
| 45 | 3.99 |
| 60 | 2.00 |
| 75 | 0.54 |
| 90 | 0.00 |

### Experiment 3

The scientists decided to polarize the original beam of light at an angle of 30° to the first polarization filter. The intensity of the original beam was kept at 8 W/m$^2$. The results are shown in Table 3.

Table 3

| Angle between axis of first and second filters (degrees) | Intensity of emerging beam (W/m$^2$) |
|---|---|
| 0 | 6.01 |
| 15 | 5.60 |
| 30 | 4.49 |
| 45 | 2.99 |
| 60 | 1.50 |
| 75 | 0.41 |
| 90 | 0.00 |

35. A beam of unpolarized light is shone through two polarizing filters with axes of polarization separated by 20°. The intensity of the original beam is 8 W/m$^2$. Which of the following could be the intensity of the emerging beam?
   A. 3.53 W/m$^2$
   B. 5.32 W/m$^2$
   C. 6.97 W/m$^2$
   D. 8.00 W/m$^2$

36. The scientists conducted a fourth experiment similiar to the first three. The two polarizing filters were placed with their axes 90° apart. Light polarized in the same direction as the axis of the first filter was then shone through the two filters, and the second filter was rotated. As the angle between the axes of the two filters decreased from 90° to 0°, the intensity of the emerging beam:
   F. decreased.
   G. increased, then decreased.
   H. decreased, then increased.
   J. increased.

**GO ON TO THE NEXT PAGE.**

**37.** Which of the following graphs best describes the relationship between the angle between the axes of the filters and the intensity of the emerging beam as determined in Experiment 3?

**A.**

**B.**

**C.**

**D.**

**38.** How does the setup of Experiment 1 differ from that of Experiment 2 ?
 **F.** In Experiment 1, the original beam was polarized, but in Experiment 2, it was unpolarized.
 **G.** In Experiment 1, the original beam was unpolarized, but in Experiment 2, it was polarized.
 **H.** In Experiment 1, the scientists tested a wider range of angles than they did in Experiment 2.
 **J.** In Experiment 1, the original beam of light was more intense than the one in Experiment 2.

**39.** The scientists hypothesize that the color of the original beam of light will affect the intensity of the emerging beam. The frequency of a beam of light determines its color. Which of the following would be the best way to test this hypothesis?
 **A.** Repeating the experiments using more than two polarizing filters
 **B.** Repeating the experiments on different planets
 **C.** Repeating the experiments using beams of both high and low frequencies
 **D.** Repeating the experiments using different intensities for the original beam

**40.** In Experiment 1, if the angle between the axes of polarization increases by 15°, the intensity of the resulting beam:
 **F.** halves.
 **G.** doubles.
 **H.** increases, but not by any constant factor.
 **J.** decreases, but not by any constant factor.

**END OF TEST 4**

**STOP! DO NOT RETURN TO ANY OTHER TEST.**

**END OF EXAM**

# 22

# ACT Practice Exam
# Answers and Explanations

# TEST 1 ANSWER KEY

| ENGLISH SECTION | | |
|---|---|---|
| 1. C | 31. B | 61. B |
| 2. G | 32. H | 62. H |
| 3. D | 33. D | 63. A |
| 4. H | 34. G | 64. G |
| 5. B | 35. C | 65. D |
| 6. H | 36. J | 66. H |
| 7. B | 37. C | 67. A |
| 8. F | 38. F | 68. F |
| 9. D | 39. C | 69. D |
| 10. H | 40. H | 70. G |
| 11. D | 41. C | 71. A |
| 12. G | 42. J | 72. H |
| 13. C | 43. B | 73. C |
| 14. F | 44. G | 74. J |
| 15. A | 45. C | 75. A |
| 16. G | 46. J | |
| 17. D | 47. C | |
| 18. J | 48. F | |
| 19. C | 49. D | |
| 20. G | 50. F | |
| 21. D | 51. D | |
| 22. F | 52. J | |
| 23. A | 53. C | |
| 24. G | 54. F | |
| 25. A | 55. B | |
| 26. J | 56. G | |
| 27. A | 57. C | |
| 28. G | 58. H | |
| 29. A | 59. C | |
| 30. H | 60. H | |

# TEST 2 ANSWER KEY

| MATH SECTION | |
|---|---|
| 1. A | 31. B |
| 2. K | 32. F |
| 3. B | 33. E |
| 4. K | 34. F |
| 5. A | 35. E |
| 6. H | 36. J |
| 7. C | 37. B |
| 8. G | 38. K |
| 9. A | 39. D |
| 10. F | 40. H |
| 11. B | 41. C |
| 12. G | 42. J |
| 13. D | 43. D |
| 14. K | 44. K |
| 15. E | 45. E |
| 16. F | 46. K |
| 17. C | 47. B |
| 18. J | 48. J |
| 19. B | 49. C |
| 20. K | 50. H |
| 21. E | 51. A |
| 22. F | 52. H |
| 23. B | 53. B |
| 24. F | 54. H |
| 25. D | 55. D |
| 26. G | 56. G |
| 27. C | 57. A |
| 28. G | 58. F |
| 29. A | 59. D |
| 30. J | 60. H |

# TEST 3 ANSWER KEY

## READING SECTION

| | | | |
|---|---|---|---|
| 1. | D | 21. | D |
| 2. | J | 22. | G |
| 3. | B | 23. | B |
| 4. | J | 24. | F |
| 5. | A | 25. | C |
| 6. | G | 26. | H |
| 7. | B | 27. | C |
| 8. | H | 28. | F |
| 9. | C | 29. | D |
| 10. | F | 30. | H |
| 11. | C | 31. | C |
| 12. | J | 32. | F |
| 13. | B | 33. | C |
| 14. | F | 34. | G |
| 15. | B | 35. | A |
| 16. | J | 36. | H |
| 17. | A | 37. | B |
| 18. | H | 38. | G |
| 19. | A | 39. | D |
| 20. | J | 40. | G |

# TEST 4 ANSWER KEY

| SCIENCE REASONING SECTION |
| :---: |

| | | | |
| --- | --- | --- | --- |
| 1. | C | 21. | A |
| 2. | J | 22. | F |
| 3. | A | 23. | D |
| 4. | G | 24. | G |
| 5. | A | 25. | C |
| 6. | H | 26. | H |
| 7. | D | 27. | B |
| 8. | G | 28. | F |
| 9. | D | 29. | D |
| 10. | H | 30. | G |
| 11. | C | 31. | C |
| 12. | F | 32. | F |
| 13. | B | 33. | A |
| 14. | H | 34. | J |
| 15. | C | 35. | A |
| 16. | F | 36. | J |
| 17. | B | 37. | B |
| 18. | G | 38. | G |
| 19. | D | 39. | C |
| 20. | H | 40. | J |

1. **C** "Destined to become the first successful flight from New York to Paris" is an incomplete sentence. Therefore it will have to be combined with the sentence that comes before it, and we need something other than a period after the word "journey." This allows us to eliminate (A) and (D). We don't want to separate "embarked" from its object, "on a journey," so we can eliminate (B).

2. **G** There is no need for the words "it was" in this sentence, so we can eliminate (F). Choice (J) can be eliminated, because "Flying in his single-engine plane" is an incomplete sentence. Between (G) and (H), choice (G) is the better choice—never use "being" on the ACT unless you really have to.

3. **D** As written, the sentence is redundant. Saying that the flight was unique is the same thing as saying that it was different from all other flights, so there's no need for the underlined portion. Moreover, choice (B) is also redundant and (C) is awkward, so the best answer is to eliminate the excess and keep it simple.

4. **H** In this sentence, what comes before the underlined word ("extremely risky") and what comes after it ("duration of the flight and the exhaustion") are similar ideas; therefore, we need a word that compares similar ideas. "Despite," "except for," and "regardless of" are used to contrast different ideas, and not to compare similar ideas, so we can eliminate (F), (G), and (J).

5. **B** This is an issue of clumsy, though grammatical, English being the wrong answer and concise grammatical English being the right answer. Choices (C) and (D) quickly fall by the wayside: (C) uses *regard* as a noun in a manner never before seen on this planet, and (D) tosses in *however* for no good reason. That leaves (A) and (B), both of which are technically acceptable. (B) is more concise, and therefore better.

6. **H** Since the sentence is discussing two pilots, we need a plural pronoun. This eliminates choice F. Don't forget that "they're" is a contraction for "they are" which doesn't make sense in this sentence. Also, the word "there" is not a pronoun, so we can eliminate choices (G) and (J).

7. **B** To answer this question, we should read a little bit of the context. The paragraph says that a "crowd descended" on Lindbergh. We need to choose a word that best describes a great deal of joy and admiration. Does a "trickle" mean a great deal? No. Does an "outpouring" mean a great deal? Yes. Does an "undercurrent" mean a great deal? Not really. Does a "murmur" mean a great deal? No. This will allow us to eliminate (A), (C), and (D).

8. **F** Let's look at what follows the punctuation mark in the underlined portion. It's not a complete sentence, so we need GO punctuation. This will eliminate (G), (H), and (J).

9. **D** Since the other verb in this sentence ("was whisked off") is in the past tense, we need another verb in the past tense. This eliminates (A), (B), and (C).

10. **H** The other verbs in this sentence and in the sentence that follows are in the past tense: "got back," "were written," and "followed." Therefore we should pick a verb that is also in the past tense.

11. **D** As written, the sentence is excessively wordy. There is no reason to say "made up of" when "of" will work fine. This eliminates (A). Likewise, (B) can be eliminated, since "consisting of" also uses more words than we need. We don't want to put a comma between an adjective and the noun it modifies, so (C) can also be crossed off.

12. **G** The "letters" and "proposals of marriage" aren't contrasting ideas, so we don't want to use "even though" or "despite," which are both ways of drawing a contrast. This eliminates (F) and (H). If we omit the underlined portion the sentence won't make any sense, so we can also cross off (J).

13. **C** "Becoming" by itself isn't a verb, and "has already become" is in the wrong tense, so we can eliminate (A) and (B). In choice (D), "remain" is a plural form, but the subject here is Lindbergh, which is singular; for this reason we can eliminate (D) as well.

**14. F** If you've been paying attention, you've figured out that parallel structure matters on the ACT. It's the key to this question: "beat...challenged ...showed" ... yeah, that's nice. Answer choices (F) and (H) offer this selection of verbs, but (H) sticks in an extra "and" so (F) gets the nod.

**15. A** The key idea in this question is "Lindbergh is emblematic of the hope and pride of America." We can eliminate (B) and (D), since these choices aren't about America. Further, we can eliminate (C) since this choice doesn't involve Lindbergh. The best choice is the sentence as written.

**16. G** This is the type of question you can do without reading the passage, because you're told exactly what to look for in the question itself. You want a word that means "appeal to a wide range of viewers." Deft? No. Wordy? No. Youthful? No. Accessible? Gee, ya think?

**17. D** The key idea in this question is "sense of the popularity of" the radio hour. Choices (A) and (B) don't really discuss the show's popularity, so we can eliminate them. While (C) mentions it was "enjoyed by many," it goes on to criticize the show. Therefore the best answer is (D).

**18. J** As written, the sentence has a misplaced comma after the word "material." This eliminates choice F. Since the word "serious" is modifying the word "literary," we don't want a comma between the two words. This eliminates choices (G) and (H), leaving us with (J).

**19. C** "So rising a promising stage director" doesn't make much sense in the sentence as written, so we can eliminate (A). Likewise, "On the promising rise" in choice (D) is unclear. Deciding between (B) and (C) is difficult—if you're not sure, take your best guess. If you read carefully, you can see that (B) doesn't quite work, because it's missing a subject —we'd need to insert "who" before the word "seemed" to make it work.

**20. G** Remember when we told you that the non-underlined portion is always perfect and you can use it to guide you in your decisions about the answer choices? Well, this is a great example of that. Because "Martian" is an adjective here, it needs to have "invasion" after it (a noun) or nothing makes sense.

**21. D** *He?* He, *who?* That's what should go through your mind every time you see a pronoun. In this case, you can't answer the question "He, who?" because it could be Wells, and it could be Welles. So, (A) and (C) are out the door. (B) is doomed for using a plural to refer to a singular (but you knew that already), so (D) is the lucky winner this time.

**22. F** The sentence before the semicolon and the sentence after the semicolon are complete sentences, so we need STOP punctuation here. This eliminates (G), (H), and (J).

**23. A** In this case, the broadcast started at a point in time in the past. Therefore (A) is the best choice.

**24. G** The key phrase in this question is "specific detail to convey the panic." We need to look for a choice that gives a specific case of panic. As written, the sentence doesn't give a specific detail, so we should eliminate (F). Likewise, choice (H) can also be crossed off. Choice (J) states that people jumped to a conclusion, but not that they were panicked.

**25. A** The comma and conjunction separate two complete statements so STOP punctuation is needed. (B) and (C) are GO punctuation and (D) places the comma in the wrong place. That leaves us with (A).

**26. J** The sentence, as written, tries to do too much. For this reason we can eliminate (F). Choices (G) and (H) are properly formed, but they add a new idea that doesn't fit with the rest of the paragraph—namely, what is true of other cultures. Therefore the best option is to leave off this unnecessary information and simply end the sentence.

**27. A** The proper idiom is "fooled by."

**28. G** We don't need a possessive in this sentence, so choices (H) and (J) can be eliminated. Further, the part of the sentence that begins with "while..." is not a complete sentence, so we need to use GO punctuation. For this reason we can eliminate (F).

**29. A** The rest of the sentence is in the past tense, with verbs like "did not" and "continued." Therefore we need a verb in past tense. This makes (A) the best choice.

**30. H** The key idea in this question is "places the response…in a larger context of other stories of alien invasion." This means that the correct answer must mention other similar stories. Only choice (H) does this.

**31. B** Since the underlined portion follows the preposition "between," we need to use an object pronoun ("me") and not a subject pronoun ("I"). For this reason we can eliminate choice (A). Choices (C) and (D) introduce a new verb at the end of the sentence just before the period, which makes the sentence incomplete. This makes (B) the best choice.

**32. H** The rest of the sentence doesn't really have anything to do with being "thoughtful," which means being nice or considerate. For this reason we can eliminate (F), (G), and (J).

**33. D** The rest of the sentence is in the past tense, so we want a past tense verb. This makes (D) the best choice. Unless there's a specific reason to change tenses, keep verbs in the same tense.

**34. G** In this case, the time at which the author expected things to be a certain way was before the time at which the author found out that things were different, so we should use the past perfect in this case. (Remember: use the past perfect to describe something that happens before another past event.) This makes (G) the best choice.

**35. C** This question asks us to link this paragraph to the following paragraph. The following paragraph is about how the author's brother changed his mind, and decided to become a doctor instead of a writer or professor. The only sentence that discusses the possibility of the author's brother becoming a doctor is choice (C).

**36. J** The other verbs in this sentence are in the past tense ("told" and "wanted") so we should use a past tense verb here. This makes (J) the best choice. Don't forget that "of" in choice (G) is slang, and not standard English.

**37. C** Sometimes quotation marks are used not only to show a direct quotation, but also to express doubt about the accuracy or truth of a statement. This is supported by the author's slightly sarcastic tone in this paragraph. Therefore both II and III are correct, so (C) becomes our answer.

**38. F** The two sentences on either side of this punctuation mark can stand alone, so we need STOP punctuation. Therefore we can eliminate (H) and (J). Choice (G) doesn't make much sense, so the best answer is (F).

**39. C** Since there are only two people in the story, the author and his brother, and the author says that his brother was getting A's, it must be the author who was getting a B+. This means that the pronoun in the underlined portion should be "I." Therefore (C) must be the answer.

**40. H** As written, the sentence has an awkward passive construction. Therefore we can eliminate (F). The word "it" in (G) is ambiguous, so it can also be eliminated. (J) is also awkward.

**41. C** As written, the comma before "to" is misplaced, so we can eliminate (A) and (B). Since the phrase that begins with "smuggling" and ends with "awake" is purely descriptive and could be removed without affecting the sentence, we will need a comma after the word "awake." This means that we can also eliminate (D). This makes (C) our best answer.

**42. J** The author's brother should be compared with other pre-meds in this sentence, which is not possible by putting "Including my brother" at the beginning of the sentence. For this reason, we can eliminate (F). In choice (G) the word "soon" is misplaced, and in choice (H) the words "grade point average" are repeated, making it extremely wordy. Therefore the best answer is (J).

**43. B** Sentences 1, 2, and 3 talk about the author's schoolwork. Sentences 4–7 talk about the author's work experience. Since the sentences before number 4 are about one topic, and the sentences after number 4 are about another topic, the most logical place to split the paragraph would be at Sentence 4. This makes (B) the best answer.

**44. G** The key words in this question are "perspective gained by experience." So we need to pick a choice that shows the benefits of experience. Only choice (G) discusses the author's experience and what was gained by it.

**45. C** The sentence as written is missing a subject, so we can eliminate (A). Choice (B) also leaves out the subject, so we can eliminate it as well. Between (C) and (D) the choice is one of verb tense. In this case, the point at which we left Chicago was "many hours before," so we're talking about a past event that came before another past event. Therefore we should use the past perfect, which is (C).

**46. J** The phrase "embarking on a great adventure" is a verb and its object, and should not be interrupted by a comma. For this reason we can eliminate (G) and (H). Further, a comma should not precede the word "that," so choice (F) can also be crossed off. This makes (J) our choice.

**47. C** It's rare that the ACT uses the word "being" correctly, and this isn't one of those cases. Choice (A) is also very wordy, so we should eliminate it. In (B) it's unclear what "having thick accents" modifies, so we can eliminate it as well. If you've got a choice between (C) and (D), you've done very well. In fact, (D) is not quite correct, since "everyone" is singular, but is used here as if it were plural. This makes (C) the best choice.

**48. F** Without a conjunction we're going to have a difficult time making a good sentence. If we have nothing at all, as in choice (H), we get a run-on sentence. If we simply put a comma, as in (J), we get two independent sentences spliced together. This means we can eliminate (H) and (J). Starting a sentence with "and" is a bit clumsy, so we should avoid (G). Our best choice is (F).

**49. D** Since there is no contrast described in this sentence, contrasting words such as "despite" and "nevertheless" don't make any sense. Therefore we can eliminate (A) and (C). Moreover, to use "in addition" we need something mentioned in the first place to which we are adding something else. But there is no such thing mentioned in the paragraph. For this reason we can eliminate (B), and our answer should be (D).

**50. F** The previous sentence gives a list of events, which ends with piling everything into the car. None of the other choices would make sense at the beginning of this sentence.

**51. D** Choices (A), (B), and (C) all have misplaced modifiers. The sentence as written makes it sound as if the writer's apprehension was watching the house. This doesn't make sense, so we can eliminate (A). Likewise, in choice (B) the sentence seems to say that it was the apprehension that was "in the distance." Finally, choice (C) says that the author watched "in the distance," when it was really the house and neighborhood that were distant. Therefore our best choice is (D).

**52. J** If we try to put the word "seeming" at the beginning of this sentence, the sentence becomes incomplete. So we can eliminate (G) and (H). Now the only question is: Should we combine paragraphs 3 and 4? We should, since paragraph 3 is extremely short, and paragraph 4 continues the idea started in paragraph 3. This makes (J) the best answer.

**53. C** The sentence as written is extremely wordy. If we can say it in a more concise way, we should. Likewise, choice (D) is also wordy. Choice (B) makes the sentence incomplete, so (C) is the best choice.

**54. F** The key idea in this question is "show she was serious." So we need to look for a choice that shows the author's seriousness about leaving the new house. Only choice (F) really shows the author doing something that makes it look like she is leaving.

**55. B** The phrase "as the first grade was called" is describing the name "P–1." Therefore this phrase needs to be set off by commas, one on each side. Choices (C) and (D) are each missing one comma, and (A) places the first comma in the wrong place, so our answer must be (B).

**56. G** Paragraph 5 discusses how the author gets used to life in Ireland. Paragraph 6 suddenly begins with her return to the US. To make the transition smoother, we need a sentence that discusses her leaving Ireland and returning to the US. Therefore (G) is the best choice.

**57. C** In the sentence as written, "one at a time" doesn't make sense, since it isn't clear what might be going one at a time. Since the author is discussing her feelings at the moment when she returned to the US, choices like (B) or (D) don't quite fit, since each of these discusses something that happens over time. This makes (C) our best choice.

**58. H** The key idea in this question is "personal relationships among the writer's family." The passage, in fact, does not mention personal relationships: It talks about the author's feelings when she moves from the US to Ireland. Only one sentence mentions the feelings or views of any other family members. This makes (H) the best answer.

**59. C** Putting this sentence at the beginning of paragraph 4 would not make sense, since paragraph 4 discusses the author's difficulty in adjusting to a new home. Nor would it make sense in paragraph 6, where the author returns to the US. Therefore we can eliminate (A) and (D). The sentence best fits in paragraph 5, but it would not work well next to the current first sentence of paragraph 5. Therefore the best answer is (C).

**60. H** The key idea in this question is "without a care in the world." What kind of word best describes this? Something lighthearted and carefree, like skipping. This makes (H) the best choice.

**61. B** In this sentence the author is expressing a contrast between what the others said and what he knew. Therefore we need a contrasting word like "but." This makes (B) the best choice.

**62. H** In the rest of the sentence, the author uses the pronoun "you" in an impersonal sense. To be consistent, the word "you" should be used throughout the sentence. This makes (H) the best choice.

**63. A** This is a great example for POE. While there may be no immediately obvious reason to pick (A), it's clearly better than the rest, which don't make sense in this sentence.

**64. G** Choice (J) leaves an incomplete sentence, so we can eliminate it. We can't use a semicolon, as in choice (H), because a semicolon requires that a complete phrase follow it. Since the sentence means to introduce a list of customers, our best choice is a colon, choice (G).

**65. D** In this case, the fact that the boy was the same age as the author's sister isn't relevant to the paragraph. So we can eliminate it, and make the paragraph clearer. This makes (D) the best answer.

**66. H** In this case, we need the possessive pronoun "their," since the sentence is talking about the behavior of the two boys.

**67. A** In the sentence as written, "barely able to remember whose order I had taken" is used to describe the word "man." No conjunction is needed, so (A) is correct.

**68. F** In this case, we need to preserve parallel construction; since the rest of the sentence uses "demanding" and "complaining," we need to use "needing" in the underlined portion. This will eliminate (G) and (J). Choice (H) is awkward, so (F) is our best choice.

**69. D** The correct idiom is to "demand something," not to demand *about*, *of*, or *for* something.

**70. G** Since the sentence already has the word "but" in it, we don't need another conjunction. This eliminates (F) and (H). Choice (J) leaves the sentence incomplete, so (G) is our answer.

**71. A** "Three years of experience" is correct as written.

**72. H** It would make more sense if the sentences that mention the manager's questions were kept together: namely, Sentences 3 and 5. This would be accomplished if the positions of Sentences 4 and 5 were reversed.

**73. C** The author's tone in this essay is generally lighthearted and humorous. Choices (A), (B), and (D) are much more serious than the rest of the passage warrants. This makes (C) our best choice.

**74. J** This sentence introduces irrelevant information and should not be included in the passage.

**75. A** The key idea in this question is "description of an employment experience." Describe an employment experience is exactly what the author does. The application process and the fact that the author was fired are irrelevant to the description of the experience.

# MATH SECTION

**1. A** To solve for $x$, we should subtract 2 from each side to get

$$4x = 18$$

Now we divide each side by 4, which gives us

$$x = \frac{18}{4}$$

So $x = 4.5$, which is choice (A).

**2. K** The easiest way to solve this problem is to draw a number line. If you draw out the line and put point $M$ at 9 and point $N$ at –5, you can simply count the points between the two. Alternately, you can subtract –5 from 9: $9 - (-5) = 14$.

**3. B** This is a great example of when you should use Plugging In. If we say the store sold two hats and three shirts, they would make $40, $x = 2$ and $y = 3$, $2 \times 5 = 10$ and $3 \times 10 = 30$, $10 + 30 = 40$. Plug two and three into the answer choices to see which one gives you $40. Plug them into (B) and you get $5(2) + 10(3) = 40$. That's what we were looking for, so B is the answer.

**4. K** This is an example of the contrapositive rule. If you ever have a statement "If A, then B" what you know to be true is "If B doesn't happen, then A doesn't happen either." In this case, if we know that $y$ is NOT equal to 4, then we know that $x$ is NOT greater than 5. This is what choice (K) says.

**5. A** Let's try Plugging In the answer choices and see which one works, starting with choice (C). If Alice began with 24 marbles and she gave away $\frac{2}{3}$ of them, that would leave her with 8. According to the question she still needs to give $\frac{1}{3}$ away and end up with 8, so we need a larger number. Let's plug in choice (B). If Alice began with 30 marbles and gave $\frac{2}{3}$ of them away, that would leave her with 10. If she then

gave away $\frac{1}{3}$, she would be left with a fraction, which is not an option. Therefore, we can eliminate (B). If she started with 36 marbles, choice (A), and gave away $\frac{2}{3}$ she would have 12 left. If she then gave away $\frac{1}{3}$, she would be left with 8, which is the answer. Our answer is (A).

**6. H** We know that $a$ is equal to $4y + 2z$, and we know that $b$ is equal to $z - y$, so to figure out the value of $a + b$ we can substitute $4y + 2z$ for $a$, and substitute $z - y$ for $b$. So $a + b = (4y + 2z) + (z - y)$. This becomes $4y + 2z + z - y$, which is equal to $3y + 3z$. The choice that says this is (H).

**7. C** To find the average, we add up the numbers to get the sum total: $56 + 47 + 43 + 55 + 64 = 265$. Now we divide by the number of days, which is 5, and get $\frac{265}{5} = 53$. Therefore the answer is (C).

**8. G** The problem tells us that $x = -2$, so we can replace every value of $x$ with –2 to solve. This means that $x^2 + 3x + 15$ will be equal to $(-2)^2 + 3(-2) + 15$, which is equal to $4 - 6 + 15$, or 13. The answer choice that says 13 is (G).

**9. A** To solve this problem, we start by figuring out 8% of 45,000. What is 8% of 45,000? We can write this as $\frac{8}{100} \times 45,000$. Put this into your calculator and you will get 3,600. This is the amount of increase in the population of Greenville. The new population will be 45,000 + 3,600, which is 48,600. Which choice says this? (A) does.

**10. F** In this figure we know that $\overline{AD}$ and $\overline{EG}$ are parallel, so on any line that crosses them, all of the small angles will have the same measure and all of the big angles will have the same measure. Since the angle just below angle $x$ is on the same line, angle $x$ must also be equal to 20 degrees. This makes (F) the answer.

**11. B** If we multiply $(x + y)(x + z)$, we get $x^2 + xz + yx + yz$. Now we need to figure out which answer choice is equivalent to this. Factoring out $x$ in the middle terms, we get $x^2 + x(y + z) + yz$, so (B) is our answer.

**12. G** In similar triangles, all sides are proportional to each other. We can figure out the ratio of the sides of the triangles by comparing their perimeters. The triangle with sides 4, 6, and 10 has a perimeter of $4 + 6 + 10$, which is 20. So the other triangle must be exactly twice its size, and have sides 8, 12, and 20. The question asks for the longest side of the triangle, which is 20. This makes (G) the answer.

**13. D** Don't forget to take the absolute value of each term before multiplying! The left term is the absolute value of $2 - 4$, which is 2. The right term is the absolute value of $-2$, which is also 2. Now we multiply 2 times 2 to get 4. This makes (D) the answer.

**14. K** The number of different outfits will be the product of the number of things John has to choose from. John can choose from 6 shirts, 4 pants, and 8 pairs of socks, so the number of possible outfits will be $6 \times 4 \times 8$, which is 192. This makes (K) the answer.

**15. E** This question gives us the formula $V = \pi r^2 h$, and then gives us the values for $r$ and $h$. In this case $r = 3$ and $h = 5$, so if we put these values into the formula we get $V = \pi \times 3^2 \times 5$, or $V = 45\pi$. Since $\pi$ is about 3.14, the volume is about 141 cubic inches.

**16. F** To see which function will have the largest value, plug $-10$ in for $x$ in each of the functions, and solve. Choice (F) becomes $-10^2 - 2(-10)$, which equals $100 + 20$, or 120. Choice (G) becomes $-10^2 + 2(-10)$, which equals $120 + -20 = 80$. Choice (H) becomes $-10^2 = 100$. Choice (J) becomes $-1000 - 100$, which equals $-1100$. Choice (K) becomes $-10^0$, which equals 1. Therefore the answer is (F).

**17. C** If we translate this into math, we get $50 = \frac{20}{100}x$. Now we can reduce $\frac{20}{100}$ to $\frac{1}{5}$, and we can solve for $x$:

$\frac{5}{1} \times 50 = x$, so $x = 250$. This makes (C) the answer.

**18. J** For the 24-minute phone call, the first minute will cost 15 cents, and the other 23 minutes will cost 3 cents each. So the total cost of the call will be $15 + (3 \times 23)$. This makes a total of 84 cents. Which choice says this? (J) does.

**19. B** To solve the slope, we take $\frac{rise}{run}$. The rise from 3 to 2 is a rise of $-1$; the run from $-1$ to 1 is a run of 2. This makes the slope $-\frac{1}{2}$, or choice (B).

**20. K** A line will intersect the $x$-axis when the $y$ coordinate equals zero. $x = -1$ is the only condition under which $y = 0$. Therefore the graph will intersect the $x$-axis only once. This makes (K) the answer.

**21. E** Be very careful when you simplify a fraction that has addition and subtraction in it. The safest way to reduce this is to remove a factor of 3 from the top of the fraction:

$\dfrac{3x+9y}{6z}$ becomes $\dfrac{3(x+3y)}{6z}$. Now we can safely reduce top and bottom by a factor of 3, and we get

$\dfrac{x+3y}{2z}$. This makes (E) the best choice.

**22. F** To make our work easier, let's just take one point on the figure and work with it first. We know that one of the corners of *BCDE* has coordinates (−4,−2). If we translate this point left 5 units, it will take us to (−9,−2). If we then translate it up one unit the new coordinate will be (−9,−1). So the correct answer must contain this point. The only answer that does is (F).

**23. B** We can find the slope of the line $2y = 10 - 3x$ by first putting it into standard form: First, we rewrite it as $2y = -3x + 10$, then we divide each term by 2, which gives us $y = -\dfrac{3}{2}x + 5$. Whenever you have an equation in the form $y = mx + b$, you know that *m* is the slope, so the slope of this line is $-\dfrac{3}{2}$. But the question asks for the slope of the line that is *perpendicular* to this line. The slope of perpendicular lines are the negative reciprocals, so the slope of the line perpendicular to the line $y = -\dfrac{3}{2}x + 5$ will have a slope of $\dfrac{2}{3}$. Therefore, the answer is (B).

**24. F** One way to solve this problem is by factoring the equation. Another way to solve it is by plugging in the answer choices. Let's start by plugging in 4; it appears in two answer choices, so POE will be faster. $4^2 + 4(4) = 32$, not 12. Since 4 doesn't work, we can eliminate (H) and (J). Now let's try 6: $6^2 + 4(6)$ is much bigger than 12, so we can eliminate (G) and (K). We could check (F), but since the other four choices don't work, (F) must be correct.

**25. D** To solve this question let's set up a proportion:

$\dfrac{\text{cups juice}}{\text{quarts lemonade}} \dfrac{3\frac{1}{2}}{4} = \dfrac{x}{10}$. Now we can solve for *x*, and get that $x = \dfrac{35}{4}$, or $8\dfrac{3}{4}$. Therefore the answer is (D).

**26. G** To figure out the hypotenuse of a right triangle, we can use the Pythagorean Theorem, but we can take a shortcut. Remember: the 3:4:5 ratio. Since this is a ratio, any multiples of these numbers also work. 12:16:? is a multiple of 3:4:5, with each term increased by a factor of 4. So the hypotenuse must measure 20 inches.

**27. C** One of the safest ways to solve this problem is to try each answer choice, and see if we can figure out which of them could be multiplied by something else to get $8x^2 + 22x - 6$. Let's start with (A). What could we multiply $(4x - 3)$ by in order to get $8x^2 + 22x - 6$? We would need to multiply it by $(2x + 2)$ in order to get an $8x^2$ term and a $-6$ term, but if we multiply $(4x - 3)(2x + 2)$ then our middle term becomes $2x$, not $22x$. So we can eliminate (A). How about (B)? If we were to use $(4x + 3)$ then we'd need to multiply it by $(2x - 2)$ to get an $8x^2$ term and a $-6$ term. But if we multiply $(4x + 3)(2x - 2)$ then the middle term becomes $-2x$, not $22x$. So we should cross off (B). Now let's try (C). If we were to use $(8x - 2)$ then we'd need to multiply it by $(x + 3)$ to get an $8x^2$ term and a $-6$ term. When we multiply $(8x - 2)(x + 3)$ then the middle term becomes $22x$, exactly as we want. So (C) is our answer.

**28. G** Let's start by solving for $x$ in the inequality $2(3x + 4) < 20$. If we multiply out the left side, we get $6x + 8 < 20$. Now let's subtract 8 from each side, and we get $6x < 12$. By dividing each side by 6, we can see that $x < 2$. This makes (G) the best answer.

**29. A** To solve this question, we need to remember our rules of exponents. Since $\left(x^y\right)^z$ is the same as $x^{y \times z}$, we know that $\left(x^{a+1}\right)^3 = x^{3a+3}$. So we can set the exponents equal to each other: $3a + 3 = 9$. Solving this gives us $a = 2$, and our answer is (A).

**30. J** To find the cosine of an angle, we solve $\dfrac{adjacent}{hypotenuse}$. In this triangle, the adjacent side is $2\sqrt{5}$ (use the Pythagorean Theorem), and the hypotenuse is 6, so the cosine is $\dfrac{\sqrt{5}}{3}$. This makes our answer (J).

**31. B** You don't have to write out the equation yourself to solve this problem; we can simply use POE. We know the question says "the cube of $y$" which means $y^3$. So we can eliminate whichever choices don't contain this, namely (C) and (D). Further, the problem asks for the "square of $z$" which is $z^2$. Choice (E) doesn't contain this, so we can cross it off. This leaves us with (A) and (B). The only difference between the two is whether $y^3$ is on the top or on the bottom. The question states that $x$ should vary as the cube of $y$ and inversely as the square of $z$, so we know that $y^3$ must go on top and $z^2$ on the bottom. This makes our answer (B).

**32. F** Whenever we have a problem with $i$ in it, all we need to do is replace every $i^2$ with $-1$. If we do this with $3i^2 + i^4$ we get $3(-1) + (-1)(-1)$. Multiply this out, and it becomes $-3 + 1$, which equals $-2$. This makes (F) the best answer.

**33. E** The problem tells us that the triangle is equilateral, and that side $\overline{BD}$ is 8 units long. Since triangle $ABD$ is a right triangle, we know that this is a 30-60-90 right triangle, and that the ratio of its sides must be $x : x\sqrt{3} : 2x$. We know the $x\sqrt{3}$ side, which is 8. So to solve for the $x$ and $2x$ sides, we should solve for $x$. We know that $x\sqrt{3} = 8$; if we solve for $x$ we see that $x = \dfrac{8}{\sqrt{3}}$. This means that $\overline{AD}$ is equal to $\dfrac{8}{\sqrt{3}}$, and that side $\overline{AB}$ is equal to twice that, or $\dfrac{16}{\sqrt{3}}$. It's not good form to leave a root symbol in the denominator of a fraction, so we can rewrite $\dfrac{16}{\sqrt{3}}$ by multiplying it by $\dfrac{\sqrt{3}}{\sqrt{3}}$ to get $\dfrac{16\sqrt{3}}{3}$. As the triangle $ABD$ is equilateral, sides $\overline{BC}$ and $\overline{AC}$ must also be equal to $\dfrac{16\sqrt{3}}{3}$. Therefore the perimeter is equal to $3 \times \dfrac{16\sqrt{3}}{3}$ or $16\sqrt{3}$. Therefore our answer is (E).

**34. F** Remember the third side rule for triangles? The rule: Any two sides of a triangle have a sum that is larger than the third side. So if a triangle has sides 4 and 7.5, then the third side plus the side that measures 4 must have a sum larger than 7.5. This means that the third side must be larger than 3.5 inches. So 3.5 inches is NOT a possible length of the third side. This makes (F) our answer. (Don't forget, we were looking for the one that did NOT work this time!)

**35. E** Angle A is a right angle. Therefore, when it is bisected by $\overline{AC}$, it is split into two 45-degree angles. Now, in triangle $ABC$, we have one angle that measures 40 and one angle that measures 45, so the third angle, angle $BCA$, must measure 95 degrees. This makes (E) our answer.

**36. J** One way to figure out whether a point is on a line is to substitute the $x$-coordinate for $x$, and the $y$-coordinate for $y$ in the equation, and see whether the equation is true. Let's try this with (F). If we substitute 0 for $x$ and 2 for $y$, is the equation true? Is $2 = \dfrac{1}{2}(0) - 2$? No, so we can eliminate (F). How about (G)? If we substitute 1 for $x$ and 3 for $y$, is the equation true? Is $3 = \dfrac{1}{2}(1) - 2$? No, so we can eliminate (G). How about (H)? If we substitute 2 for $x$ and 4 for $y$, is the equation true? Is $4 = \dfrac{1}{2}(2) - 2$?

No, so we can eliminate (H). Let's look at (J) now. If we substitute 2 for $x$ and $-1$ for $y$, is the equation true? Is $-1 = \frac{1}{2}(2) - 2$? Yes, so (J) is the answer.

**37. B**  In this picture, since triangles *ACE* and *BCD* share angle C, and since $\overline{BD}$ and $\overline{AE}$ are parallel, we know that these two triangles are similar. This tells us that their sides will be proportional to each other: $\frac{CD}{CE} = \frac{BD}{AE}$. Substituting in the numbers we know, we get $\frac{4}{6} = \frac{6}{x}$. When we solve for $x$, we find that $\overline{AE}$ must equal 9. This makes (B) our answer.

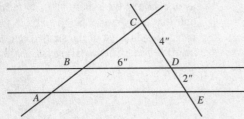

**38. K**  This is a right triangle, so the Pythagorean Theorem will tell us the relationship of the lengths of the sides. This means that, if we use $x$ for the length of $\overline{AC}$, $8^2 + x^2 = 17^2$. We can transform this into $x^2 = 17^2 - 8^2$. By taking the square root of each side we can solve for $x = \sqrt{17^2 - 8^2}$. This makes (K) our answer.

**39. D**  Since the basic equation for a circle is $x^2 + y^2 = r^2$, and we know that the radius is 5, the correct formula must have a 25 in it. This will allow us to eliminate (A), (B), and (C). To choose between (D) and (E), let's look at one of the points that we know is on the circle. If the circle has a center $(-4, 3)$ and a radius of 5, then one of the points of the circle will be at $(-4, 8)$, since this point is at a distance of 5 units from the center. If we plug in $-4$ for $x$ and 8 for $y$, which of these equations is true? (D) says $(-4 + 4)^2 + (8 - 3)^2 = 25$, which is true. Therefore (D) is the answer.

**40. H**  We know that the sine is the same thing as $\frac{opposite}{hypotenuse}$ and that tangent is the same as $\frac{opposite}{adjacent}$, so now we know that the opposite side to angle $\theta$ must be 9, the adjacent side must be 40, and the hypotenuse must be 41.

Since cosine is the same as $\frac{adjacent}{hypotenuse}$, we know that the cosine must be $\frac{40}{41}$. Therefore our answer is (H).

**41. C** Since the left side of the figure has a length of 19, and all of the angles are right angles, we know that the sum of the sides that make up the right side of the figure must also have a length of 19. Likewise, since the length of the top of the figure is 12, we know that the sum of the sides that make up the bottom of the figure must also have a sum of 12. Therefore the perimeter will be 19 + 19 +12 + 12 = 62 feet. The answer is (C).

**42. J** Normally two different equations will graph two different lines; however, if the two equations are two versions of the same equation, then they will define a single line. If $b = 9$, then the second equation is the same as the first: $9x + 12y = 45$ is the same equation, simply multiplied by a factor of 3, as the equation $3x + 4y = 15$. This makes (J) the answer.

**43. D** We know that triangle $ACD$ is a 30-60-90 right triangle, because it has a right angle and one angle of 30 degrees. We also know that the hypotenuse in a 30-60-90 right triangle will be twice the shorter leg. So the hypotenuse $\overline{AC}$ will measure 12 inches. The problem states that triangle $ABC$ is isosceles, so since $\overline{AC}$ will measure 12 inches, then $\overline{AB}$ will also measure 12 inches. We know that triangle ABC is a 45-45-90 triangle, since it is a right isosceles triangle, and we know that the ratio of the sides of a 45-45-90 right triangle are $x:x:x\sqrt{2}$. This means that the sides must be $12 : 12 : 12\sqrt{2}$. Therefore our answer is (D).

**44. K** This is a good example of a question for which you should try plugging in the answer choices. Start in the middle with (H); suppose that the width of the rectangle is 6. The problem says that the length is two feet less than 4 times the width, so if the width is 6, the length will be 22. Does 22 times 6 make 240? No, it's much smaller, so we can eliminate (H). Now we should try choice (J). If the width is 7, then the length will be 2 less than 4 times 7, or 26. Does 26 times 7 equal 240? No, it's still too small. So let's try (K). If the width is 8, then the length will be 2 less than 4 times 8, or 30. Does 30 times 8 equal 240? Yes, so (K) is our answer.

**45. E** The easiest way to solve this problem is to draw it. Start by drawing draw a circle with center (−1,2) and the point (−6,5).

Now let's draw the lines that would get us from the center to the point (−6,5). To get there we go left 5 units and up 3 units. So to find the opposing point, we start from the center, and go right 5 units and down 2 units. This takes us to the point (4,−1). This makes (E) the answer.

**46. K** To solve this problem we need to remember that $x^2 - y^2$ can also be expressed as $(x + y)(x - y)$. We know that $(x + y) = -3$ and that $(x - y) = -4$, so $(x + y)(x - y)$ will be equal to $(-3)(-4)$, or 12. Therefore (K) is our answer.

**47. B** To find the area of the shaded region, we need to take the area of the square and subtract the area of the circle. The area of the square will be length times width. Since the length and width are both 10, the area of the square will be $10^2$. The area of the circle will be $\pi r^2$, and since the circle's diameter is the same length as one side of the square (10), its radius will be half that length, or 5. So the area of the circle is $5^2\pi$. So the area of the shaded region will be $10^2 - 5^2\pi$. Choice (B) says this, and is our answer.

**48.  J**   We can break up this figure into other figures we know. The center of the figure is a rectangle, with length 16cm and height 12 cm. We know the height is 12, because it is the third side of a right triangle with hypotenuse 13 and one leg 5: This is one of our 5:12:13 Pythagorean triples.  So the area of this part of the figure is $12 \times 16$, or 192.  Now all we need to do is add the areas of the two triangles on the ends. Each of them has height 12 and base 5, so each of them has an area of 30, because the area of a triangle is $\frac{1}{2}$base $\times$ height. 192 + 30 + 30 = 252, which is choice (J).

**49.  C**   First let's draw the figure. If we draw a line from her ending point to her starting point, we get the hypotenuse of a right triangle with base 80 and height 60. This means that the shortest path (the hypotenuse of the triangle) is 100 feet. (Remember your 6:8:10 Pythagorean triple?)  Going the long way, Miko actually walked 20 + 70 + 60 + 10, or 160 feet. Therefore the shortest path, which would have been 100 feet, is 60 feet shorter. Therefore the answer is (C).

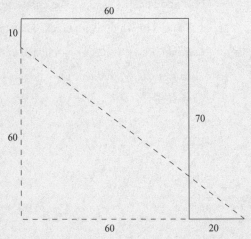

**50.  H**   If $\log_x 64 = 2$, then we know that $x^2 = 64$. Which value for $x$ makes this true?  $8^2 = 64$, so (H) is our answer.

**51.  A**   For $\dfrac{x}{x^2 - 7}$ to be undefined, the denominator must be zero. This means that $x^2 - 7 = 0$, and that $x^2 = 7$.  Now we can solve for $x = \sqrt{7}$.

Therefore the value of $x^3 - 7x$ will be equal to $7\sqrt{7} - 7\sqrt{7}$, or zero. This makes (A) our answer.

**52.  H**   Let's plug in on this problem. What would be an easy number to plug in for $n$? Any small round number will do. Let's try plugging in 10 for $n$.  If Bob drives 3 miles in 10 minutes, how long will it take him to drive 14 miles?

We can set up a proportion: $\dfrac{3}{10} = \dfrac{14}{x}$. Solving for $x$, we get $\dfrac{140}{3}$. Which choice also says this? Remembering that $n$ is 10, choice (H) also reads $\dfrac{140}{3}$.

**53.  B**   Let's try a few sample points to see which will satisfy the inequality $|x| \geq 5$. If the $x$-coordinate is 6, 7, or 8, that will satisfy the inequality. −6, −7, or −8 will also satisfy the inequality.  It isn't satisfied if the $x$-coordinate is −3, −2, −1, 0, 1, 2, or 3.  This is what graph (B) shows.

**54.  H**   Plugging in is a great way to solve this one. What if we try $x = 2$?  Choice (F) becomes 4, choice (G) becomes 12, choice (H) becomes 9, choice (J) becomes 13, and choice (K) becomes 20. (F), (G), and (K) are even numbers in this case, so we can eliminate them. Now let's try $x = 3$.  In this case, choice (H) becomes 19, and choice (J) becomes 28. Since (J) is an even number, we can eliminate it. The only choice that is always an odd integer is (H).

**55. D** The way to think about this question is to ask which of the answers could be plugged in for $k$ and would allow the equation to be factored with one value of $x$. Let's start with choice (C), and plug in 12 for $k$. Can we factor $x^2 - 12x + 12 = 0$? If it doesn't seem like it can be done, let's move on. How about choice (D)? Let's try assuming that $k$ is 36. Now let's factor $x^2 - 12x + 36 = 0$. We can factor it as $(x - 6)(x - 6) = 0$, which leaves only one possible value for $x$, which is $x = 6$. Therefore (D) is our answer.

**56. G** Since $AE = \frac{1}{2} BE$ and the hypotenuse of $AEB$ is $\sqrt{5}$, we can figure out the lengths of $AE$ and $BE$. The Pythagorean Theorem tells us that $(AE)^2 + (BE)^2 = \sqrt{5}^2$. Since $AE = \frac{1}{2} BE$, we can replace $AE$ in the equation by $\frac{1}{2} BE$, and get $\left(\frac{1}{2} BE\right)^2 + (BE)^2 = \sqrt{5}^2$. If we solve for $BE$, we get that $BE = 2$. Now to find the area of the parallelogram, we take the base (7) times the height (2), which gives us 14, or choice (G).

**57. A** Remember that the tangent of an angle is equal to $\frac{\text{opposite}}{\text{adjacent}}$. In this case, we can say that the $\tan 29 = \frac{\text{height of pole}}{40}$. So now we can solve for the height of the pole, which will be equal to $40 \times \tan 29$. This makes (A) the best answer.

**58. F** The maximum value of the function $\sin \theta$ is 1. Even if we ask for $\sin 2\theta$, the maximum value is still 1. Therefore the maximum value will be $y = -1 + 4(1)$, which is 3.

**59. D** If the average of 6 integers is 65, then we can solve for their total, which must be $6 \times 65$, or 390. If an average of 7 integers is 66, we can solve for their total, which must be $7 \times 66$, or 462. The difference between these two totals is 72, which must be the value of the seventh number.

**60. H** This probability problem has two steps. When Jamie pulls out the first sock, there are a total of 28 socks to choose from, 10 of which are black. When she pulls out a black sock on the first draw, and goes back in the drawer for another sock, she will be choosing from 27 socks of which 9 are black. Thus on the second draw she has a $\frac{9}{27}$ chance of drawing a black sock. $\frac{9}{27}$ reduces to $\frac{1}{3}$, making (H) the answer.

**1. D** Let's look at how these words are used in context. On the last line of the first paragraph, Mick is wondering whether to climb the ladder, and the passage says that she *screwed up nerve and began to climb*. What word could we put in place of the words screwed up? Something like found or gathered. The choice that comes closest to this idea is (D).

**2. J** In the first paragraph, Mick does not find Mr. Singer, so (F) can be eliminated. She doesn't make breakfast for her family, so (G) can also be crossed off. While the passage says that Bubber goes to Sunday School, it doesn't say that Mick does, so (H) won't be right either. The paragraph does, however, describe how she cares for her younger brothers; this makes (J) the best choice.

**3. B** In the third sentence of the third paragraph, Mick is on top of the roof and thinks to herself this is *where everybody wanted to stand*. This supports choice (B).

**4. J** In the first paragraph we find that Mick cares for Ralph and Bubber, so they aren't her father. The first paragraph also states that her father tells Mick that Mr. Singer came in late the night before. Therefore we can eliminate (F), (G), and (H), which leaves us with (J) as our answer.

**5. A** According to the fourth paragraph, other children also climbed the roof, so we can eliminate (D). While choices (B) and (C) might be true, there isn't really any evidence in the paragraph to support them. (A) has some support, since the sixth paragraph tells us that Mick was finally somewhere *by herself. No one was around and it was quiet and she could think for a while*. This makes (A) the most plausible choice.

**6. G** This is a good example of using POE to solve a problem. There is nothing in line 31 that tells us that Mick felt she had a poor singing voice, or that she did not want to scare her brothers, so we can eliminate (F) and (J). While there is some reason from the first paragraph to believe that she was slightly afraid of climbing the ladder, we need to find an answer that has support in this particular line, which doesn't mention fear of heights. Therefore we should avoid (H) as well. Even if it's not entirely clear what (G) is saying, since we're sure that the others aren't correct, we should pick it.

**7. B** The first paragraph tells us that Mick *waited for Mister Singer a long time. All the other boarders came down...* This is evidence that Mr. Singer is a boarder in Mick's house.

**8. H** In the next-to-last paragraph of this passage, Mick dreams of inventing a tiny radio, a flying machine, and a tunnel through the earth. The passage mentions big balloons but doesn't state that Mick intends to invent them. This makes (H) the best choice.

**9. C** Toward the end of the first paragraph it states that the house was being built, and the fifth paragraph says *soon the work would all be finished*. This tells us that the house is unfinished, so our answer is (C).

**10. F** The passage doesn't mention getting good grades in school, or wanting to spend more time with parents, so choices (H) and (J) can be eliminated. Moreover, while Mick does care for her younger brothers, the passage doesn't actually state that she wants to have children of her own. This makes (G) not very promising either. In the seventh paragraph, Mick spends time thinking about what she would do when she was very famous. This makes (F) the most reasonable choice.

**11. C** This is another great example of how POE works on the ACT. From the first paragraph we know that the author thinks that television has had a negative effect on news reporting. This will allow us to eliminate (B) and (D); choice (A) states that he is defending news stations, which also can't be right. This leaves us with (C) as our best answer.

**12. J** Let's look at how this word is used in context. The sentence in question says *the world as mapped by the speeded-up electronic media has no order or meaning and is not to be taken seriously.* What word could we put in place of the word mapped? Something like described or presented. The choice that comes closest to this idea is (J).

**13. B** Let's try to eliminate what we know is wrong and work our way to the best answer. The question of live television as opposed to recorded television isn't addressed in the passage, so we can eliminate (A). The passage also does not discuss how television brings families together, so we can also eliminate (C). While the author might believe that television reporters should also write articles, he doesn't actually say that anywhere in this passage, so choice (D) can also be crossed off. There is evidence to support choice (B) on lines 30–34, so our best bet is (B).

**14. F** The point of the paragraph immediately preceding these lines is that television reporters are chosen based on how they look. Then Christine Craft is cited as an example of someone who was fired because people did not like how she looked. This makes (F) our best choice.

**15. B** The author doesn't talk about the future of newspapers, so choice (C) can be eliminated. Since the passage argues that television has significantly changed the nature of news, (D) isn't likely either. Choice (A) might be something the author thinks, but he doesn't discuss actors in these paragraphs. We can find support for (B) in the third paragraph, where he states that on television *we are presented not only with fragmented news but news without context… and therefore without essential seriousness.*

**16. J** The author doesn't really discuss the unbiased reporting of facts, or informing the public about new products. For this reason we can eliminate (F) and (H). While (G) might be tempting, nowhere does it actually state that the point of television is to make individuals popular. At the end of the third paragraph, however, the author says that television news has become *pure entertainment.* This makes (J) the best choice.

**17. A** Let's look back to the passage where the author mentions "talking hair-do's" and re-read just these lines. There the author says that television executives will *exclude women who are not beautiful or who are over the age of fifty, men who are bald, all people who are overweight or whose noses are too long…* and this best supports choice (A).

**18. H** Let's look back to the beginning of the passage. It says "Now...this" *is commonly used on radio and television newscasts to indicate that what one has just heard or seen has no relevance to what one is about to hear or see.* Answer choice (H) sounds closest to this.

**19. A** At the beginning of the last paragraph, the author claims that *the perception of the truth of a report rests heavily on the acceptability of the newscaster.* This best supports choice (A).

**20. J** In the second paragraph, the author states that *television sells its time in seconds and minutes,* that it *must use images rather than words* and that *viewers are rarely required to carry over any thought or feeling from one parcel of time to another.* Therefore choices (F), (G), and (H) are cited; the one that is not is (J).

**21. D** By reading a few lines above and a few lines below, we can get a better understanding of the context. The author mentions the *photographic motion study* to emphasize the movement being suggested in the painting. The best answer is (D).

**22. G** The first paragraph mentions students burning Brancusi in effigy and one of America's more distinguished artists, Kenyon Cox. Lines 30–31 state that Hughes was an art critic. Therefore, the answer is (G).

**23. B** Lines 11–12 state that Kenyon Cox saw modern art as the *total destruction of the art of painting.* Which choice best paraphrases this idea? (B) does.

**24. F** Lines 34–35 discuss Duchamp's painting with the words *to the degree that it looked at all like what it was supposed to be…* The author thereby implies that the painting does not, in fact, look much like a nude person at all. Therefore (F) is the best answer.

**25. C** Let's go back to the passage and re-read the word *abhorrent* in context. The lines in question compare the word abhorrent with absurd and unnatural. The word that best matches these is (C).

**26. H** According to lines 48–49, modern artists *saw themselves as articulating an ideology*, that art was not intended to be pretty but instead to be bold and challenging. The choice that best re-states this idea is (H).

**27. C** Lines 23–24 say that Roosevelt declared *in a loud voice his disapproval of all but the American entries*. Therefore we know that he did not like much of it, but did like some of it. This best supports choice (C).

**28. F** On line 17, we see that modern art was considered *perverse fantasies of the foreigner*. This implies that the artists were mostly foreign-born. The best paraphrase of this idea is (F).

**29. D** The last paragraph states that the organizers took action to encourage viewers to *greet the new art with an open mind*. This tells us that they expected people not to like the art that was displayed, which is choice (D).

**30. H** In the final paragraph, we find that some of the supporters described modern art as art that is *a sign of life. There can be no life without change, as there can be no development without change*. This means that they felt that modern art was associated with change and development. The choice that best paraphrases this idea is (H).

**31. C** The point of the first paragraph is contained in the first line: namely that great discoveries may come from very small beginnings. The choice that best paraphrases this idea is (C).

**32. F** According to the final paragraph, it was Berzelius who used the initial of the Latin name of the elements. This makes (F) the best answer.

**33. C** The author's attitude toward Dalton is generally positive, so we can eliminate choices (B) and (D). Evidence for the author's interest in Dalton can be found at the end of the first paragraph, where the author states that Dalton's work was the beginning of the *wonderful theory* of atoms. This makes (C) our best choice.

**34. G** Lines 59–60 state that Gay-Lussac was *the rising authority of the French chemical world*. Therefore the best answer is (G).

**35. A** The beginning of the fifth paragraph states that Avagadro discovered the *true explanation of Gay-Lussac's law of combination by volumes*. Even if you're not sure exactly what this says, (A) looks like a close paraphrase.

**36. H** While it's true that Berzelius improved upon Dalton's work, the last paragraph doesn't say that he disproved Dalton's view; therefore we can eliminate (F). Nor does it say that Berzelius was an influence on Avogadro and Gay-Lussac, so we can also eliminate (G). The final paragraph does say that Berzelius's discoveries were facts that *all harmonized with the atomic theory of Dalton*. This makes (H) the best choice.

**37. B** Lines 53–55 state that Dalton gives an atomic weight of 5.5 to oxygen, and lines 52–53 say that the unit of weight is based on the hydrogen atom. Therefore we know that Dalton believed oxygen to weigh 5.5 times as much as hydrogen. Choice (B) is the best paraphrase of this idea.

**38. G**   Lines 65–70 discuss Gay-Lussac's work. They
describe his discovery that gases, when kept
at constant temperature and pressure, always
combine in definite proportions as to the
volume.

**39. D**   Lines 40–45 describe Dalton's assumption.
This caused Dalton to underestimate the weight
of oxygen because he thought there was only
half as much hydrogen as there really was. This
is contradicted in lines 74–76 and 79–80. The
answer is (D).

**40. G**   On lines 80–82, the passage states that
Avogadro devised the name of the molecule.

# SCIENCE REASONING SECTION

1. **C**   If we look at Table 3, and find the entry where the length is equal to 4.0 and the cross-sectional area is equal to 2.0, we see that the change in length is 2.8. If both the length and cross-sectional area are doubled, such that the length is 8.0 and the cross-sectional area is 4.0, the change in length remains 2.8. The change in length has stayed the same so the answer is (C).

2. **J**   The passage tells us that *if the force on the bar exceeds the yield strength...permanent deformation will occur, and the bar will not resume its original shape*. Under Experiment 1, we see that aluminum returned to its original shape in all trials except the final one. This means that the yield strength is not as great as 400 but greater than 200. The only value that fits in this range is choice (J).

3. **A**   According to Table 2, we see that the Young's modulus of glass will fall somewhere between the Young's modulus of concrete (which is 30 $\times 10^9$ N / m$^2$) and that of steel (which is 200 $\times 10^9$ N / m$^2$). This means that the change in length should be somewhere between that of concrete (6.6) and that of steel (1.0). The only answer choice in this range is (A).

4. **G**   From Table 1, we can see that if the applied force increases, so does the change in length. This will allow us to eliminate (F). In Table 2, we can see that decreasing the Young's modulus is associated with an increase in the change in length. This allows us to eliminate (J). If we look at the fourth and fifth rows of Table 3, we find a case where the cross-sectional area remains constant but the length of the bar increases. The change in length also increases, so this must be due to the increasing length of the bar. Therefore we can eliminate (H). We can see from the first two rows of Table 3 that increasing cross-sectional area does not increase the change in length: instead, the change in length decreases from 0.7 to 0.4. This makes (G) our answer.

5. **A**   We don't know anything about density, so choice (B) couldn't be the correct answer. Choice (C) actually hurts the hypothesis, as it says that temperature would not affect the Young's modulus, which we know does have an effect on the change in length. Finally, while (D) is a true statement, it would not help the hypothesis that temperature would affect change in length. Therefore the best answer is (A).

6. **H**   We can tell from Table 3 that a bar 16 meters long with a 4 meter square cross section would change about 5.6 mm, and that this is double the change from a bar with the same cross-section and half the length. We can therefore infer that if we double the length to 32 meters and keep the same cross section, the bar will change about twice as much, or about 11 mm. This makes (H) the best answer.

7. **D**   If we look just at the first two rows of the table, we see that the distance between similarly sized plates doubles from 5 mm to 10 mm; at the same time the capacitance is cut in half. This makes (D) the best answer.

8. **G**   The eighth row of the table shows a 20mm distance between plates of porcelain that are 2 meters square. Its capacitance is given as 6.17 pF. The question tells us that the dielectric constant of mica is similar to that of porcelain, so its capacitance should be about the same as porcelain. This makes (G) our answer.

9. **D**   The question almost answers itself. It mentions that the plates cannot touch, and (D) is the only choice that addresses this issue.

**10. H**   If we look at the seventh and eighth rows of the table we find a case where both the area of the plates and the distance between them doubles. On these lines we see that the capacitance is, in each case, 6.17. Therefore we know that doubling the area and the distance between them have no effect on the capacitance, and (H) is our answer.

**11. C**   The fourth and fifth lines of Table 1 show a paper dielectric with a separation of 15mm and areas of 1.0 and 2.0 square meters. The question asks for the capacitance if the plates measured 1.5 square meters; this will fall somewhere between the values for the capacitance of plates with areas of 1.0 and 2.0 square meters, or between 2.07 and 4.13. The only value that falls in this range is (C).

**12. F**   From Figure 1, we can deduce that mitosis will take 15% of the time, as the other values add up to 25% + 25% + 35% = 85%. Therefore the fibroblast should spend 15% of its 24 hours in mitosis, which is 3.6 hours. This makes (F) the best choice.

**13. B**   According to Figure 2, if we look at the levels of Cyclins E, A , B, and D at the point where the letter M indicates, we see that E has dropped off to zero, D is low and steady, A is dropping off to zero, and B is coming down from its highest point. Therefore our answer is (B).

**14. H**   According to Figure 2, Cyclin D is fairly steady throughout every phase. This makes it likely that Cyclin D has the least effect on the phases.

**15. C**   According to Figure 2, the beginning of the cycle goes along with a rapid increase in Cyclin E. Cyclins A and B change only in the middle of the cycle, so they probably are not responsible for initiating the cycle. This makes (C) the best answer.

**16. F**   Figure 2 tells us that an increase in Cyclin A comes at the beginning of stage S. From Figure 1, we know that during stage S, DNA synthesis takes place. Therefore the most likely answer is that Cyclin A triggers DNA synthesis.

**17. B**   According to the first paragraph, we can figure out $K_m$ by figuring out half the maximum rate of the reaction ($V_{max}$) and then finding the corresponding substrate concentration. Since this question asks about bMAO, we need to look at Figure 2. In Figure 2 we see that the maximum value of the reaction is at approximately 100. This makes half of it equal to 50. However, 50 is not our answer—we need to find the corresponding substrate value where the reaction rate equals 50. Looking at the line that represents the use of Drug X, we see that it hits 50 where the substrate concentration is about 20. Therefore the best approximation for $K_m$ is 20.

**18. G**   Since this question asks about hMAO, we need to look at Figure 3 to find our answer. In Figure 3 we see that without Drug X, the maximum reaction rate is approximately 100. With Drug X, the maximum reaction rate is approximately 50. This means that Drug X cuts the maximum reaction rate in half. The choice that best describes this is (G).

**19. D**   The paragraphs that describe experiments 1 and 2 are very similar—they describe the same quantity of enzyme and the same method of increasing the amount of drug used. The significant difference is that Experiment 1 was performed with the enzyme bMAO while Experiment 2 was performed with the enzyme hMAO. This makes (D) the best answer.

**20. H**   According to Figure 2, the maximum value of the reaction is about the same whether Drug X is used or whether it is not used. Therefore $V_{max}$ doesn't change. This is enough to get our answer, since this will eliminate (F), (G), and (J). We can also see that the curve with Drug X is slightly shifted to the right; this means that that $K_m$ will be slightly increased. Therefore (H) is the answer.

**21. A**   Comparing Figure 2 and Figure 3 shows us that Drug X does have an effect in both cases, but the effect is much more pronounced in the case of hMAO than in bMAO. The choice that best paraphrases this is (A).

# SCIENCE REASONING SECTION

**22. F** In these experiments, the reaction rate was variable, so we can eliminate (G). The substrate concentrate was increased steadily, so we can eliminate (H). Finally, tissue homogenation is not a variable. Both experiments used 10 micrograms per milliliter of enzyme, so our best answer is (F).

**23. D** In the final sentence of Scientist 1's statement, we see *it is possible that similar bacteria could be living on present-day Mars*. Scientist 2, on the other hand, claims *any forms of Martian life...would have died out billions of years ago*. The choice that best paraphrases this difference is D.

**24. G** Scientist 2 claims that one of the reasons for the extinction of life on Mars is that the *thick Martian atmosphere, which also would have protected the planet...has long since disappeared*. If Mars had a weak magnetic field that allowed the atmosphere to erode, this would support Scientist 2's statement.

**25. C** If we re-read the statement of Scientist 3, we can find wind, volcanic activity, and liquid carbon dioxide cited as reasons for the gullies. While expansion of the planet's crust is mentioned, it is mentioned as an explanation for the appearance of a coastline, and not as an explanation for the gullies.

**26. H** Scientist 3 claims that whether water is present or not, the harsh ultraviolet radiation would prevent all life from growing on the surface of Mars. But if there were water below the surface, out of range of the ultraviolet rays, then Scientist 1's claim would be stronger. This makes (H) the best answer.

**27. B** The bacteria in the meteorite seem to show that there was, at some time in the past, life on Mars. Scientist 1 thinks that there are bacteria on Mars now that are similar to those on Earth. Therefore the meteorite helps Scientist 1's claim. Scientist 2 claims that there was once water on Mars that could have supported life; so the meteorite also supports Scientist 2's claim. Scientist 3 contends, however, that life does not exist on Mars, so the meteorite does not help Scientist 3's claim.

**28. F** Both Scientist 2 and Scientist 3 cite harmful ultraviolet radiation as a factor that would prevent life on Mars today.

**29. D** One of Scientist 3's claims is that the gullies were formed by liquid carbon dioxide, which forms at very low temperatures. It would help this claim to know that Mars never had a warm climate.

**30. G** From the opening paragraph we know that respiration at rest is called tidal volume (TV). In Figure 1, tidal volume is marked out as the region between 3.5 and 5 liters. Therefore we know that TV, and respiration at rest, is about 1.5 liters.

**31. C** This is a good case for POE. We know that restrictive lung diseases are pulmonary diseases, so we can eliminate (A). If FEV is reduced, then the ratio will certainly be smaller than 0.8, so we can eliminate (D). FEV and FVC would not be increased in a patient with lung disease, so choice (B) is out. That leaves us with (C).

**32. F** If the FEV/FVC ratio is about 0.8, this means that the top number should be about 20% less than the bottom number. Since these numbers are all around 2.5–3, a difference of 20% would be approximately 0.4–0.6. Patients 2, 3, and 4 all have FEV numbers that are approximately 0.4–0.6 less than their FVC number; however, Patient 1 has an FEV number that is more than a 1.0 difference from the FVC number. This makes (F) our answer.

**33. A** According to the table, tidal volume has no direct relationship to vital capacity, so choice (B) can be eliminated. Nor does vital capacity have any relation to total lung volume, so (C) can also be crossed off. The sum of inspiratory reserve volume and the tidal volume only makes up about half of the vital capacity, so (D) can also be eliminated. However, the residual volume is what is left over in the lung aside from vital capacity, so any increase in residual volume will decrease vital capacity. This makes (A) our answer.

**34. J** According to the passage, a build-up of fluid in the lungs is characteristic of an obstructive lung disease, which results in a reduced FEV/FVC ratio. This will eliminate (F) and (H). Emphysema will not reduce the ratio, since it is a restrictive pulmonary disease and tends to increase the FEV/FVC ratio. Therefore we can eliminate (G). This leaves us with (J) as our answer.

**35. A** This experiment begins with unpolarized light, so we need to look at Experiment 1. Table 1 shows us that the intensity of the beam at 15 degrees is 3.73 and the intensity at 30 degrees is 2.99. We know that at 20 degrees, the intensity will be between these two values. Therefore the answer is (A).

**36. J** In each of the tables, as the angle between the axes of the filters increases, the intensity decreases. Therefore we have good reason to believe that as the angle is decreased from 90 to 0 degrees, that the intensity of the resulting beam will steadily increase.

**37. B** If we look at the values of intensity on Table 3, we see that as the angle goes up, the intensity drops off consistently. In fact, it drops more rapidly as the angle gets greater. The only graph that shows a consistently dropping intensity is graph (B).

**38. G** The first line of Experiment 1 states that the scientists were using unpolarized light; the first line of Experiment 2 states that the scientists used the same setup but used polarized light. The choice that best re-states this idea is (G).

**39. C** The question tells us that the frequency of the beam determines its color, so to know whether color has any effect on the intensity of the emerging beam, we will need to try beams of different frequencies. The choice that paraphrases this idea is (C).

**40. J** It's clear from the table that the intensity decreases as the angle of axis increases, so we can eliminate (G) and (H) right away. To choose between (F) and (J) we should first look at the difference between 0 and 15 degrees. According to the table, the intensity changes from 4.00 to 3.73, a difference of 0.27. Now let's look at the difference between 15 and 30 degrees. In this case, the intensity changes from 3.73 to 2.99, a difference of 0.74. Therefore the difference isn't constant, and our answer is (J).

# SCORING YOUR PRACTICE EXAM

## STEP A

Count the number of correct answers for each section, and record the number in the space provided for your raw score on the Score Conversion Worksheet below.

## STEP B

Using the score conversion chart on page 476, convert your raw scores on each section to scaled scores. Then compute your composite ACT score by averaging the four subject scores: Add them up and divide by four.

| ACT Score | | |
|---|---|---|
| Section | Raw Score | Scaled Score |
| 1 | _____/75 | _____ |
| 2 | _____/60 | _____ |
| 3 | _____/40 | _____ |
| 4 | _____/40 | _____ |

# SCORE CONVERSION CHART

## SCALED SCORE

## RAW SCORES

| Scaled Score | English | Math | Reading | Science Reasoning |
|:---:|:---:|:---:|:---:|:---:|
| 36 | 75 | 60 | 39-40 | 40 |
| 35 | 74 | 59 | 38 | 39 |
| 34 | 72-73 | 58 | 37 | 38 |
| 33 | 71 | 57 | 36 | — |
| 32 | 70 | 55-56 | 35 | 37 |
| 31 | 69 | 53-54 | 34 | 36 |
| 30 | 67-68 | 52 | 33 | — |
| 29 | 65-66 | 50-51 | 32 | 35 |
| 28 | 62-64 | 46-49 | 30-31 | 33-34 |
| 27 | 59-61 | 43-45 | 28-29 | 31-32 |
| 26 | 57-58 | 41-42 | 27 | 30 |
| 25 | 55-56 | 39-40 | 26 | 29 |
| 24 | 52-54 | 37-38 | 25 | 28 |
| 23 | 50-51 | 35-36 | 24 | 27-26 |
| 22 | 49 | 33-34 | 23 | 25 |
| 21 | 48 | 31-32 | 21-22 | 24 |
| 20 | 45-47 | 29-30 | 20 | 23 |
| 19 | 43-44 | 27-28 | 19 | 22 |
| 18 | 40-42 | 24-26 | 18 | 20-21 |
| 17 | 38-39 | 21-23 | 17 | 18-19 |
| 16 | 35-37 | 18-20 | 16 | 16-17 |
| 15 | 32-34 | 16-17 | 15 | 15 |
| 14 | 29-31 | 13-15 | 14 | 13-14 |
| 13 | 27-28 | 11-12 | 12-13 | 12 |
| 12 | 24-26 | 9-10 | 11 | 11 |
| 11 | 21-23 | 7-8 | 9-10 | 10 |
| 10 | 18-20 | 6 | 8 | 9 |
| 9 | 15-17 | 5 | 7 | 7-8 |
| 8 | 13-14 | 4 | — | 6 |
| 7 | 11-12 | — | 6 | 5 |
| 6 | 9-10 | 3 | 5 | — |
| 5 | 7-8 | 2 | 4 | 4 |
| 4 | 5-6 | — | 3 | 3 |
| 3 | 3-4 | 1 | 2 | 2 |
| 2 | 2 | — | 1 | 1 |
| 1 | 0 | 0 | 0 | 0 |

# ACT Diagnostic Software

## ABOUT THE SOFTWARE

The diagnostic tests (or practice tests) on the CD-ROM were designed to be as much like the real ACT as possible. However, since the real test can only be taken using pencil and paper (at this time), we recommend practicing with the written assessment test as well, to better prepare you for an actual ACT.

Of course we know you got the book with the CD inside so you could benefit from its obvious advantages, such as immediate scoring, detailed score reports, and easy review of question explanations—so you definitely want to use it! Therefore, we have incorporated a few features into our software to simulate some of the experiences of the written test.

- You can cross out answers you've eliminated by right-clicking the answer choice (or pressing SHIFT while clicking if using a Macintosh).

- You can skip around and do the questions in whatever order you like by taking advantage of the *Review Test* button, which shows you a list of all the questions in a section at once.

Also, don't forget to have scrap paper handy. Just because you are taking a test on the computer doesn't mean you can't write things down.

Although the software does have a feature that lets you suspend the test in the middle and finish it later, we recommend that you try to take an entire test in one sitting. Remember—you want to simulate real testing conditions. We also advise making good use of the review features—look at the explanations for questions you missed, and figure out the sections with which you are having the most trouble.

If you have any trouble, call our technical support center at (800) 546-2102.

## SYSTEM REQUIREMENTS

WINDOWS™
866 MHz or higher
Windows 95, 98, 2000 ME, XP
32 MB RAM
12 MB Hard Disk space
SVGA Monitor (256 Colors)

MACINTOSH®
Power PC
System 7.6.1 or higher
32 MB RAM
12 MB Hard Disk space
256 Color Monitor (640 x 480 pixels)

# INSTALLATION AND START-UP

## Windows:

Close all other applications.

1. Insert the CD in your CD-ROM drive.

2. From your Start Menu (or File menu if using Win 3.1), select Run.

3. Type D: setup and press Enter. (If your CD-ROM drive is not drive D:, type the appropriate letter).

4. Follow the onscreen instructions until installation is complete.

To run the software, make sure the CD is in your CD-ROM drive, and simply select ACT Diagnostic from *The Princeton Review* folder in Programs from the Start Menu (or in *The Princeton Review* Program Group, if you are using Win 3.1).

## Macintosh:

1. Insert the CD in your CD-ROM drive.

2. Double click the ACT—Installer icon.

3. Follow the onscreen instructions until installation is complete.

To run the software, make sure the CD is in your CD-ROM drive, and simply double click the *Tester* icon located in the *ACT Diagnostic* folder in *The Princeton Review* folder on your hard drive.

# USING ACT DIAGNOSTIC TESTS

## THE MAIN MENU

Each time you launch your ACT Diagnostic, you will begin with the main menu screen. From this screen, you can either **Start a Test**—one of four ACT Diagnostics—or **Review a Test** you've already taken. You can also exit the software by clicking **Quit** on the upper-right corner.

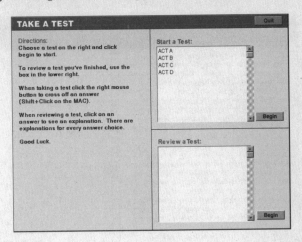

## TAKING A TEST

Each ACT consists of 4 sections: English, Math, Reading, and Science Reasoning. There is no experimental section included on these diagnostic tests.

To start a test, select one from the list and click **Begin**. You will go directly to the Directions Screen of the first section of your selected test.

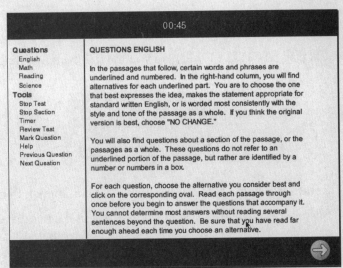

This is also the **Help screen**. If you need to review the directions for any type of question or the functions of any of the buttons on your screen, simply click the Help button at the bottom of any active testing screen and this screen will reappear. You can then click on the topic with which you need help.

Since the timer starts as soon as you click Begin, you should not spend unnecessary amounts of time on the Directions Screen. Review all of the section directions (provided in the book) before taking the diagnostic tests. The buttons on the toolbar are explained below.

Here is a sample test question screen:

To select an answer, click on the oval next to the answer or the answer itself. To cross out an answer, right-click the answer itself (press Shift and click if using a Mac). You can change an answer as many times as you want.

## THE TOOLBAR

*Stop Test icon*     Clicking **STOP TEST** will give you the following warning:

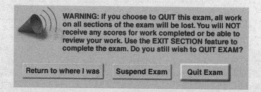

**Return to where I was** does exactly what you think it does.

**Suspend Exam** allows you to stop the test in the middle and return to it at a later time. The suspended test will appear on the Main Menu. Obviously, this option would not be possible if you were taking an actual ACT.

**Quit Exam** terminates the testing session and erases any work you have done on the test you are taking.

*Stop Section*

Clicking **STOP SECTION** will give you the following warning:

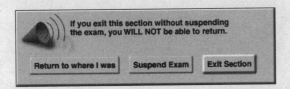

> If you exit this section without suspending the exam, you WILL NOT be able to return.
>
> **Return to where I was**   **Suspend Exam**   **Exit Section**

**Return to where I was** does exactly what you think it does.

**Suspend Exam** allows you to stop the test in the middle and return to it at a later time. The suspended test will appear on the Main Menu. Obviously, this option would not be possible if you were taking an actual ACT.

**Exit Section** ends the present section of the test. You can use this button if you complete the section and have extra time left. However, you may want to use the extra time to review your work because once you move on to the next section, you cannot return to previous sections.

 *Clock icon*

Clicking **TOGGLE TIMER** will turn the clock display on or off. The time will continue to count down either way.

 *Review icon*

Clicking **REVIEW TEST** will allow you to see a chart of every question in the section. This feature is especially helpful in giving a big picture of how the section lays out. You can jump around and do the questions in whatever order you choose. The chart lets you see the questions you have answered and the ones you have not.

 *Print icon*

Clicking **PRINT** will print the question presently on the screen. You cannot print out the entire test.

 *Help icon*

Clicking **HELP** will bring you to the Directions Screen (see above).

 *Previous icon*

*Next icon*

Clicking **PREVIOUS QUESTION** or **NEXT QUESTION** allows you to move throughout the section question by question.

## ENDING A SECTION AND FINISHING THE TEST

When you reach the end of a section, you will see this message:

**Return to where I was** allows you to continue working on the section.

**Exit Section** will end your time on the section. Choose this option if you are finished with the section. If you have another section remaining, you will now have a five-minute break and then the computer will start the next section. If you would like a longer break, you can also wait until time runs out on this section.

When you reach the end of the last section of the test and choose **Exit Section,** you will receive a message that reads, "You have reached the end of the exam." Select **Exit** to proceed.

# THE SCORE REPORT

When you have completed a test, you will see a screen that asks you to wait while your exam is scored. Then you will see your **SCORE REPORT.** This report gives you detailed information about your test. You can view the results of each section by selecting a section from the pull-down menu in the upper-right corner, or you can print the full report by clicking the Print button.

| SCORE REPORT | | | | Print | | Exit Review |
|---|---|---|---|---|---|---|

**Exam Name** ACT Diagnostic 1  **Date** 10/9/01  **Subject** English ▼

**Scores** English=23  Math=3  Reading=32  Science=19  Composite=19

**Section Performance** (Click on a question to review.)

| Q# | Corr Ans | Your Ans | Category | QID | Time Spent |
|---|---|---|---|---|---|
| 1 | C | C | ENG | 7994 | 02:11 |
| 2 | B | B | ENG | 7883 | 00:17 |
| 3 | D | D | ENG | 7772 | 00:18 |
| 4 | A | B | ENG | 7661 | 01:48 |
| 5 | A | A | ENG | 7550 | 01:12 |
| 6 | A | B | ENG | 7439 | 00:24 |
| 7 | D | D | ENG | 7101 | 00:03 |
| 8 | B | B | ENG | 7212 | 00:24 |
| 9 | C | C | ENG | 7319 | 01:38 |
| 10 | C | C | ENG | 7993 | 00:15 |
| 11 | C | C | ENG | 7982 | 00:22 |

**Performance Summary**

| Category | #Right | #Wrong | %Right | Average Time |
|---|---|---|---|---|
| English..(ENG) | 54 | 19 | 72 | 00:27 |
| Math..(MATH) | 0 | 0 | 0 | 00:00 |
| Reading..() | 36 | 4 | 90 | 00:39 |
| Science..(SCI) | 21 | 19 | 52 | 00:36 |

You can view this **SCORE REPORT** at another time by selecting this test from the **Review a test** section of the main menu.

You may review any question from your test by clicking on the question number in the **SCORE REPORT.** The review mode will show you a green check mark to indicate the credited response and show your answer as the darkened oval. Answers you crossed out are also shown. To view an explanation for an answer choice, click on the answer (the words in the answer, not on the oval). These explanations do not print. To return to the **SCORE REPORT,** click on the **STOP SECTION** button.

# ABOUT THE AUTHORS

Geoff Martz attended Dartmouth College and Columbia University, joining The Princeton Review in 1985 as a teacher and writer. His first book for The Princeton Review was *Cracking the GMAT*, published in 1989.

Kim Magloire is a graduate of Princeton University. She joined The Princeton Review in 1984 as an SAT teacher, and has since taught The Princeton Review's SAT II, LSAT, GMAT, GRE, and MCAT programs. Magloire is currently attending graduate school at Columbia University.

Ted Silver is a graduate of Yale University, the Yale University School of Medicine, and the law school at the University of Connecticut. He has been intensely involved in the fields of education and testing since 1976, and has written several books and computer tutorials pertaining to those fields. He became affiliated with The Princeton Review in 1988 as the chief architect of The Princeton Review's MCAT course. Dr. Silver's full-time profession is as Associate Professor of Law at Touro College Jacob D. Fuchsberg Law Center.

# Find the Right School

**BEST 345 COLLEGES**
**2003 EDITION**
0-375-76255-8 • $20.00

**COMPLETE BOOK OF COLLEGES**
**2003 EDITION**
0-375-76256-6 • $26.95

**COMPLETE BOOK OF**
**DISTANCE LEARNING SCHOOLS**
0-375-76204-3 • $21.00

**AMERICA'S ELITE COLLEGES**
Choosing Wisely, Getting in,
Paying for It
0-375-76206-X • $15.95

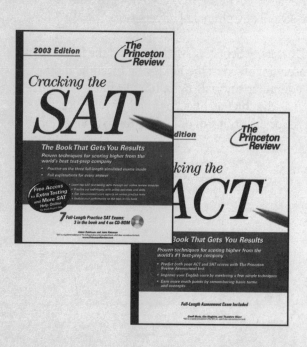

# Get in

**CRACKING THE SAT**
**2003 EDITION**
0-375-76245-0 • $19.00

**CRACKING THE SAT**
**WITH SAMPLE TESTS ON CD-ROM**
**2003 EDITION**
0-375-76246-9 • $30.95

**MATH WORKOUT FOR THE SAT**
**2ND EDITION**
0-375-76177-2 • $14.95

**VERBAL WORKOUT FOR THE SAT**
**2ND EDITION**
0-375-76176-4 • $14.95

**CRACKING THE ACT**
**2003 EDITION**
0-375-76317-1 • $19.00

**CRACKING THE ACT WITH**
**SAMPLE TESTS ON CD-ROM**
**2003 EDITION**
0-375-76318-X • $29.95

**CRASH COURSE FOR THE ACT**
10 Easy Steps to Higher Score
0-375-75326-5 • $9.95

**CRASH COURSE FOR THE SAT**
10 Easy Steps to Higher Score
0-375-75324-9 • $9.95

# Get Help Paying for it

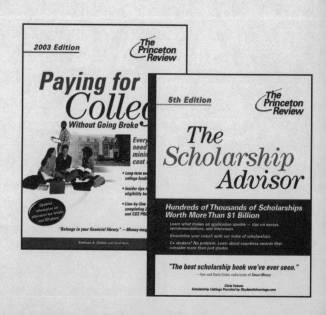

**DOLLARS & SENSE FOR COLLEGE STUDENTS**
How Not to Run Out of Money by Midterms
0-375-75206-4 • $10.95

**PAYING FOR COLLEGE WITHOUT GOING BROKE**
**2003 EDITION**
0-375-76273-6 • $20.00

**THE SCHOLARSHIP ADVISOR**
**5TH EDITION**
0-375-76210-8 • $26.00